The University of Nebraska-Lincoln
Study Commission on Undergraduate Education
and the Education of Teachers
Andrews Hall #338
Lincoln, Nebraska 68508

JUL 17 1974

Reform and Organizational Survival

Reform and Organizational Survival

THE TEACHER CORPS AS AN
INSTRUMENT OF EDUCATIONAL CHANGE

RONALD G. CORWIN
Professor of Sociology
The Ohio State University

FOREWORD BY MELVIN TUMIN

Conducted under a grant by the Ford Foundation to the National Education Association, National Commission on Teacher Education and Professional Standards, in cooperation with The Ohio State University. Published in conjunction with the National Education Association

A WILEY-INTERSCIENCE PUBLICATION

JOHN WILEY & SONS
New York • London • Sydney • Toronto

Library of Congress Cataloging in Publication Data:
Corwin, Ronald G.
    Reform and organizational survival.

    "A Wiley-Interscience publication."
    "Published in conjunction with the National
Education Association."
    Bibliography: p.
    1.   United States. National Teacher Corps.
2.   Socially handicapped children—Education—United
States.   I.   Title.
LC4091.C67   371.9'67   72-10367
ISBN 0-471-17519-6

Printed in the United States of America

10 9 8 7 6 5 4 3 2 1

To my wife Bonnie Jean Corwin

Prepared with the assistance of

KENNETH KISER
Assistant Professor of Sociology
Oklahoma State University

JOHN STEPHENSON
Assistant Professor of Sociology
California State University at San Diego

and

ELIZABETH HANNA
Lecturer
State University of New York at Albany

Advisory Committee to the Project

Melvin Tumin, Committee Chairman, Professor of Sociology, Princeton University

Albert Beaton, Chief, Data Analysis Research Division, Educational Testing Service

D. D. Darland, Division of Instruction and Professional Development, National Education Association

Roy A. Edelfelt, Division of Instruction and Professional Development, National Education Association

James Hall, Dean of Students, New York City Community College

Morris Keeton, Vice President, Antioch College

Gerald Lesser, Professor of Education, Harvard University

Herbert Schueler, President, Richmond College

Donald Sharpe, Director, Professional Laboratory Experiences, Indiana State University

Bernard Watson, Chairman, Department of Urban Education, Temple University

Foreword

The Teacher Corps Program is an archetypical model for all federal programs. First, it is global in scope, its reach being no smaller than the totality of all possible goals of education. Second, though it pretends to a special target—the improvement of education of disadvantaged children—it prefaces, surrounds, and supports that target with so many ancillary ones that it ends up as a multipurpose, diffuse complex of targets. Third, while it specifies a group with special needs to serve, it invokes the need for total reform of all connected agencies and institutions if those needs are to be met. Finally, while it is phrased in the ennobling, rolling rhetoric of the modern language of "identity" theory, there are frequent reassuring references to more traditional goals of education.

The formulation of program objectives in the way just described serves a number of important purposes, perhaps chief of which is that friends of the Program cannot fail to prove that at least some of its aspects have worked reasonably well. It is equally impossible that enemies of the Program should not be able to prove that some aspects have failed miserably. Moreover, the aims of the Program are diverse enough so that the most heterogeneous mass of Congressional forces can endorse it, even if they find certain parts distasteful, while the Program resonates with enough nobility of intention to allow its supporters to invoke the highest sounding moral philosophy as they defend it. Also important is the fact that the aims are stated sufficiently generally and ambiguously to permit almost anything and everything to be done in their name. Finally, provisions are made for the inclusion of agencies at all levels of government (local, state, and federal), all strata in the socioeconomic class structure, and all levels of functionaries in the educational system. This last feature makes it possible for the Program to recruit the widest possible constituency, for it seems to ensure that everyone will have a piece of the action.

The statement of Program objectives is therefore an ideal political instrument. One could use its basic outline for programs of health, national defense, enrichment of the arts and humanities, establishment of law and order, elimination of ecological despoilation, or what not. In one sense, the fact that the Program focuses on desired outcomes in the field of education is incidental, since the concern for education seems not to have required a form different from what could have been used for all other programs, except for certain obviously needed specifics from the language of education. In that regard, the statement of objectives is like an all-purpose lease or contract, in which one only need fill in the names of the parties, the date of agreement, and the specifics of costs and penalties.

At first, these features of the Program seem utterly negative. How can anything useful be accomplished under so broad a mandate, embracing so diverse a constituency? Reflection, however, reveals a very important sociological fact: if the federal government is going to intervene in the domestic affairs of the society, it simply must seek the widest possible support; it must provide for the widest possible participation; it must allow diverse political elements to find grounds for support of the program; it must make provision for flexibility and volatility so that directions can be changed, if need be, in midstream; it must scatter its targets so that at least some of them can be accomplished, to some degree; it must be sufficiently ambiguous to permit different interpretations as various actors involved in the Program try to integrate the "innovations" with their own established practices. Finally, it must be wildly overacclaimed in the rhetoric of the Great Society, or it cannot triumph over parochial objections based on partisan interests. In an important sense, then, the Program objectives epitomize the basic ingredients of a pluralistic society and embody the requirements of any program aimed at securing cooperation and support from all the diverse forces that make up such a society.

But there is a price to pay for those advantages, namely, no sound evaluation of such programs is possible. All the complexities that plague evaluation studies are operative here, even if not intentionally. Even assuming there were some well-measured outcomes, who could possibly say which of the many interacting forces was responsible, and to what degree, for those outcomes?

At the same time, it is evident that significant and useful analyses of portions of the Program may be possible, if one deliberately renounces any intention at completeness or precision. It is therefore a mark of the eminent good sense and sociological perspicacity of Dr. Ronald Corwin and his colleagues that they recognized from the outset that their mandate to evaluate the Teacher Corps Program had to be construed in relatively narrow terms. Ideally, of course, one would want to know whether the Program made any difference in the educational lives of the children at whom the program was ultimately aimed. But as is now well known by professionals in the field of evaluation of the effectiveness of educational programs, any attempt to measure the impact of programmatic features on educational outcomes is about as difficult, time consuming, and expensive a project as can be undertaken in the social and behavioral sciences. This of course assumes that we agree on what is meant by improved education. But as the current debates among friends and opponents of "community control" amply reveal, even this minimum, indispensable clarity about program objectives is subject to the most opposed kinds of interpretations. Are improved reading scores more or less important than or as important as some signs of increased ethnic pride? And if reading scores go down but ethnic pride goes up, how does one add those two outcomes into some meaningful score to compare with a situation where reading scores improved but ethnic pride decreased?

Well aware of these difficulties, Dr. Corwin wisely renounced any intention to study "student outcomes" of the Program and instead focused on the impact of some aspects of the Program on the student interns themselves, that is, the Teacher Corpsmen who had been recruited as the primary agents of educational change. Dr. Corwin, in effect, has asked, What has happened to these corpsmen as they have gone through the Program? On the assumption that the agents of change must function effectively, if the desired changes are to be achieved, this was an eminently wise decision and one to which all members of the Advisory Commission assented.

It should not be thought, however, that even such a narrowed version of the objectives made it much easier to do an adequate evaluation study. For the complexities here are not sufficiently fewer than those that would beset a study of student outcomes to give grounds for much optimism about what such a study can achieve.

What Dr. Corwin has done, therefore, strikes me as extraordinarily sensible. He has chosen to locate this analysis within the framework of a body of theory concerned with the structure and functioning of complex organizations. Because that body of theory is grounded in a fairly well-developed empirical literature, Dr. Corwin could examine the most important hypotheses in organization theory and determine to what extent, with their use, the complexities of the Teacher Corps Program could be conceptualized, formulated, and clarified. In my judgment, that aim has been as fully accomplished as one might dared have hoped, given the limited time and resources available to the study. We have here a set of valuable understandings of some aspects of the Teacher Corps Program that would otherwise not have been available and, reciprocally, as one always hopes for in all good scientific work, the hypotheses of the general theory are tested by empirical materials from a well documented case study. When the causes of social reform and sociological theory both profit from a research study, we must consider ourselves fortunate, indeed, and in this case there is no doubt that we are fortunate in that regard.

But Dr. Corwin's achievement is even more substantial. He has recognized that the formal structure generated by the intrusion of the Teacher Corps Program into the established educational community created a *network* of complex organizations rather than only one such specimen. That network, then, in the author's analysis, becomes a system of its own, showing some central features of complex organizations, but exhibiting additional features—mostly strains and stresses—that arise in the process of interaction among the various organizations that make up the network system.

This development is of interest and importance to governmental officials and sociologists alike. For the former, it serves as a reminder—and one that is badly needed—that however nobly intentioned a program of federal intervention may be, and however high the initial enthusiasm among potential participants, all such programs unavoidably must interfere with the normal, relatively smooth workings of established organizations and agencies. That being the case, such an intrusion must carry a very high promise of generous rewards to those whose daily schedules are interfered with, if they are to cooperate in attempting to make the intrusive element an organic part of their ongoing systems.

As Dr. Corwin shows, one of the most important factors that made the Program difficult to implement was that it could not promise the members of agencies and institutions whose cooperation was needed that it would be worth their while. Innovation is a charming word, beguiling and rousing. But it is like other terms such as relevance, concern, sensitivity. One cannot be against these on principle. But they are almost always privately read as warning signs that there is trouble ahead for those who are fulfilling their accustomed routines. Moreover, since most innovation efforts fail sooner or later, wise masters of ongoing enterprises have learned how to live and wait until such innovations speed themselves to their ultimate demise. While not many other earthly travails can be safely waited out, with any hope of relief, innovative programs do have that special quality of a high probability of failure, so that "this too shall pass" is a reasonably sound prediction about most of them.

Dr. Corwin shows in a variety of ways that the enthusiasm of Teacher Corps interns for their mandate "to improve the education" of minority children was often met with a considerable reserve by those already involved in that education. Frequently, a fundamental hostility was quickly generated. He summarizes these trends in his concluding chapter:

They were encouraged in the recruiting publicity and by the national office to view themselves as "catalytic change agents," while it was implied that veteran educators were traditionalists obstructing needed change. Interns were to be the colleagues of veteran teachers; and socialization was to be a two-way process, with interns helping to resocialize their professors and veteran classroom teachers. Presumably, the greater the difference between these newcomers from the outside and the veteran teachers, the more innovation would take place.

However, it did not usually work that way. The more aggressive the interns were, the more defensive and inflexible the schools became. Their image only threatened teachers and irritated the professors. This produced confusing role reversals, compromised traditional teaching and learning roles, and paralyzed the innovative thrust of the program.

In part this hostility was due to the absence of diplomatic, organizational skills among corpsmen interns. Where, indeed, should they have acquired these skills? And how could they be diplomatic and also maintain a high level of innovative enthusisam? Again, Corwin comments:

But these questions arise: Is it possible to train people who are passionately committed to the need for reform *and* who are calculating and patient enough to work effectively within the system? Can they become *sophisticated* about the system without losing their zest for change? Can they learn to temper their *romanticism* without losing their *compassion* for and *optimism* concerning the children? In many instances these ingredients did not mix.

Nor was the interns' compassion for the children necessarily an unmixed blessing. The interns were discounting the importance of cognitive achievement for precisely the group of youngsters who most needed to improve their academic skills.

These findings of course are of equal interest to the sociologists, who perhaps need fewer warnings than political figures who are prone to convince themselves by their own enthusiasms. For some time now, social scientists have been trying to convey the importance of realizing that structural features in organizational life—identities, statuses, roles, resources, and sanctions—are deep rooted and difficult to alter. Yet government officials charged with devising innovative programs chronically seem to forget this injunction, hoping against hope that the infusion of new blood in existing organizations will work wonders. As. Dr. Corwin reminds us, however, his analysis of this idealism on the part of innovators reveals that "it is still doubtful that personal characteristics of new people alone can change a profession as long as there are structural features that inhibit innovation."

Since federal intervention in education cannot hope to avoid working with existing structures, its sights about possible innovative reforms must be lowered considerably in view of this sociological reminder of structural resistance to innovation. It is indeed curious that, in the final analysis, social scientists are far more realistic about what is possible than most government officials. The traditional charge has been that "those people in their ivory towers" simply do not understand the limits of the practical, everyday world.

The politics of social innovation being what they are, and the practice of journalism being what it is, the usual public version of the outcome of an innovative governmental program is almost always phrased in terms of blame for failure and credit for success. In that milieu, of course, heroes and villains must be identified. As Lewis Mumford once wrote, blame avoidance is as deep lying a characteristic of the American people as any other. Since career success in organizations depends on such blame avoidance, and since most lives are conducted within the framework of such organizations, it makes good sense that the attempt to avoid blame should be so deep rooted and ubiquitous.

Dr. Corwin has assiduously avoided the language of success and failure and, instead, has analyzed the respective contributions to various outcomes of the numerous elements in complex networks of forces. Thus "blame" for the outcomes could not be attributed to the professional status-orientation of the university professors; or the reluctance of teachers to make ample room for the Teacher Corps interns; or the insistence by existing teaching staffs on being concerned with the cognitive development of children; or the militance of a number of the interns; or their refusal to deal diplomatically with the fears and anxieties of the teaching staffs and principals. Rather, the interaction among these quite understandable forces, and many others, produce the outcomes. In other words, the inability of the interns to implement their visions was not any more due to the resistances they encountered than to the forms and manners in which they "introduced" the innovations. Sociological understanding of *interactive processes* is therefore crucial here to rescue the understanding of how programs work from the ambiguity that would pervade the atmosphere if the language of blame and failure were applied.

Did the Teacher Corps Program succeed? To ask this question is to belie the understanding of system-interaction just recited above. Moreover, one crucial term is left undefined in that question, namely, "the program." As Dr. Corwin shows, the "program" was many things. For while there exist a set of guidelines for conducting programs in their various scattered locales, the guidelines are neither so specific nor so protected by sanctions that they cannot be altered at every site where the Program is attempted.

This is exactly what happened with the Teacher Corps Program, as it has with every such program: VISTA, Peace Corps, Headstart. Even if one should care to try to answer whether the Program worked, it would not be possible, since the Program is not a homogeneous entity. The various versions of the Program differed in numerous basic features: the number of people involved, the kinds of universities, schools, and communities in which they were located, the quality of the corpsmen and their versions of their mandate, the understandings of the cooperating agencies as to their roles, and the like. In short, one does not know what *the* Program was, hence one cannot say whether *the* Program worked.

What can be done, however—and this Dr. Corwin has done and done well—is to identify certain variables present in all programs, such as the militance of the corpsmen, their frequency of contact with their professional mentors, the ideologies of those mentors, or the qualities of the teaching staffs in the schools in which the corpsmen were located. Dr. Corwin then treats these variables as system factors that are present to specifiable degrees in the various programs and statistically analyzes the variable influence of these factors as they interact with others. This is, after all, the only possible and sensible thing to do when a program is as diverse in its forms of implementation as the Teacher Corps.

The failure to recognize this elementary fact about other programs, such as Headstart, was significantly responsible for a disastrous overinterpretation of the results of a brief "evaluation" study of Headstart that was commanded by the federal government a few years ago. With more than 90 different versions of "Headstart" at work in as many different communities, it would have been preposterous to insist on any generalizations about Headstart as such. Yet the government rose to the challenge of the preposterous and issued official ukases to the effect that Headstart programs were a failure. This led to the shockingly erroneous claim by Professor Arthur Jensen, in his now ill-famed article on Negro intelligence, that compensatory education has been tried and failed. Though Professor Jensen withdrew that statement in response to his critics, his first assertion remains in the public memory far more forcibly than his subsequent modest revision. This is just one instance of how dangerous loosely formulated and ineptly conducted evaluations of programs can be.

Dr. Corwin's study will give no such possibilities to those seeking to denounce the Teacher Corps Program as another example of government bungling. Neither friend nor critic of the *idea* of a Teacher Corps can find comfort in this well-measured analysis of the impact of a number of different variables on various aspects of the Teacher Corps Program. Precisely because it is so frustrating a study from the viewpoint of the politics of praise and denunciation, it is a rewarding one from the viewpoint of anyone concerned with sound knowledge about interventional programs. Moreover, it will be difficult for subsequent government planners to insist on knowing whether a particular program has worked or failed, that is, if they have a sense of obligation to work done in the field of evaluation. *All government programs, we see, are both doomed to failure and guaranteed success.* All depends on what one wants to stress in the outcomes of those programs.

For these many contributions to both government planning and the theory of complex organizations, we are in debt to Dr. Corwin and his staff. Moreover, those concerned with improving the quality of education of disadvantaged children will surely benefit from this study—if they choose to be rational, of course—since they will appreciate how extremely difficult it is to alter existing practices and outcomes even a small amount. Apocalyptic beliefs in instant salvation through the magical removal of villains and the introduction of new heroes may still be the dominant mode in which desperate people think about solving educational problems. But one dare hope that over time these magical ways of thinking about the complex social world will yield to a mature understanding of the complexities we face.

Only this new understanding can save us from the disastrous fluxes in public opinion as the public comes first to hope beyond reason and then to despair beyond fact when their bright, shiny visions encounter the difficulties of ongoing institutional arrangements. This is not to be interpreted as a counsel of despair of its own kind. Quite to the contrary. True freedom lies in the recognition of necessity, as our best philosophers have continued to remind us. Dr. Corwin's work describes, analyzes, and clarifies certain basic necessities in the field of education that must be recognized if we are to find the freedom to alter things to approximate more closely the visions we all share of equal quality education for all.

MELVIN M. TUMIN
Professor of Sociology
Princeton University

August 1972

Preface

This book reports the findings of a longitudinal study of the Teacher Corps and reviews the theory and methods that guided the study. It was written for social scientists, scholars, educators, policy makers, and other informed citizens to give a better understanding of this complex program. A companion volume, *Lessons from the Teacher Corps*, which deals with the practical implications of the study for teacher education and proposes specific recommendations about the program, is being published by the National Education Association (NEA).

The present study is being published in collaboration with NEA. Funds were provided by a Ford Foundation grant to NEA's former National Commission on Teacher Education and Professional Standards (NCTEPS), now merged with other units into the Division of Instruction and Professional Development. NCTEPS served as the primary fiscal and administrative agent, and functioned as a liaison among the research group, the universities and school systems, and the Teacher Corps office in Washington, D.C. The project staff also was guided by an Advisory Committee (p. vii), which functioned independently of the Teacher Corps and NCTEPS. I am grateful for the assistance of the members of this committee. Together, NCTEPS and the Advisory Committee helped to establish a neutral research atmosphere, despite the politically controversial nature of the program under study.

I am greatly indebted to the committee's members, Albert Beaton, David Darland, Roy Edelfelt, Morris Keeton, Gerald Lesser, James Hall, Herbert Schueler, Donald Sharpe, Melvin Tumin, and Bernard Watson. We spent many hours together in frank discussions, pondering research strategies, debating the merits of alternative interpretations, and exchanging candid criticisms. They read what I wrote and reacted with penetrating comments. Although I am responsible for this book, the committee deserves credit for having steered me into fruitful directions.

This project would not have been possible without the diligent assistance of Roy Edelfelt and David Darland, of NEA-TEPS, and Mario Fantini and Edward Meade of The Ford Foundation. The full extent of their contribution is immeasurable.

I also am indebted to Melvin Tumin, chairman of the Advisory Committee and a respected colleague, who guided the study. His comments on earlier drafts of the manuscript (Chapter 11, in particular) were most helpful. Albert Beaton, of the Advisory Committee, assisted with technical aspects of the statistical analysis. His balanced perspective on the role of statistical procedures was useful. Wen Li and Kent Schwirian, of Ohio State University, helped with certain aspects of the regression analysis.

Charles Bidwell read the manuscript and made several good suggestions, which I accepted.

I appreciate the cooperation of Richard Graham, Mrs. Lucy Conboy, William Moulden, and more than 1400 dedicated members of the Teacher Corps staffs and classroom teachers who made my visits pleasant and productive.

I thank the members of the project staff—the interviewers, coders, and typists—who painstakingly carried out the study, sometimes under trying conditions. I especially thank Lois Brooks and Evelyn Pease for their secretarial assistance and devotion to the project. John Stephenson, Kenneth Kiser, and Beth Hanna directed portions of the field work and analysis. I am indebted to each of them for assistance and constructive advice. Kathy Hudson and Nancy White handled the details of coding and statistical analysis efficiently. Kathy Hudson also collaborated on parts of Chapter 7. My admiration goes to Larry Shirk for his skill in taming the computers on our campus.

Finally, I acknowledge the contributions of my colleagues in the Department of Sociology at Ohio State University. I thank the university administration for endorsing this research and for granting me the necessary time and latitude to undertake it.

RONALD G. CORWIN

Columbus, Ohio
June 1972

Contents

Tables and Figures

Introduction

Lewin stated that if someone wants to understand how something works, he should try to change it. He probably will learn something about the object changed and also about the change process itself. Although social scientists seldom have been able to manipulate the major structures of the society through systematic experimental design, massive federal-intervention programs are providing unprecedented opportunities to observe attempts to change large-scale institutions. The subject of this study—the Teacher Corps—is this kind of program. By studying it, something can be learned about the general processes of organizational change and, particularly, about how professional services to the poor can be improved.

In a changing and heterogeneous society the need to keep professional organizations vital and adaptive is a pressing practical problem as well as a significant theoretical area for research. As Griffiths (1964) observed, "The observer of social organizations is forced to the conclusion that organizations are not characterized by change." Indeed, a large portion of the energy expended by most organizations appears to limit the impact of outside influences. Several years ago, Mort (1964) concluded from approximately 200 studies that the time required from the inception to the diffusion of an innovation in educational institutions was about 50 years. Barrington (1953), surveying the diffusion of innovations in 161 teacher-education institutions and associated laboratory schools, found a similar time span for the adoption of an innovation and the same diffusion curve. However, in the past few years, diffusion has occurred at an accelerating pace. Bushnell (1957) found that only 20 years were needed to achieve 50-percent diffusion and, more recently, Carlson (1964) ascertained that diffusion of modern math was 88 percent complete in 6 years.

What accounts for these variable rates of change? More important, why are many innovations resisted at first, and why do some fail, while others succeed? There are many plausible explanations of the reluctance of educational systems to change. First, innovations disrupt established routines

1

in complex organizations. For instance, programmed learning, which allows students to progress at their own rate, tends to increase the gap between the advanced and slower student in a classroom, and thus requires the teacher to find something to occupy the time of students who complete the course before the end of the term.

Second, a change might alter the status structure and benefit one individual or post of the organization over others. The gap between the aspirations of teachers for full professional status and the modest status they actually occupy makes them especially sensitive to any action that could widen the gap. For example, proposals to use teacher aides might be regarded by some teachers as a threat to their professional position.

Third, many universities and most public schools, which are the focus of this analysis, exist in what Carlson (1964) called a "domesticated" environment, where they do not have to compete strenuously for clientele and are guaranteed a certain level of funding and other necessary resources. Domesticated organizations are not compelled to adapt quickly to a changing environment.

Furthermore, schools and colleges are trapped within a web of other organizations. Since elementary schools must mesh their activities with high schools, and high schools must mesh their activities with colleges and industry, their freedom to make changes in their procedures is reduced. The force for change, in these instances, must be strong enough to mobilize the entire web of organizations to which schools and colleges belong.

Finally, innovations are often costly and risky, and there is no guarantee that they will be effective. There are no clear guidelines to determine when an innovation should be accepted, no assurances that because it worked in one situation it will work in another. Also, innovations are often very expensive and place heavy burdens on a system. Perhaps they will require the entire restructuring of current procedures or the hiring of new staffs.

The Teacher Corps (a federally initiated reform effort, created during the poverty-conscious 1960s to improve the welfare of low-income people) can illuminate these and other issues. Perhaps it can provide lessons about the reform process in general. Several perspectives run through the study.

First, the Teacher Corps is sociologically significant because it represents an unprecedented attempt to mobilize temporary networks of *organizations*. The Corps is an affiliation of organizational units within schools and colleges, and it cooperates with community and federal agencies to accomplish changes and reforms in the host organizations. This concerted effort assumes even greater significance because leadership and coordination were provided by an agency of the federal government. The involvement of a federal agency not only increased the legitimacy of the program but also subjected it to direct political controls.

Second, the way an organization (or, in this case, a set of organizations) actually functions is assumed to depend on the compromises made among alternative norms that make up organizations. The choice of alternatives is governed by a combination of status and economic and political considerations, and the choice is influenced by other organizations in the network. In view of these assumptions, the process of deliberate change can be understood better in terms of conflict and exchange theories than in terms of the more rational or bureaucratic models of organization.

Social reform, then, like the organizations in which it takes place, is essentially a bargaining process. Reform, in other words, must be considered as a natural product of the power conflicts and compromises that are inherent in social organizations. The distinct sociological task is to identify the organizational structures that act as incentives and barriers to change. Different *conceptions* of organization influence the strategy that is adopted, but once a strategy is adopted, the fundamentally political nature of organizations will determine how well it works. In this political context, also, organizations develop alternative strategies for their protection and survival, which can be identified.

Finally, organizational goals and structures, being subject to bargaining and change, have fundamental implications for the nature of "evaluation." That term implicitly assumes that there is a dominant, static goal and that new programs can be rationally implemented and controlled. Both of these assumptions are at variance with the political nature of organizational reform.

The Teacher Corps is a strategic opportunity for the application of these perspectives. The original purposes of the program, as provided in the authorizing legislation, were (1) to strengthen educational opportunities for children in areas with concentrations of low-income families, (2) to attract and prepare persons to become teachers in such areas through co-ordinated work-study experiences, and (3) to encourage colleges and universities, schools, and state departments of education to work together to broaden and improve teacher-education programs. The Corps resulted from the premise that there are critical differences between the skills required to teach in low-income schools and middle-class schools. But this premise does not imply that unique *principles* of learning are involved in the two different settings. Another justification for the Teacher Corps is this: the differences in values, prior experiences, and environments among children from various income, ethnic, and racial subgroups are so great that teachers need special training in order to *apply* the principles and fashion the procedures for each group.

John Kenneth Galbraith is credited with the original idea for the Teacher Corps. President Johnson gave it a name, and Senators Gaylord Nelson of Wisconsin and Edward Kennedy of Massachusetts drafted the legislation for it. The Higher Education Act of 1965, which embodied the program, was formed from a merger of two separate bills. One bill, introduced by Senator Nelson, was based on the Cardozo Peace Corps Program in Urban Teaching, an internship for returned Peace Corps volunteers in Washington, D.C. The second bill, sponsored by Senator Kennedy, sought to create a corps of experienced teachers who could go into disadvantaged areas and teach for one or two years. Congress authorized $100 million to start the Corps and to finance it for two years. However, the funds were not appropriated until the last moment, and only a small part of the authorized amount—$9.5 million—was actually appropriated in the first year, 1966–1967. During 1970, only $21.7 million was appropriated.

The Teacher Corps had its detractors from the outset. Less than one-half of the school administrators polled in 1967 wanted to see it expanded, and one-third of these advocated its termination (*Nation's Schools*, 1967). But despite its controversial birth, the program began under a banner of hope. Lyndon B. Johnson commented:

> Our country is blessed with young men and women who desire to serve those less fortunate than themselves. In the ranks of experienced teachers there are others who would devote part of their lives to children in most critical need. The Teacher Corps offers a practical means of uniting the idealism and wisdom of each—young graduates and accomplished teachers—and thus enriching the lives of coming generations.

In the view of the National Advisory Council on the Education of Disadvantaged Children (Wilson, 1967) the main value of the Teacher Corps program was that it recruited "an unusual group of young people who, but for the Corps, would never have been drawn to the teaching profession." U.S. Congressman John Brademas of Indiana (1967) expressed the opinion that "at the same time it presents an opportunity for young college graduates who wish to render service here at home in the same way that young people have served abroad in the Peace Corps." In essence, then, the program's purpose was to channel the creative energies of critical and idealistic young people into constructive, socially acceptable outlets—to temper their passion for reform with the knowledge, tools, and experience needed to exercise wise and effective leadership for change.

Although the missions of the Corps were complicated, it developed a broad scope of activities and goals, and a structure for carrying them out. Actually, the Corps is an affiliation of federal agencies, state governments, universities, public school systems, and community agencies. According to its brochure, it seeks (1) to extend to two years a work internship in the schools for new teacher trainees, (2) to utilize the team approach for training purposes, (3) to provide for special and continuous supervision of interns, (4) to incorporate the spirit of the Peace Corps, (5) to establish a closer relationship between theory and practice, (6) to set up a route into teaching for some who might otherwise be excluded, and (7) to extend the walls of the classroom into the community so that the community can be used as a training ground. Its program is divisible into two main parts with several components: a preservice program for interns, which includes graduate courses in education as well as some observation of schools and the community; and a tripartite, in-service period consisting of university study, a work-experience internship in poverty schools, and community-work experience with poverty children and their families.

The typical Corps program involves from 30 to 40 liberal arts graduates (interns) and five professional teachers who act as team leaders. The group receives about eight weeks of special preservice training at a college or university, after which it is divided into five teams, each composed of at least six interns and one team leader. Each team is assigned to a school that serves a poverty area, usually an elementary school, where the team spends at least 60 percent of its weekly time. In the beginning the team may work with small groups of students on specific lesson plans but, as the team gains experience, its tasks become more complex. It spends about 20 percent of its time in academic work at the university (some of this work is interdisciplinary and leads to teacher certification and a master's degree in two years). Finally, the interns also are expected to spend 20 percent of their time on community activities, learning as much as they can about the environment of their students.

Several thousand interns and experienced teachers have graduated from the program since the first cycle began in 1966. Corps teams serve in from 30 to 70 universities at one time, but they have served in more than 100 universities and 250 school systems in 37 states and Puerto Rico at various times. About half of the programs are in city school systems, including 17 large cities, and about half are in small towns and rural areas. There have been programs in New York, Chicago, Detroit, Philadelphia, Los Angeles, Kansas City, Miami, Atlanta, Seattle, and Dallas; in Appalachian towns, in the Ozarks, and in the rural South; in migrant communities, in Indian schools; and in Spanish-speaking communities in New York, Florida, and the Southwest.

Chapter 1 describes the sociological dimensions of the program and raises three vital questions. To what extent is it feasible to deliberately change organizations? What targets of the educational system must be changed to effect significant institutional reforms? What role does the federal government play? Also the goals of this book are discussed.

Procedures are described in Chapter 2—the samples and the measurement procedures along with a rationale for a wide range of variables that were selected for study.

Chapters 3 and 4 give a composite picture of the Teacher Corps. Chapter 3 deals with the people involved and, particularly, with the status identities and values of the interns. The interns are compared to the veteran teachers and other students and teachers in the colleges and schools associated with the program. The interns are then compared with an "ideal type" humanistic, change-minded teacher. I conclude that the interns typify a larger humanistic transformation than is under way in teaching. The potential problems and advantages of this transformation are considered.

Chapter 4 considers the places involved and the social contexts in which the interns found themselves. It tells how the various local programs operated, how they attempted to reform teacher education, and how conflicts and compromises resulted. It points out that the program was confronted with the difficult task of preparing interns for an unknown future and for nonexistent roles. Several structural sources of problems are indicated.

Chapters 5 to 7 consider the consequences of the program: what happened to the people and places. Chapter 5 analyzes the changes that occurred in interns' attitudes and values during the program, and the characteristics of the interns who dropped out. I conclude that the interns tended to become, simultaneously, more liberal and disillusioned. One of the unintended effects of the program was the radicalization of liberal interns who joined the venture with high expectations and found relatively little change occurring. However, the program may have produced a few role "hybrids" who retained their commitment to reform, although they adapted to the constraints of the profession.

Chapter 6 gives an inventory of what happened to the participating organizations: the schools and colleges. The assessment relies heavily on the way in which the participants themselves reported and assessed the changes that took place. Although there was usually a degree of consensus, the respondents were sometimes polarized among themselves. This polarization reflected substantial variability among the local programs as well as differences in perspective and the lack of clear-cut evidence of change.

Chapter 7 documents the variability among local programs by using two case studies. It provides a concrete picture of how the people and components of the program converged in particular places. The cases identify the main structural characteristics that might account for the variable outcomes.

Chapters 8 to 10 probe analytically and place the study in its broader social and theoretical context. Chapter 8 explores the structural sources of technological innovation in schools included in the program, and several theories of change are identified and tested. I conclude that a combination of theories is needed to explain the innovation process. The influence of the larger social context is also considered—regional variations and differences between rural and urban districts. It is demonstrated that small rural school districts are less able to defend themselves against the influence of aggressive newcomers than large urban school districts. For this reason, strategies of change that are not effective in one setting might be effective in another.

Chapter 9 analyzes local programs and considers the structural sources of change in colleges, in community activity, and in relationships between schools and colleges. It also explores the sources of organizational flexibility and conflict.

Chapter 10 places the Teacher Corps in its national setting. It focuses on the role of the national office, the social context in which it was operating, and the constraints under which it labored. This chapter identifies several tactics used by the national office to promote innovation in a hostile environment and to keep the program alive. The fate of the bureaucratic and professional organizations involved is reviewed.

Finally, Chapter 11 reinterprets the program in retrospect. The questions of sociological dimension are reexamined. Because social reforms must be implemented through organizations, I contend that these reforms are subject to the principles and processes inherent in complex social organizations. Since power is considered to be a central component of organizations, it is argued that reform will be subject to the power struggles and compromises associated with power. A sociological model is introduced, and it serves as a framework for the remainder of the chapter. The model has five elements: power, resources, status, task structure, and the occupational setting. It discusses the things that evaluation can and cannot be expected to accomplish and explains the concept, "political economy."

I

Background for the Study

CHAPTER 1

Teachers and the Poor: A Case of Federal Intervention for Professional Reform

In my experience, in practice, most explicit and implicit conceptions of change derive from the language and vocabulary of an individual psychology that is in no way adequate to changing social settings. The fact that one can be the most knowledgeable and imaginative psychoanalytic, learning, or existentialist theoretician gives one no formal basis for conceptualizing the problem of change in social settings. The problem is simply not one to which these individual theories address themselves.

SARASON, 1971, p. 59

Modern society is so complex, and its social problems are so formidable that neither the informed citizen, the politician, nor the social scientist can fully grasp all of the diverse issues that are plaguing us. But even though we cannot study each problem as it arises, we can select certain critical events, which illuminate the major social forces that shape the future, and examine them.

The Teacher Corps is such an event. It has been called "possibly the most radical experiment in teacher education ever tried" (Sharpe, 1968), and it is a clinical case whose importance extends beyond the immediate program.

Its fate can shed light on the larger issues that brought the program to life and that continue to shape it. It can act as a barometer for the future of federal-local relations and provide lessons on how to change complex organizations and the professions in the hope that man can learn to control his future better. The Teacher Corps is a microcosm that, perhaps, can serve as a means of studying the larger concerns of the nation and of social science, and as a strategic avenue for learning more about these concerns.

AN ANATOMY OF THE PROGRAM

From a sociological standpoint, the Teacher Corps program has a fascinating, complex structure. It works as a coalition of schools and universities, mediated by a federal agency and held together by an exchange of funds and services (see p. 28). Certain units within the schools and colleges and some units that bridge the two institutions form a somewhat autonomous, temporary system; among the units that make up the system are selected departments and professors in the university, the program director's office and staff, and teams composed of leaders and interns who function in the schools and communities. This coalition acts as a unique kind of change agent whose mission is to promote reform within the member organizations. Universities are expected to broaden their programs as a condition for receiving federal funds, and the schools are supposed to help interns try out new ideas, but final control remains at the local level with the schools and colleges. Instead of creating entirely new organizations to implement the program or an artificial "laboratory" environment that might have protected it from certain types of pressures, Congress designed the Corps to work within the day-to-day operations of schools and colleges. Presumably, in that way, the activities of the Corps members could be of direct benefit to these institutions. Also the advocates of the Corps hoped to elicit broad support for the program and to demonstrate that it could exist outside of "hothouse" conditions. However, this meant that opposition and red tape would be faced from the beginning.

A second feature of the Teacher Corps is its internal complexity. The program is divisible into four discrete parts: an eight-week preservice training workshop, a two-year period of on-the-job work experience, a two-year college program leading to an M.A. degree, and community projects. This divisibility creates the possibility that local systems will accept some parts and reject others.

The chief premise behind the program is that a profession can be changed by recruiting unconventional, change-oriented newcomers from nontraditional sources. The newcomers, with the benefit of special training, will act as catalysts for change within the local systems. Pursuant to this precept, the program deliberately has attempted to recruit the altruistic, reform-minded liberal-arts graduates.

Furthermore, the program relies on the strategy of using marginal increments of funds to trigger the presumably latent forces for change within a system. (The funding for the 10 programs in this study averaged approximately $300,000 each, or a mean cost of $7000 per intern.) The college receives a nominal 8 percent for overhead and must waive tuition. The uncertain, outside, temporary nature of the funding leaves few incentives for professors and teachers, who operate the program, to develop long-term career commitments. They look on their positions as interim jobs or stepping-stones.

Finally, the program has many objectives and purposes, and a diversified and variable role structure. Teams have a vague mandate to improve education and to provide service to local schools. The national office claims at least nine objectives with unknown, shifting priorities. Introducing liberal, aggressive newcomers into a program that is already plagued by ambiguous goals and unstructured roles compounds the problems.

THE UNDERLYING ISSUES

The following sketch conveys some sense of the range of issues that are potentially involved in the Teacher Corps program. Three problem areas are discussed.

What is the role of the federal government with respect to current efforts to reform this country's educational system?

There is a long tradition of local autonomy in the United States, and local authorities continue to have an important hold on educational policies. This control structure was designed for early American life when local communities were the basic integrating units of society. Conflicts arose and were resolved within community boundaries. Since the beginning of this century, however, the importance of the local community has diminished because of other forces. Striking improvements in transportation and communication, the emergence of a national labor market, concentration of the nation's wealth in a few Eastern-based corporations, and rapid population mobility have destroyed the sanctity of local community boundaries. A national society has emerged around the locally controlled school boards. Local organizations are usually branches of national parent organizations, and a great many special-interest groups (the NAACP, the National Association of Manufacturers, AFL-CIO, the Jewish Congress, and the National Education Association, for instance), in making demands on schools and universities, have placed national backing and resources at their disposal. Accordingly, the issues that affect education are national in scope, and attempts by local school boards to retain local control are largely ineffective. To the extent that they are effective, they may be obsolete.

Educational organizations, as they have become assimilated into the social mainstream, have had to evolve an informal national system of coordination and control. In response to the anomalies resulting from local control in the midst of the nationalizing trends, an informal national system of education has emerged. It consists of accrediting agencies, agencies of the professional organizations, textbook publishers, and many other groups (Wayland, 1964). B. Clark (1965) has described how the new math program was originated and rapidly disseminated by subtle forms of collaboration among college professors, the National Science Foundation, textbook publishers, and the U.S. Office of Education. But this system has seldom been *dominated* by the federal government, which usually has played a passive role compared to other groups in the coalition. This situation may be changing, however. The government has access to vast resources and can influence accreditation and other major policies. In the past few years the proportion of the growing cost of education borne by the federal government has more than doubled. Moreover, government agencies furnish guidelines and disseminate information; they help to coordinate programs and to set universal standards for many local groups.

The Teacher Corps is significant because it is an explicit attempt by the federal government to establish and to guide a network of educational organizations within its jurisdiction. Thus, it indicates an emergence of trends that may lead to a more fully federalized society. An analysis of the Corps can give clues about the changing role of the federal government, particularly as an agent for change in local institutions.

Can complex organizations be deliberately changed?

The Teacher Corps will not be remembered simply as an act of federal intervention in local educational institutions; nor will it be remembered only as a historical specimen of an action program of the poverty-conscious 1960s. Although both of these features are notable, the Teacher Corps raises a question that is fundamental to the existence of modern man: Have social organizations, created by man, become so powerful that they are beyond his control and, therefore, impervious to deliberate change? Certainly, the capacity of modern man to control his destiny in a changing, organizational society hinges on his ability to change, deliberately, its key formal organizations.

However, in comparison to the importance of the topic, systematic empirical studies of deliberate efforts to change organizations have been rare. One reason is that there have been few chances to undertake such studies. Also, the fact that sociologists attribute an independent life to social systems is another reason why they have devoted scant attention to strategies of deliberate organizational reform (Blau and Scott, 1962). However, the assumptions behind the Teacher Corps and many other current government programs are at variance with this fatalistic image of history. Because these programs attempt to manipulate precisely some of the structural variables that theory suggests are important, they should be of great interest to sociologists. They can provide clues about how to deliberately change social systems, such as professions, schools, and colleges.

The Teacher Corps adds an important dimension to the few cases that have accumulated, which describe how a variety of organizations adapt to changing or hostile environments by various means, including goal adaptation, selection of membership and audience, and reinforcement of organizational structure.[1] With some exceptions (Moynihan, 1969; Selznick, 1949), these studies have concentrated on a single organization or have viewed large sets of organizations as a collective. Incidental attention has been given to the dynamics of change that involve an organizational network. Recent developments, reported in the literature, indicate that research should focus more directly on the interorganizational processes. A series of coping strategies (described later) that has enabled the Teacher Corps to survive against formidable external and internal constraints suggests general patterns that might also apply to other cases.

ORGANIZATIONAL STRUCTURE AND INNOVATION. On the basis of previous research and theory, we can expect that the ability of the Teacher Corps to introduce change will be influenced by the organizational context in which it is implemented. Certain organizational characteristics and external forces cause the various local programs to be receptive or resistant to change and determine the amount of initiative that the participants are permitted to take. Although this problem is considered in Chapter 8 and other chapters, it is helpful here to enumerate the major parameters to be considered.

A case study reported by Gross and his colleagues (1968) suggests the key negative role that bureaucratic procedures sometimes have played in many aborted attempts to change educational organizations. They found that, even though teachers in the systems studied endorsed a proposed innovation, it was aborted because of obstacles posed by the organization: red tape, the failure of some members of the role set to fulfill their roles adequately, and the interdependence of individuals. In a more systematic study, Cillie (1940) found that decentralized schools had adopted more new programs than centralized schools. Decentralized schools were more likely to have experimented with new methods, to have obtained more recent instructional materials, and to have made continuous revisions in courses of study.

Innovation probably has been studied most frequently in business and service organizations, in which the environment is a compelling force for adaptation. Certain studies provide clues to the situation in education. For example, a study of 16 social-welfare agencies (Aiken and Hage, 1967) revealed that several types of organizational variables are related to the rate of program change:

- Number of occupational specialties in the organization.
- Level of training of personnel.
- Number of outside professional activities engaged in by personnel.
- Number of hierarchical levels in the organizational structure.
- The extent to which decision making is decentralized.
- The extent to which work is formalized through rules and regulations (which was the only variable that was negatively related).

Only the latter three variables remained significant after others were controlled. By comparison, a personality scale, measuring individuals' self-attitudes expressing interest in and resistance to change, was not related to program change, and a measure of pro-change ideals was inversely related. Rate of change, in other words, did not depend strongly on individual attitudes in *favor* of change.

Evan and Black (1967) asked respondents in business organizations to describe successful and unsuccessful proposals for change. They found that innovation was more likely to occur in large, standardized organizations, in which decisions are made at the top, where there are well-trained professional staffs and a high rate of communication between line and staff personnel. Studying another setting, Carroll (1967) concluded that innovative medical schools had large faculties and more departments than conservative schools.

These studies indicate the nature and state of the research in this area. On the one hand, there are parallels among the available studies. For example, several studies have confirmed that large, complex organizations with professionally qualified staffs tend to be innovative. Generally, innovative organizations are loosely structured, "open," and have well-trained staffs. Burns and Stalker (1961) perceived a model of organization with these characteristics, which they labeled the "organic model." This type of organization has few rules; decisions are made at all levels, although the organization is staffed by experts. In contrast, the "mechanical" organization is characterized by precise definition of rights and obligations, approved procedures, and a hierarchical structure of control. Burns and Stalker, on the basis of extensive research, concluded that innovative organizations conform to the organic model.

On the other hand, inconsistencies can be observed, even among the few studies cited. Whereas Aiken and Hage (1967) revealed that unstandardized organizations with decentralized decision-making structures tend to be innovative, Evan and Black (1967) found the opposite to be true in their sample. Although the discrepancies might be attributable to differences in the types of organizations studied, the situation reflects the primitive state of knowledge and theory in this field.

The complexity of the issues is illustrated by frequent disagreements about the role that centralization of authority plays in the innovative sequence. Several writers have noticed a basic dilemma in decentralized organizations: although competition among autonomous departments can stimulate *proposals* for changes that will enhance their respective positions, the same competitive relationship makes each department reluctant to *accept* proposals made by other departments (Wilson, 1966). In other words, the factors that increase the probability that innovations will be proposed decrease the probability that they will be adopted. The situation is illustrated in a study of several retail department stores (Sapolsky, 1967). Diversity of task structure within stores and divisional autonomy in accounting matters clearly facilitated the presentation of new proposals: (1) a proposal for the separation of buying and selling functions within merchandise units, and (2) a proposal to use electronic data processing in merchandising operations. Yet, because the units could not agree among themselves, attempts to implement these proposals were continually frustrated.

In view of complexities of this type, various writers have reached different conclusions about decentralization. Some believe that decentralized organizations are more innovative (Thompson, 1967; Aiken and Hage, 1967). In this connection, Shepard (1967) observes that innovative ideas are most likely to occur to persons who are familiar with the situation to which the innovations apply. Because these persons are likely to be some distance from the center of power in a centralized organization, their proposals are usually screened out in the flow of upward communication. Moreover, it is argued that persons in power are less likely to favor a change because their power rests on the existing structure and, therefore, changes proposed by subordinates could jeopardize their own status security (Aiken and Hage, 1970). On the other hand, other observers concur with March and Simon (1958) that any innovation falling outside the province of an existing department will take place at the top levels of the organization because only the top levels are powerful enough to force an innovation on reluctant members of the organization. Griffiths (1964), speaking specifically about educational organizations, states bluntly that innovations are implemented from the top down.

There are parallel disagreements about other dimensions of organizations. For example, it can be reasonably argued that organizations with well-trained, specialized staffs are more innovative because education expands the employee's awareness of alternatives and because conflict among different occupational specialties promotes program development (Aiken and Hage, 1970). But some critics disagree. They point out that groups of experts have their own vested interests and tend to lose sight of overall goals. This causes them to become defensive about changes that could threaten their status prerogatives. Professionalized groups can (and often do) use their strong associations to block proposals.

There is perhaps less dispute about the negative effect of formalization on innovation. The argument is made that rules set limits on the acceptable alternatives and thus increase the risk of proposing new ideas. Also, the more rules there are in an organization, the more likelihood there is that a new procedure will break them (Aiken and Hage, 1970). But, even in this case, it can be argued that some rules are needed to protect the persons who propose change and to clarify the procedures for introducing it. Since these issues will be discussed in detail in later chapters, the purpose here is to introduce the issues briefly.

ORGANIZATIONAL GOALS. In addition to structural factors, the nature of the organization's goal system is likely to influence its capability to adapt to a changing society. Organizations are linked to their environments through their goals, which usually are imposed by the outside society. Consequently, they are held accountable for their contributions to the society and toward their own self-defined objectives. However, the concept of "goals" is one of the most perplexing concepts in the literature on complex organizations. Goal concepts, considered as statements of an ideal condition, seldom provide clear prescriptions of what should be *done* to achieve the goal. Another practical question is: How do we determine whose goals in the community, neighborhood, or society are to be accepted? Moreover, separate parts of an organization often develop their own goals and goal priorities. Therefore, despite the apparent significance of the *idealized* ultimate objectives, goals are translated into programs by practical, immediate contingencies and priorities.

In view of the vagueness in the concept, goals, at best, can have an indeterminate effect on the change process. A related obstacle to research on new programs is confusion among different *levels* of objectives. Some investigators believe that it is sufficient to evaluate outcomes, for example, by observing that "the student has learned his lesson well"; other investigators insist that it must first be proved that the student's learning has actually resulted in better job performance. The resolution depends on the level of the objectives chosen.[2]

How can the professions be changed to improve service to low-income clientele?

The reason for changing organizations, of course, is to improve service to people. During the poverty-conscious 1960s, the quality of professional service to the poor became a focus of criticism, and the professions became a prime target for social reform. Until recently the professions have not been eager to make radical departures from their basic procedures and premises but, as society has assumed greater responsibility for rehabilitating individuals (who, in the past, were held responsible for their own fate), professional training programs are being forced to change accordingly. The usual image of the professional—a technically skilled practitioner who treats a receptive, often docile client and who teaches new generations of professionals in the same techniques—must be adjusted to the reluctance of many clients to accept treatment. A new model is emerging that gives priority to certain ways of involving clients in the treatment process and of establishing more effective rapport. The Teacher Corps, as one of the few national efforts to produce such a model for educating the poor, provides an unprecedented opportunity to study a major effort to bring about innovation in a significant profession. There are few instances in which a new approach to public education has included so many institutions, such diverse settings, and such a concerted effort among as many different organizations as has the Teacher Corps. The program illuminates the way new roles are accommodated by a profession; the effectiveness of an outside influence, such as a federal agency, in promoting the changes; the results of experimentation with a wide variety of new teaching techniques and modes of organization; and the potentials of collaboration among schools, local communities, and colleges as a means of improving the profession of teaching.

Specifically, the Teacher Corps attacks two of the most challenging problems confronting public education today: (1) finding effective designs for improving the education of the children of poverty, and (2) guiding the impending changes in the role of the teacher. The intimate relationship between these two problems was underlined in the survey on *Equality of Educational Opportunity* (Coleman et al., 1966), sponsored by the U.S. Office of Education. This study found that the test achievement of children was more highly correlated with their home backgrounds than with school characteristics. Nevertheless, of those variables over which the school has some control, the quality of teachers was one of the most significant factors affecting the quality of education of minority groups. Although, overall, teacher characteristics had relatively little effect on test achievement (10 to 20 percent of the variable could be explained by teacher characteristics), even a small effect means that the teacher can make a difference in whether a *large number* of borderline children in the United States pass or fail their school subjects. Moreover, the positive effects of teacher characteristics occasionally were relatively large among children in the lowest socioeconomic groups in some regions of the country, accounting for up to 40 percent of the achievement of some children. In other words, teachers can make the most difference for children who do not have other advantages. Sometimes, an effective teacher is their only hope.

In comparison with most programs for disadvantaged children, which have focused on the development of techniques for changing the *child*, the Teacher Corps is designed to change the system of teacher training and of schooling itself in order to improve the *condition* of disadvantaged children. Before this program, only a handful of colleges offered a complete course of study geared to teaching in ghetto schools. A major objective of the Corps has been to prod schools of education into modifying their curriculums so as to give more attention to the teaching of the disadvantaged (Douty, 1968). Indeed, stress on institutional change is built into the guidelines of the Corps. To receive funds, a college or university must provide evidence that various departments are participating in the planning and staffing of the Teacher Corps program, that the Corpsmen will be enrolled in related courses focused on the disadvantaged, and that changes in the approaches to education arising from the Teacher Corps experience will be incorporated into the regular education curriculum. In this way, the program attempts to alter key components of the profession, including the type of new members recruited, the authority structure, the status and role system, knowledge content, ideologies and philosophies, socialization practices, and relationships among the profession, community, and university.

NEED FOR INNOVATION IN THE PROFESSIONS. In recent years, the public has become more and more aware of disaffection between professionals of many types and their clientele from low-income families. The problem is so widespread that it is endemic to the professional mode of organization.[3] Today, a confluence of developments has brought the problem to a head: an increasing number of low-income clients are using professional services; the professions are playing a bigger role in the welfare of the individuals in a government-regulated, interdependent economy; more power and improved organization are available to groups living in poverty, who have expressed more and more vocal criticism of the professions; and the number of young professionals is growing—especially the college graduates coming from the swelling noncommercial sector of the economy (government service, communications and the arts, and education, for instance), who are sensitive to the problems of their poor clients, who are often critical of established society, and who identify with the disenfranchised poor. The glaring failures with the poor not only represent a menacing "social problem" but reflect a fundamental condition of today's society: a crisis of faith in the professions. This crisis challenges the convention of granting the professions a license to control their own work and raises anew the question of their proper function in society.

The teaching profession has not escaped this crisis. In this technological age, many children who, a generation ago, would have dropped out of high school are remaining. Education furnishes the only hope for low-income blacks and whites to break the vicious cycle of poor housing, unemployment, and job discrimination. Thus, it is no accident that the schools have been a primary target of the civil rights movement.

SOURCES OF THE PROBLEM. The devastating critiques of ghetto schools, written by Friedenberg (1967), Kohl (1967), Kozol (1967), Coles (1967), and others, and damaging evidence that a great many teachers in ghetto schools have negative attitudes toward their students and have lost faith in them (Coleman et al., 1966; Herriott and St. John, 1966; Corwin and Schmit, 1970) focus on only one part of a highly complex problem. These critiques often have been misleading because they imply that the problems are *unique* to teaching and that they are caused by the type of *people* who enter the profession. There are more generic problems. As already pointed out, not only teaching but every profession—medicine, psychiatry, law, social work, and nursing, for instance—is being criticized for failures with lower-income clients. In addition to the personal characteristics of practitioners, several features of professional work itself have been criticized:

(1) characteristics of the professional structure; (2) the bureaucracy that houses employed professionals; (3) the social disadvantages suffered by many clients because of their family situations; (4) the social distance between professional persons and their clients, including ignorance about their home and community life; and (5) isolation of the profession from professional schools. These problems are now discussed.

1. *Structure of the Professions.* Various writers have attributed the problems to the professional's disproportionate concern for the opinions of colleagues or superiors, compared to his concern for the welfare of his clients (Corwin, 1970); to his formal education, to the differences in his fundamental assumptions and those of his clients (Becker, 1951); and to his own self-interests and those of his colleagues. The status aspirations of occupational groups tend to make them want to disaffiliate themselves from the stigma of working with exclusively lower-class clientele (Goffman, 1963). Professionals have been accused of having degrading and fatalistic conceptions about low-income clients that could adversely affect a child's aspirations and expectations of himself (K. Clark, 1965). People in a specialized society not only depend on professional help but often are required by law to use professional services (for example, school children and applicants for welfare and rehabilitation funds). Differences between the professional and his client are accentuated in this compulsory, one-to-one situation. Also, many helping professions, such as social work and psychology, use techniques that presume that problems can be resolved through the talking process and "self-understanding." This presumption is not always fully accepted by the poor, who are more interested in environmental changes and concrete, impersonal services such as care for children, housing, unemployment compensation, and old-age assistance.

Recognizing that many of these problems are by-products of professionalism itself, some observers have advocated deprofessionalization by relying more on noncareerists, paraprofessionals, and indigenous laymen (Reissman, 1962). Other investigators advocate a different type of training to reduce the social distance between professionals and their low-income clients, such as the Teacher Corps attempts to do.

2. *Bureaucratic Structure.* Bureaucracy is an often-ignored factor that contributes to the problems of low-income clients (Corwin, 1965). Blau (1960) reported that bureaucratic patterns sometimes inadvertently reinforce the middle-class value system at the expense of poor clients. Professionals with procedure-oriented supervisors were likely to be less oriented to service than those who worked for less procedure-oriented supervisors. Blau (1955) also found that the tendency for supervisors in large-scale orga-

nizations to evaluate their employees on the basis of the number of clients processed and on their adherence to given procedures predisposes professional employees to give preference to achievement-oriented clients, who promise to be more "receptive" to treatment and more willing to conform to bureaucratic procedure. Moreover, as other observers have pointed out (Sjoberg, Brymer, and Farris, 1966), the low-income client is at a further disadvantage because he is not likely to be sophisticated about alien bureaucratic rules. Finally, because the poor are more likely than persons from the middle class to be afflicted by multiple problems, they are the least well served by specialized bureaucratic systems in which related problems are treated by different agencies functioning in isolation from one another.

3. *Family Disadvantage.* Some observers deny that either the professions or the bureaucratic procedures are, in themselves, the major causes of the problems. They point, instead, to the client's disadvantage that stems from his own family structure and his lack of motivation to achieve in an environment of poverty (Moynihan, 1965). According to this argument, many lower-class children are deprived of a positive "role model" because of the absence of a permanent father. Although this is a somewhat dubious argument, it is true that the loose-knit family and community structure not only deprive the poor of a source of organized self-help (which other ethnic groups used to good advantage in their climb up the social ladder) but also force them to rely almost exclusively on outside professional assistance, which they often cannot afford and are not in a position to control.

4. *Social Distance Between Profession and Community.* Although all of the foregoing factors are involved in one way or another, some commentators argue that the heart of the problem is the social distance between profession and community. Professional status and bureaucratic controls impose formidable barriers to any meaningful collaboration with clients from an alien subculture. The key to improving service to the poor, therefore, is to integrate professional organizations more fully into the life of their clients and their surrounding communities. It is widely assumed that closer relationships between home and school will provide a greater incentive for children to learn, will help teachers to develop a better understanding of the children's interests and problems, and will assure more assistance from the parents, who are in a better position to reinforce the teachers' instructions. Thus, many of the experimental training programs, designed especially for inner-city schools, have incorporated efforts to establish closer relationships between the home and school (Fusco, 1964).

There *is* some evidence that a child's performance is positively related to his parents' support for, and participation in, school activities (Luszki and Schmuck, 1963; Schiff, 1963; Duncan, 1964; and Himmelweit and Sealy, 1966). Another study showed that the value of education was heightened for parents who visited the school or participated in parent-teacher associations, particularly for the working classes (Cloward and Jones, 1963). Of course, since community relations usually constitute only one aspect of broader programs, it is impossible to attribute gains to school-parent contacts alone.

Although, in recent years, teachers have been exhorted by their professional leadership to become more familiar with their communities, they actually tend to remain aloof from the lower-class neighborhoods in which they teach. Lower-class respondents, more so than those from the middle and working classes, feel that teachers are uninterested in their children and that the schools do not pay enough attention to children from poor families (Cloward and Jones, 1963). A survey of Columbus, Ohio, indicated that teachers, from all parts of the city, felt that parents *should* have an opportunity to sit down and discuss education with teachers and administrators. However, a smaller proportion of inner-city teachers than outer-city teachers stated that parents actually *do* have such an opportunity (Corwin and Schmit, 1970). It has been found that parents with the lowest incomes (for any neighborhood) participate least in school activities, lack contact with people who do participate in these activities, lack the ability to communicate in group situations, have few cultural expectations that would lead them to participate, do not feel that participation is relevant to their needs, and lack the time and energy required for participation (Foskett, 1959). After studying school-parent programs of 20 depressed urban-area schools, Fusco (1964) reported that the "parents, as revealed in the interviews, were reluctant to visit the schools their children attended, did not become involved in the activities of school-related organizations, and were generally shy with school personnel and suspicious toward them." Perhaps the typical activity draws no more than 20 percent of the parents. But racial militancy in the big cities, with its demands for community control, can quickly change this picture.

5. *Relationship Between Profession and University.* The profession's relationship with the community, however, represents only one dimension of its external environment—and not necessarily the most important one. The link between the profession and its parent training institutions is, in the long run, perhaps an even more decisive factor in the profession's capacity to adapt to change. Unfortunately, the attention now being given to the issue of community control, and to school-community relations in

general, may have obscured the primary role that professional schools can (and, sometimes, do) play in the change process. Very little attention has been given to this dimension in the literature, but I think that it should be examined extensively.

IMPLICATIONS. The prospect of improving professional service to low-income people may depend on the ability of society to reform the professions, to alter bureaucratic structures, and to close the social distance between professionals and the communities and other innovative institutions. The question is: Can solutions to these problems be found without destroying what is valuable in the present structure?

APPROACH TO THE RESEARCH

I have commented on the general issues that form the framework of this study. Obviously, a single work cannot deal adequately with all of the facets of such complex matters. Consequently, I have selected aspects of each issue for consideration. However, I have tried to maintain a comprehensive view of each aspect by using a variety of research strategies. I shall clarify, now, what can and cannot be expected from my approach.

Alternative Modes of Inquiry

To place the study in context, it is useful to identify several modes of social-science inquiry that an investigator might follow. Thompson and his colleagues (1960) developed a typology to distinguish between these various modes. It is based on (1) the reliance that the researcher places on his own personal observations or "sensory experience" (high or low), and (2) the kind of reasoning used to analyze and arrange the experience (codified and systematic or uncodified). These two dimensions underlie four types of "truth strategies." At one extreme, high reliance is placed on personal observation (data) and codified reasoning; the authors call this the "scientific" type, as exemplified by experimental psychology. At the other extreme, a more "inspirational" or speculative mode is relied on; that is, when the observations are imprecise and largely uncodified. There are two intermediate types. One of them (called the "direct" strategy) relies on data that are largely uncodified but that can be directly confirmed through sensory experience, as is done in cultural anthropology. The other type (called the "analytic" mode) uses abstract and codified knowledge forms, as exemplified by mathematics.

The *codified* mode of inquiry is most useful with very focused studies, confined to a few precisely measured, logically related variables derived from general propositions. It is helpful for extending abstract, hierarchically organized theory in which the specific events are treated as representative of general classes of events. Because the main utility of this mode is to contribute to an abstract system of knowledge, it usually provides only incomplete and segmental information about the objects studied. *Uncodified* inquiry, on the other hand, proceeds by collecting a wide array of information pertaining to some social unit, such as a group, community, organization, or program. The variables considered and the focus of inquiry are very broad, since the primary objective is to understand the social unit itself. Abstract concepts are systematically employed, but only as a means of describing and helping to interpret specific patterns of events. The success of this approach must be measured in terms of how well the analysis helps one to comprehend a specific situation instead of in terms of its contribution to general theory.

With respect to the other major dimension of the typology—the reliance placed on sensory data—it need only be observed that the type of inquiry that is closely tied to direct observation is useful for confirming or denying well-formulated propositions. By comparison, inquiry that is not closely tied to systematic observation can be a valuable source of new directions for seeking information and a source of general propositions and speculations.

Each mode of inquiry has distinctive advantages. Conversely, it has disadvantages. Considered together, they provide *alternative* approaches that can supplement one another and, in concert, provide a rather comprehensive attack on a topic. However, in practice, social scientists rarely have experimented with eclectic approaches to research that rely on a combination of approaches. There are both sound and indefensible reasons for this "purist" attitude in the social sciences. A sound reason is that each form of research makes special demands on the researcher, that is, each form requires special data, unique methods of data collection, and the like. Moreover, the conclusions reached from different forms are subject to different types of qualifications and reservations. But some of these problems might be overcome if it were not for other, more dubious bases for the purist tendencies. Foremost are the compelling dogmas and ideologies that are associated with each form of research and that discourage combined attacks. Because of these blind dogmas, a researcher's prestige and reputation become linked to the form of research he uses, which discourages experimentation with combined approaches. As a result of these pressures, each piece of research becomes forced into a mold; any deviation from the methodological stereotype is considered as a sign of weakness and is doomed to the disadvantages inherent in the approach. There is little incentive within the social sciences to benefit from the advantages offered by alternative modes or to synthesize the results obtained from different modes of inquiry.

Nevertheless, I prefer an eclectic approach that attempts to cut through the stereotyped research designs that are so typical of social-science research—even at the risk of compromising the presumed "integrity" of any given approach and of producing results that "fall between two or more stools." If an eclectic methodology is subject to the *problems* associated with the various approaches, by comparison to the purist attitude it can also capitalize on the *strengths* of several alternative truth strategies. Only by using multiple approaches can the researcher view the subject from different angles, and only in this way can research begin to fulfill more effectively the highly diversified demands made upon it. In other words, I believe that the comprehensiveness achieved from an eclectic attack on research outweighs the compromises that must be made in the integrity of each approach to achieve the comprehensiveness.

Research Objectives and Strategy

Now let us consider the objectives behind this research and the overall strategy used to achieve them. Generally the research should be considered as a multiple case study whose objective is to describe the natural history of a reform program and to explain some of the variable program outcomes. This broad statement embodies at least four additional specific purposes:

1. To provide a comprehensive *description* and *interpretation* of the Teacher Corps program itself in the hope that the fate of this program will provide lessons that can be used not only to improve it but that can help other programs to avoid the pitfalls that this one encountered.

2. To use the Teacher Corps as a specific case of a more general class of organizations and programs in order to derive general propositions that might be tested in subsequent research.

3. To use data from the Teacher Corps to test specific hypotheses that can be derived from sociological theory.

4. To use the personal insights and informal observations gained from the study as a basis for speculating about general issues.

This is clearly a large order. It was therefore necessary to draw on a variety of proxy indicators rather than to concentrate on a few precisely measured concepts. It has required the use of elements of a natural-history approach, of statistical analyses, and of comparative case-study methods. Moreover, the study necessarily encompasses a range of concerns: occupational socialization, organizational change, the political and economic context of the program, and the like. Therefore, it was necessary to make a shift in focus and in methodology from one chapter to another. However, I believe that this constant shift of focus is the only method of explaining such a complex program in any meaningful way. As a whole, the study should provide one of the few available relatively comprehensive and balanced descriptions of a national reform program.

Scope of the Study

I have kept in perspective both the national dimensions of the program and the variety of local forms that it assumed. I also have focused, alternatively, on simple descriptions and on more analytic interpretations and explanations of both the national and local programs. It was necessary to include a sufficient number of cases to make sure that the scope of the national program would be represented. Yet the number of cases will permit an in-depth, comprehensive study of each case. A multiple-case approach reveals the significant general patterns in modes of organization, problems encountered, and strategies used to overcome the problems, and also permits a study of the variations. The ten colleges and 42 cooperating schools discussed, will provide a profile of the national program and permit a statistical analysis (although statistics are merely a convenient way of dealing with patterns and variations among multiple cases). The description of two extreme cases (in Chapter 7) illuminates the more abstract comments on general patterns and the detailed statistical treatments in other chapters.

Much of the focus has been on organizational changes that took place within the schools and colleges that were participating in the program. However, it is not possible to understand these internal changes without considering the broader interorganizational context of the program as a whole. Consequently, the Teacher Corps program can be viewed as a network of organizations, with its own structure and dynamics, consisting of:

1. The U.S. Congress, which created the program.

2. The national Teacher Corps office, which was responsible for interpreting the legislation and administering the program.

3. The colleges, which were responsible for directing the local programs and which acted as the primary link between the national office and the local school districts.

4. The local school districts, especially the specific schools cooperating with the colleges.

5. A variety of local community groups and organizations cooperating with the schools.

In general it was necessary to consider the interplay between the intra-organizational change and changes and tensions that occurred within this interorganizational network.

The structure of this interorganizational network is very complex. Officially, the relationships take place in a chainlike form; that is, the Congress exerts influence directly on the Teacher Corps office, which works directly with colleges, which work with local schools. Actually, however, local school districts often had direct access to the federal agency and, in some cases, to Congress itself; and the federal agency itself was embedded in a web of complex relationships within the federal bureaucracy. These and other subtleties in the interorganizational structure will become clearer during the course of this study.

As stated previously, this book deals with the problems of change both in organizations and in the professions. Since each of these problems is a complex topic in itself, the study focuses on the organizational changes that overlap the changes in the professional structure and the practices used to socialize new professionals. The data show that organizational change is necessary if certain professional reforms are to take place. Moreover, since the injection of socialization into the profession is regarded as an important condition for long-term change in professional practice, attention is given to *personal* changes that occur during the program.

Nature of the Data

Changes in the individuals were inferred from a profile of values and attitudes measured at the beginning and at the end of the two-year program. Although the time span involved is relatively short, it includes the critical points at which any changes induced by the program itself are most likely to be detected. However, the present data do not indicate whether there might have been changes that did not materialize until much later, or how permanent the changes that were observed might have been. (It will be possible to make long-term comparisons from longitudinal studies, in progress, of the interns after they graduated.)

The measures of organizational change are based on an index derived from an analysis of respondents' reports. These reports are largely retrospective in nature; the respondents were asked to describe the changes they had observed since the Teacher Corps program had been introduced. This index was validated by visits to five of the programs at the beginning and at the end of the program.

It has been necessary to rely heavily on the reports of participants in the program for many measures of change and other critical variables. Some colleagues will feel that too much reliance was placed on respondents' reports, and I tend to agree. However, there was no "hard," objective, or precise way of documenting the evidence on the type of questions that were considered important. The alternative of ignoring the difficult issues seemed irresponsible. Instead, several compensating steps were taken. First, when the respondents reported different perceptions of the program, these differences were incorporated into the overall estimates by stratifying the weighting of the pooled responses. Second, respondents' reports were spot-checked against the observations of our interviewers who spent several weeks at each program; some measures were informally checked at two different times. Third, for at least some of the key measures, somewhat complex indices were constructed that relied on data from several sources and, in some cases, required the judgment of the principal investigators. These precautions will minimize some of the drawbacks of relying on informants, but the source of most of the measures must be kept in mind. There are other reservations inherent in this type of research, which will now be examined.

CONDITIONS FOR THE RESEARCH

I must mention the limitations of this study. Any study of an ongoing action program will necessarily be subjected to pressures growing out of the program's political context. Administrators understandably view research as a way of demonstrating the successes and failures of their own programs and have a great deal to lose from negative findings. It is especially important to recognize these constraints if the findings are to be used as a basis for making policy decisions about the program (including a determination of whether to continue or terminate it). Although much may be expected of social-science research, it is usually conducted under circumstances that are least favorable to the production of fully reliable information. Even though academic colleagues may be aware of the limitations imposed by the state of the art, laymen, seeking valid and reliable knowledge on which to base decisions, are less likely to be fully aware of the technical deficiencies and tentativeness of most conclusions of social-science research.

Obstacles to Field Research

Action programs, by their very nature, must be tentative, noncommittal, and adaptive, whereas research requires a clear and constant purpose and a continuity of procedure (Marris and Rein, 1967). The number of variables over which the investigator has control is minimized appreciably in field research, while the number of contingent factors is maximized. The changing operational setting often can force the researcher to make compromises in the design in order to meet administrative contingencies imposed by the groups being studied. Research on action programs, in comparison to other forms of field research, must be closely tied to the time schedules and administrative procedures of the program being evaluated; the relevant variables are predetermined by the nature of the program; the chain of events between the program treatment and outcomes is usually complicated by a range of variables influencing human behavior. Therefore, many more variables must be taken into consideration.

1. *Multiple and Ambiguous Objectives.* According to the canons of methodology, action programs are supposed to have a clearly stated objective and, where several objectives exist, there should be clearly stated priorities. In practice, however, action programs are designed to accommodate diverse expectations. The program director often finds it strategically wise to intentionally leave the program's objectives ambiguous so that it cannot be judged against a single, clear-cut criterion that could expose failure as well as success. It is the researcher's responsibility to identify a range of stated and implicit objectives.

2. *The Criterion Problem.* Policy makers and informed citizens want to know how "effective" a program is, but it is difficult to identify measurable variables that clearly reflect vague, multiple objectives. No one knows what kinds of skills prospective teachers need to accomplish a given objective such as improving the quality of instruction in poverty schools. Whether it is possible to train individuals to be "innovative" is not certain and, even if it were possible, it does not follow that "innovative people" are more effective teachers. Finally, there is the problem of determining whether the improvements that have been made will persist.

3. *The Measurement Problem.* The above problems are difficult, but the behavioral sciences have not reached a stage at which even simple variables can be measured with a high degree of precision—methodological magic notwithstanding. This is particularly true of research on complex organizations. Only 112 scales and indices have been developed to measure characteristics even remotely related to complex organization, and

most of them are single indices; by comparison, 435 attempts have been made to measure socioeconomic status (Bonjean, Hill, and McLimore, 1967). More important, there has been little continuity in efforts to measure facets of complex organization. The available measures have been used on the average of only once or twice; by comparison, the Edwards occupational scale was used 91 times, and the California "F Scale" 53 times. Unfortunately, therefore, each project must develop its own modest measures.

The critical measurement problems include separating the effects of the program from other sources of change in the dependent variable, untangling the members of the target population who are involved in more than one experimental program from the members who are involved in only one, and identifying changes that take place in the character of the sample during the course of the program (Freeman and Sherwood, 1965).

4. *Heterogeneous and Changing Nature of Experimental Programs.* Programs such as the Teacher Corps, which consist of a multitude of stimuli imposed over an extended period of time, are much too complex to fit the classical "independent-dependent variable" model. They also change and fluctuate over time, and there is likely to be an enormous variation in the way these programs are implemented from one location to another.

5. *Complexities of Social Life.* The foregoing difficulties are compounded by several conditions of life that make any social research difficult, including these elements: few aspects of social life are caused by a single factor; complex multiple causation is the normal situation; causation is rarely completely linear in social life; many social situations involve feedback from their effects to their causes, which makes the total process reciprocal or spiral; and the factors that initially cause a social phenomenon often are not the ones that perpetuate it (Olsen, 1968).

6. *Ideological Factors.* Borgatta (1966) has identified several self-defeating rationalizations that can undermine a new program from the start. These include the assumption that the effects of the program are long-range—thus the results cannot be measured in the immediate future; the assumption that the effects are general rather than specific—thus a single criterion cannot be utilized to evaluate the program and, indeed, the use of many measures would not really evaluate complex general consequences intended; the assumption that the effects are small but important —thus they cannot be measured effectively because instruments are not sufficiently sensitive; the assumption that the effects are subtle and that circumstances may not be ordered appropriately to evaluate the qualities

that are being changed; and the assumption that measurement would disturb the process involved.

7. *Charismatic Effects.* Finally, programs very often are initiated by charismatic individuals who have great confidence in them. These individuals attract equally devoted subordinates who sometimes develop such a level of enthusiasm that they "sell" the program despite its problems. This pioneering spirit makes it difficult to separate the effects of the program itself; a program that has been successful in one location may not be as successful in other locations in which the staff views it with less enthusiasm.

Compensating Factors

What makes such studies difficult? It is not their unique principles of research but the practical problems of adhering to standard research principles in the face of administrative constraints. By comparison, when a problem is theoretically defined, it can be arbitrarily limited in scope and ambition. Yet it is precisely this limited scope that often makes such research trivial. Therefore, despite the obstacles, research on action programs offers many advantages; for instance, the fact that action projects are "natural field experiments." Even though they are not likely to meet many of the conditions of the classical design, since it is almost impossible to control the gamut of environmental variables that are likely to influence the setting, they do represent an improvement over most studies. They have in common with the classical design a focus on the consequences of systematic changes in certain independent variables and attempt to manipulate variables in a field setting. Additional rigor can be added through the use of statistical controls and correlation inferences.

THE APPROACH TO BE TAKEN

The above considerations necessarily will influence the feasibility of different approaches that can be taken. Four approaches to the study of an action program are: the goal model, the comparative model, the program-testing approach, and the variable-testing approach. Let us discuss these approaches.

Goal Model versus Comparative Model

The goal-model approach defines program success as a substantial realization of the organizational goal or goals. By contrast, in the comparative model the performances of existing organizations are assessed relative to one another instead of to an ideal state. Etzioni (1964) points out that the comparison of existing organizations to ideals of what they might be is analogous to an electrical engineer rating all light bulbs as ineffective because they convert only 5 percent of their electrical energy into light, the rest being "wasted" on heat. In practice it is more meaningful to compare light bulbs to one another than to a superbulb.

The comparative model, then, provides a more realistic assessment of what might be hoped for in a particular situation. Its drawback is that it requires many more factors, other than goals, to be taken into account; furthermore, the means to those goals must be analyzed. Therefore, this approach is more exacting and expensive.

Program Testing versus Variable Testing

Simplistic evaluations that concentrate only on the outcomes without considering the processes involved produce dubious and often totally deceptive conclusions. Unless the underlying factors responsible for the outcomes are identified, the study cannot yield knowledge that will be applicable beyond the specific program being evaluated. It will not provide useful guidance for other programs and is therefore, in the long run, far less practical and more expensive than research that is more broadly grounded in theory.

Compared to the program-testing approach, the variable-testing approach is less concerned with determining general success or failure of a program and is more concerned with singling out specific components and identifying the conditions under which each contributes to various outcomes of the program (Hovland, 1949). Also, as Cronbach (1962) points out, such research can perform a valuable service by determining where revision is desirable. In the long run these considerations are more important than learning whether the program, on the average, produces better or worse results than conventional programs. The role of theory is to direct the search for the key variables and the conditions that affect them.

In short, the objective is not only to ask whether the program "works" but to identify the conditions associated with specific changes. Therefore, a comparative analysis of the crucial underlying variables is the most fitting approach for a study of this kind.

SUMMARY

The Teacher Corps was a product of the widespread disaffection between professionals and their clients from the lower socioeconomic classes. It was intended to help improve teaching in low-income schools. Although the subject of the study is teaching and university teacher-training programs, the discussion is cast within a more general framework. By comparison to most programs for the disadvantaged, which usually have been aimed at changing the client, the Teacher Corps attempts to change the system itself. It therefore provides an excellent case for learning more about how to deliberately change organizations; it can also illuminate and guide impending changes in the roles of other professionals and teachers, who are needed to improve conditions and prospects for youngsters from low-income homes; and, since the Corps is a federally sponsored program involving a coalition of schools and universities mediated by a federal agency, its fate also can shed light on the larger forces producing an increasingly federalized, national society.

It is not my intention to determine how well the program as a whole achieved its abstract goals, and I shall not attempt to arrive at overall, simplistic judgments. Moreover, I shall not catalog each component in detail. Instead, I shall focus on the program components to identify the conditions that are responsible for variable outcomes and to arrive at a general awareness of the overarching, but variable, patterns within and among the local Teacher Corps programs. This kind of research must rely partly on theory for direction.

There are several obstacles to this kind of study: multiple and ambiguous objectives and the heterogeneous and changing nature of the program; the problem of identifying appropriate performance criteria and measures for assessing performance; the lack of control over critical variables and other complexities of social life; the exploratory character of most social research; and the self-defensiveness and charismatic qualities of the particular people involved in the program. However, as compensation, such programs attempt to manipulate precisely the structural variables that are of great practical and theoretical significance. Despite the obstacles, more can be learned about significant issues by studying action programs than by ignoring them in the name of scientific purity. Although loosely structured, they are "natural field experiments" involving the manipulation of critically important variables that researchers seldom have enough resources to alter by themselves and that therefore are seldom included in "pure" research designs. In view of the objectives of the study and the obstacles that it must face, the research must be largely exploratory rather than definitive. Large-scale, survey-analysis techniques will be combined with case-study analyses. It is advisable to "cast a large net" and explore many dimensions of the problem, providing ample opportunity to detect unanticipated outcomes. But the introduction of a large number of variables compounds the measurement problem; it becomes necessary to rely on crude indicators of certain variables. Intensity of analysis, in other words, necessarily must be exchanged for a larger scope, which is in contrast to the common practice in survey research of testing in detail specific hypotheses based on a few variables and refined measurements. As Hertzog (1959) points out, it is not profitable to lavish time and money on being extremely precise in one feature when it is out of proportion with the exactness that can be claimed for the project.

NOTES

1. For example, see Sills, 1957; Selznick, 1949; Gusfield, 1955; Messinger, 1955; B. Clark, 1956; Moynihan, 1969; Marris and Rein, 1967; Watson, 1968; Zald, 1970; B. Clark, 1960; B. Clark, 1965.

2. One way of circumventing some of these problems is to concentrate on an organization's ability to obtain scarce resources needed to attain goals, whatever they may be—for example, the ability to compete for the desired people—and to examine the way these resources are actually employed (Yuchtman and Seashore, 1967).

3. Koos (1954) observed a prevalent feeling among poor people that physicians do not want them as patients. Several investigators have reported that less-adequate medical care is given to poor patients (Hollingshead and Redlich, 1958; Myers and Schaffer, 1954). Hollingshead and Redlich found that the type of agency in which mentally ill patients are treated and the type of treatment they receive are adversely associated with having a lower socioeconomic status. The number of therapists who saw patients each month, as well as the length of the visits, differed markedly by social class. Sudnow (1967) concluded that the care one gets in medical emergency rooms of the two cities he studied is partly determined by one's social standing in the community, although not purely by racial considerations. Simmons (1957) observed that the greater the social distance between the professional and his patient, the more likely it is that they will perceive each other in terms of their rights and obligations. Willie (1960) found that nearly half (30) of 64 public health nurses surveyed preferred to work exclusively with middle-class patients; only nine stated a definite preference to work with lower-class patients. And from a survey of the selection of applicants for treatment in a social-work clinic and a family agency, Coleman and others (1957) found that, regardless of diagnosis, lower-class clients were less likely to receive continued treatment, particularly at the clinic. A report on a tax-supported child guidance clinic also showed that even though income level did not influence intake, the probability of being accepted for treatment was nearly twice as great for children from high-income homes as for children from middle-income or low-income homes (Stevens, 1954).

CHAPTER 2

Procedures

Don't indulge in lop-sided research.

HERTZOG, 1959, p. 82

From October 1968 to March 1969, 10 Teacher Corps training programs were visited for one week each by teams of interviewers; five of these program sites were revisited during the spring of 1970. During these visits interns, team leaders, cooperating school personnel, program administrators, and university faculty completed lengthy questionnaires developed for this study by the principal investigator in cooperation with the Advisory Committee and the Teacher Corps office in Washington, D.C. Approximately two thirds of the respondents also were interviewed.

THE SAMPLE

Teacher Corps Sites

The 10 sites were selected on the basis of informed estimates about the characteristics of each program. Four programs were selected because they were new and provided the opportunity to observe the development and evolution of a new program; a fifth program, even though it was not new, was selected primarily because it had a new third cycle, which was of primary interest. (These were the five programs revisited in 1970 to observe changes that had taken place during one and one half years of operation.) The other five programs had been established since the Teacher Corps

began in 1967 and had operated for at least one year at the time they were
visited.

At each site, at least three local cooperating schools were included in
the study. In selecting these schools the research staff made a special effort
to represent the various types of low-income groups served by the system.
A fourth school, not participating in the Teacher Corps but resembling
the mode of the cooperating schools, was included for comparative purposes. These comparison schools, of course, do not provide a matched
sample, but they can provide an indication of systematic differences within

Table 2-1 Characteristics of 35 third-cycle programs and of the
study sample

Program characteristics	Third-cycle programs[a]		The study sample[b]	
	Number	Percent	Number	Percent
Urban [c]				
Established [d]	13	36	4	40
New	10	31	3	30
Total	23	67	7	70
Rural [c]				
Established [d]	9	25	2	20
New	3	8	1	10
Total	12	33	3	30
Total	35	100	10	100

[a] This breakdown was estimated from preliminary information on 35
scheduled third-cycle programs.

[b] The variables considered in this choice were ongoing versus new
programs, geographical location, urban versus rural, and ethnic
group served.

[c] Two programs, one in each of the urban and rural categories, included both urban and rural elements. Categorization reflects the
major emphasis of the two programs.

[d] Only programs that had been in from the beginning of the Teacher
Corps were included.

a city between schools without Teacher Corps teams and schools to which teams are assigned.

An effort was made to represent, proportionately, the rural and urban programs, programs located in different regions of the United States, and programs servicing different minority groups. Four of the programs primarily serviced black children, and two serviced a portion of Mexican-Americans and Indians (see Table 2–1).

A range of quality is also represented in the selected programs according to ratings made by Teacher Corps personnel, interns, team leaders, and a panel that rated them for re-funding; but none was rated as being of poor quality at the time the selection was made, and all were ranked in the upper third of the programs. In other words, in recognition of the odds against the Teacher Corps, a deliberate effort was made to select the programs that had a chance to make a measurable impact on the schools and colleges involved. It was assumed that there would be a natural tendency for programs to cluster around a point of little or no change and, therefore, that the safest way to maximize the variance was to stack the sample in favor of programs most likely to move beyond this point.

Respondent Sample

Two forms of the questionnaire were distributed to all interns in new programs and to the second wave of interns who had joined in 1967 and were still in established programs, to the principal and to all regular classroom teachers in each cooperating school, to the university program directors, to school-system coordinators and to university faculty members who were associated with the program, and to a comparable group of graduate students in education at each college who were not in the Teacher Corps. Between one half and three fourths of the persons who returned questionnaires were interviewed.[1]

QUESTIONNAIRES. Table 2–2 reports on the first visit and shows the total number (in parentheses) of 1785 possible respondents available at all programs visited. A total of 1298 questionnaires (for the two forms combined) were returned from among all position groups, a total response of 73 percent. On the second visit to 5 of the 10 sites, 305 of the possible respondents returned questionnaires, a rate of about 92 percent.

There were some differences in rates of return from different programs that are not reflected in the table. The total number of questionnaires returned from the different programs on the first visit ranged from 97 to

Table 2-2   Number of questionnaires and rate of return, and number
of interviews, by position

Event	Intern	Team leader	Classroom teacher
First visit			
Total number of questionnaires	266 (332)[a]	53 (56)	872 (1255)
Percent completing questionnaires	80	95	69
Number of interviews	153[b]	48	531
Second visit			
Total number of questionnaires	117 (126)[a]	24 (25)	107 (119)
Percent completing questionnaires	92.9	96	89.9
Number of interviews	67	17	54
Percent interviewed twice	44	35	10

[a] Numbers in parentheses report total number of possible respondents. The rate of questionnaire return is higher than reflected in these figures as questionnaires were not distributed to every possible respondent (only to about 90 percent of this number).

[b] In addition, 66 graduate students not in the Teacher Corps but enrolled in the 10 colleges in the sample were interviewed in depth.

180. This represented a rate of return of between 42 and 100 percent. The rate of return on the second visit varied between 80 and 100 percent.

Because two different forms of the questionnaire were used, the sample size varies widely for different items. Some items were included on both forms, others on only one form. Since the two questionnaires were distributed randomly among the incumbents of each position at each program, this variance should not be a major source of error.

INTERVIEWS. At each site a random sample of approximately 15 interns, 5 team leaders, 6 principals, 53 classroom teachers, and 4 university faculty members were interviewed; in most cases the sample included the teachers in the school who were currently working with interns. A total of 923 persons were interviewed during the first visit, including two thirds of those who completed questionnaires and 66 graduate students not in the program. On the second visit, 186 members of the third wave of interns,

Position				
Principal	Coordinator and assistants	Program director	University faculty	Total
53 (56)	9 (14)	16 (21)	29 (51)	1298 (1785)
95	64	76	57	73
54	10	19	42	857
20 (21)	2 (5)	4 (5)	31 (34)	305 (335)
95.2	40	80	91.2	91.9
14	5	5	24	186
24	50	21	57	22

who had joined in 1968, were interviewed again, including more than half of the interns and teachers who returned questionnaires and over two thirds of the team leaders, principals, and university faculty members.

OBSERVATION. In addition to the questionnaires and interviews, official records were used, systematic field notes were kept by interviewers, a few interns kept field diaries, and some members of the project staff acted as informal observers. One member of the research staff spent 20 days observing teams of interns at four of the sites; a substantial part of each day was devoted to recording extensive notes on the activities of the teams and the persons with whom they associated. Patterns of relationships among team members and between them and the classroom teachers and other persons with whom they associated were noted (Hanna, 1970).[2]

Characteristics of Interns and Teachers in the Respondent Sample

Fifty-eight percent of the interns were male, 16 percent were nonwhite, and 59 percent had come to their training programs from outside the region. The first two figures are identical to a survey of all graduating second-cycle Corps members (Cort, 1968). By comparison to the interns, only 25 percent of the teachers were male, over 34 percent were nonwhite, and only 20 percent were new to the system.

One third of the interns (the mode) had earned their degrees in one of the social sciences, and 30 percent held degrees in psychology, the physical sciences, music, art, mathematics, or philosophy. Less than 3 percent had majored in education, whereas three fourths of the teachers declared an education major. But 13 percent of the interns had obtained a degree from either a teachers college or a college of education in a large university, and one in four had graduated from a liberal arts college with a program that included work in education courses. A total of 37 percent had taken courses in education before joining the Teacher Corps. Cort (1968) reported that about half of the second-cycle interns had taken courses in education.

RATIONALE FOR THE DESIGN

As the public has become more aware of the decisive influence that schools and colleges can have on the learning process, it has turned to the behavioral sciences for reliable information and for new perspectives. This twist of fate, although flattering to social scientists, has placed an imposing burden on these fledgling disciplines, which is hardly warranted by the state of the art. This new faith results from the fact that there are few alternative sources of help, but it is also an acclamation of the social scientists' preparedness to undertake the demands being placed on them. Not only is it difficult to identify the variables that most appropriately reflect the wide range of outcomes that might be desired of a program as complex as the Teacher Corps but, once they are selected, it is even more difficult to develop precise measurements in view of the primitive state of measurement procedures in this field.

We have proceeded in full recognition that sociological theory is not sufficiently developed to completely determine in advance the variables that are likely to influence the outcomes of a program such as this. We have had to grope our way through the morass of possibilities by making certain assumptions about what the various Teacher Corps programs are attempting to do. One of the considerations in selecting variables, of course, was the presumed goals of the Corps itself. The difficulties in identifying organization and program goals already have been discussed.

Assumptions

The little that is known about the sociology of learning provided some guidance. Since there is some evidence that teachers' education is associated with the academic achievement of their pupils, this factor was considered. As another tack, we drew upon general theory. For example, in a changing heterogeneous society, we assumed that there would be a preference for organizational flexibility and teachers who are open-minded, who respect children from low-income homes, who are tolerant of others, and who desire to exercise leadership rather than teachers with the opposite characteristics. Therefore, priority was given to variables related to organizational change and to individuals' attitudes toward change and initiative-taking. The basic assumption was that, at this particular stage of knowledge, the *capacities* of organizations to change must be enhanced before education can be improved.

Value and Limits of Opinion Measurement

Because this study relied on the views of the participants as one way of assessing program outcomes, perhaps it should be noted here that the correlation between opinions, attitudes, and actual behavior has been disputed, so much so that some writers would dismiss attitudes and opinions entirely (Deutscher, 1969). Although the degree of correspondence is not so great as some early attitude theorists seem to have assumed, Ehrlich (1969) has summarized a convincing body of evidence that opinions do provide insight into *behavior*. Although the degree of correspondence is often confounded and sometimes erased by intervening circumstances, opinions can tip the balance when people are confronted with conflicting pressures. Generally, the more determined the opinions are, the more powerful the intervening circumstances must be to offset the opinion-behavior correlation. Hence, while personal opinions cannot be justified as the sole criterion of program outcomes, it is not sensible to dismiss them entirely.

Conversely, however, the emphasis that has been given to personal attitudes and opinions in the literature can be very misleading if it conveys the notion that one can solve the problems only by persuading people to change their opinions or by replacing the individuals involved with people who express more favorable attitudes. An attempt to solve problems by getting rid of, or changing, the individuals involved can be seriously inadequate unless it is accompanied by plans for making deliberate changes in the structure in which these people must operate.

Scope and Limits of the Study

Since all research must select certain facets of a problem for study, oversimplification is almost inevitable. However, this does not justify limiting attention to a single outcome. All programs will have multiple effects and both unintended and intended consequences. A fair assessment of a program must take into account the effects and consequences, since failure to achieve one objective is easily masked by success in another direction (Cronbach, 1962). Cronbach maintains that, ideally, one should include measures of all the types of proficiency that could be desired, not just the selected outcomes to which the particular program is directed. It is desirable to know not only how well the program is achieving its objective but also whether it is serving some broader interest.

One important type of outcome was *not* directly assessed in the study—the program's impact on students. The reason is that the objectives and roles in this program were too highly diversified, and the interns' responsibilities to children were too varied within and among programs to accurately assess how the program, as a whole, affected learning.

MEASUREMENTS

Scales and Indices

Scales and indices were developed to measure a battery of variables. Some of the more complex measures are discussed in Appendix 1, which lists the specific items used in each measure. A summary of measures is included in Table 2–4 at the end of this chapter (p. 54).

1. *Commitment to Teaching.* The intentions of interns to continue teaching in poverty schools were elicited from the sum of three questionnaire items asking the respondents to estimate how likely it was that they would be working in a low-income school the next year, in five years, and indefinitely (see Appendix 1, p. 399). The expression of career plans while in graduate school reflects only an initial guess.

2. *Attitudes Toward Racial Integration.* Three Likert-type items (adapted from the 1966 *Equality of Educational Opportunity* survey and other sources) were used to ascertain teachers' attitudes toward the expected advantages of integrated schools and their support for proposals to reduce racial segregation (see Appendix 1, p. 399).

3. *Initiative and Compliance in Education.* A scale consisting of nine hypothetical incidents in which a teacher finds himself opposed to the administration was developed to estimate the tendencies of teachers to use "initiative" or show "compliance" with respect to their administrators (Corwin, 1970). The incidents are based on actual conflicts that have been reported in public education. For example: "The assistant principal told a teacher that he was too outspoken in criticizing certain policies of the

school and that this was causing unrest among the faculty members." (See Appendix 1, pp. 399 to 407). Respondents were asked to imagine themselves in each situation and to indicate (1) what they would do, and (2) the sanctions likely to be imposed in their school for failure to comply with the administration's wishes. Six alternatives, rated from 1 to 6, are possible for each item on each part. The alternatives for the first part range from "comply with the superior" to "quit" and, for the second part, from "no disapproval or mild disapproval from administration" to "dismissal." The corrected split-half reliability for each part is $r_n = .85$. The items on each part are also internally consistent, based on the "scale value difference" method of computing total respondent scores.

A typology was then constructed, consisting of six types of initiative and compliance. It was derived by comparing each respondent's total scale scores on the two parts. The anticipated actions of teachers were labeled "initiative-taking," "discreet-support-seeking," and "compliance-compromising." Each of these was divided into "severe" or "moderate" constraints on the basis of sanctions that the respondents anticipated would be imposed for failure to comply. Since the scale takes into account the amount of constraint under which an act occurs, and since respondents were not asked for their beliefs but were asked to anticipate their behavior in specific situations, the typology pertains to probable *behavior* and does not describe general personality traits or personal orientations.[3]

4. *Professional and Employee Role Conceptions.* Scales developed for another study were used here to measure the professional and employee role conceptions of teachers (Corwin, 1970). The professional role conception scale consists of 16 Likert items, and the full employee scale consists of 29 Likert items selected from several hundred statements that were judged for internal consistency and reliability. Respondents were asked to indicate on a scale from 1 (strongly agree) to 5 (strongly disagree): (a) how strongly they personally agreed with each statement, and (b) how characteristic the statement was of the situation at their particular school. The items were summed for each respondent, and the mean of all respondents was computed for each school.

The professional scale is composed of four role segments: (a) orientation to the client (that is, regard for the welfare of students), (b) orientation to the profession and professional colleagues, (c) belief that competence is based on knowledge, and (d) belief that teachers should have decision-making authority. The corrected split-half reliability is $r_n = .65$ (see Appendix 1).

The full employee scale is composed of six segments: (a) loyalty to the administration, (b) loyalty to the organization, (c) belief that teaching competence is based on experience in addition to the notion that personnel can be treated interchangeably, (d) enforcement of standardization, (e) emphasis on rules and procedures, and (f) loyalty to the public. For this study only two of the subscales were used: loyalty to the administration and emphasis on rules and procedures.[4] The corrected reliability for the two subscales is $r_n = .81$ and $r_n = .84$, respectively (see Appendix 1).

Each scale discriminated in the expected direction among select groups of school teachers with a reputation for professionalism.

5. *Pupil Control Ideology Index.* Five items were adapted from a 20-item scale developed by Willower et al. (1967), which was based on a dichotomy (scored 1 and 2) between humanistic and custodial treatment of children in the classroom and which was found to be related to Rokeach's (1960) dogmatism scale and to the judgments of principals about their teachers. The items concern the right of pupils to influence teaching methods and school policy, to criticize their teachers, and to move freely through the school. The 5 items used here represent the first component of a factor analysis of all 20 items in the original scale (variance explained is $r = .47$). Items were summed for each respondent. For interns the mean interitem correlation among the 5 items is $r = .30$; for teachers it is $r = .33$ (Appendix 1).

6. *Indices of Alienation from the Program.* Two components of alienation were assessed: the individual's sense of powerlessness and influence with respect to (a) the university program (two items) and (b) the school (two items). The correlation coefficient for interns for the two university items is $r = .63$; for the school items it is $r = .59$. Items were summed for each respondent and means computed for each position (Appendix 1).

7. *Liberalism.* The liberalism scale is a political-economic-social value dimension that involves sympathy for an ideology either of change or of preservation. It consists of nine Likert items adapted from a longer scale developed by Peterson at the Educational Testing Service (1968). Respondents indicated the extent of their agreement with each item (scored 5 to 1). The items used here represent the first component loading of a factor analysis (variance explained is $r = .54$). The correlated internal consistency of the total scale is .60 (corrected). Items were summed for each respondent and averaged for each position. For some purposes in this study the distribution of the scale scores for the total sample will be divided into approximately equal groups (high, middle, and low) (Appendix 1).

Interns were also requested to identify themselves as either highly liberal, moderately liberal, moderately conservative, or highly conservative. The self-classification was significantly correlated with the above scale distribution (divided into four equal parts) ($X^2 = 52.1$, $p < .00$). For example,

49 percent of those who ranked in the "very liberal" category on the liberalism scale also ranked themselves as highly liberal, and 41 percent placed themselves as moderate liberals; only 10 percent considered themselves as being conservative. Similarly, half of those who ranked as "fairly conservative," on the above scale, rated themselves moderate conservatives, and another one third considered themselves as being highly conservative; only 16 percent classified themselves in one of the liberal categories.

8. *Satisfaction with the Faculty.* This scale refers to the interns' general esteem for their instructors' competence and the characteristic manner of student-faculty relationships at the college. It was adapted from 6 items of a 10-item Likert scale (scored 5 to 1) developed by Peterson (1968) that loaded in the first component of a factor analysis (variance explained is $r = .68$). The mean interitem correlation for interns is $r = .48$, with a range of $r = .36$ to $r = .56$ (see Appendix 1). For some purposes in this study the distribution of scale scores for the total sample will be divided into three approximately equal groups (high, middle, and low).

Notice that this measure is based on the subjective impressions of the interns, who are likely to be swayed by their own values, self-interests, and scholarly ability. Also, notice that the items in this index emphasize the locally based *teaching* reputations of the professors rather than their external reputations as scholars or researchers. Although this is probably the dimension that is most relevant to the students and most appropriately evaluated by them, the professors' own colleagues might have used different criteria of competence. External scholarship, however, is probably correlated with the index of resources and selectivity described below.

There is a significant relationship between the way interns rate their college (that is, the way it compares to all colleges in the nation) and the way they rate their satisfaction with the faculty as measured by this scale ($X^2 = 8.99$, p < .06). Sixty percent of those who were least satisfied with the faculty rated the college in the bottom third of the nation's colleges; only 13 percent of the least-satisfied group rated the college among the top third.

9. *Teaching Competence.* Four indices of the teaching competence of interns were developed. A total of 18 criteria were used by classroom teachers and team leaders to rate each intern. The four dimensions rated are (a) innovativeness in the classroom (4 items), (b) respect for and understanding of pupils (5 items), (c) rapport with pupils (5 items), and (d) relationship with the community (4 items). The means of the intercorrelations for each scale are all above $r = .50$ (see Appendix 1).

These items were selected through factor-analysis techniques from a great many items adapted principally from an index for rating elementary teachers developed by Sontag (1966), who selected criteria on the basis of consensus among juries composed of various groups of educators. Twenty-four items with the highest value array in Sontag's analysis were included on the original form; 18 with high correlations ("loadings") when interns were evaluated by team leaders and classroom teachers were retained in the final scale. The possible responses for each statement were "poor," "below average," "average," "good," and "excellent" (weighted from 1 to 5). Raters also had the option of checking the category "no opportunity to observe," but these responses were not figured into the final scores. The ratings for most of the items were high ("good" or "excellent").

There is an empirical intercorrelation among many of the items in the different indices, but the overall magnitude of these correlations did not seem high enough to warrant combining the separate indices into a single, "generic teaching ability" scale score.

The caveats usually applied to rating forms need to be emphasized here. There is no way of knowing exactly what criteria teachers are using to form judgments about various teaching abilities. Moreover, the assumption that teachers who have experience in poverty schools *know* how to rate the competence of beginning teachers working in such settings is subject to question. Partly with this in mind, and as one means of gauging the mutual respect between interns and teachers, interns were asked to evaluate teachers and team leaders. Also, for other analyses, the ratings of only those classroom teachers who themselves received a high rating were used, and for some purposes a select group of teachers who were judged by the field work staff to be knowledgeable informants were analyzed separately.

10. *Preferred Teaching Style.* An index of teaching style, developed by Sieber and Wilder (1967), was included in the questionnaire. Two important aspects of the teaching role, derived from the literature—the extent to which the subject matter is emphasized and the extent to which adult authority is exercised—yielded four distinct styles of teaching: (1) control oriented, (2) content oriented, (3) discovery oriented, and (4) sympathy oriented (see Table 2–3).

11. *Organizational Innovation.* The term *organizational innovation* has been used in several different ways in the literature. As Hage and Dewar (1971) have noted:

In the study of organizations, innovation has been used to refer to the first use ever of a new product, process, or idea by any organization, with subsequent uses being called imitation (Mansfield, 1963); to the first or early use of an idea by one of a set of organizations with similar goals (Becker and Whisler,

Table 2-3 Types of teaching styles

Relations between teacher and child	Emphasis on Subject Matter	
	High	Low
Adult centered (authoritarian)	Content oriented	Control oriented
Child centered (permissive)	Discovery oriented	Sympathy oriented

1967); and to the first use ever of a new procedure, product, service, or idea by a given organization (Evan and Black, 1967; Mohr, 1969). . . . Mansfield's and Becker and Whisler's definitions are rejected since their focus is more on the innovation and not enough on the organization adopting it. Their definitions would have some utility, if one were examining the history of some particular invention. Since the object of analysis in this study is the individual organization, innovation new to the particular organization will be our interest. We are concerned with innovations that have been successfully incorporated into an organization's structure, although they might conceivably be discontinued at some later point in time.

In concurrence with these observations, for the purposes of this study one usage of the term was adopted. This usage was identified by Thompson (1969, p. 6) as "the generation, acceptance, and implementation of new ideas, processes and products or services *for the first time within a given organization.*" In other words, the organization and not the profession as a whole will be the focus of the analysis. This means that a practice such as the use of audiovisual aids might be relatively widespread, but it could represent an innovation for a given school the first time such materials were used.

Two types of procedures were used to measure the amount of change produced by the program—the "global assessment" technique and the "objective weighted index."

Global assessment technique: Several questionnaire items requested interns, teachers, team leaders, school administrators, university faculty members, and program officials to estimate the extent of change produced by the program on each of four dimensions: school-college cooperation, techniques used in school classrooms, the school's involvement in community projects, and changes at the college such as the introduction of new courses or modification of existing courses and the introduction of new training procedures. Responses ranged from "The teacher is largely responsible" (weighted 4) to "the teacher is not responsible" (weighted 1). Disregarding the responses of those who disqualified themselves, the means of the responses of each type of personnel who could be assumed to have some acquaintance with the behavior in question were added for *each position* (that is, category of personnel); each position therefore was given equal weight regardless of the number of individuals in the position. Disregarding those who disqualified themselves, there was a high degree of agreement among the majority of each of the different categories of personnel who responded, although some perceptions did vary by the respondents' positions; generally, team leaders were the most optimistic and classroom teachers the least optimistic about the impact of the Teacher Corps.

Objective weighted index: Respondents were also asked, in open-ended interviews, to describe specific changes they had observed that could be attributed to the Teacher Corps (see Appendix 1). It was assumed that the respondents' knowledge, memory, and perception would provide a reliable (but crude) indication of the Teacher Corps' impact (as opposed to other sources of change). Although this is not entirely satisfactory, our own spot checks in five programs that were visited at the beginning and end of the program yielded the same rank order among the colleges and schools involved. Again, the same four types of change were probed: the introduction of new techniques into schools, change in the college program, school-college cooperation, and community activity. Then each school and university was given ratings by judges on the basis of a content analysis of the interviews. Several dimensions were taken into account and scored separately. For instance, to measure new techniques introduced into schools, an index was derived for each of the 42 schools involved, based on both all *planned* changes and all secondary by-products (unplanned changes) that resulted from the planned changes. Each planned change identified was then rated on a five-point scale on each of five dimensions: methods, materials used, clientele, personnel involved, and creativity of the activity. Secondary by-product changes were scored in a similar way but included the dimensions of improved attitudes or self-conceptions on the part of professors, students, teachers, or interns. A school's scale score is the product of the number of planned and by-product changes times the weights assigned to each applicable dimension of change associated with the innovation.

The ratings were based on the assumption that complex changes requiring new or altered role relationships—those affecting the basic curriculum and those requiring structural reorganization—are more important than simple additive changes affecting a few individuals, or peripheral activities.

For example, team teaching or a new unit on black history, mixed-age grouping, cross-age teaching, and use of indigenous laymen received higher ratings than did use of a new film or establishment of a photography club. School scores were obtained in a similar way for community projects. Scores were also obtained for each of the 10 programs for changes in the college and school-college cooperation.

There was a small positive correlation between the above two procedures used to score the introduction of new techniques among the 42 schools (Spearman rank order correlation is $r_s = .61$). It appears that they might be tapping a similar phenomenon but are identifying some different *aspects* of that phenomenon. Furthermore, the global-assessment technique probably weights subtle attitude changes among members of the program more heavily than does the objective technique.

12. *College-Quality Index.* The Bureau of Applied Social Research at Columbia University collected information on five types of "resources" possessed by universities: the number of volumes in the library, ratio of library books to students, ratio of financial support to students, faculty-student ratio, and proportion of the faculty with doctorates. On the basis of available information, each dimension was scored on a scale from 1 to 10. The total index for each college was computed by adding the five scales. Scale scores range from 5 to 50 (Nash, 1969).

All colleges that have had Teacher Corps programs were classified on this Resource Index. Although the index is based on superficial criteria of quality, there is evidence that the criteria have validity. One study of 95 colleges (Rock et al., 1970) reported that two college characteristics— college income per student and the proportion of faculty with a doctorate—identified colleges with differences in student achievement controlling for the ability of the students recruited. Specifically, of three groups of colleges, those with higher incomes and with more Ph.D.'s on the faculty tended to achieve more than the two other groups.

This index was supplemented with an Index of Student Selectivity, based on the college's admission requirements, as reported by Cass and Birnbaum (1970–1971). The selectivity index categorizes several hundred colleges as "selective," "very selective," "very (+) selective," "highly selective," or "highly (+) selective," based on percentage of applicants accepted by the college, average test scores of freshmen classes, and related data. All colleges that have had Teacher Corps programs, including the 10 in our sample, were assigned weights (50 for the most selective to 0 for the least selective).

The College Selectivity Index, it should be noted, was designed solely to indicate the academic capability of an institution's student body and therefore to provide prospective students and their parents an indication of the degree of competition they must expect in seeking admission and in compiling a satisfactory college record. It was *not* intended to be used as a system to rate colleges. A college's rating on this academic measure does not imply that it is "good" or "bad," since this is only one of many bases on which colleges can be ranked and since such judgements are meaningless apart from the college's own objectives. Nevertheless, the index adds a crucial dimension to the usual measures of college quality based solely on the proportion of Ph.D.'s on the faculty and other resources. The quality of a college can never be much better or worse than its student body. Although this is probably not a perfect measure of selectivity, it is the best available measure.

Finally, these two indices were combined into a "quality index" for rating all colleges that have had Teacher Corps programs. This index rates the institution as a whole rather than the college of education separately, which would have been more directly relevant to the present study. As a check, we asked members of the Advisory Committee for this project to independently identify the teacher-education institutions that they considered to be the nation's best in terms of three criteria—prestige, quality, and innovativeness. The 15 colleges of education identified by them (based on the combined scores) scored high on the resource and selectivity indices, which adds confidence in the application of these indices to teacher-training institutions:

	15 Top Institutions Rated by Judges (%)	National Population of Institutions (%)
Resource Index (%)		
Mean	34.2	28.1
High or upper middle	69.0	39.0
Selectivity Index		
Most selective	40.0	18.5
Selective	30.0	37.2
Least selective	30.0	44.3

13. *Regional Modernization Index.* Variations in the social contexts in which the different programs were located were estimated with an index of "modernization," developed by Herriott and Hodgkins (1969). This index assesses the level of technological, ecological, and occupational development that a state or region has achieved. The 48 continental states were rank-ordered on five correlated indicators: percent of males in the labor force engaged in nonagricultural work, percent of the population in

urbanized areas, per capita annual income, number of physicians per capita, and number of telephones per housing unit. Each indicator was assigned a weight based on a principal components factor analysis of the five indicators. The composite index for each state consists of these summed weights. Each of the 10 programs was located in a different state.

SUMMARY

The study, then, is based on a few selected programs that were examined as comprehensively as possible over a two-year period. Because of the sparse knowledge about this relatively new program, it was felt that a comprehensive, in-depth study of a small number of sites would be preferable to a more superficial, extensive coverage of the entire spectrum of Teacher Corps programs.

Ten Teacher Corps training programs, representing a range of regional and social contexts and quality, were selected for in-depth study. Five of the new programs were visited twice. Rural and urban programs were represented, as were programs in different regions of the country and those servicing different minority groups. At each site, in addition to the university, at least three local cooperating schools serving low-income groups were included in the study.

Questionnaires were distributed to all interns in new programs and to second-cycle interns in established programs, to the principals and all regular classroom teachers in each cooperating school, to the university program directors, to school-system coordinators, to university faculty members who were associated with the program, and to comparative groups of graduate students in education at each college who were not in the Teacher Corps. Approximately 1300 people associated with the program completed questionnaires; over 300 of them in the five new programs completed the same questionnaire at the beginning and at the end of the two-year period. These totals represent a 73 percent return on the first visit and a 92 percent return on the second visit. Also, over 900 of the respondents were interviewed on the first visit. One half of the coordinators and university personnel, one third of the team leaders, one fourth of the principals and program directors, and 10 percent of the teachers were interviewed twice. In addition to the questionnaires and interviews, official records, systematic field notes kept by interviewers, interns' field diaries, and participant observation were used.

A great many indices were included in the questionnaires to measure several dimensions of this complex program. These and other measures are summarized in Table 2–4 and are described in more detail in Appendix 1.

Table 2-4 Summary of indices and scales developed from questionnaires and interviews

Name of index or scale	Items	Scoring	Other comments, source, reliability
1. Commitment to teaching index	Three items—intention of respondent to work in low-income school: (a) the next year (b) the next five years (c) indefinitely Likert-type scale—(1) very likely to (4) very unlikely. Sample item: "How likely is it that you will work in an impoverished school next year?"	Three items added for each respondent. Means for each position computed for schools. Low score = high commitment.	Correspondence of intentions with actual commitment to be assessed after graduates have taken positions.
2. Endorsement of racial integration index	Three items measuring attitudes toward desirability of integrating schools. Likert-type scale—(1) strongly agree to (5) strongly disagree. Sample item: "If children of different races went to school together, this would lead to better academic achievement for all students concerned. . . ."	Three items added for each respondent. Means for each position computed for each school. Low score = high endorsement.	Adapted from 1966 Equality of Educational Opportunity survey.
3. Initiative-compliance scale	Nine hypothetical incidents of teacher-administrator conflict. A two-part response for each item:	Six-part typoloty derived. Three categories of anticipated action.	Corrected split-half reliability for each part, r_n = .85.

54

Table 2-4 (Continued)

	(a) What would respondent do? (b) Sanctions likely to be imposed for failure to comply with administration's wishes. Six alternative responses for each part of response, rated 1-6.	Two categories of level of constraint--severe and moderate. Percent of respondents type 1 (high initiative) computed for each position for each school.	Internal consistency of items in each part determined by scale difference value method. An index of probable behavior.
4a. Professional role-conception scale	Sixteen items measuring attitude toward four separate role segments: (a) client orientation, (b) orientation to profession and professional colleagues, (c) orientation to knowledge as a basis of competence, (d) belief teachers should have decision-making authority. Likert-type scale--(1) strongly agree to (5) strongly disagree. Sample item: "A teacher's skill should be based primarily on his acquaintance with his subject matter."	Items added for each respondent. Means for each position computed for each school.	Developed by Corwin, 1970. Corrected split-half reliability, $r_n = .65$.
4b. Employee role-conception scale	Two subscales consisting of twelve items: (a) loyalty to the administration (b) emphasis on rules and procedures Likert-type scales--(1) strongly agree to (5) strongly disagree.	Items added for each respondent. Means for each position computed for each school. Low score = high administrative orientation and high rules and procedures orientation.	Scale developed by Corwin, 1970. Corrected reliability of two subscales: a) $r_n = .81$ and b) $r_n = .84$.

55

Table 2-4 (Continued)

	Sample item: "The school should have a manual of rules and regulations which are actually followed."		
5. Pupil-control ideology index	Five items measuring attitudes toward the rights of students to effect the school practices and policies. Likert-type scale—(1) strongly agree to (5) strongly disagree. Sample item: "The opinions of students should not influence teaching methods."	Items added for each respondent. Means for each position computed for each school. Low score = high pupil control.	Items adapted from 20-item scale developed by Willower, which was related to Rokeach's dogmatism scale. Mean interitem correlation among five items: for interns, r = .30; for teachers, r = .33.
6. Indices of alienation from Teacher Corps program	Two items to assess individuals' sensed powerlessness and influence with regard to Teacher Corps program. Likert-type scale—(1) strongly agree to (5) strongly disagree. Sample item: "What I personally think doesn't count very much in the way the Teacher Corps program is managed."	Items added for each respondent. Means for each position computed for each school. Low score = high alienation.	Means interitem correlation coefficient: for university alienation, r = .63; for school alienation, r = .59.
7a. Liberalism scale	Nine items assessing attitudes of sympathy for an ideology either of change or of preservation.	Nine item scores added for each respondent. Percent high and $\bar{X}$ computed	Items adapted from scale developed by ETS (Peterson, 1968).

Table 2-4 (Continued)

	Likert-type scale—(1) strongly agree to (5) strongly disagree. Sample item: "The welfare state tends to destroy individual initiative."	for each school. High score = high liberalism.	Corrected correlated internal consistency coefficient of total scale = .60.
7b. Self-identification with political beliefs	Respondent identified self as highly liberal, moderately liberal, moderately conservative, or highly conservative.	Percent identified as very liberal in each school computed.	Self identification significantly correlated with the scale distribution (divided into four parts) (X^2 = 52.1, p < .00).
8. Satisfaction with the faculty index	Six items measuring a general attitude of esteem for the faculty and education received at the college. Four alternative responses for each item varying by item, namely, very dissatisfied, very satisfied, unsuccessful, successful. Sample item: "What proportion of the college faculty members who have taught you during the past year would you say are superior teachers?"	Low score = low satisfaction. Percent high and $\bar{X}$ computed for each program.	Items adapted from 10-item scale (Peterson, ETS, 1968). Mean interitem correlation for in terns, r = .48.
9. Teaching-competence scale	Four indices of teaching competence of interns based on ratings by classroom teachers and team	Items added for each index. No overall score due to loss among the four dimensions.	Items adapted from Sontag's index (1966) for rating

57

Table 2-4 (Continued)

	leaders: (a) innovativeness in the class-room (four items) (b) respect for and understanding of pupils (five items) (c) rapport with pupils (five items) (d) relationship with community (four items) Five response alternatives ranging from "poor" to "excellent," weighted 1 to 5; response of "no opportunity to observe" unscored. Sample item: "Makes efforts to try new ideas in the classroom."		elementary school teachers. Means of intercorrelations within each scale—all above $r = .50$.
10. Preferred teaching style index	Four different styles of teaching, based on variations in two aspects of the teaching role, emphasis on subject matter and exercise of adult authority, were presented. Three items indicated respondents perceived own style and styles perceived by respondents as preferred by students' mothers and principals. Sample item: "Teacher 1 is most concerned with maintaining discipline, seeing that students work hard, and teaching them to follow directions."	Perceived self-style indicated by single score corresponding to one of four types described. Disparity of role preference determined by difference between perceived self-style and perceived styles preferred by others.	Index developed by Sieber and Wilder (1967).

58

Table 2-4 (Continued)

11. Indices of organizational innovation	Four indicators of organizational change: (a) school-college cooperation (one item) (b) introduction of new techniques into local schools (one item) (c) involvement of the school in community projects (one item) (d) change in college (three items)	Method No. 4--positions used varied by change indicator, for example: (a) school-college cooperation--six positions: principal, coordinator, team leader, faculty, interns, and program director. (b) introduction of new techniques--I, TL, P, and cooperating teachers.
A. Questionnaire measures Global change index	Sample item: "Has the TC program been in any responsible for . . . the introduction of new courses into the curriculum?" Three alternative responses: no; yes, largely responsible; and yes, partially responsible.	Weights varied by position: Interns--No + 1, Yes LR + 3, Yes PR + 2 TL and PD--No - 2, Yes LR + 2, Yes PR + 1 CO, F, CT, and P--No - 1, Yes LR + 2, Yes PR + 1 Percentages of weighted scores obtained for selected positions by school (or by site). School means compiled only for (b) introduction of new techniques and (c) community projects.
B. Interview measures Objective weighted index	Changes and innovations cited by interview respondents rated. Scale I--Introduction new techniques (a) Dimensions (primary change) (1) method (2) materials used (3) clientele (4) implementary personnel (5) activities Ratings 1-5	Scale I (a) Each primary change rated on applicable dimensions. Totaled ratings divided by number of dimensions used.

Table 2-4 (Continued)

B. (Continued)

Scale II--School-college cooperation

Dimensions

(1) frequency of contact
(2) quality of relations
(3) amount of cooperation
(4) attitudinal change in relations

Rating categories: quality of relations (positive-negative), and participants (TC-school and school-college).

Scale II

Positive

Rating categories scored.
TC-school = +1, school-community = +5

Negative

TC-school = -1, school-community = +5

Site scores computed from all changes rated +100.

High positive score = more cooperative relationships between school and college.

Negative score = deteriorated relationship.

Scale III--Change in college

Dimensions

(1) instructional changes (six subcategories)
(2) administrative changes
(3) relational changes (two sub-categories)
(4) attitudinal changes (three subcategories)
(5) noninstructional activities

Scale III

Each change categorized and scored on relevant dimension: Dimensions 1 and 2--ratings by organizational unit involved in change: 1--TC only, 2--TC and/or college, 3--college.

Dimensions 3-5--each change scored 1.

Site scores computed by totaling scores of all changes rated x 10.

High score = greater change in college.

Scale IV--Community projects

Dimensions

(1) activities
(2) clientele
(3) Teacher Corps-community relations
(4) change in parent/community/school relations.

Ratings 1-4.

Scale IV

Average rating score computed for each school x 10.

Site scores computed by totaling all school scores.

High score = greater school involvement in community projects.

Table 2-4 (Continued)

C. Composite measure

12. Quality (and selectivity) of college	The quality of all colleges or universities hosting a Teacher Corps program was determined from two measures: (a) College Resource Index, which scores institutions on the basis of: 　(1) number of volumes in library 　(2) ratio of library books to students 　(3) ratio of financial support to students 　(4) faculty-student ratios 　(5) proportion of faculty with doctorate. (b) Selectivity Index categorizing colleges on admission requirements as: 　(1) selective 　(2) very selective 　(3) very (+) selective 　(4) highly selective 　(5) highly (+) selective	College Resource Index--for all institutions with TC program, each of five dimensions scored on scale from 1 to 10. Total index computed by adding the five scales. Scale scores range from 5-50. Selectivity Index--for each college which has had TC programs, five categories were assigned weights of 50 for most selective to 0 for least selective. A quality index, rating all colleges having TC programs, is a combination of Resource and Selectivity Indices.	Rating scores (B) were combined with percentage scores (A) for each area of change. Original (A) scores + 100, multiplied by 2, were added to (B) scores and result divided by 2. College Resource Index from the Bureau of Applied Social Research (Nash, 1969). Selectivity Index from Cass and Birnbaum (1970-71). Selectivity Index is based on percent of applicants accepted in the college, average test scores of entering freshmen and related data.

61

Table 2-4 (Continued)

| 13. | Regional modernization index | Assesses variations in the extent of modernization among the different states in which TC programs were located. Forty-eight continental states were rank ordered on five correlated indicators:

(a) percent of males in labor force engaged in nonagricultural work
(b) percent of population in urbanized areas
(c) per capita annual income
(d) per capita number of physicians
(e) number of telephones per housing unit | Each indicator assigned a weight based on a principal-components factor analysis of the five indicators. Composite index for each state consists of the summed weights. | Index developed by Herriott-Hodgkins (1969). |
| 14. | School centralization index | Seven school operation issues are presented, such as grading system, selection of textbooks, use of team teaching, and ability grouping. Seven possible responses to the question, "To what extent can schools follow different practices in each of the seven issues?" Responses range from "Schools are permitted to pursue different policies without informing the central office" to "Schools are never permitted to pursue different policies." | Seven items added for each respondent. Means for each school computed. Low score = decentralized system. | Completed by teachers, team leaders, and principals. |

62

Table 2-4 (Continued)

15.	Evaluation of principals and team leaders	Six items assessing interns' and teachers' opinions of both the team leader and the principal in their school. Likert-type scale--(1) never to (4) always. Sample item: "He (she) refuses to explain his (her) actions." Two sets of responses per item, for team leaders and principals.	Response No. 5 "Don't know," unscored. Six items added for each respondent. Means for each position computed. Low score = low evaluation of competence.	Interns' mean, r = .52 (evaluation of team leader). Teachers' mean, r = .56 (evaluation of principal).
16.	Flexibility index	Five items assessing satisfaction of school personnel with the amount of restrictions and opportunities they experience in personal and professional activities. Sample item: "The amount of flexibility that is permitted in the curriculum." Likert-type scale--(1) very dissatisfied to (6) very satisfied.	Low score = inflexibility. Five items added for each respondent. Means computed for each school.	Interns' mean, r = .56. Teachers' mean, r = .47.
17.	Quality of local school index	Four items measuring interns' and teachers' satisfaction with various aspects of the school. Sample item: "How satisfied are you with the attitude of the faculty toward the students in this school?" Likert-type scale--(1) very dissatisfied to (6) very satisfied.	High score = high quality. Four items added for each respondent. Means for each position computed for schools.	Interns' mean, r = .61. Teachers' mean, r = .47.

Table 2-4 (Continued)

18. Respect for school administration index	Three items assessing interns' and teachers' satisfaction with the administration's position toward them. Likert-type scale--(1) very dissatisfied to (5) very satisfied. Sample item: "How satisfied do you feel with . . . evaluation process which my supervisors use to judge my effectiveness."	Three items added for each respondent. Site means for each position computed. High score = high respect. Interns' mean, r = .51. Teachers' mean, r = .57.
19. Long-range career plans index	One item--all respondents asked to indicate their expectations regarding their future career plans. Five alternative responses, ranging from (1) "expect to continue teaching until retirement" to (5) "expect to leave education for another vocation."	Proportion of responses by position and site computed.
20. Preference for racially mixed school	One item--all respondents asked to indicate their preference for the racial composition of schools in which they work. Six alternative responses, ranging from (1) "in an all-white school" to (5) "in a school with all non-whites." Response No. 6, "no preference."	Responses 1 and 2 combined and 4 and 5 combined. Percent of responses by position and site computed.

64

Table 2-4 (Continued)

21.	Index of principal support	One item--I's, TL's and CT's rate "the adequacy of the . . . support of the program by the principal." Likert-type scale--"excellent" to "nonexistent."	High score = excellent support (Response no. 5, no opinion-- unscored). $\bar{X}$'s computed for each site and school from all positions com- bined.
22.	Participation index	"Did you participate in preparing the proposals for the Teacher Corps program?" 1. Yes 2. No	Percent of teachers and principals who participated in the proposal combined to obtain site $\bar{X}$'s.
23.	Index of status difference	Four indices used to compare statuses of teachers and interns: (a) sex (b) race (c) education (d) quality of undergraduate college.	High prestige score--greater status differences with I's of higher status. Differences were obtained in the percent of I's and CT's having low-status characteristics by school and site, such as female, black, without liberal arts degree (I's) and without MA degree (CT's) Average "quality of college" scores obtained for each position in each school. Low-quality undergraduate colleges scored in lowest quartile of the Quality Index.

NOTES

1. The total number included all Teacher Corps personnel at each site, all of the university faculty members closely associated with the program, and the total professional staff (both teaching and administrative) at four local schools, three of which had Teacher Corps interns assigned to them. In each of the local schools, only regular classroom teachers and the administrators were included in the distribution of questionnaires; counselors, art teachers, and music teachers were excluded. Respondents were paid $5 to $7 for completed questionnaires. The rate of return for team leaders was above 80 percent and, for interns, about 90 percent in all but three sites (6, 9, and 10). Only about one third of the interns from site 6 returned questionnaires, but almost twice that number were interviewed. Although the response rates of coordinators and program directors fell below 90 percent, all were interviewed.

2. The contributions of the interview team leaders were particularly helpful. They include John Stephenson, Ken Kiser, Beth Hanna, Robert Kennedy, Harold Treharne, Frances Willison, and Larry Adams. Elizabeth Hanna was the participant observer.

3. This is not a typical attitude scale. Respondents were not asked to state their generalized beliefs. Instead, they were asked to anticipate what their actual behavior was likely to be in specific situations described. The resulting typology pertains to probable situationally defined behavior and is not a description of general personality traits or personal orientations.

4. This and related measures, of course, place heavy reliance on the respondents' *perceptions* of structure and therefore cannot be considered as being entirely "objective." However, some steps were taken to correct these perceptions for possible bias. First, scores were computed separately for each position—interns, experienced teachers, and team leaders, for instance. The means for the positions were then averaged. This permitted each category of respondent to contribute equally, regardless of the number of respondents in the category. The procedure prevented a single type of bias from having a disproportionate influence on the measure and perhaps served as a self-correcting mechanism to cancel out extreme bias. Second, "informants" were identified by interviewers, that is, one or two persons in each position at each program who seemed especially knowledgeable and informative about the type of issues in question. Informants' scores were computed separately and, where there was a marked discrepancy between their responses and those of others in the same position, the respondents' answers were given equal weight. Third, the interviewers were asked to complete the same questionnaire items that were used to measure the various dimensions of organizational structure on the basis of their own impressions gained informally during their week-long stay at the program and from their general sense of the interviews. The ranks assigned by the questionnaire method were compared with those assigned from the interviewers' responses. The rank-order correlations were as follows:

   Centralization: $t = .87$
   Emphasis on rules and procedures: $t = .78$
   Principals' support for the program: $t = .92$
   Quality of the school: $t = .68$
   Control of the program by local schools: $t = .81$

II

The Teacher Corps: An
Experiment in Change

CHAPTER 3

A Statistical Portrait of the New Teacher Interns

The administrators are apt not to know exactly how the desired change will manifest itself. Although they can be prevailed on to list the changes they hope will result, they will nevertheless be opportunistic in their program management and will direct program resources to changes which appear within reach. . . .

WEISS AND REIN, 1970, p. 102

Now I shall begin to describe the program—that is, the people and the places. This chapter focuses on the status identities of the interns and their personal values and aspirations. The following chapter describes the major dimensions of the local programs.

As is pointed out in Chapter 6, there are various ways in which changes in schools might be attempted. A major one is an alteration of the kind of people recruited into the occupation. Altering the kind of training that these people receive is another. Changing the moral and social order of the occupation itself is a third alternative. Changing the structure of the school and school system is another possibility. Today, the effectiveness of each approach is entirely problematic. However, the Teacher Corps policy seemed to rely heavily on the assumption that a profession can be changed by changing the patterns of recruitment in order to bring different types of teachers into the profession. Therefore, we shall consider the type of teacher that an analysis of ghetto schooling indicates might be the most "desirable" type (usually based on the criterion of improved academic performance, although other criteria could be used). Then we shall consider various models of teachers. The questions raised here are: Who is recruited? What are the characteristics of the interns, and how do they compare with other new recruits into teaching? How do they compare with practicing teachers? Chapter 5 considers the changes that occurred during the training program and the way in which the program reinforced or accentuated existing predispositions.

I emphasize that an overarching strategy of the Teacher Corps is to encourage new types of people to enter teaching—people who otherwise might not consider this career—particularly graduates from the liberal arts colleges and members of minority groups. This strategy assumes that good teachers are the key to successful learning and that a teacher's effectiveness is largely a product of his perspectives, values, and prior socialization experiences. Yet, despite the almost universal importance attached to the professional role, little is known about the kind of teacher and teaching that produce the best learning results (Boocock, 1966). Therefore, let us review the speculation and available evidence and, from this, sketch an ideal teacher. Then we shall focus on the status identities of the Teacher Corps interns, their personal values, and aspirations.

DIMENSIONS OF TEACHER COMPETENCE

The competence of teachers is a product of several dimensions of their personal qualities and their situations.

Training and Background

A most extensive research concerning organizational change in education was conducted on "school adaptiveness" by Mort and his colleagues at Teachers College, Columbia University (Ross, 1958). On the basis of a scale consisting of 176 new educational practices in 43 school systems, it was concluded that the adoption of new techniques was highly correlated with the amount of professional training and experience of teachers. A recent review of the research in this area summarized studies that also found teacher attributes to be significantly associated with measures of student achievement, after having controlled for factors representing the students' home background and environment (Guthrie et al., 1969).

The *Equality of Educational Opportunity* survey of 600,000 school children in 5000 schools in the United States revealed that teachers' years of experience and education, socioeconomic background, and verbal facility were all positively correlated with student achievement (as measured by standard test scores) (Coleman et al., 1966). Correlations were higher in schools with large proportions of minority-group children from the lower socioeconomic class. Moreover, the influence of teachers apparently became progressively greater at higher grades, indicating their cumulative impact. The quality of teachers showed a stronger relationship to achievement than nearly every other characteristic of schools, with the major exception of the social-class composition of the student body. Of the teacher characteristics assessed, scores on a "verbal facility test" were most highly correlated with pupil achievement. Educational background (both the teacher's own level of education and that of his parents) was second in importance. Teachers of minority-group children tended to score lower on all of these measures. The teacher's preference for teaching in middle-class, white-collar schools showed a slight negative effect, and his years of teaching experience were equivocal.

Other studies have produced evidence that student achievement is related to the teachers' training and home background although, unlike the *Equality of Educational Opportunity* survey, most of these studies have not systematically considered the socioeconomic and ethnic differences among student bodies. The 1967 report of the Central Advisory Council for Education on 171 primary schools in England found that pupil performance was related more closely to a configuration of personal characteristics of teachers (such as level of education, teaching evaluations, and home background) than to any other school variables considered. Benson's (1966) study of 392 school districts in California concluded that the caliber of teachers was the single most important school factor for predicting achievement scores. Anderson (1950) found that improvement in individual students' test scores was positively related to the institution in which the teacher had done his undergraduate work. Results were more positive where teachers had attended institutions other than teachers colleges and had taken a larger proportion of science courses.

Project Talent data indicate that one of the most important variables closely and uniquely associated with school outcomes—such as achievement, going to college, and staying in school—is the number of years of experience in teaching (Flanagan, 1964).

Finally, the international study of achievement in mathematics in 12 countries, controlling for a large number of related factors, established a slight relationship between pupil performance and the length of teachers' training (Husén, 1967).

RACE AND VERBAL FACILITY. I have just stated that the *Equality of Educational Opportunity* survey found verbal facility of teachers to be significantly correlated with student achievement. I also reported that college students, who were preparing to teach, demonstrated relatively high levels of verbal competence reflecting an important trend toward improved quality. White college seniors in both the North and the South and black college seniors in the North scored several points higher on the test than did experienced teachers; black freshmen scored lower. But there was little indication that the test-score differences between future black and white teachers is narrowing, despite some gains in both groups.

TEACHING EFFECTIVENESS. One of the implicit assumptions behind programs like the Teacher Corps is that the quality of teachers has more effect on children from poverty homes than on middle-class children who have other advantages that can offset poor teaching. But the assumption is not easy to prove because of the difficulty of measuring "teaching effectiveness." The criteria usually used may be inappropriate for assessing teaching in low-income schools, and the reliability of such methods in any setting is open to suspicion. Nevertheless, attempts have been made with alarming results. The Herriott and St. John study (1966) is an illustration. When the principals of 100 schools in 41 cities were asked to rate teachers, it was found that principals in the lower-socioeconomic-status schools were relatively unsatisfied with the effectiveness of their teachers and were less convinced that the teachers had mastered the skills necessary to present their subjects with a high degree of competence.

Professional and Employee Teaching Roles

A profession consists of an organized group of people who have mastered a body of knowledge and the techniques necessary for coping with allied social problems and who have an exclusive license to apply that knowledge. Professional roles revolve around at least four dimensions: emphasis on knowledge, orientation to colleagues, concern about the welfare of clients, and the quest for authority to make critical decisions regarding the work process (Corwin, 1970). It might be expected that professionally oriented teachers, compared to other teachers, will be more conscious of the needs of pupils, more skillful and knowledgeable about the problems they encounter in teaching (or more willing to search for and adapt such knowledge), and more alert to developments in their field. Presumably, too, they will be less subject to local administrative pressures, more willing to take the initiative in solving problems, and more receptive to changes likely to benefit clients. It seems plausible that organizations with a high proportion of professionals will be more innovative than organizations with fewer professionals. There is some evidence that "cosmopolitan" persons are more likely to adopt innovations than are "locals" (Rogers, 1962). Carlson (1962) has shown, more specifically, that school superintendents, recruited from outside the system, are more likely to propose innovations than superintendents recruited from inside.

On the other hand, realistically, professions have monopolies over select groups of clientele, which would tend to make them conservative toward changes that affect their vested interests. A study of staff conflicts in the public schools (Corwin, 1970) revealed that at least a small portion of the sample (estimated to be only about 15 percent of the 1500 teachers included in the study) was determined to improve the status of the profession and, although they expressed more concern about the welfare of their pupils than did the rank-and-file teacher, it was clear that their own authority was their foremost concern. The question is whether they will apply their new-found influence in such a way that the children will be helped.

Teachers who show the most concern about their colleagues' opinions and who desire the recognition and authority accorded to professionals sometimes are not highly committed to teaching in low-income schools. Because students' conduct and achievement reflect on the teacher, teachers are inclined to prefer students who exhibit a capacity to improve and a willingness to conform to the teacher's expectations (Becker, 1951). Wayson (1964), dealing with the reasons why teachers stay in slum schools, reported that the leavers were achievement-oriented and desired professional recognition. They wanted pupils to acquire academic skills and knowledge and therefore preferred children "who could learn." They resisted "watering down" the curriculum, did not like having to meet the children's emotional and physical needs, and were frustrated by the low academic achievement of disadvantaged pupils. Almost half of the stayers, on the other hand, wanted recognition from pupils and gained personal satisfaction from close personal relationships with them.

Certain facets of the Teacher Corps, such as recruiting from outside traditional channels and putting novices in a change-agent role, might help to offset some of these problems by "deprofessionalizing" teaching to some extent.

POWERLESSNESS AND PARTICIPATION IN DECISION MAKING. It is plausible that teachers who feel powerless will only underscore the sense of alienation in their pupils, which the *Equality of Educational Opportunity* survey reported as being highly correlated with student achievement. A recent Louis Harris poll reported that alienation is a widespread problem afflicting Americans, especially the poor, the old, the blacks, and the people who never went beyond the eighth grade in school. Therefore, as the opportunity for teachers to participate meaningfully in decision making increases, they might be in a better position to contribute toward educational policy and to set better examples for their students.

INITIATIVE-TAKING AND COMPLIANCE. Educational institutions must change before the people who operate in them can change. However, some people must be prepared to lead institutional change. Therefore, reform cannot be accomplished without the presence of at least a few individuals who are not entirely committed to the existing system and who are willing to exercise leadership and take risks to implement their own ideas.

The majority of teachers in the public schools today probably are not prepared to lead institutional change, and this is perhaps even more true in the low-income schools. Herriott and St. John (1966) reported data suggesting that the lower the socioeconomic status of a school, the smaller the proportion of teachers who consistently try out new ideas in the classroom. In a survey of Columbus, Ohio teachers, the inner-city teachers were less satisfied than their colleagues in the outer belt of the city with willingness of the administration to support innovation, and they were reportedly more reluctant to "stick out their own necks" in the event of trouble (Corwin and Schmit, 1970).

COMMITMENT TO TEACHING. There is evidence dating back to Becker's (1951) study of Chicago public school teachers that new inner-city teachers disproportionately request transfer to middle-class schools, their places being filled by other new teachers who must wait their turn for transfer. On this point, Herriott and St. John (1966) found few teachers in low-income schools who said they enjoyed their work and desired to stay in their present school for the remainder of their school years; indeed, the lower the school's socioeconomic status, the greater the proportion of teachers who would prefer to move to a school in a "better neighborhood." Similarly, whereas the vast majority of Columbus, Ohio public school teachers in the outer-city schools were satisfied with their present teaching assignments, a majority of inner-city teachers were not as satisfied and disproportionately requested transfer; one out of five inner-city teachers wanted to move to a better neighborhood (Corwin and Schmit, 1970). A special report on the Los Angeles school system, made shortly after the Watts riots in the middle 1960s, also revealed that lower-class schools, where performance was the lowest, not only had fewer teachers on permanent status and more inexperienced teachers, but the teachers were less eager to stay in those schools (Martyn, 1965).

Data from the *Equality of Educational Opportunity* survey
compared to middle-class pupils, the average minority pup
school in which teachers were less likely to remain if giver
change and would be less likely to reenter teaching if a decɪsɪ.
made again. There was also evidence that inner-city teachers were less committed to continuing in their present school or to continuing in teaching in
general. After analyzing the characteristics of college students who planned
to enter teaching, the authors of that survey were not very optimistic about
the future. They concluded that "the preferences of future teachers for
certain kinds of schools and certain kinds of pupils raised the question of
the match between the expectation of teacher recruits and the characteristics of the employment opportunities" (p. 26). Few teachers, either white
or black, preferred to teach in predominantly minority schools. The situation could change rapidly as the supply of teachers increases but, irrespective of the supply, there remains the problem of recruiting more teachers
dedicated to poverty area schools.

Teachers' Opinions

People's opinions can have a vital influence on the *value climate* of an
organization such as a school. They indicate a predisposition on the part of
groups to act, which in some circumstances can tip a situation one way or
another. Thus, the presence of even a few teachers who want change might
trigger other liberalizing forces in the school that otherwise would remain
dormant. This does not mean, of course, that opinions will always override
other influences. Recruiting more liberal people into teaching is not likely,
in itself, to produce change, but it could help.

LIBERALISM AND HUMANISM. Although the evidence is equivocal, it
might be expected that, other things being equal, people who hold liberal
political opinions or express humanitarian attitudes will be supportive of
institutional change specifically designed to benefit children from poverty
backgrounds. But several studies suggest that students in education are
among the least liberal of university colleges and departments (Selvin and
Hagstrom, 1960; Crotty, 1967; Bereiter and Freedman, 1962). In comparison to students in the liberal arts, those who are preparing to be teachers
usually were found to have "other-directed" and conservative attitudes toward politics and civil liberties (Bereiter and Freedman, 1962).

Also, as a group, schoolteachers are perhaps less "humanitarian" than
certain other occupational groups. According to the Herriott and St. John
(1966) data, the lower the socioeconomic status of a school, the more

teachers there were in it who complained about students being difficult to work with. Also, there were fewer teachers who made themselves available to students at a sacrifice of their own time, who planned courses so that different types of students could benefit from them, or who said they got real satisfaction from working with young people. Another recent study of one city indicated that, compared to social workers, teachers were more inclined to hold the *individual* rather than the society or state responsible for social problems. Teachers were less supportive of the idea that the family and the government have responsibility for helping individuals who are in trouble and that the group is responsible for the welfare of its members (Meyer, Litwak, and Warren, 1968). They were more likely to endorse system goals, the responsibility of the individual for his own welfare, the value of struggle and self-denial for self-realization, traditionalism, and individual autonomy. It was felt that in contrast to social workers, most teachers were concerned with transmitting the culture from one generation to the next and, therefore, were relatively unconcerned about change. However, the same study also suggested that in recent years teachers participating in experiments in the inner-city schools had become more humanitarian than other teachers, with a definite leaning toward the values ascribed to social workers.

The Teacher Corps might help to reverse these patterns. It has been compared to the Peace Corps and VISTA, both of which are in some sense "liberal," humanitarian, social-reform programs. We shall return to this issue later.

ATTITUDES TOWARD CHILDREN IN POVERTY SCHOOLS. Somewhere in the socialization process, teachers learn how to reconcile their roles as teachers with conflicting values held by various ethnic and lower socioeconomic groups. It is possible that teachers who are more tolerant and liberal toward deprived children will be more effective in working with them. But a large body of literature suggests that teachers are predominantly middle class by background and, even more important, by present values and style of life (Riessman, 1962). Because they have definite conceptions of moral acceptability, their students often act in ways that offend deeply felt moral standards centered around such areas as cleanliness, sex, aggression, ambition, and relations among age groups (Becker, 1951).

Some of the differences in attitudes among teachers were reflected in the Columbus, Ohio survey (Corwin and Schmit, 1970). The majority of teachers in the middle-class outer belt of the city did not believe that racial integration would lead to better academic achievement or improve the self-confidence of low-income children, whereas a majority of teachers in the inner city endorsed these beliefs. Also, outer-city teachers were more supportive of a racially segregated faculty than those in the inner-city schools, and nearly half of the outer-city teachers would prefer the predominantly white school. A majority of outer-city teachers were opposed to assigning the most experienced teachers to the "most difficult" schools and were opposed to spending more money on compensatory education for inner-city school children. By comparison, the majority of inner-city teachers were in favor of the first practice and a near majority favored the second practice. Although a majority of all teachers endorsed neighborhood schools, a smaller proportion of inner-city teachers were in favor of neighborhood schools while the larger proportion of these teachers were in favor of busing. The *Equality of Educational Opportunity* survey revealed similar comparisons between teachers in predominantly black and predominantly white schools (Coleman, 1966). That is, the inner-city teachers were more favorably disposed toward children from low-income homes than were their counterparts in the suburbs.

Focusing more specifically on Teacher Corps interns and team leaders, a study at the University of Pittsburgh revealed that their knowledge about low-income people and their problems varied substantially at the beginning of the program and remained somewhat variable at the end (Fitzpatrick and Blum, mimeograph). It was conceded that a few individuals clearly had not learned some of the major facts about poverty during their training, although others seemed to have learned a great deal. An opinion inventory suggested that the interns became somewhat more liberal and tolerant of deviant behavior during their training, while team leaders tended slightly in the opposite direction. Interviews with 37 public-school teachers were equally indeterminate. The majority were favorable toward interns, many of them feeling that interns possessed highly positive and accepting attitudes toward the "deprived" and that none exhibited negative attitudes; but other teachers were unimpressed, feeling that the attitudes of interns toward the deprived were no better, and were perhaps worse, than the attitude of the typical teacher. Others felt that Corpsmen lacked the proper preparation for teaching. Even the more favorable teachers tended to feel that interns were too idealistic, that they had a tendency to oversimplify the problems and to inflate their own ability to help.

CONFIDENCE IN CHILDREN. People learn their self-conceptions and general estimates of their ability from "significant others" (people regarded as examples who are looked to for cues). Teachers, although perhaps they are not as important as parents or children's peers, are in a position to act as significant examples for young children. Analyzing the *Dark Ghetto*, Clark (1965) concluded:

> In the light of available evidence, the controlling factor which determines the academic performance of pupils and which establishes the level of educational efficiency and the overall quality of the schools is the competence of the teachers and their attitude of acceptance or rejection of their students.

Possibly, student performance improves when the teachers are provided with information on their students' abilities, home environments, and emotional problems, and are encouraged to use this information in planning their class work. In a study by Ojemann and Wilkinson (1939), a sample of ninth-graders was individually matched on age, I.Q., achievement, and home background and then randomly assigned to experimental and control classes. In the experimental classes only, teachers were given comprehensive data on their students and participated in small-group sessions in which pupil problems and possible solutions were discussed. The researchers' conclusion was that the experimental classes made significantly greater academic gains and manifested more motivation. Parallel studies produced similar results. Recently, in a methodologically vulnerable study, Rosenthal and Jacobsen (1968) attempted to demonstrate the self-fulfilling effect of teachers' definitions of students. When told that some children were brighter than others, teachers purportedly graded those children somewhat higher; their lack of confidence in the ability of certain types of children to learn seemingly affected the way they treated them, which presumably caused the children to expect less of themselves.

I suspect that many teachers are negative toward the motivation of pupils from low-income homes and about their ability to learn. Teachers in low-income areas around Los Angeles were more likely than their counterparts in middle-class areas of the city to judge that their students were unmotivated or lazy (Martyn, 1965). Wayson (1964) interviewed 42 women teachers who had taught in inner-city schools for five years or more and 20 teachers who were learning. He found that white teachers who stayed had reduced their academic expectations of the children and had increased their acceptance of nonmiddle-class behavior. The Columbus, Ohio study of school teachers in the inner city also revealed certain elements of self-fulfilling prophecy. Nearly two thirds of the inner-city teachers said they believed their students' motivation was average or poor, compared to only one quarter of the teachers in the middle-class, outer-city area who held this belief (Corwin and Schmit, 1970). The majority ranked home background as the major reason for poor academic performance, and one third blamed the limited ability of the children themselves; only 17 percent ranked inadequate curriculum or poor teaching in previous grades as a major contributing factor to the poor performance. The *Equality of Educational Opportunity* survey also indicated that, compared to the majority of pupils, the average minority pupil was more likely to attend a school in which the teachers probably would rate him low on academic motivation and ability. The teachers had less preference for students of this kind.

The Teacher Corps could make a contribution by attracting people who identify more closely with children from poverty backgrounds and who have more confidence in their potential than have a large proportion of teachers now working in low-income neighborhoods.

STRESS ON CONTROL. Finally, many critics have charged that custodial goals have displaced therapeutic and humanistic ones in many poverty-area schools. The alienation of the children and the teachers' negative attitudes toward them may be manifestations of this more basic condition. Turner's (1965) study of more than 200 beginning teachers in 13 Indiana school systems found that, according to Ryan's teacher-characteristics schedule, teachers in school systems with predominantly working-class pupils placed high value on discipline, organization, and task performance in the classroom. It found that the teachers who needed help with discipline were rated lower by their superiors than the teachers who did not. The parents reinforced the value of strict discipline. This stress on discipline probably aggravates pupil-teacher conflicts in these schools, minimizing the child's incentive to learn. In the predominantly middle-class school districts, by comparison, teachers were evaluated on the basis of their personal warmth and social skills, and problems with discipline did not influence their ratings.

AN IDEAL TYPE OF TEACHER

It is widely assumed that, ideally, teachers who possess the characteristics just described should be better represented in the teaching profession. The image of the ideal teacher that emerges is humanistic, but it also includes a great deal of liberal skepticism about the viability of the present system and is tempered by thorough training, technical competence, and professional commitment to teaching children. This does not mean that there is conclusive evidence that ideal teachers would be more effective (in some sense) than their not-so-ideal colleagues; some of the characteristics involved might be incompatible with those of the children. For example, the humane, compassionate teacher might smother a child with sympathy or disorient him with too much permissiveness when he needs to be challenged and given firm direction; moreover, the liberal person is just as susceptible as the conservative person to the temptation to stereotype individuals classed within a common socioeconomic strata and thus to gloss over individual differences; and unqualified confidence in a child, on the part of his teacher, could lead both parties to a sense of defeat if the child's performance does not meet the teacher's high expectations. In other words, the ideal qualities, in themselves, are not a substitute for the kind of teacher who has perception and attacks his work with sophistication. But the model is promising, and it is receiving social support. Not only is the image promoted by the Teacher Corps but, generally, new professional careers are being developed and new roles are being fashioned within established occupations to appeal to idealistic, creative young people who fit the ideal type.

Based on the literature, some characteristics of the "ideal type" of teacher are given below. This kind of teacher:

1. Demonstrates a deep-seated social consciousness and is confident of the need to change the social environment.

2. Is confident of his power to influence his environment.

3. Demonstrates willingness to experiment in the classroom and displays readiness to take initiative toward improving education even in the face of administrative obstacles.

4. Prefers to work with minority-group children and is dedicated to a career of teaching low-income children.

5. Endorses the desirability of racially integrated schools.

6. Maintains a professional orientation toward his own work role, especially a strong sense of dedication to students' welfare.

7. Shows understanding of and maintains rapport with students and maintains effective relations with the community.

8. Stresses the desirability of unleashing the creative capacities of children over the need to maintain discipline and to assert the authority of the teacher.

9. Expresses confidence in the ability of disadvantaged children to learn and is predisposed to place blame for learning failures more on the school and society than on the child.

Some Focal Questions

With this ideal type in mind, we can determine, by the following questions, how well the model fits the Teacher Corps interns.

Did the interns more closely approximate each dimension of the model than new and experienced teachers and other graduate students in education?

The answer will also have a bearing on the strategy of changing a profession by recruiting new members from outside the traditional channels on the assumption that bringing in new blood will expand awareness of alternatives and shift the balance of forces responsible for maintaining the status quo.

Did the Teacher Corps interns who were recruited into teaching from outside the traditional sources more closely approximate the model than the ones recruited through traditional channels?

The Teacher Corps systematically attempted to recruit more teachers from the liberal arts who did not have extensive exposure to colleges of education. Also, there were disproportionately more male elementary teachers in the Teacher Corps, and some programs were making concerted efforts to recruit more blacks. Finally, in some programs, interns had been recruited from outside the immediate geographical region. Did interns from each of these backgrounds differ in the extent to which they approximated the ideal type?

Did the model as a whole exist empirically; that is, were there examples of the ideal type and were they more typically found among interns or among experienced teachers?

Did interns approximate the ideal type more closely as they progressed through the training program, and did differences persist after they graduated and accepted employment?

The answer to this last question can only be inferred from changes in third-cycle interns who were tested in the first weeks of training and who were retested at the end of their program. This subject is discussed in Chapter 5.

ANALYSIS

The instruments developed for this study draw upon several dimensions of the model. Using them, we shall answer the questions by comparing specific characteristics of the interns with the characteristics of other new teachers and veteran teachers.[1]

Did the Teacher Corps attract a different type of person into teaching?

There was evidence that the programs served this function to a limited extent.

Reasons for Joining

Less than one third of the interns (30 percent) said that they would not have entered teaching if it had not been for the program; another 30 percent were not certain. The proportion of interns who would not have entered teaching ranged from a high of 42 percent, in one program, to 24 percent in another.

When interns were asked to estimate why they and most of their colleagues joined the program, nearly one half (43 percent) of the 145 respondents interviewed gave, as their primary reason, their desire to work with or help improve the condition of the disadvantaged.[2] However, over one third (37 percent) of the interns indicated that getting an M.A. degree or learning a new career was the primary reason. The classroom teachers perceived interns' motives in the same way, but they sometimes added that the interns were seeking economic gain, job security (17 percent), or wanted to avoid the draft (16 percent).

Previous Experience

Of the interns who probably would not have entered teaching without the program, a disproportionate number had not taken prior course work in education (83 percent versus 50 percent). There were slightly more non-whites than whites and more females than males. Interns, more frequently than other teachers, had assisted impoverished people before entering the program—two thirds compared to one half. The difference held true when interns were compared to new teachers (65 versus 43 percent), but they did not differ greatly from other graduate students (57 percent). The proportion of interns with such experience was as low as 42 percent in some programs. Only 10 to 15 percent of the interns in the sample had been with the Peace Corps or VISTA, but this figure fluctuated from 0 to 45 percent in different programs.

Commitment to Teaching

The long-range career plans of the interns indicated that the ones who had been attracted into teaching by this program were also the ones who were the most prone to drop out of teaching. They less frequently planned to continue teaching (20 percent versus 48 percent) and more frequently planned to move to some other field of education (32 percent versus 54 percent). A survey of 112 dropouts from the first cycle, conducted by the national Teacher Corps office, revealed that almost three fourths were originally liberal arts majors. Only one half of the liberal arts majors, compared to three fourths of the education majors, continued in the teaching field after dropping out of this program.

Social Backgrounds

The interns were predominantly from the white upper-middle class. Fifty-eight percent of them came from professional or managerial homes, and only 24 percent were from homes where the father worked as a skilled or unskilled laborer or unskilled service worker. An additional 18 percent had technical, sales, or skilled clerical home backgrounds. By comparison, only one fourth of the experienced teachers and one third of the other new teachers were from professional or managerial homes. The interns, nevertheless, did not differ greatly from other graduate students, 45 percent of whom were from professional or managerial backgrounds.

Several programs made determined efforts to recruit more black interns, but only 10 percent of the interns in the study sample were nonwhite; by the fourth cycle, reputedly over half were nonwhite. While recruiting minority-group members undoubtedly is beneficial in many respects, white interns in many Southern schools were among the few white persons who had frequent contact with the black children, and most of these interns seemed to have established reasonably good rapport with the children. In those settings, at least, white Teacher Corps teams served as positive vehicles for desegregation in certain schools.

Academic Quality

There appeared to be a slight tendency for programs to select applicants with relatively good academic records outside of education, although the evidence is mixed. Of the 1967 applicants with a grade point average of B or better (54 percent of all applicants), 60 percent were selected. There was a modest under representation of applicants from education; 18 percent of the applicants, compared to 13 percent of those selected, had degrees in education.

Generally, the interns' aptitudes were considerably below those of the typical graduate student but were comparable to, or slightly above, the aptitudes of other graduate students in education. On the verbal Graduate Record Examination, different cycles of interns scored between the thirty-first and fortieth percentiles, compared to the mean of 50 for all graduate students and 27 for graduate students in education (based on norms derived by the Educational Testing Service).

The general impression of participants in the program also was that interns were somewhat more competent than other education students, although the difference was not overwhelming. Less than half (40 percent) of the faculty members, program directors, principals and coordinators, and interns and one fourth of the team leaders rated the overall quality of interns as "excellent." Also, in most programs, although the majority of both the university faculty members and the classroom teachers were impressed by a greater-than-average intellectual ability of interns, only a small minority of any group felt that interns were among the brightest students in the college.

When asked to estimate the level of prestige of interns in comparison to the rest of the university student body, all groups placed them as being neither particularly high nor particularly low in comparison to other students, although substantial minorities of the interns, principals, and coordinators, and nearly one half of the team leaders considered the prestige of interns to be relatively high. Moreover, only a minority of interns believed that they had relatively high prestige within the college.

Recruitment from Outside the Region

One factor that might influence a profession is the number of sources from which recruits are drawn.[3] The fewer restrictions that are placed on an organization to stay within specific territorial limits for recruiting purposes, the wider is the selection of possible recruits and the greater is the probability that new recruits will hold conceptions different from the conceptions prevailing in the organization.

Approximately 60 percent of the interns in the study came to the program from another state. The proportion in a program from outside the state was correlated with the proportion with VISTA and Peace Corps experience ($r = .27$), their initiative scores ($r = .30$), the percentage who considered themselves to be liberal or radical ($r = .20$), the proportion who were male ($r = .38$), the difference in liberalism between them and the teachers ($r = .30$), and the proportion of teachers for whom the program had created problems ($r = .18$). Recruiting from outside the region, then, seemed to attract socially conscious, aggressive males, who were often a source of problems for teachers.

Were the new teachers who were recruited from the liberal arts less committed to the present system and more change-oriented than those drawn from traditional sources?

Conceivably, teachers recruited from nontraditional sources would be less committed to the existing system and more personally receptive to change than those recruited from more traditional sources. A range of evidence drawn from many opinion scales suggested that the interns were more predisposed than the typical teacher to work for change. Each scale will be discussed. (See Table 3–1 for selected summary figures referred to in the discussion on this question and following ones.)

Initiative-Compliance Predispositions

Interns' scores on the initiative-compliance scale indicated that, on the whole, they were less submissive and slightly more predisposed to take initiative than the veteran teachers. The difference, however, could be primarily attributed to the relative conservativeness of the veteran teachers rather than to any difference between interns and other new teachers or other graduate students (although the differences were in the expected direction in both cases). Almost 24 percent of the interns (but less than half that proportion of experienced teachers) were classified as being in the "rebellious" category.

Another tabulation, not reported, indicated that interns also were more rebellious than their team leaders who, significantly, had fewer tendencies toward being compliant than other experienced teachers.

PATTERNS AMONG THE PROGRAMS.* Differences between teachers and interns, which ranged from 37 to only 2 percent in the different programs, were in the expected direction in 8 of the 10 programs, all but one of these being statistically significant. The proportion of "rebellious" interns ranged from 6 to 47 percent of all interns in a given local program.

Loyalty to the Local Administration

Interns expressed less loyalty to the administration of the local schools than did new teachers, veteran teachers, or graduate students. Only 12 percent of the interns were in the upper one third of the distribution on this measure, compared to 40 percent of the new teachers and 25 percent of the other students who scored high.

Rules and Procedures

Similar differences appeared among these groups on the subscale measuring their endorsement of the rules and procedures in the school. Eleven

* Figures for the individual programs are not reported in the tables.

Table 3-1 Role conceptions of interns, new and experienced teachers, and graduate students: a summary of chi square and critical ratio analyses [a]

| | Position | | | | Chi square | | | |
| | Teachers | | | | | | | |
Type of role conception	1 Interns	2 New	3 Experienced	4 Graduate students	Total	1 vs. 2	1 vs. 3	1 vs. 4
Initiative and compliance pre-dispositons (6)								
Percent rebellious	23.6	19.8	9.5	22.2	.01	.05	.01	.05
Percent submissive	9.7	18.0	27.0	11.1				
Administrative orientation (3)								
Percent high	12.0	39.9	44.7	24.7	.01	.01	.01	N.S.
Rules and procedures orientation (3)								
Percent high	10.8	35.6	42.6	24.7	.01	.01	.01	N.S.
Social and political liberalism (4)								
Percent highly liberal	32.2	11.1	6.4	8.8	.00	.01	.05	.01
Percent highly conservative	4.1	15.4	23.0	17.5				

86

Table 3-1 (Continued)

Changes that might have to occur to combat poverty (9)								
Guaranteed annual income	3.4	0.0	1.5	--	--	--	--	--
Better educational opportunities	17.9	11.3	10.1	--	--	--	--	--
Changes in basic social structure	24.0	9.4	5.4	--	.00	--	--	--
Endorsement of racial integration (5)								
Percent high or moderate	51.5	41.9	29.9	28.5	.04	.01	.01	.01
Level of alienation (3)								
Percent high	52.6	32.7	35.5	29.2	.00	.06	N.S.	N.S.
Plans to teach in a low-income school								
Percent certain (4)	39.8	23.7	20.4	7.0	.00	.01	.01	N.S.
Type of school preferred (5)								
Percent all or mostly white	5.9	38.7	49.0	69.8	.00	--	--	--
Long-range career plans (5)								
Continue teaching								
Males	34.1	26.0	54.7	29.7				
Females	34.5	25.4	55.3	31.5				
Move to another field of education								
Males	44.9	--	25.7	39.8	.00	--	--	--
Females	39.3	--	21.3	23.3				
Leave teaching for another vocation								
Males	10.8	--	4.2	4.7				
Females	4.8	--	2.7	2.7				

87

Table 3-1 (Continued)

Professional orientation (3)							
Percent high	30.5	--	32.7	31.9	N.S.	N.S.	N.S.	N.S.
Client orientation (3)							
Percent high	47.1	--	22.6	29.7	.001	.01	.01	.05
Pupil control ideology (4)							
Percent low control	36.1	15.4	10.9	42.7	.00	.01	.01	.01
Percent of students considered capable of graduation from high school--91 or more (8)	30.6	10.8	18.3	--	.00	--	--	--

a Space does not permit reproducing each chi square separately. Therefore, selected rows were taken from different chi-square analyses to provide an indication of patterns in the data. Numbers in parentheses after type of role conception refer to the number of categories into which the variable was divided. Where possible, both chi-square and critical ratios (based on means) were computed.

percent of the interns were in the upper one third of the distribution, compared to 36 percent of the new teachers and 25 percent of the other graduate students in education. The differences between the interns and new teachers were statistically significant.

PATTERNS AMONG THE PROGRAMS. In all of the programs, teachers consistently expressed more loyalty to the administration than the interns, but the magnitude of difference between the two groups in the "high" category ranged from 5 to 45 percent.

Social and Political Liberalism

Interns ranked disproportionately high on the social and political liberalism scale, compared to new and veteran teachers and graduate students. About one third were classified as very liberal, and only 4 percent were "highly conservative." The ratio of interns to new teachers in the "highly liberal" category was 3 to 1.

But, in another analysis, the proportion of university faculty (38 percent) and program directors (33 percent) in the highest category of liberalism was equal to or exceeded that of the interns. The proportion of team leaders in this category was comparable to new teachers (11 percent).

PATTERNS AMONG THE PROGRAMS. The patterns just described were uniform throughout the 10 programs, although the differences in the proportion of liberal interns and teachers varied from 5 to 25 percent; in only two of these instances were the differences not statistically significant. As many as two thirds of the interns were classified as highly liberal in one program and as few as 11 percent in another.

Prescription for Combating Poverty

Interns and teachers also differed in their prescriptions for combating poverty. Interns were more likely to prescribe changes needed in the basic structure of the society and to observe a need for better educational opportunities, but they were less likely to mention training in marketable skills or the ideology that the poor do not have enough drive to get out of poverty and to get ahead. However, a substantial number of both interns and teachers stressed the personal factor of self-respect and, even though they were more liberal than teachers in certain respects, they tended to discount the importance of job opportunity and guaranteed income.

PATTERNS AMONG THE PROGRAMS. The proportion of interns believing the need for greater drive among the poor to be the most fundamental way of combating poverty varied from one fourth in one program to none in another.

Endorsement of Racial Integration

A comparison of new teachers, veteran teachers, and interns on many items concerning the desirability of certain practices leading to racial integration revealed slight tendencies for interns to endorse school integration more frequently. On the three-item index, 52 percent of the interns ranked "high" or "moderate," compared to 42 percent of the new teachers and 30 percent of the experienced teachers. The interns also differed from other graduate students in this respect (29 percent of whom were "high" and "moderate").

An examination of the separate items in this index (not shown in Table 3–1) revealed the following: (1) Almost 80 percent of the interns and 75 percent of the teachers and graduate students agreed that the difference in intelligence between the races will disappear under conditions of racial integration. (2) Only 28 percent of the interns agreed that neighborhood elementary schools should be maintained regardless of racial balance, compared to more than twice that proportion of teachers and other graduate students.[4] (3) Sixty-three percent of the interns, compared to 50 percent of the teachers and 59 percent of the graduate students, believed that integration would increase the achievement of all students. When interns were compared specifically to new teachers on these individual items, only the difference on the value attached to neighborhood schools was sustained.

PATTERNS AMONG THE PROGRAMS. Interns were more highly or moderately supportive of integration than were teachers in all 10 programs, although in four cases the differences were not statistically significant. Differences between the two groups ranged from 8 to 39 percent. The proportion of interns classified as highly or moderately supportive of racial integration varied from 70 to 29 percent on the different sites.

Alienation

On a multiple-item index, used to assess the alienation (or sense of powerlessness) of the respondents, interns placed in the highly alienated category more frequently than other graduate students. They were also significantly different from both new and experienced teachers in this respect.

PATTERNS AMONG THE PROGRAMS. The differences between interns and teachers were in the expected direction in 7 of the 10 programs, but they were not statistically significant in most of these cases. Differences between the proportion of interns and teachers classified as low on alienation ranged from 35 to only 3 percent among the various programs.

Were Teacher Corps interns committed to teaching in poverty schools?

An array of evidence suggested that interns were relatively committed to the idea of teaching in low-income schools on a short-term basis, but many of them expected to move to other fields of education and therefore had not made a long-term career commitment to classroom *teaching*.

Short-Term Plans To Teach in Low-Income Schools

DATA FROM OTHER SOURCES. A questionnaire mailed by the Teacher Corps office to graduates of the first cycle revealed that 80 percent were teaching their first year after graduation and an additional 8 percent were in education but were not teaching. Three fourths of those teaching (or 62 percent of the total) were teaching the disadvantaged, most of them (two thirds) in the same geographical area as the Teacher Corps program where they trained. Over half of the male graduates (58 percent) were teaching at the elementary level.[5] Forty-three percent of the team leaders in the first cycle were still teaching, and 46 percent were in the field of education working as supervisors, principals, and the like; 84 percent were working with the disadvantaged.

The Teacher Corps also mailed questionnaires to second-cycle Corpsmen at the time of their graduation but before many had taken jobs. Three fourths of those who replied (or 55 percent of the total contacted) planned to be working in schools having concentrations of students from low-income families. Asked how likely it was that they would teach in a disadvantaged school next year, the interns and team leaders responded as follows:

	Interns (%)	Team Leaders (%)
Very likely	48	74
Probably	27	12
Maybe	14	4
Very unlikely	11	9
Do not plan to continue in education	—	1

THE COMMITMENT TO TEACHING INDEX. Examining the present sample, then, we find a comparably high level of commitment to low-income schools. More frequently than either experienced teachers or other graduate students, interns said they were certain that they would continue working in impoverished schools during their careers (40 versus 20 versus 7 percent). The comparison with new teachers (24 percent) was smaller but still significant (Table 3–1). Also, the trends were similar for each of the three items in the commitment to teaching index (not reported in the table). However, it is significant that the differences diminished as the period of time involved became protracted. Seventy-eight percent of the interns said that it was very likely that they would be working in impoverished schools next year, 40 percent in five years, and 25 percent indefinitely; the comparable figures for teachers were 56, 22, and 17 percent.

Differences were found in the commitment of interns who had taken courses in education and interns who had not. When the tests were repeated for each of these groups, differences were found between each type of intern, teacher, and graduate student on the first two items on the index.

PATTERNS AMONG THE PROGRAMS. The differences between teachers and interns were in the expected direction in 8 of the 10 programs. The highest difference was 55 percentage points in some programs, but in three cases there was a difference of only a few percentage points. The proportion of interns classified as being highly committed to teaching in impoverished schools varied from 64 to 13 percent in different programs. The comparable figures for teachers ranged from 43 to 9 percent.

Preferences for Working with Minorities

Interns were also less likely to prefer working in all-white or mostly white schools than either classroom teachers or graduate students in education.[6] Only 6 percent specified all-white or predominantly white schools, whereas nearly 70 percent of the graduate students and 49 percent of the experienced teachers preferred such schools.[7] Moreover, differences between interns and the new teachers, although smaller (6 versus 39 percent specifying all or predominantly white schools), remained statistically significant (Table 3–1).

PATTERNS AMONG THE PROGRAMS. Interns were uniformly more favorable than teachers toward minority schools in all of the programs; in 9 of the 10 programs, differences were statistically significant. The percentage difference between the two groups, however, ranged from 50 to only 4 percent among the different programs.

Another analysis indicated that interns were less likely than teachers to want to move into a school in a "better neighborhood," but the differences were statistically significant in only 4 of the 10 programs. The differences between interns and teachers on this item ranged from more than 20 to less than 3 percentage points in the different programs. The proportion of interns who were strongly opposed to moving to a school in a better neighborhood varied from 60 percent in one program to as low as 17 percent in another.

Long-Range Career Plans

The interns, in contrast to their preference for working temporarily in low-income, ghetto situations, were not as highly committed to a career in classroom teaching. In fact, compared to the experienced teachers, interns in the sample *less* frequently expected to continue teaching (34 versus 55 percent) and more frequently expected to move to another field of education (45 versus 26 percent).[8] However, the difference between the proportion of interns and new teachers who expected to continue teaching indicated a reversal of the above pattern; more interns than new teachers expected to continue teaching (34 versus 25 percent).

The differences between interns and graduate students were smaller but similar; 30 percent of the graduate students expected to continue teaching, and 40 percent expected to move to some other field of education.

Did Teacher Corps interns define their roles and objectives differently from other classroom teachers?

In many respects, they did. But the picture is somewhat complex.

Professional and Client Orientation

The groups in the sample did not differ significantly in their total *professional* orientation scale scores. About 31 percent of the interns, 33 percent of the experienced teachers, and 32 percent of the graduate students scored in the high range of the total professional orientation scale. However, interns' *client* orientation scores were significantly higher than the scores of experienced teachers or other graduate students. Forty-seven percent of the interns, compared to only 23 percent of the teachers and 30 percent of the graduate students, ranked in the upper third of the client subscale distribution. They differed significantly from both new teachers and experienced teachers.

PATTERNS AMONG THE PROGRAMS. Teachers, more frequently than interns, were in the high end of the professional orientation distribution in 8 of the 10 programs, but consistently the interns were statistically more client oriented than teachers in all programs. The difference in proportions of these groups in the high category ranged from 7 to 44 percent. The proportion of interns in the highest category varied from 70 to 34 percent in the different programs.

Teaching Roles

There were also some notable differences and similarities between the teaching practices and philosophies of interns and teachers.

TEACHING OBJECTIVES. In an analysis not reported in the tables, almost half of both the interns and the teachers said that teaching children basic knowledge (arithmetic, reading, and the like) was the most important objective in teaching. One fourth of both groups placed primary emphasis on teaching children to think for themselves. But they were nearly reversed in the priority that they placed on two other factors: (a) teaching children to respect the authority of the teacher and to follow instructions, and (b) helping children to do what *they* wish to do. Only 11 percent of the interns ranked factor (a) first or second in importance, compared to 42 percent of the teachers. By contrast, over half (53 percent) of the interns but only 15 percent of the teachers ranked factor (b) as first or second in importance. Team leaders were intermediate on factor (b)—21 percent ranked it first—but they placed more emphasis than the teachers did on factor (a).

PATTERNS AMONG THE PROGRAMS. In 6 of the 10 programs, interns were more liberal than teachers about discipline, the differences between the two groups ranging from 33 to 0 percentage points in the different programs; but there was only one program where more interns than teachers stressed discipline. The proportion of interns who ranked as their first objective the helping of children to do as they wish varied from a high of 23 percent in one program to less than 5 percent in another.

PREFERRED TEACHING STYLE. The majority of all groups preferred the type of teacher who encourages creative, independent thought (see Teacher 3, Table 3–2). However, a disproportionately large number of interns chose this type of teacher (88 percent compared to 56 percent of the new

Table 3-2 Style of teaching preferred by interns, new and
experienced teachers, other graduate students, and team leaders

Teaching style [a]	Total	1 Interns	2 New teachers	3 Experienced teachers	4 Graduate students	5 Team leaders
Teacher 1	14.1	0.6	16.7	19.0	5.4	3.3
Teacher 2	15.1	6.2	20.0	17.4	17.2	13.2
Teacher 3	66.4	87.5	55.8	60.6	69.9	76.7
Teacher 4	4.4	5.6	7.5	2.9	7.5	6.7
Total	654	160	120	373	93	30

$$1 \text{ vs. } 2 \text{ vs. } 3 -- X^2 = 58.69, P = 0.00$$
$$1 \text{ vs. } 4 \text{ vs. } 5 -- X^2 = 61.87, P = 0.00$$

[a]
Teacher 1 -- is most concerned with maintaining discipline, seeing
that students work hard, and teaching them to follow directions.
Teacher 2 -- feels it is most important that students know their
subject matter well, and that he cover the material thoroughly
and test students' progress regularly.
Teacher 3 -- stresses making the class interesting and encourages
students to be creative and figure things out for themselves.
Teacher 4 -- thinks it is most important that a teacher be friendly
and well liked by students and able to understand and to handle
their problems.

Instrument adapted from Sieber and Wilder (1967).

teachers, 70 percent of the other graduate students, and 77 percent of the
team leaders). Less than 1 percent of the interns chose the disciplinarian
(Teacher 1) in comparison to 17 percent of the new teachers and 19 percent of the experienced teachers. Similarly, only 6 percent of the interns
chose the subject-oriented teacher (Teacher 2), but this type was preferred by 20 percent of the new teachers and 17 percent of the experienced
teachers and graduate students.

PUPIL-CONTROL IDEOLOGY. The pupil-control index also indicated that
interns were more likely than teachers to be among the more laissez-faire
type of teacher who prefers not to exercise rigid control over pupils in
the classroom (see Table 3–1). They were more liberal in this respect
(36 percent) than either new teachers (15 percent) or experienced teachers

(11 percent). Less than 1 percent of the interns were in the "high-control" category, compared to 9 percent of the new teachers and 11 percent of the experienced teachers (not shown in Table 3–1). However, in certain respects, other graduate students seemed to be even more laissez-faire than the interns, since more than 43 percent were in the "low-control" category.

These differences were reflected in responses to particular questions in the ideology index (not shown in the table). For example, teachers more frequently than interns agreed that beginning teachers are not likely to maintain enough control over their pupils (32 versus 48 percent); they less frequently agreed that teachers should consider revising their usual teaching methods when criticized by pupils (88 versus 58 percent); and they less frequently agreed that opinions of students should influence teaching methods (91 versus 79 percent).

PATTERNS AMONG THE PROGRAMS. The differences on these items were in the expected direction in 8 of the 10 programs. Differences between the proportions of teachers and interns who were classified in the lowest range of the scale varied from 6 to 56 percent. The proportion of interns in the lowest category ranged from 13 to 67 percent in the different programs.

Were interns more optimistic about children than other teachers?

Confidence in Children's Ability To Learn

On two indicators, interns expressed more confidence than teachers in the learning potential of their pupils; team leaders tended to score between the interns and the teachers. First, nearly three times as many interns as new teachers estimated that over 91 percent of their pupils were capable of graduating from high school (31 versus 11 percent). Table 3–1 does not indicate the fact that 60 percent of the interns, compared to 43 percent of the team leaders and 47 percent of the teachers, estimated that more than three fourths of their pupils were capable of completing high school.

Second, Table 3–1 does not show that, although the majority in all groups disagreed with the statement, "There are some groups in this country to whom you cannot teach anything," interns were more likely than teachers and team leaders to express strong disagreement with the statement (59 percent of the interns versus 38 percent of the teachers and 47 percent of the team leaders).

PATTERNS AMONG THE PROGRAMS. In 7 of the 10 programs the percentage differences between the estimates of interns and teachers of the ability of their pupils to graduate were statistically significant, with interns more positive in each case; the magnitude of the differences between the two groups, however, varied from 54 to less than 5 percent in the different programs. The proportion of interns who were optimistic also varied considerably: from 50 percent to a low of 9 percent in the different programs.

Interns in nine of the programs were also more optimistic than teachers about the ability of children to learn, although in three cases (including one in which the direction was reversed) the differences were too small to be statistically significant. The differences between the two groups varied from 46 to less than 5 percent.

Explanations of Poor Performance

Another analysis (not shown) indicated that all three groups, when asked to rank nine possible explanations for the poor educational performance of their pupils, stressed "poor home background" as their first or second choice (70 percent of the interns, 78 percent of the teachers, and 67 percent of the team leaders). The groups differed, however, in the priority placed on the limited capacity of children to learn, as opposed to inadequate curriculum and teaching. Whereas more than one in three classroom teachers and one in five team leaders rated the limited personal capacity of children as first or second, less than 1 percent of the interns chose this explanation. Teachers also placed more emphasis than interns on large classes (27 versus 16 percent). Instead, interns were more likely to blame the schools by stressing inadequate preparation in previous grades (49 versus 22 percent) and inadequate curriculum and instructional materials (32 versus 12 percent); team leaders ranked in between. Interns were only slightly more ready than teachers to blame the lack of imagination and unwillingness of the administration to carry out teachers' suggestions (9 versus 2 percent).

PATTERNS AMONG THE PROGRAMS. Interns in every program, with the exception of one statistically insignificant case, were more charitable toward the children than were teachers. The percentage difference varied from 54 to 10 percent. The proportion of interns that used "the limited capacity of the pupils" as their first or second explanation for poor performance in school ranged up to 33 percent in one program but, in other cases, only 15 percent endorsed this explanation.

DIFFERENCES WITHIN THE TEACHER AND INTERN GROUPS

Concerning the earlier question about differences between interns from conventional and new sources, a series of more refined internal comparisons was repeated for most of the opinion scales already discussed here. Space does not permit the inclusion of these detailed tables, but the conclusions are summarized below.

Sex

Among interns, females more frequently than males (a) were certain of their plans to continue *teaching* in poverty schools (60 versus 28 percent on the total index), (b) had assisted the impoverished prior to joining the Teacher Corps (70 versus 61 percent), and (c) planned to leave teaching temporarily (21 versus 9 percent). But males less frequently planned to leave teaching for another vocation (5 versus 17 percent). A larger proportion of women planned to leave the profession temporarily (18 versus 0 percent), and a smaller proportion intended to move to some other field of education (21 versus 39 percent). Over half of the women (55 percent) but only one fourth of the men (27 percent) considered it likely that they would be teaching in five years, and only 31 percent of the women and 18 percent of the men planned to continue teaching in the indefinite future.

This pattern of evidence raises some questions about the receptivity of men to classroom teaching in low-income elementary schools. The men were not as likely to leave the field within education, but they were more likely to leave classroom teaching for another "field" of education, probably administration or college teaching. In other words, men were more likely than women to use the Teacher Corps as an avenue of mobility within the broad field of education. This does not imply, of course, that attracting more men was a mistake. They will probably attain positions where they can exercise an important long-range influence on education. But it does raise questions about the feasibility of attracting large numbers of male liberal arts graduates into classroom teaching for extended periods.

Race

There were also some systematic differences between the white and black interns and teachers in the program. One difference was that the blacks were less permissive toward the children than were the whites, a difference that also separates ghetto and suburban residents. There is a widespread feeling on the part of ghetto parents that children should be treated fairly but strictly and should be challenged to work hard if they are to make it in white society. Thus, compared to the white interns, the black interns expressed a lower client orientation (23 versus 45 percent ranked in the lower third of the scale distribution) and endorsed stricter discipline (76 versus 33 percent ranked low on the pupil control scale). More generally, there were conflicts in philosophy and style of teaching between the white liberals and the black teachers. The blacks seemed less concerned about making schools more "humane" places in the sense that the white middle-class liberals wanted to "humanize" the schools, although, of course, the blacks disapproved of discriminatory practices. These differences have implications on the effects of recruiting blacks and whites into teaching.

Another difference was the greater acceptance of the existing situation on the part of the blacks in the program, which probably stemmed from the lack of alternatives open to them in other jobs or occupations. Thus, black interns were more frequently compliant toward the administration than were whites (percentage compliant: 37 versus 20 percent). Black interns also were more committed to teaching (percentage with high commitment: 83 versus 63 percent); they less frequently planned to leave education for another career (3 versus 24 percent); and they were more certain than whites of their plans to continue teaching in an impoverished school. On the latter measure, there was a two-to-one difference with respect to both plans for five years (64 versus 35 percent) and for the indefinite future (43 versus 21 percent), but there was not a significant difference in their plans for next year (83 versus 77 percent).

Comparable analyses were made for the teachers. More blacks than whites planned to teach next year (63 versus 52 percent), planned to teach for five years (28 versus 20 percent), and planned to be teaching in the indefinite future (23 versus 15 percent). There was only a slight tendency for black teachers to plan more frequently to move to some other field of education (37 versus 21 percent). Nineteen percent of the white teachers specified an all-white school, compared to only 3 percent of black teachers. Over half of the white teachers (57 percent) preferred either all-white or predominantly white schools, compared to 10 percent of the blacks.

A majority of both white (64 percent) and black (58 percent) teachers "agreed" or "strongly agreed" that integration would improve the academic achievement of all concerned and would minimize the existing I.Q. differences between the races (75 percent for blacks versus 60 percent for whites). Nevertheless, a majority of both groups (71 percent of the whites and 78 percent of the blacks) would not sacrifice neighborhood schools to achieve integration. Perhaps blacks were not convinced that true integration could be achieved.

Region

Interns from outside the region had more frequently worked with the disadvantaged before joining the Teacher Corps (73 versus 58 percent), but interns who had lived in the region prior to the program were more committed to teaching in impoverished schools than interns from outside of the region (53 versus 30 percent). Again we find that the type of intern that the program attempted to recruit (in this case, the cosmopolitan) was least likely to stay in teaching, once he was recruited.

The region of origin, however, appeared to have a unique influence only on the interns who had taken courses in education. Of these interns, a higher proportion from the region considered it very likely that they would teach in poverty schools during the next year. But region made no difference to interns without education courses. In short, region seemed to make a difference primarily for interns who had had education courses; coming from outside colleges of education seemed to have an effect comparable to coming from outside the region.

Educational Background

Interns who had not taken courses in education were slightly more committed to teaching in *impoverished* schools than interns who had prior contact with education courses (43 versus 38 percent ranked high), but the latter expressed more *certainty* about their intentions to commit themselves to teach in impoverished schools (45 versus 31 percent). Also, the graduates of teacher-training institutions more frequently expressed preference for schools consisting primarily of white pupils (25 versus 8 percent).

Liberal Arts Degrees Versus Others

Despite the importance attached to attracting liberal arts graduates as a way of liberalizing teaching, a series of chi square statistical tests revealed no significant differences, in any of the scales discussed above, between interns who did and did not major in the liberal arts as undergraduates. Self-selection into the Teacher Corps program perhaps moderated the differences that might have been expected if a random sample of each group were compared. That is, perhaps the most liberal students from outside the liberal arts and the moderates from the liberal arts were attracted to the program.

Attracted to Teaching by the Teacher Corps

Interns who said that they would not have considered teaching if it had not been for the Teacher Corps were compared with interns who said they would have entered anyway. The former expressed lower commitment to teaching (percentage low: 48 versus 32 percent) and less frequently expected to continue teaching to retirement (13 versus 26 percent). More-over, the program itself did not draw a more liberal type of new teacher than would have entered on his own volition. On the contrary, of the interns who said that the Teacher Corps was responsible for their going into teaching, a disproportionate number were moderately conservative on the liberalism scale (42 versus 33 percent of the sample).

Team Leaders

When team leaders were compared to teachers and interns on some of the items, it became apparent that in many respects they were in an inter-mediate position. For example, although it is noteworthy that none of the team leaders were in the most rebellious category, there were proportion-ately more team leaders than teachers in the second most rebellious cate-gory and proportionately fewer in the most submissive category.[9] Also, team leaders were more client oriented than experienced teachers, but less client oriented than new teachers and interns. They were also inter-mediate between teachers and interns on the measures of loyalty to the administration, endorsement of rules and procedures, and in the pro-portions who preferred all-white or predominantly white schools. In the latter case, 24 percent of the team leaders expressed preference for all-white or predominantly white schools, compared to 49 percent of the experienced teachers but only 6 percent of the interns. Moreover, the proportion of team leaders who expressed high or moderate racial tolerance was more similar to interns than to teachers.

These findings tend to confirm my interpretations of the important link-age role played by team leaders, discussed in Chapter 4. Although the team leaders, in some sense, were a select group, they were not the most con-servative or even the typical teachers. Compared to the teacher group, they were relatively liberal; this probably enhanced the teachers' ability to relate to the interns (in comparison to other teachers who might have been selected for this role if the administrators' *sole* purpose had been to co-opt the program). In short, the team leaders were a good choice for the kind of mediating role they had to play.

TEACHER PROFILES

These questions arise: Do a person's scores on one of the measures reviewed above predict his scores on another? Do the variables form patterns that describe teacher "types"? Several approaches were used to answer these questions.

Table 3-3   Summary of patterns among nine variables

Correlated at r = .25 scale	Interns
Client orientation	+Professional orientation (.54) −Administrative orientation (−.40) −Rules and procedures (−.32) +Initiative-compliance (.35) −Pupil control (−.43) +Liberalism (.34)
Professional orientation	+Client orientation (.54)
Administrative orientation	−Client orientation (−.40) +Rules and procedures (.60) −Initiative-compliance (−.53) +Pupil control (.53) −Liberalism (−.70)
Rules and procedures orientation	−Client orientation (−.32) +Administrative orientation (.60) −Initiative-compliance (−.41) +Pupil control (.37) −Liberalism (−.58)
Racial integration	−Pupil control (−.33) +Liberalism (.39) −Commitment to teaching (−.23)

Intercorrelations

First, patterns among the variables showed up in (zero order) computer intercorrelations among 10 of the key measures discussed in this chapter.[10] The pattern that emerges in the matrix will reveal whether or not the separate dimensions cluster into an "ideal type" of teacher as described earlier, the extent to which teachers approximate the ideal, and the variables that are central to the type. Table 3–3 summarizes the correlation matrix; the matrix itself can be found in Appendix 2. A correlation had to correlated at r = .25 or above, by position

Position	
Teachers	Team leaders
	+Professional orientation (.42)
+Initiative-compliance (.26)	+Initiative-compliance (.28)
+Liberalism (new teachers only) (.33)	
+Client orientation (.55) +Initiative-compliance (.26) (experienced teachers only)	+Client orientation (.42) +Rules and procedures (.26) −Liberalism (−.25)
+Rules and procedures (.61) −Initiative-compliance (−.39) −Commitment to teaching (new teachers only) (−:34) −Liberalism (−.33) −Racial integration (new teachers only) (−.33) +Pupil control (new teachers only) (.30)	+Rules and procedures (.48) +Pupil control (.46)
+Administrative orientation (.61) −Initiative-compliance (−.31) +Pupil control (.26) −Liberalism (−.35)	+Professional orientation (.26) +Administrative orientation (.48) +Pupil control (.50) +Liberalism (.70)
−Pupil control (−.29) +Liberalism (.38) −Administrative orientation new teachers only) (−.33)	+Initiative-compliance (.52) +Liberalism (.38)

reach an arbitrary criterion of $r = .25$ to be included in Table 3–3. The table indicates that interns, and to a lesser extent teachers, who have one given characteristic (such as concern for students or loyalty to the administration) have other predictable characteristics as well. This tendency for clustering to occur among these dimensions suggests that complex types of teachers do "exist." But, more important, the patterns indicate that *any effort to recruit new teachers on a single criterion can have unintended*

Table 3-3 (continued)

Correlated at r = .25 scale	Interns
Initiative-compliance	+Client orientation (.35) −Administrative orientation (−.53) −Rules and procedures (−.41) −Pupil control (−.31) +Racial tolerance (.30) +Liberalism (.43)
Commitment to teaching	−Racial tolerance (−.23)
Pupil control	−Client orientation (−.43) +Administrative orientation (.53) +Rules and procedures (.37) −Racial integration (−.33) −Initiative-compliance (−.31) −Liberalism (−.52)
Political and social liberalism	+Client orientation (.34) −Administrative orientation (−.69) −Rules and procedures (−.58) +Racial integration (.39) +Initiative-compliance (.43) −Pupil control (−.52) −Commitment to teaching (−.27)

effects. For example, suppose a university makes an effort to recruit only new teachers who express great concern for children. This client-oriented teachers also will tend to be more socially and politically liberal and more prone to take initiative against the administration. They are not likely to exhibit a great deal of loyalty to the administration or to the rules, and they will tend to run permissive classrooms.

As another alternative, suppose administrators make a deliberate effort to recruit teachers who are socially and politically conservative, on the assumption that they will fit in better. These recruits also are likely to place lower priority on racial integration, to be less concerned with students, to be less prone to take initiative, to exert more pupil control, and to be more loyal to the system.

Position	
Teachers	Team leaders

+Client orientation (.26)
 −Administrative orientation (−.39)
 −Rules and procedures (−.31)
 +Liberalism (.33) (for new
   teachers) (.50)
 +Professional orientation
   (experienced teachers only)
   (.26)
 	
 +Administrative orientation
   (for new teachers only) (.34)
	+Client orientation (.24)
	
	 +Racial integration (.52)
	 +Liberalism (.39)

+Administrative orientation (new teachers only) (.30) +Rules and procedures (.26) −Racial integration (−.29) −Liberalism (−.41)	+Administrative orientation (.46) +Rules and procedures (.50)
−Administrative orientation (−.44) −Rules and procedures (−.35) −Racial integration (−.38) +Initiative-compliance (.33) −Pupil control (−.41) +Client orientation (new teachers only) (.33)	−Professional orientation (−.25) +Rules and procedures (.70) +Racial integration (.38) +Initiative-compliance (.39)

If the administration stresses the importance of attracting teachers who emphasize discipline (pupil control), these teachers will tend to be compliant and loyal to the system, but they will also be less concerned about students, less supportive of racial integration, and less politically liberal.

If efforts are made to recruit interns who are prone to take initiative, the system will have to cope with student-oriented, liberal teachers who are inclined to be disloyal to the administration, to conform less to the rules, and to tolerate more permissive classrooms.

If the administration wants teachers who will support racial integration policies, they will also tend to be more liberal and to run more boisterous, permissive classrooms. Moreover, they are not likely to be highly committed to teaching.

Interns who were committed to teaching tended to be more politically

Table 3-4   Proportion of correlations among nine variables which reach r = .25 or above

	Interns			Teachers		
Total (percent)	2nd cycle	3rd cycle	Total	New	Experienced	Team leaders
55[a]	58	47	33	42	22	30[b]

[a] Total interns--53 percent significant in expected direction.
[b] Team leaders--22 percent significant in expected direction.

conservative and less supportive of racial integration. But the selection of interns on the basis of the other characteristics will not necessarily assure that the ones recruited will be committed to teaching.

Alienation from the Teacher Corps was not included as part of the ideal type. However, the interns who otherwise approached the ideal type also tended to be alienated from the program. Thus, interns who were not committed to the administration and to school rules also tended to be alienated from the program, whereas interns who were less alienated tended to become more committed to teaching. Disillusionment with the program and with schools appeared to be associated with disillusionment with teaching.

Ideal Types

If the assumed ideal teacher were completely congruent with reality, all 36 correlations in the matrix among the set of variables would be statistically significant in the expected directions (excluding those dealing with alienation). If the construct were not valid, few of them would be statistically significant, and many of them would be in the unexpected directions. The actual patterns are summarized in Table 3–4. The table indicates that the interns approximated the ideal type more closely than did teachers. For interns, 20 of the 36 correlations (55 percent) reached an arbitrary criterion of $r = .25$ or above, 19 of which were in the expected direction (53 percent). By comparison, only 33 percent of the correlations among teachers reached this figure. The new teachers approximated the ideal type more closely than did experienced teachers (42 versus 22 percent of the correla-

Table 3-5 Composite scores of second cycle interns compared to other groups on six dimensions of the ideal-type teacher

	Mean	Percent of maximum possible	Rank
Interns	32.33	60.61	1
New teachers	29.65	55.34	2
Experienced teachers	27.26	51.11	3
Team leaders	24.95	46.30	4

tions at $r = .25$ or above); but they still ranked lower than the interns. Team leaders' scores (30 percent) were similar to those of other teachers. (Interns in the second cycle scored higher than those in the new third cycle, 58 versus 47 percent.) The pattern, then, does provide some support for the ideal type, although clearly all dimensions were not simultaneously present among large groups of both interns and teachers.

The question of how closely interns resembled the ideal type of teacher also can be answered in another way—by constructing profiles for *individuals*. The five ongoing second-cycle programs were selected for a more detailed analysis of eight of the variables:[11] client orientation, professional orientation, administrative orientation, rules and procedures orientation, racial tolerance, initiative and compliance, commitment to teaching, and liberalism.

The actual mean score and the maximum possible mean score for the eight scales were computed for each group. A third score, a percentage, was also computed, which indicates the proportion of the potential mean actually achieved by each group. One hundred percent would represent the "ideal type." Table 3-5 reports the results. Interns achieved the highest mean score (32.3) of the four groups in the comparison. They ranked first in all five programs. The new teachers ranked second, and the team leaders ranked last on the composite score in four of the five programs; in the fifth program, team leaders and experienced teachers changed places.

Table 3-4 also reflects again the intermediate position of the team leaders whose scores fell between the scores of experienced teachers and interns on six of the dimensions: client orientation, administrative orientation, initiative predisposition, pupil control, liberalism, and rules and procedures orientation. However, the scores of the team leaders were among the lowest of the three groups on racial integration and total professional orientation measures.

TEACHING COMPETENCE

The question that now must be raised is whether these liberal, change-oriented new recruits to teaching were any more effective as teachers than their traditional counterparts. The evidence on this point was necessarily indirect and inferential. It will be assumed that the way interns were evaluated by their team leaders and other teachers reflected on their ability to teach. This assumption, of course, is open to question, particularly if it is recognized that the Teacher Corps itself was introduced in order to compensate for the presumed relatively low effectiveness of teachers in low-income schools, who now are being asked to judge good teaching. We have assumed that, on the average, teachers are as qualified as anyone to judge, and as an added precaution, the evaluations made by the team leaders—who were generally considered to be among the most competent teachers in each school—were separate from the evaluations made by the rank-and-file teachers.

A review of literature and a scale analysis of a battery of items developed for this study suggested that there are at least four crucial dimensions of good teaching: innovativeness, understanding of pupils, rapport with pupils, and relationship with the community. These four dimensions were used to evaluate all interns who had been in the program 18 months at the time they were evaluated by team leaders and cooperating classroom teachers who worked directly with them. The interns evaluated team leaders and cooperating teachers, and team leaders also were evaluated by classroom teachers.

Since the numbers involved, particularly in individual programs, were small, and there was some variability among and within the programs included, extreme caution is needed in interpreting the mean estimates reported here. However, if the data are interpreted with the appropriate discretion, suggestive patterns show up.[12]

Differences in Rating Among Programs

Several analyses (using analysis of variance methods) indicated that there was more variability in the composite ratings given to interns by classroom teachers and team leaders *within* particular programs than occurred *among* programs. An analysis of the overall ratings of classroom teachers by interns and team leaders (not reported) yielded similar results. There were no significant differences in ratings among the programs on any of the four scales as measured by critical ratio and analysis of variance methods. By contrast, there was some variability from program to program in the competence of team leaders as evaluated by their colleagues and interns, although the numbers involved were small.[13]

In short, while there were not large differences between programs, the fact that at least some difference existed calls for caution in interpreting subsequent analyses.[14]

Differences in Ratings Given by Persons in Various Positions

Disregarding for the moment the variation among the programs, there appeared to be systematic differences in the way interns, classroom teachers, and team leaders rated one another (Table 3–6). On all four scales the team leaders rated the interns statistically higher than did the teachers. With a few exceptions, each of the five programs displayed a similar pattern (although in most cases, at the program level, the differences were not statistically significant). There appeared to be no uniform differences between the way interns and other personnel rated either team leaders or teachers.

Lines 3, 5, and 7 (Table 3–6) further suggest that on three out of four scales, the team leaders' favorable evaluations of interns were reciprocated by the interns, who rated team leaders more favorably than they rated other teachers. With several exceptions, this pattern was also found in the individual programs. Classroom teachers confirmed these favorable ratings.

The fact that classroom teachers rated interns favorably was even more noteworthy in view of the relatively low opinions that interns had of the classroom teachers' teaching ability. On all four dimensions in which teaching competence was rated, the interns rated classroom teachers lower than the teachers rated the interns (line 2 versus 5, Table 3–6), although the differences were statistically significant only for the two scales measuring innovativeness and understanding of pupils.

In summary, interns were judged by team leaders to be relatively competent, and although team leaders were more favorably impressed with the interns than were classroom teachers, the teachers nevertheless evaluated the interns more favorably than the interns evaluated them. Team leaders received relatively favorable ratings from both the interns and the teachers.

Areas of Strength and Weakness

These evaluations were generally skewed in a favorable direction; no group scored in the "poor" range. But, of the four dimensions rated, all three groups evaluated—teachers, team leaders, and interns—ranked lowest on

Table 3-6 Evaluation of interns' teaching competence, by position

	N = members being rated	Scale I[a] Innovativeness		Scale II[b] Respect and understanding		Scale III[c] Rapport with pupils		Scale IV[d] Community relations	
		$\bar{X}$	V	$\bar{X}$	V	$\bar{X}$	V	$\bar{X}$	V
Total									
N = 181 Ratings of interns-- by number of raters									
1. All positions	78	16.56	17.7	20.3	26.3	20.13	23.3	12.7	32.0
2. Teachers	67	16.11	19.0	19.25	39.7	19.2	31.5	10.35	53.1
3. Team leaders	40	17.8	6.8	21.7	22.4	21.65	11.8	12.3	34.9
N = 81 Ratings of classroom teachers--by number of raters									
4. All positions	50	13.4	26.2	16.8	52.6	18.08	40.6	8.42	48.6
5. Interns	49	12.91	29.1	16.57	51.7	17.95	40.5	8.51	47.0
N = 51 Ratings of team leaders-- by number of raters									

110

	N	Scale I[a]		Scale II[b]		Scale III[c]		Scale IV[d]	
6. All positions	16	13.75	40.0	21.68	12.7	21.75	18.8	10.56	36.5
7. Interns	16	12.62	53.4	21.67	13.3	20.37	48.3	10.5	63.4
8. Teachers	5	15.0	71.5	19.80	12.7	19.4	118.3	10.8	97.7
1 vs. 4 vs. 6 (critical ratios)		(1,4) = 3.644		(1,4) = 3.049		(1,4) = 1.941		(1,4) = 3.657	
		(1,6) = -.201		(1,6) = 1.210		(1,6) = 1.334		(1,6) = -.522	
		(4,6) = 1.702		(4,6) = 3.591		(4,6) = -2.599		(4,6) = -2.854	
1 vs. 2 vs. 3 (cricital ratios)		(2,3) = -2.486		(2,3) = -2.276		(2,3) = -2.756		(2,3) = -1.504	
6 vs. 7 vs. 8 (critical ratios)		(7,8) = -.565		(7,8) = -.565		(7,8) = .188		(7,8) = -.061	
2 vs. 5 vs. 8		(2,5) = 3.409		(2,5) = 2.088		(2,5) = 1.093		(2,5) = 1.393	
		(2,8) = .293		(2,8) = 1.102		(2,8) = -.038		(2,8) = -.097	
		(5,8) = .539		(5,8) = .400		(5,8) = -.291		(5,8) = -.505	

a Scale I maximum score--20; minimum--4.
b Scale II maximum score--25; minimum--5.
c Scale III maximum score--25; minimum--5.
d Scale IV maximum score--20; minimum--4.

community relations. For example, team leaders and interns were rated as "good" and teachers as "average" or "slightly above average" on the two scales measuring understanding of pupils and rapport with pupils; and on the scale measuring innovativeness, interns were again rated as "good" and team leaders and teachers as "average." By comparison, on the scale measuring community relations, teachers were rated "below average" most often, with team leaders only slightly higher, whereas interns were rated as "average" on this scale.

Of the three groups being compared, interns received the highest overall ratings on innovativeness in each of the five programs (line 1 versus 4 versus 6, Table 3–6), and they also outranked classroom teachers on three of the other scales. One must be cautious about drawing conclusions; the cards were essentially stacked against the teachers because a larger number of interns than team leaders participated in evaluating them. Nevertheless, even when the interns' ratings of teachers were excluded (line 4, Table 3–6), teachers still rated lower than the interns on all four of the scales.

SUMMARY

The program attracted a limited number of new types of recruits from the liberal arts, one in three of whom otherwise would not have entered a teacher-preparation program. Comparisons of interns' and teachers' re-

---

A Note on Table 3-6

The table represents the total composite scale scores for the various groups being rated by categories of persons doing the rating. The means under the various scales (I, II, III, and IV) are the composite scores for the particular group being evaluated. The N of 181 in "Rating of Interns" indicates the number of respondents who rated interns. It should be noted that one person may have rated only one intern while others may have rated more than one. Sixty-seven interns were rated by teachers, while 40 interns were evaluated by team leaders. Again, it must be kept in mind not only that a teacher and a team leader may be rating the same interns but also that they may be rating more than one intern.

Critical ratio tests were then calculated first for the variation in the composite evaluation of all interns, all classroom teachers, and all team leaders for each of the four scales. The final tests were calculated on the difference of rating scores assigned only to interns by teachers (line 2); second, to teachers by interns (line 5), and finally to team leaders by teachers (line 8).

sponses to a series of opinion scales indicated that new teachers from liberal backgrounds can be attracted through this type of program and that new teachers drawn from middle-class liberal backgrounds are likely to differ substantially in many respects from veteran teachers and other new teachers from conventional programs. However, the self-selectivity into the program seemed to be a more crucial determinant of the difference than whether the new teachers were formally trained in a liberal arts program. Their aptitudes were below the national standards for graduate students but were comparable to or slightly above the aptitudes of other graduate students in education.

Compared to new and experienced teachers and other graduate students, the interns were relatively attracted to working with low-income, mixed racial groups, but they were less committed to classroom teaching and often planned to move to other fields of education. They expressed great concern for the welfare of their students, believed that children should be helped to do what they want to do, were permissive toward discipline, and admired teachers who encourage creativity and independent thought. They expressed a high degree of confidence in the intellectual abilities of their pupils.

Politically and socially they were more liberal than other teachers; they exhibited little sense of loyalty to the school administration and to school rules but instead were inclined to be rebellious. They tended to view the solution of poverty to be in the structure of society rather than in personal drive. They also frequently expressed a sense of alienation.

A correlation analysis, based on scores of a great many opinion and role-conception indices, indicated that interns approximated an "ideal type" of liberal, humanitarian teacher more closely than it was approximated by either the experienced or new teachers, although the new teachers were more like the ideal type than the experienced teachers. The interns also scored higher than new teachers, experienced teachers, or team leaders on a composite measure of the fit between their scale scores and the ideal type.

The teachers' profiles indicated that when new teachers are recruited along one dimension, such as "concern for students," they will also tend to have other characteristics that schools and colleges may not have bargained for. For example, change-oriented interns were not only more oriented to children (which teachers approved) but they also took a laissez-faire policy toward classroom discipline (which irritated the teachers); they were socially and politically liberal (which often got them into trouble in the community); and they disregarded school rules and the authority of school administrators (who resented the fact).

There was as much variability within as among programs on some of the dimensions. In general, however, classroom teachers rated the teaching competence of second-cycle interns and team leaders relatively high:

• Interns were judged by teachers and team leaders to be relatively competent on four dimensions of performance in the classroom: innovativeness in the classroom, respect for and understanding of pupils, rapport with pupils, and community relationships.
• Interns were rated higher than the teachers on community relations, received the highest overall ratings on innovativeness, and outranked teachers on the other dimensions as well.
• Team leaders rated interns more favorably than did the classroom teachers.
• Interns rated their team leaders more favorably than they rated classroom teachers on three of the four dimensions rated. Classroom teachers also were favorably disposed toward the teaching ability of team leaders.
• Interns rated classroom teachers less favorably than teachers rated them.
• All groups rated one another lower on the community relations dimension than on the other three dimensions rated.

CONCLUSIONS

Historically, the occupation of teaching has been looked upon by aspiring teachers as an avenue toward social mobility. It undoubtedly still serves that function. According to NEA estimates, about one half of the teachers today have come from the homes of farmers, or skilled and unskilled workers; one third are from families whose fathers are in managerial occupations or are self-employed; only 15 percent have fathers with professional or semiprofessional jobs (NEA, 1963). But the available information also indicates that the younger teachers who have joined the teaching ranks in more recent years are coming from middle-class backgrounds with increasing frequency.

Buried in these figures and the ones reported in this chapter are perhaps some implications for *a new kind of occupational transformation that seems to be under way as a result of new recruiting patterns in teaching—a trend toward humanistic liberalism*. The majority of interns in this study not only were from middle-class homes (58 percent had fathers in professional or managerial occupations) but frequently came from families at the growing edge of the middle class—the rapidly growing and bureaucratized professional, service, communications, and technological sectors of the economy as opposed to the entrepreneurial sector that historically has been the backbone of the individualistic, conservative, middle-class ethic. These individuals very likely were socialized in relatively secure but changing, forward-looking homes. They are bound to infuse teaching with a unique liberal, humane value system and perspective. Accordingly, our data indicated that the more politically and socially liberal the intern was, the higher his socioeconomic status was likely to be. Whereas 58 percent of the interns were from the upper middle class, only 15 percent of the more conservative interns were from that class.

Generally, there was a consistent pattern: *The upper-middle-class, white intern from the better colleges conformed more closely to the various components of the liberal, humanistic ideal type identified in this chapter* than did interns with lower-socioeconomic-class backgrounds. Moreover, while some of these young, middle-class liberals were probably attracted to teaching through this special program, the same figures suggested that there is probably a much more pervasive, natural influx of comparable people who are going into teaching through other channels. There is little difference between interns and other graduate students in education with respect to their rebelliousness and their disregard for rigid discipline. Between one third and one half of the interns in the sample said that they probably would have gone into teaching even if the Teacher Corps had not been available. It is possible, of course (as we shall discuss later), that the most unique people in this group will not stay in classroom teaching very long; but, to the extent that they do, they will help to create a new, forward-looking, humane value climate in teaching.

It is not difficult to anticipate what this value climate will be like. The socially mobile aspirants to teaching who traditionally came from the lower classes had reason to be cautious and loyal to the established system, since they had placed themselves in an uncertain, marginal, high-risk position by their very efforts to be mobile. But the already secure middle-class youth who want to participate in social reform are not likely to feel so constrained. The data consistently point to an inextricable relationship between broad social and political attitudes and values of the individual and attitudes and predispositions toward teaching. It is almost impossible to separate a teacher's classroom behavior from his more general attitudes and values. Since these broader values also may be related to his social origins, this connection has important implications for both recruitment and training. A shift can therefore be expected in teaching philosophy and style—from the authoritarian, rigid, and impersonal to the flexible and informal—as more middle-class liberals enter teaching through a variety of channels.

This matter of general *style* will probably make more difference in the value climate of schools and in the outcomes of schooling than the *techniques* used.

We, of course, must be careful not to exaggerate the amount of difference that can be made simply by recruiting various types of people into teaching. In view of the overwhelming controls over teachers (Corwin, 1970), their personal characteristics at best can have only a modest influence on the profession. Nevertheless, if a critical mass of new types of teachers were to accumulate in a sufficiently large number of schools, they might provide other new teachers with an alternative point of reference, in addition to the conservative environment into which most of them are now being socialized. Thus, to the extent that new teachers from the Teacher Corps and other programs are able to exercise some discretion in their teaching style (as they often can behind the doors of their self-contained classrooms), and to the extent that these teachers are able to withstand the crushing socializing forces that now favor the conventional mode, classrooms across the nation will perhaps slowly and subtly become more humane, and schools will become more flexible and progressive.

Probably the prime achievement of this program was to provide a channel to attract this new type of teacher. While the program could not claim full credit, since many interns said that they would have entered teaching anyway, it did provide an available, visible channel of entry for such persons. Moreover, the data in other chapters seem to indicate that, to the extent that there was a force for change within the program, the force often emanated from this idealistic, hypercritical group. Without their optimism, their impatient criticism, and their sustained pressure on team leaders, classroom teachers, and university faculty, it is doubtful that the program would have produced *any* momentum for change in some circumstances, or *as much* in others.

But conjecture begs the critical question: Will it be beneficial if these changes do produce the transformation predicted? I came away from my visits to schools—in city after city in several regions of the country, in rural and urban settings, serving black, Indian, and white children—convinced that most classrooms are the grim, joyless places described by Silberman (1970). The teachers' almost universal preoccupation with cognitive achievement, discipline, and regimen created a stifling and dogmatic environment that assaults human dignity. A depressing lack of enthusiasm for learning and the dismal disrespect that prevailed between teachers and students in the public schools was repeatedly impressed upon me. Too many schools were run on blind, deadly routines, girded by little more than a preoccupation with order. With few exceptions, monotonous regimen-

the county in which they currently teach and to have finished high school in that county (Coleman et al., 1966, Table 2.31.1, pp. 122, 125).

4. The percentage of teachers agreeing (57 percent) is lower than the 84 percent of the Coleman sample, which felt that neighborhood elementary schools should be maintained in spite of racial imbalance (Coleman, 1966, Table 2.35.1, p. 167).

5. Less than two thirds of the teachers trained in the United States actually enter teaching. Stone (1969) reported that an even lower portion—54 percent—of graduates of conventional programs in his sample were in education the year after graduation. Forty-nine percent of them were teaching. However, the fact that 85 percent of the graduates of 42 experimental programs in his study had entered education (78 percent of them teaching) suggests that the Teacher Corps does not necessarily exceed other experimental programs in this respect.

6. According to Coleman's (1966) study, 30 percent of all elementary teachers prefer teaching white students, although only 5 percent of teachers in predominantly black elementary schools prefer to teach white students (Table 2.35.1, p. 167).

7. While 58 percent of all classroom teachers in Coleman's sample preferred all-white or mostly white schools, 47.7 percent of the present sample preferred such schools. Since Coleman's sample, for these figures, consisted of teachers in their first three years, they were compared to the "new teachers"; this yielded a difference of 58 versus 38.7 percent.

Much of this difference can be accounted for by the differences in the type of schools in which the teachers taught, particularly among white teachers. Sixty-six percent of Coleman's sample consisted of white teachers teaching in all-white schools. By comparison, the present sample consisted of mostly nonwhite schools. By deleting from Coleman's sample this all-white bias, the percentages of new teachers from both samples preferring all-white or mostly white schools are 32 (Coleman) versus 38.7.

The deletion of white teachers teaching in all-white schools also shifts the percentage of white teachers who prefer white schools from 66 to 49 percent as compared to 47 percent of the white teachers in the present sample preferring such schools. Ten percent of the black teachers in this sample preferred all-white or mostly white schools, compared to 3.7 percent of the black teachers in Coleman's sample (Coleman Report, Errata Sheet, Table 4.10.3, p. 8).

8. While 54.7 percent of the teachers in this sample planned to continue teaching until retirement, only 39 percent of Coleman's sample planned to remain in teaching to this point (Coleman, Table 2.34.5, p. 153).

9. The 20 university faculty members in the sample who filled out this form are nearly twice as likely as the Teacher Corps program staff at the university to fall in the most rebellious category (30 versus 17 percent) and are much less likely to be classified as "submissive" on this form (5 versus 17 percent). This, together with the above pattern for team leaders, indicates that the selection process may extend into the Teacher Corps program staff in favor of more conservative members of colleges and schools.

10. In the case of the initiative-compliance index, a dummy variable was constructed from six unequal categories in the typology. The racial-integration and commitment-to-teaching measures are based on indices of three questions each, none of which have the degree of internal consistency characteristic of scales. Despite these

reservations, however, the correlation procedure provides a better indication of coherence among the variables, while violating fewer assumptions, than could be obtained by most other methods.

11. Individuals who did not answer at least six scales were omitted from this analysis. Potential and actual means were computed only for the scales that individuals actually answered.

12. Because this does not represent a random sample, the probability estimates presented in Table 3–5 should be viewed as approximations.

   The N listed in the tables represents the number of persons being rated, and the means are averages of all persons rating. Variance ratios were calculated on the amount of variation occurring among the composite scale scores for each site, not the variation occurring on the evaluations of those rated within each site.

13. The t tests, which are more appropriate than critical ratios for samples of this size, were not computed, but there is little reason to believe that conclusions would change.

14. A subsequent analysis, which included all ten programs, revealed significant inter-program differences in the way interns were evaluated by team leaders on all four scales and differences in the way they were evaluated by classroom teachers on two scales (respect for children and community relationships).

CHAPTER 4

Local Programs in Action: Strategies for Change

The Teacher Corps should not be judged on what it did to improve the education of the children of poverty—what can 1200 people do for 28 million in one year?—but on what it has taught about the problems of effecting change in the schools of poverty and in the teacher education establishment.

SHARPE, 1969, p. 207

The local programs took shape as they coped with local sources of resistance and other contingencies, such as the idiosyncratic goals imposed by local personnel, variations in the type and level of poverty from community to community, and variable skills and experiences of the people involved. Whereas the preceding chapter focused on the status identities of the people in the program, this chapter describes the context in which they found themselves. The reforms introduced by the program and the implicit strategies through which they were introduced will be discussed.

INTRODUCING PROGRAMS AT THE TOP

Usually, negotiations with the national office were handled by a few administrators of the participating universities and school systems; only coordinators and program directors were involved from the beginning. An average of only one out of three university faculty members reported having helped in preparing the proposal; fewer than one out of five school princi-

121

pals had been involved; and only 3 percent of the classroom teachers and none of the team leaders in the sample participated in writing their proposal. Moreover, only one fourth of the teachers and 40 percent of the faculty said that they had ever been in *meetings* devoted to explaining the Teacher Corps program; this ranged from 17 to 34 percent in different programs. However, the proportion of cooperating teachers working directly with interns who had been in such meetings was much higher—from 50 to 80 percent.

The 10 programs were scored on the basis of a combined index consisting of the proportion of teachers and principals who participated in the proposal-preparation stage. It was found that participation in the proposal did not increase the likelihood of change, as might be supposed. On the contrary, the participation of more teachers in the proposal resulted in fewer new techniques being introduced in the schools $(r = -.38)$, less cooperation between the college and schools $(r = -.36)$, and fewer community projects being undertaken $(r = -.59)$. On the other hand, the more the participation, the more teachers there were who reported that the program created problems for them $(r = .52)$. Apparently, participating in the initial decisions only illuminated the potential problems and provided persons who did not support the proposal's objectives with a better opportunity to co-opt it and to undermine it.

CHANGE BY ADDITION

When a new program was introduced into an ongoing system, it was placed in direct competition with that system. The time, energy, and funds devoted to the new program threatened to detract from the normal activities. If additional resources had been provided, it was tempting to convert the new program into supplemental forms of assistance. This was done in two ways: (1) by making alterations or minor, superficial adaptations to what already existed (Chin, 1963); or (2) by making *additions* to the existing systems without systematic integration of what was added. Both methods are substitutes for more fundamental changes. Although it is difficult to quantify the distinction between a minor, surface change and a more fundamental change, the distinction nevertheless helps to make sense out of data that often seem to point to opposite conclusions.

The interviews repeatedly indicated that the same need for money that presumably prompted universities and schools to seek outside funds also tempted them to use slack funds surreptitiously to underwrite the pressing costs of normal operation. Universities and schools could maximize their benefits if they received funds for new activities without having to give up any aspect of the existing program. It was in this sense that innovation could be viewed as a process of *adding to* the existing programs rather than a process of reallocating resources or revising priorities in order to accommodate the objectives of the Teacher Corps.

In the schools this often meant that cooperating teachers were not given the time or financial incentive to set up systematic training experiences for interns. In the universities it usually meant that changes were limited to more courses and more requirements within existing programs. Thus, the majority of all groups sampled agreed that the Teacher Corps was largely responsible for the addition of new college courses (at least three out of four, in most cases). Nearly all of these courses focused on the impoverished child. A majority of most groups (that is, faculty members, program directors and their staffs and coordinators, principals, teachers, interns, and team leaders) also reported that they had observed modifications in the existing college courses and increased attention to the impoverished. Moreover, in 7 of the 10 programs a near majority of teachers agreed that the Teacher Corps had been chiefly responsible for introducing new techniques into the schools. (In the other three programs, nearly one half of the teachers denied it.)

However, these changes did not seem to entail modifications in other parts of the program. Instead of a shift in priorities, the effect was to add work for the interns who, in nearly every program, not only completed the normal amount of course work for an M.A. (and often much more; 160 hours in some programs) but also worked on community projects without academic credit and served as regular staff members of schools in which they were assigned regular responsibilities.

Criticism of the University

The interns, expecting by the program's publicity that they would participate in an educational reform, became critical of the program upon learning of the modest alterations taking place. Indeed, they were more critical toward the university than toward any other phase of the program. Over half of them (53 percent) were dissatisfied with the choice of college courses and the availability of suitable field experiences; 17 percent were "very dissatisfied" with these aspects of the program.

COMPETENCE OF THE PROFESSORS. Interns not only regarded course work as far less relevant than their experiences in the schools but over half of both interns and team leaders expressed dissatisfaction with the competence of their supervisors, especially their supervisors' knowledge about teaching the disadvantaged. Professors were named as poor supervisors more frequently than any other group (mentioned by 30 percent of the interns). The majority of interns (57 percent) estimated that "almost none" of their professors were superior teachers; more than four out of five interns rated less than half of their teachers as superior. There was, however, some variation from program to program.[1] Furthermore, at least half of the interns in every program judged that the Teacher Corps faculty members were less academically qualified than the professors who taught them in their area of specialization as undergraduates; only 8 percent of them believe that the Teacher Corps faculty members were superior academically. Whereas more than half of them said that their undergraduate professors encouraged them to become actively involved in social issues and problems of American society, only one in five (but as high as one in three in some programs) said that most of their present faculty members encouraged active involvement.

One of the major problems was that the programs continued to focus on abstract knowledge without translating it into pedagogical skills that would be immediately useful to interns. The interns complained that most of their professors had no previous experience with the disadvantaged and were unfamiliar with disadvantaged schools; the interviews confirmed that few professors were visiting schools on a regular, systematic, sustained basis. In fact, the interns charged that neither the professors nor the team leaders were teaching or demonstrating practical, concrete techniques of teaching. Moreover, in no case did local school teachers have a real influence on the course work that interns were taking at the university. Interns also frequently complained that most of their professors ignored racial and other minority-group problems. To cite one example, where there was a serious language problem connected with the disadvantaged group, the university typically did not offer courses in the second language.

CURRICULUM. In light of the above assessments, insofar as the interns were concerned, university training was still too close to the existing standard training programs; it still turned out teachers who were ill-equipped to deal with the immediate problems and needs of the disadvantaged. Interns often referred to the courses as "glib." One intern, for example, in describing a course entitled, "The Sociology and Anthropology of Disadvantaged Children," claimed that the instructor required the students to clip articles from *Time* on ghetto problems for use in class reports. In a diary kept for this study another intern complained of a professor who "lectured" on the subject of creativity. The professor was reportedly on the verge of tears, saying that she wanted to be liked and respected by the interns but felt that she was not. The intern wrote: "We had heard everything that she talked about. These people come in and expect to tell us something that we have not heard before. It doesn't happen very often, really." Another wrote: "I had my test tonight. It was really easy. I have yet to stay awake in this course, but I know I got a B at least. Any knowledge came on my own. This guy has been teaching since 1929."

A former Teacher Corps director, Donald Sharpe (1969), reflecting on his experience with the program, said:

We learned that traditional courses of the college do not satisfy the needs of interns. We college people tried our best to provide the kinds of help they wanted and we could not do it. We do not know that much about teacher education. . . . We conclude that the Teacher Corps has demonstrated that educators can learn a lot about how to educate disadvantaged children and how to educate teachers if we recognize that we do not know very much to start with but are willing to learn. *The interns came asking for easy answers or bags of tricks. We did not have them. The team leaders do not have them.* We have all learned that they do not exist—but we are convinced that we may find some answers if we keep on searching together. [pp. 207, 208]

When respondents were asked to rank three activities in the Teacher Corps program that they would reduce, 42 percent of the interns, 33 percent of the teachers, and 44 percent of the university faculty mentioned first the university course work. The primary problem area mentioned (by one fourth of the interns and teachers) was the irrelevance of the college curriculum in the lives of the students in the program. Also, when asked what was least relevant about the program, three fourths of the interns specified course work; there was similar agreement among all groups queried. Only one in six respondents mentioned university course work as the most useful part of the program. Generally, it was the program directors (over 50 percent) and the university faculty members (40 percent) who had the high opinion of courses; they usually rated university-conducted preservice experiences as excellent (compared to only 15 percent of the interns and team leaders who were as favorable).

OTHER REASONS FOR DISSATISFACTION. Although university faculty members tended to be middle-class-oriented and traditional in their approach, there were other reasons why the interns rejected them so completely. In part, the interns' complaints simply reflected the fact that very little is known about how to teach the disadvantaged. In part, too, the complaints reflected this problem: even though interns were being instructed in behavioral, psychological, and social-science approaches to education, they themselves subscribed to an altruistic, ideological, and humanitarian frame of reference that was not entirely compatible with behaviorism. Many interns believed that cognitive skills were less important for teachers in low-income schools than were certain personal empathetic qualities such as the personal ability to understand and relate to children, a sincere desire to help children, respect for students, and love of children.

But something else seemed to be involved. Interns may have become more disillusioned with colleges than with schools precisely because they had expected more of their professors than of the schoolteachers. In interviews, some of the interns indicated they had assumed that the schools would be traditional, but they had hoped that professors at least would be progressive and flexible. Instead, nearly all interns (90 percent) and over half of the university faculty members said they had observed some faculty members who were unwilling to depart from traditional methods of teacher education; interns could not justify this rigidity to themselves. In most programs interns accused at least half of the faculty of being rigid and, in two programs, a majority of interns believed that nearly all of the faculty members were too traditional. The university faculty members generally believed that only a few of their colleagues were too traditional. Some of this tension probably was a by-product of the status insecurity characteristic of the less prestigious institutions—and of education faculty members in general who, in many universities, must contend with a relatively low professional status on the academic ladder.

Ironically, too, interns may have been more inclined to direct their criticisms toward the university because it was more tolerant of the criticism than were the public schools and because professors were more physically and socially remote, since interns spent so much of their time working in the schools and communities.

Finally, the interns' level of dissatisfaction was related to certain personal characteristics of the interns themselves. Dissatisfaction was especially acute in programs in which a high proportion of interns held degrees in the liberal arts and were from outside the region. Their satisfaction diminished with the quality of their own undergraduate college ($t = -.66$ controlling for quality of present college). Half of the interns who rated their undergraduate colleges among the top ones in the United States expressed low satisfaction and rated the present Teacher Corps institution at the bottom of the college hierarchy; 57 percent of this group said that the faculty had been wholly unsuccessful in challenging their intellect and creative capacities. Interns who rated their present Teacher Corps institutions higher were more favorable; 22 percent of this group expressed high satisfaction, and only one third felt that they were not being challenged. Nearly all the former group—92 percent—compared to 56 percent of the latter group, said that only a few of their professors were superior teachers.

There were also political differences that could account for some of the expressed dissatisfaction. Although 80 percent of the university faculty members (and 72 percent of the classroom teachers) considered themselves to be at least "fairly liberal," only from 10 to 12 percent of either group identified themselves as "very liberal" or "radical" (and these occurred primarily in two programs). By comparison, 38 percent of the interns considered themselves as "very liberal," and 17 percent considered themselves as "radical"; the combined proportions varied considerably among the different sites (from 3 to 40 percent). Of the interns who were classified as "highly liberal" (on the liberalism scale), only 10 percent were highly satisfied with the faculty of the university; by comparison, 40 percent of the "highly conservative" interns were satisfied. Thirty-six percent of the liberal interns expressed low satisfaction with the faculty, compared with 20 percent of the most conservative group.

Reactions

In view of their dissatisfaction with the university, interns often felt that it was up to them to bring the "nitty-gritty practical problems" into the more "idealistic" discussion groups in the university classrooms. Accordingly, they frequently confronted professors with their underlying assumptions. The vast majority of the interns in every program (an average of 80 percent for the sample as a whole) and most of the university faculty members (64 percent) believed that some professors had perceived the program as potentially disruptive because of the appearance and attitudes of some of the interns; two thirds of the interns themselves (but only one fourth of the faculty members) reported that they had actually attempted to disrupt classroom routines. Most of the interns (two thirds) believed that the university faculty members did not welcome disagreement; one third maintained that disagreement actually had been penalized. (In two programs the majority of interns believed that disagreement was penalized; in only one program did the majority believe that disagreement was accepted by the faculty.)

Faculty members reported that they often, indeed, had been shaken by interns' criticisms. Interviews indicated that the professors became defensive as often as they became introspective. Like their colleagues in the public schools, professors expressed considerable animosity toward many of the interns, complaining that they were "too radical," "too hippie" in appearance, tactless, and unduly critical and rude in the classroom. In every program there was a suspicion that many interns had merely drifted into the program, had entered it to avoid the draft or to obtain an advanced degree, and had no enduring commitment to teaching.[2] By stigmatizing interns as troublemakers, change-for-change-sake crusaders, cynical, naïve, or draft-dodgers, professors could deny the validity of the interns' criticisms.

Yet more than self-defensiveness was involved because the interns had touched off some issues about which professors were legitimately concerned. For one thing, professors had grounds to believe that interns had frequently used school classrooms to indoctrinate children with a closed-minded liberal ideology, which often was only remotely related to subject matter. Also, underlying the professors' specific criticisms was a sense that interns were, in principle, anti-intellectual and so profoundly naïve and superficial about social problems that their good intentions could actually hurt the persons they wanted to help. Characteristic of many contemporary, middle-class liberals, the interns were concerned about the immediate problems and were impatient toward knowledge that might be useful only in the long run. Even some of the professors who admired other nonconventional character- istics of interns frequently expressed the suspicion that all of the talk about the "irrelevance" of the curriculum was a rationalization for the interns' ultimate disregard for academic and scholarly standards and an excuse not to study the fundamental materials.

THE INTERNSHIP

As a means of bridging the gap between theory and practice, between uni- versity and school, interns worked in the school and the community. After the successful completion of preservice training, Teacher Corps members were employed by local schools and received salaries for their services during the school year. The in-service program included study toward certification and a college degree, service in low-income area schools, and community service to the low-income families and their children. University studies during this period were intended to be closely related to the interns' work and experiences in the schools. During in-service training an intern could progress from tutorial and small-group instruction to large-group instruction and then to team teaching. At the end of the second year, when he had exhibited sufficient competency, he could progress to solo classroom teach- ing. At no time was an intern supposed to replace or supplant the regular teacher (or to be used as a "substitute" teacher). A survey of first-cycle interns showed that, each week, the average Teacher Corps intern spent 25 hours working directly in the local school, 9 hours in university classes, 14 hours studying and preparing for school work, and 7 hours working in school-related community work.

In comparison to university work, there is reason to believe that interns were better prepared by their internship experiences, although there were many problems. Nine out of 10 persons believed that when interns completed the program they would be better prepared to teach in low-income schools than they would have been if they had enrolled in any other program. The primary advantages were considered to be the more direct experience with children in actual school settings and the opportunity to develop a better understanding of disadvantaged children and their community and home life. A few program directors also believed that the interns had developed a more genuine interest in teaching as a result of the experience. However, only 1 in 10 interns mentioned that they had learned to be more innovative.

Many teachers believed that interns' participation in the classrooms was by far the most effective part of the in-service program (mentioned by 38 percent). Various facets of community work (18 percent) and the tutoring of small groups (10 percent) were mentioned less frequently. Asked to rank the three most important activities that deserved an expanded role in the program, both teachers and interns most frequently wanted to increase the opportunity to conduct individual instruction (mentioned by 17 percent). The experienced teachers also stated that actual experience with disadvantaged schools (33 percent) and their own personal disadvantaged backgrounds (33 percent) had helped them most in preparation for teaching in low-income neighborhoods. Only 6 percent mentioned university training or a knowledge of teaching methods as useful preparations for their situations.

However, the internship was not without its problems. The "shortcoming" mentioned most frequently by interns was simply that they still did not spend *enough* time in the classroom. But teachers were more specific. They complained that interns still had not learned how to "maintain control" over their classes, and a few thought that interns were unrealistic about the changes that can be accomplished within a conventional school system. Interns seemed to enjoy most working with individual children, but they seemed less confident about, or appreciative of, teaching classes on a day-to-day basis. The experiences provided by the program tended to be limited and artificial. The small group sessions and tutorials provided interns with only limited responsibilities and an atypical view of teaching. Interns, working so closely with a few children, were spared the pressures of day-to-day teaching before a large group. They sometimes developed so much rapport and became so involved and possessive of "their" children that the regular teachers began to resent another person in the classroom; that person was a threat to the teachers' monopolistic hold over the children. At times interns were unwilling to obtain a broader range of experience if it meant switching classes and leaving "their" pupils. Also, the presence of both cooperating teachers and team leaders in the classroom, and the fact that the students had access to the professors represented an atypical teaching situation. The question is whether, after graduation, interns would be able to adjust to the self-contained, large and often unruly classrooms that are typical of disadvantaged schools.

INCORPORATING INNOVATION ROLES INTO TRAINING PROGRAMS

I mentioned previously that the prevailing model of socialization, which portrays the socialization agent as someone who molds the novice to fit the prevailing role conception, is no longer viable in complex and changing societies. Because the teaching profession is undergoing a marked transformation, professionals are being socialized for roles that do not yet exist and, therefore, the professionals are actually helping to develop the role itself (Gogswell, 1968). In this setting, socialization becomes a two-way process: interns may help to resocialize the agents and give new meanings to their roles. The Teacher Corps attempted to incorporate these facts into the program. Teams were defined as "change agents," and the internship was touted as an opportunity for interns to contribute to the improvement of education.[3]

Tension Between Teachers and Interns

Many of the problems within the program resulted from the innovative objectives that were tied to a training internship. As new teachers, interns were the least potent forces in the entire educational system. Although their temporary assignment and university connections may have given them some courage, their dual role posed challenging identification problems. Teachers generally viewed interns as additional manpower who were functioning in the conventional role of apprentice student-teachers and aides; the interns were assigned to the teachers' classrooms primarily to assist and to learn from the teachers—the master craftsmen. But the interns, influenced by the recruiting appeals and the program's public image, came to the program viewing themselves as agents of change, not as autonomous colleagues of regular classroom teachers, whose purpose was to experiment in the classroom and, generally, to act as catalytic change agents even though they did not receive special training for this role. Accordingly, the interns wanted more authority and more support for their ideas. One interviewer wrote of an intern in the South:

Several interns admitted coming south with a determination to change everything as fast as possible. All seemed to have tempered their ideals quite a bit with the realization that any change that will come along will come about so slowly that one has to be very cautious about what one does, because the end result might hurt the black community. . . . These interns said that they were told in class by their instructors that the black students and their teachers were very slow and backward, and that it was up to the Teacher Corps interns to go into the schools to teach the teachers how to teach.

This dual role created confusion over what interns were supposed to be doing. Between 5 and 20 percent of the teachers in different programs reported that the Teacher Corps had created problems for them. Sixty percent of the principals and from one fourth to one half of the interns and cooperating teachers in different programs reported disagreements, in most cases with team leaders, about the interns' role. These differences of opinion most frequently concerned the amount of time interns should spend in the schools, lesson plans, permissiveness in the classroom, supervision of interns, and teachers' resistance to interns' proposals.

It seems inherent in the very structure of internship programs that part of the interns' duties will be determined as much by the needs of the system as by the training objectives. A majority of interns reported having been asked to serve as substitute teachers, typically several times; one third of the interns in the first cycle also complained that they were being used as full-time teachers or substitutes (Cort, 1968). In some cases they were told by a principal to teach full time, but were told not to teach full time by the university program director. In one such case, the intern, feeling that the director did not give him sufficient support, resigned from the program to join the staff of the school. In this connection, Watson (1968) also concluded that the regular classroom teachers generally perceived the intern as an adjunct to local programs:

It has been shown that the activities assigned to interns may be reasonably described as helping or auxiliary activities designed to implement existing programs and assist regular teachers in the performance of their duties.

One of the interns in this study wrote:

One of the teams has been doing more substituting this year than the rest of us. Last night I found out that one of the members has been informed she must substitute on a daily basis. Her principal told her and that's that. Isn't that sweet? Her team leader won't stick up for her because she is such a wishy-washy bowl of jelly who is only concerned with pleasing the hierarchy.

Other problems mentioned by some teachers and principals concerned the already noted tendency of Corpsmen to "overidentify" with their students, sometimes supporting the students against the regular teacher. Some teachers seemed to resent the freedom of interns to move about the school because they were not as tied to a particular classroom or schedule as were the teachers. Still others, who perhaps had to struggle for a college degree, resented the fact that interns were being paid to go to college. In one program, teachers were so resentful of the time available to interns to attend university classes that they managed to get equal time off for their own "professional preparation" while the interns manned their classes. Indeed, in some programs, teachers had become so dependent on interns in the classrooms that they tended to resent the time the interns spent on tutorials and community work.

One of the major differences between teachers and interns was that interns tended to encourage more student participation and to conduct more "permissive" and noisy classrooms than did regular teachers. Interns ranked the objective of experimentation in classroom activities higher than the objective of maintaining orderly classes, whereas teachers placed priority on order in the classroom. Interns encouraged group activities, sociodrama, unmonitored hallways, optional class attendance, or simply "helping children to pursue their own objectives."[4] Their teaching style is reflected in the comments of interns. One wrote:

Language arts was hyper today. The kids would not settle down, so I told them anyone not finished with their work would remain after school—they finished. I have been doing dictation on Negro history, and some students decided they were not going to write it—they wrote it after school. When you set definite boundaries, the children limit themselves to activities within that range. No confrontations, even.

Another intern wrote:

We started on biographies today in language arts. I brought in copies of biographies of James Brown for the kids to get the feel of it. They are writing them later in the week. . . . the children were interviewing each other for their biographies. The noise level in the room hit an all-time high, but in all honesty, I must say they were working. All finished their assignments. We had two shifts, so that those who were interviewing the first half could be interviewed in the second. Oh brother, it was loud, but productive. For students not occupied during both sessions, we had an overhead projector and they made silhouettes. It was a good day, but loud.

In schools with high faculty and student turnover rates, and in which assault, rape, extortion, and drugs were prevalent problems, teachers simply regarded interns' permissiveness as naïve and self-destructive. The teachers wanted practical assistance, not change agents.

Remote colleges were not in a position to support interns when confronted with these role conflicts. Although a majority of interns (57 percent) felt that reasonable disagreement was tolerated within the Teacher Corps program, they also reported that they were thrown on their own meager resources with very little positive support. Between 10 and 50 percent of the interns in different programs reported that innovation was discouraged; one in four reported that he had personally encountered resistance to an attempted innovation. Only one in four interns felt that he could count on the Teacher Corps administration to back him if he were to get in trouble in the course of a worthwhile activity. Their isolation was even more pronounced because they were not yet well integrated into either a professional society or a career ladder.

Reactions of Interns

Interns' responses to the program varied. Two extremes of response are discussed below.

RADICALIZATION. As one response to their role conflict, some interns became radicalized; they gave up entirely working within the system and were now looking for more radical means to achieve change. A few others organized and, in some programs, formed student unions. At one point the interns became so dissatisfied with their condition that something had to be done by the national office. Interns were invited to form a National Intern Advisory Council. Predictably, the need for a parallel Directors' Council was expressed at a conference a year later. The Intern Council was authorized to make recommendations for changes in program guidelines. A long list of their requests included: authority to play a major role in the recruitment and selection of team leaders, interns, and cooperating teachers; authority to initiate community projects; access to all financial reports, budgets, and statements of program condition; participation in drafting new proposals; and more relevant curriculums focused on the specific groups served. The interns' black caucus expressed concern about the apparent inability of the Teacher Corps to recruit black Corpsmen, the absence of a reasonable number of black directors and supervisors in the national office, and the small number of black institutions participating in the program.

In response to these demands the director of the Teacher Corps indicated that guidelines were being changed to require that interns be included on panels to select interns and team leaders but that selection of cooperating teachers be left up to those who write the proposal. The guidelines also would require that budgets be made available to all members of the program, including interns, and that interns participate in the drafting of new proposals and amendments. Interns from previous cycles were also appointed to five-man teams to evaluate proposals for the fourth cycle. But even with these concessions, the interns continued to protest that they had been shunned and relegated to a minor role in some of the national conferences. Having prepared a list of proposals to improve the program, interns complained that no one had listened.

WITHDRAWAL AND ASSIMILATION. At the other extreme, some interns withdrew, having lost complete interest in teaching. They had decided pragmatically to "serve out their time" with little commitment to their actual duties. Finally, still others became fully integrated into the system. The patterns in these responses are analyzed more fully in Chapter 5.

Perhaps adaptation and full assimilation were the typical responses. Indeed, aside from their "hippie" clothes, long hair, and reputations, most interns (with a few major exceptions) were not being particularly "troublesome" but were concentrating their efforts on safe experiments within the classroom. A situation that could frequently be observed was reflected by an intern who wrote:

Today was a slow day . . . I've just moved into a new classroom situation, and as yet, I only teach a reading group. The group consists of the slowest readers in this top second grade, which means that they are not too far below grade level. I work with them for 45 minutes or an hour a day, but that is not enough to keep me busy. The rest of the morning I observe and help students with their homework. I need to teach more. I've got to get more involved in this new classroom, for the inactivity is driving me crazy. I only taught my reading group for about 50 minutes.

After complaining to his cooperating teacher, he was permitted to teach three classes instead of one. Another intern wrote:

I'll study whenever I'm not teaching. . . . today was rather uneventful. My social studies class gave their reports, and the class got "squirmy." They are getting tired of the format, I think. The reports have gone fairly well, but the students could have done a better job. In this same room the people are writing poems for the contest at school. I started to read them and they are really good. . . . I decided to give my language arts class the opportunity to write for the contest. . . .

Not much going on today. It was kind of quiet. My social studies class was kind of noisy. I started to arrange them in a circle, instead of rows for social studies and they all kind of went for it. But today I wondered if the period of adjustment would last for the rest of the year. They weren't that bad. I expect more out of that group. . . .

Social studies today was a breeze. Because of the nature of today's work, I had the students remain in their own seats in rows. It was so quiet, and they were so busy. One would be very tempted to go back to that method. I can see why teachers get so attached to it. Alas, however, I will return to the circle Monday to give the kids a chance to make that a workable situation. Such tenacity.

By the middle of the second year, as they assumed more responsibility over the classrooms, some interns closely identified with the problems of teachers. One intern, who had been asked to remain in the system the following year, sided with teachers and administrators in a controversy that had been started by a small group of parents about the right of teachers to paddle children. According to some sources, by the time the Teacher Corps graduates took full-time positions, they had recovered from the "reality shock" and had learned to live with, if not fully accept, the red tape, time pressures, problems of disciplining, and the curriculum plans from which they had been sheltered under the rather artificial conditions of the internship.[5]

THE USE OF LINKAGE ROLES

If an innovation is to be successfully institutionalized, roles must be established with fixed responsibility for overseeing its implementation. Without such roles the new program has no protection against the existing system. Accordingly, each local Teacher Corps program was required to establish several new roles that together provided for an intricate system of linking the different institutions and groups involved.

Each program was administered by a director, usually from the university staff. The director was assisted by a parallel program coordinator located in each cooperating school system. These two persons acted as points of liaison for the principal, teachers, professors, and interns and supervised the activities of interns while at school. Team leaders were teachers released from full-time duties in the local school system, with authorization to serve on the instructional staff of the university program during the preservice period. Universities were encouraged to design special seminars or course work for them.

The Team Leader's Role

The role of the team leader can be described as a combination of master teacher, supervisor, counselor, methods instructor, intervener with local administration, and guide to the community. The leaders were expected to play the dual role of educational innovator and diplomat, capable of smoothing over friction between interns and classroom teachers. In most cases this was the only way a team leader could establish the legitimacy of his position, and consequently the role assumed precedence. One interviewer wrote:

> Mrs. ———— maintains constant contact with her interns as well as their cooperating teachers. She mediates between them (interns) and the cooperating (often not so) teachers, using her friendliness, insider-status, and implicit authority to smooth the way for the interns. This task is made easier by virtue of the fact that she asks very little of the classroom teachers—they need not abdicate any of their classroom sovereignty.

Generally, team leaders seemed to be functioning primarily in an administrative capacity, assigning interns to cooperating teachers and performing other logistical and control functions. Conversely, they did not seem to be fulfilling the roles of model teacher or educational innovator. They seldom gave demonstration lessons, for example. The interns' esteem for the team leader depended on the team leader's ability to protect them, to cut red tape, and to support what they wanted to do, which in turn depended on the team leader's authority and influence within the school system itself. All team leaders seemed to define their role operationally as administrators of intern activities within the school, with varying degrees of emphasis on supervision and teacher training. Being recognized as master teachers did not appear to be necessary for either the establishment or the maintenance of team leaders' authority, since they could rely on other bases. Also, the team leaders' position seemed to be in no way affected by their role in community projects, since their position was anchored entirely within the school. Because a team leader could firmly entrench his position strictly within the school itself, he had everything to lose and very little to gain by venturing into community activities.

THE QUESTION OF CO-OPTATION. Generally, two types of teachers seemed to become team leaders: (1) teachers who were using their position as a stepping-stone into administration; and (2) teachers whose principals wished to move them out of the classroom or out of their school, in some cases because of their creativity and, in others, because of their lack of it.

In most cases team leaders were selected partly as a reward for good teaching and hard work in the local system and for their loyalty to the local administration.

Interns, teachers, and principals all believed that team leaders were selected primarily for their years of teaching experience, although they also believed that some consideration was given to excellence in teaching, special experience with the disadvantaged, and an M.A. degree. One third of the interns also felt that factors such as acceptability to the community power structure, reward for loyalty to the local school system, or personal favoritism had entered into the decision.

Watson (1968) concluded that school principals had used the team leaders to co-opt the program. Some evidence supports this interpretation. In some cases team leaders were simply working for the same school in another capacity, and usually there was little contact between the team leaders and the university faculty. Team leaders themselves were often explicit about the fact that they did not work for the university but for the school; they maintained that they were primarily concerned about finding activities that would help the school and were not simply "using the school" for university purposes. Several team leaders stressed that the school was neither a clinic nor the intern's personal province. Accordingly, team leaders were often accused by interns of being overly conservative and anxious to please the schools.

On the other hand, more than co-optation was involved. It is misleading to view team leaders solely as the handmaidens of the school principals. As insiders they also provided a form of leverage and a sense of legitimacy to the otherwise marginal team. Their presence on teams helped to offset the suspicion teachers felt toward the interns, who were looked upon as aliens. Not only did team leaders lend a dimension of balance within the team but, in their marginal roles, they were in a position to mediate the conflicts that arose between interns and the other teachers. Although they often tried to "tone down" interns' proposals, they also acted on behalf of the interns and provided the essential legitimacy and assistance without which the proposals would not have had a chance.

THE INTERMEDIARIES. Together with the program director and coordinator, as well as the interns themselves, team leaders occupied important "boundary" positions. It was their job to establish the linkages among the various components of this system. They articulated demands, coordinated schedules, and adjusted their own organizations to outside constraints and contingencies not directly under the principal's control. In marginal positions, subjected to the pressures and expectations of outside groups, they were the intermediaries who worked out the necessary compromises. This kind of status gave them some independence from the administration.

The importance of the team leader as a link in the system is reflected by the fact that over half of the interns said they had daily contact with the team leader; 71 percent rated their communication effective. By comparison, only one in five interns had daily contact with the principal, and one in three reported that such contacts with principals, program directors, or university officials were effective.

As mentioned in the previous chapter, team leaders ranked between teachers and interns on many of the attitude scales used in this study: submissiveness, loyalty to the administration, endorsement of rules and procedures, preferences for predominantly white schools, racial tolerance, and commitment to teaching in inner-city schools (see Hanson, 1962). The fact that they were personally and officially marginal subjected them to criticism from both sides but facilitated their mediating role.

The team leader, however, was only one of a series of intermediaries in the chain of persons whose cooperation was necessary. It is in the nature of a linkage system that differences between the extremes tend to be progressively graduated through intermediaries. Through a series of bargains made at each successive stage, intermediaries articulate and compromise the differences. The persons in any particular role tend to hold attitudes that fall "between" the immediately adjacent roles on which they are most dependent. For example, where extreme differences existed between the university faculty and the classroom teachers regarding whether interns ought to engage in community-action programs, the opinions of the program director, coordinators, and team leaders all shaded between these extremes and more moderate beliefs. A series of indirect linkages of this kind can moderate conflicts that would be severe if persons in the extreme positions had to associate directly with one another.

COMPETENCE OF TEAM LEADERS. Several interviewers concluded that at least a few team leaders apparently were not well prepared for their jobs. In a few cases these leaders had no prior experience in a disadvantaged school and, occasionally, in one or two programs, interns felt that their leaders had outmoded beliefs about black people. But probably as many cases could be cited of exceptionally competent team leaders. Generally, team leaders seemed to be highly motivated to make the Teacher Corps succeed.

Team leaders were more experienced than typical teachers. Eighty-three percent of them had taught at least 10 years, compared to 33 percent of the other teachers in the study. Only 12 percent of the interns were very dissatisfied with their team leaders; only 4 percent rate them as less capable than other teachers, while 45 percent rated them superior in effectiveness with low-income children. This opinion was confirmed by the classroom teachers, who rated the team leaders as superior teachers (varying from 27 to 61 percent in different programs).

Interns were generally positive about their team leaders in other ways as well, though not always enthusiastic. Over half of them indicated that their team leaders always went out of their way to help them, and the bulk (62 to 73 percent) said their team leaders had sound ideas about curriculum materials suitable for children in poverty schools, understood the personal problems of such children, and were excellent educational leaders with sincere interest in the interns' professional development. A smaller proportion, though still a majority or near majority, also said their team leader understood sources of the important problems they will face as teachers in low-income areas, that he was one of the most competent educators in the system, and that he demonstrated innovative approaches to teaching low-income children.

On the negative side, between one fifth and one third of the interns expressed unfavorable evaluations on each of the above dimensions. (In the study of the first cycle, 30 percent of the interns complained of inadequate assistance from their team leaders and 60 percent said that team leaders had not satisfactorily met their role specifications.) "They need to select better team leaders" was the most frequently suggested change in the team approach mentioned by interns. Over one half of the team leaders had no previous supervisory experience prior to joining the Teacher Corps, and they felt they were handicapped in their knowledge of the appropriate techniques for teaching the disadvantaged. Moreover, it is significant that nearly 50 percent of the interns disagreed and only 10 percent agreed with the statement that interns learn much about teaching from their associations with the team leader.

In short, team leaders were generally regarded by interns as helpful, interested, and competent, with sound ideas about an appropriate curriculum for poverty children, but interns did not report that they actually had learned about teaching from team leaders.

Sources of Tension in the Team Leader's Role

The team leader's authority and the respect accorded him by the interns were sources of threat to other teachers. Consequently, some teachers stressed that team leaders should be selected from inside the system (19 percent), while others (11 percent) wanted the authority of the team leader more clearly defined.

There was also some tension between team leaders and university professors, although it was minimized by the fact that they seldom saw one another. Since team leaders were closely identified with the school administration and were responsible for supervising interns, they had a controlling position, which professors did not have. University faculty members had to depend on team leaders to provide students with the time and opportunity to carry out course assignments. Since they had little control, professors did not tend to give assignments that would require coordination of this type.

The primary friction, however, came with the interns. The two groups were highly critical of one another. Thus when asked to suggest changes in procedures, the most frequent response for team leaders (31 percent) was the need to select better interns; 42 percent rated the practices used to recruit interns as unsatisfactory.

One source of problems arose from status and value differences. In many programs a majority of interns had been recruited from liberal arts programs, often from superior universities outside the region, whereas team leaders were more likely to have attended lower quality colleges and departments of education. They were usually recruited from within the system. Interns came from significantly higher quality universities than teachers in 9 of the 10 programs ($\overline{X} = 31.5$ vs. 25.0); the mean college quality scores for interns ranged from 5 to 8 points above the median college in all programs, whereas teachers' scores were below the median in five of the programs and above the median in only three of them. These differences also reflect a fundamental difference in social-class life styles of the interns and the teachers.

A second problem was that a disproportionately high number of males (over 60 percent in this sample) were assigned to female team leaders in elementary and junior high schools. This sometimes led to inconsistencies in the statuses of the teams. The authority problems were further aggravated by age differences. One half of the interns were between 21 and 35 years of age, whereas nearly one half of the team leaders were over 40.

Third, until recently there was an unbalanced racial composition in the Teacher Corps teams: 43 percent of the first-cycle team leaders were nonwhite as compared to only 23 percent of the interns. In the present sample, over half of the team leaders were black, while three fourths of the interns were white. In 5 of the 10 programs the majority of the team leaders were nonwhite, while the majority of interns were white. The ratio of nonwhite team leaders to nonwhite interns was as high as 5 to 1 in some programs. Race sometimes contributed to special anxieties, especially for older black teachers in some Southern communities. These teachers were threatened by the interns' idealism and enthusiasm for working in lower-class areas and were fearful that the better educated white liberals would take over their jobs at the end of the program. This fear was heightened by the failure of many administrators to explain the program before the interns were assigned. Many of the black teachers, who graduated from Southern segregated black colleges and were happy to have reached a middle-class position, did not appear to be relating to their pupils and to the younger white interns. Furthermore, some *white* teachers in the South also resented the fact that white interns were being assigned as subordinates to black teachers, who were getting extra assistance that was not available to white teachers.

Fourth, interns and team leaders frequently had gained different types of experiences before entering the program. Nine tenths of the first-cycle team leaders studied by Cort (1968) had worked with disadvantaged children before joining, and two thirds of them had lived in a disadvantaged area. By comparison, one half of the interns had never worked with disadvantaged children or adults before joining the program, and nearly two thirds had never lived in a disadvantaged neighborhood. Consequently, many team leaders tended to consider interns as being naïve, immature, and unrealistic. Although guidelines stipulated that Corpsmen should live in the school community during their internship, only one out of five during the first cycle said that their program either encouraged or required them to do so. In some communities, interns expressed fear of living in the community because of high crime rates in the area. In the present sample, only one third of the interns and team leaders were living in impoverished neighborhoods, but the percentage varied from 75 in one program to 0 in another.

Finally, tension arose because teams were formed early in the program, occasionally without regard to "personality" differences. But, more important, this tension arose before interns had an opportunity to experience the problems that might make them more cognizant of the need for assistance from a team leader. Team leaders found that interns did not readily take advice until they had encountered such problems. Teams found themselves in an awkward position: although they had been established, they were searching for a meaningful task. Usually, there were no formal provisions for changing the composition of the teams without creating ill feelings.

THE TEAM APPROACH

The key training unit of the Teacher Corps was the team, composed of from five to eight inexperienced teacher-interns led by a veteran teacher working in the school system. The majority of those interviewed at each program responded favorably when asked how effective the team approach was; only 8 percent were not positive. Fifty-one percent considered it to be very effective, the proportion ranging from 33 to 62 percent in the different programs. Only 8 percent of the interns and 4 percent of the team leaders recommended that the Teacher Corps should discontinue the use of the team approach, although between one quarter and one half of each group was not sure what to recommend.

Advantages

Some of the advantages of team training most frequently mentioned were: the combination of ideas, talents, techniques, and methods that the team provided (53 percent); increased teacher effectiveness (42 percent); more individual instruction for the child and more teacher-pupil contact; and reduction in teaching loads afforded by additional personnel in the classroom.

Problems

A majority at each program, however, also recognized some disadvantages in the team approach. Two thirds of those interviewed complained about: a tendency for too many approaches to be used, thus confusing the child; the creation of scheduling problems and unequal work loads; and an undue amount of responsibility for some of the less competent members assigned to the team. Those who expressed the latter complaint seemed to be implying that one of the latent functions of the self-contained classroom has been to insulate some bad teachers from most children.

When asked to rank the changes needed in their respective programs, interns stressed that more attention should be given to defining the functions of the team more clearly (the modal response, 23 percent). Other interns placed primary stress on more careful screening of team members for compatibility (14 percent) and selecting better interns (14 percent). In practice, "teaching teams" were seldom observed to actually function as viable social units in the classroom. They were, at best, administrative groups that handled scheduling and planning. One intern wrote:

We had a small team meeting with Mrs. ——— today, since two of our interns were absent. She made a couple of announcements, asked if there were any problems, and it was over. She took over for our team leader who left and does not have that much to do because your last couple of months you can handle a lot yourself.

The interns' team training experience, then, amounted to tutoring individual children in isolation, outside of classrooms, and some group tutoring within classrooms in the presence of one cooperating teacher. There was an occasional responsibility for teaching a full class in specific units of a given subject, usually with a teacher present at the back of the room. This is more accurately characterized as "turn teaching" instead of team teaching; that is, there is one teacher and one intern to each classroom, and each takes his turn teaching.

In view of the administrative focus of the teams, interns seldom shared teaching experiences with one another during formal meetings. They were also isolated from other students in the college of education (only 8 percent of the interns in the sample reported daily communication with other students outside the Teacher Corps program) and from more experienced cycles of interns in the same program. Some interns voiced the suspicion that the program staff was purposely keeping them separated.

Difficulty in scheduling meeting times was only one of several barriers to closer team work. The most fundamental problem stemmed from the practice, specified by the national program's design, of assigning interns to work individually with cooperating teachers in self-contained classrooms. In effect this policy transferred responsibility from the team leader to several teachers working independently. The team leader's authority was thus undermined, and control was diffused among many teachers who were marginal to the program. This had serious consequences because the teachers' interest was in the individual assistance that interns could provide, and they resented the disruption involved when interns tried to experiment, were rotated among classrooms, or were assigned to functions beyond the teachers' control.

The fact that team leaders were rated as being more competent than their colleagues is not particularly relevant because the actual teaching models were being provided by cooperating teachers. Whereas only 10 percent of the interns strongly agreed that they had learned much about teaching from their team leaders, twice as many (22 percent) strongly agreed that they learned much about teaching from their cooperating classroom teachers (a range of 0 to 36 percent at different sites).

In an effort to correct some of these problems, the 1970 Teacher Corps guidelines specified that team leaders, and not cooperating teachers, were responsible for the guidance of interns. A supplementary statement also encouraged districts to shift team leaders' responsibilities from supervision to those of a master teacher. But without necessary changes in the program structure, it was almost impossible to implement these revisions.

Potentials

Despite these problems, two illustrative situations were identified in which teams did function effectively as such. In one case a team was given complete responsibility for implementing a packaged science program at a school, with the team leader as the teacher in charge. Since this class was not already under the preserve of another teacher, the team could function outside the confines of the typical self-contained classroom. The interns developed a sense of purpose and devotion to their work that was seldom observed elsewhere. They willingly looked to the team leader for guidance because they had a wide latitude of responsibilities and had come to recognize the problems for which they would welcome assistance.

In the second case a team worked together on a community project setting up an after-school tutoring center in cooperation with parents and older children who acted as teachers. Because community work of this kind was not constrained by teacher monopolies and daily time schedules that afflicted classroom activities, the project offered a unique opportunity for interns to experiment. They were excited about the *idea* of the project and, together with the team leaders, spent many hours organizing the venture and discussing its outcomes. But precisely because these activities were not yet institutionalized as part of the daily schedule, the interns complained that they had too little time to maintain the center. They felt squeezed by pressures to complete other work. In most other cases, therefore, community projects were usually left to the discretion of individual interns.

COMMUNITY FIELD WORK

The conditions of the internship required each intern to engage in some form of involvement in the local community. Individuals or teams developed activities suited to their own interests and talents, which promised to make the Corpsmen more responsive to the expressed needs of the indigent community. In concept this was one of the most innovative aspects of the entire program: by making the community a legitimate concern, the teacher's role was extended beyond the limits of the classroom.

But in practice it was one of the most varied, difficult, and controversial phases. The university was given primary responsibility for this part of the program, with the understanding that the school would provide necessary time (10 to 12 hours per week) and would be kept fully informed of all community action. The national office identified two objectives of this phase: (1) to provide the intern with thorough knowledge of the particular community from which the children come, and (2) to "reach out to the child and his parents to help stimulate motivation for learning, and to convince parents that the teachers and school can help." But the underlying objectives were to bring about constructive change in the relationship between school and community and to broaden the teacher's role.

Types of Activity

Exemplary community activities, cited by the national office, included: interns living in the community, home visits, projects requiring parent involvement, work in community health programs, cross-age student tutoring (where younger pupils are instructed by older ones), recreation programs, revitalization of local PTA's, and parent or community education classes in child development. Activities that merely involved "observation" were not encouraged, nor was the practice of assigning interns as additional manpower for ongoing community programs. The latter practice presumably prevented the intern from "developing the natural relationship that should exist between teachers and community," especially when the work of these groups was unrelated to education.

Guidelines issued by the national office identified four levels of involvement. At the highest level the objective was the complete involvement of the community in the design, implementation, and supervision of programs that met its educational needs. Corps members were to assist the community in defining its educational needs and were to serve as "catalysts" for new activities, but in a supporting role rather than in a leadership role. For instance, Corps members encouraged adult members of the community to implement and supervise cross-age tutorial programs with the assistance of the school. At the other extreme, in the substandard program, Corps members did not meet with parents or work with members of the community served by the school, and home visits were infrequent, although interns might tutor an after-school study hall. At intermediate levels, interns might have been involved individually in the community (for example, assigned to work in several agencies or to survey existing community services) or, preferably, might have worked individually or in team projects with community members in developing new programs, in meeting with or organizing parent groups, or in assuming leadership in developing structures for parent involvement.

The community activities most frequently described in interviews were adaptations of the traditional after-school, extracurricular activities with the children, such as arts and crafts, clubs, and sports. These activities seldom involved direct contact with adults in the community, with the notable exception of home visits, which frequently were mentioned. Less frequently mentioned were: participating in community organizations (such as churches, the YWCA, and community-action agencies), tutoring outside of school settings, and establishing parent self-help projects (such as leadership training, crafts, and adult-education classes). Occasionally there were community surveys and field trips involving parents and children; in a few instances, interns participated in voter-registration drives or were active in model-cities programs.

Evaluations

Forty-three percent of the first-cycle interns (and 33 percent of the team leaders) believed, without qualification, that the Teacher Corps should attempt to make changes in the area of school-community relations (Cort, 1968); yet, one third of the interns (and over half of the team leaders) said that they had made no attempt, or only a few attempts, to extend these activities. Similarly, although 30 percent of the faculty and program directors in the present study and over 25 percent of the interns rated community activity as excellent, only 13 percent of the teachers and 15 percent of the team leaders were so positive. Over one fourth of the interns rated community activity as unsatisfactory or nonexistent, and they uniformly regarded it as less valuable than classroom teaching experience.

The majority of all persons interviewed believed that it is important for interns to become involved in some type of community activity as a part of their training (81 percent); 41 percent believed it very important. Yet, 22 percent of the teachers indicated they were opposed to community work, and between one fourth and one third of the classroom teachers wanted to see it reduced; in one program nearly every teacher wanted it reduced. Over one half of the total sample, including one fourth of the interns and one third of the team leaders and university faculty, said that if any phase had to be reduced, it should be the community projects. Over one fourth of the total sample (including interns) would reduce home visits as well.

When asked what changes should be made in this community aspect of the program, the first choices of all groups were "better planning be-

tween the university and local school system," "better definition of how
the community activity relates to teaching," and "more contact with
parents."[6] Interns and team leaders also sometimes mentioned the need
for better liaison with existing community programs. Only 15 percent of
the interns wanted more innovation in community programs and, interest-
ingly, the same proportion wanted to make the community phase optional.

Problems

The disparity between the promise that many people saw in this phase of
the program and the low priority they actually gave it can be explained by
several problems that plagued efforts to implement community activities.
Typically, too little time had been allotted for it. Interns had to spend
a certain amount of time at the school and also had to complete university course work. Because community work was less well incorporated
into the daily routine, it tended to be the first activity slighted. Although
there was a great deal of potential for innovation outside the classroom
because of fewer institutional constraints, the very absence of institutionalization made community work most subject to neglect in the face of
more persistent pressures. (As a partial stopgap, the 1969 guidelines issued
by the national office specifically required universities to give credit for
courses or practicums in community activity and required interns to live
in the community in most instances.)

Since teachers felt that the interns' time would be better spent on
learning teaching methods and how to handle discipline problems, the
teachers would have preferred that the interns prepare for their classroom
activities. The time interns spent in the community reduced their value
as assistants to the teachers. Also, in rural and mountain areas, sheer
commuting time was an obstacle. Similarly, in some of the larger cities
the problem was heightened by the fact that married interns and team
leaders often lived in different parts of the city and preferred to spend
evenings at home. One program director expressed the fear that in requiring the prospective teacher to engage in community work, teachers were
being discriminated against. He recalled the time when teachers were
required to teach Sunday school as a condition of employment.

In light of these time constraints, individuals tended to work in isolation on their community projects; one team leader even felt that she
needed to establish her own community project, separate from the interns.
These individual projects had widely varying value, although many program directors believed that they had a cumulative effect.

Another set of problems arose over disagreement about the propriety of different types of community activity. There were two overlapping issues: (1) How much encouragement should be given to "social action" as opposed to "social service"? (2) How much should communitywide activities be encouraged as compared to activities directly related to classroom teaching? Social action was exemplified by participation in voter registration and open housing drives, whereas communitywide service included work with community recreation departments, adoption agencies, or helping to organize a consumers' buying cooperative. On the other hand, tutoring, supervising children's recreation, conducting community surveys, or visiting with parents at the school or in the parents' home were more directly related to the school's immediate needs.

Teachers almost universally viewed community activity exclusively as a means to better acquaint the interns with the problems of the individual children in their particular classroom. Interns, however, often had a broader conception of their own role. More frequently than either teachers or principals, interns believed they should become involved in projects to remedy housing conditions [69 (interns) versus 50 (teachers) versus 40 percent for principals], in voter registration drives and sensitive legal civil rights activities (69 versus 47 versus 40 percent), and in campaigning for political candidates (52 versus 33 versus 27 percent). Program directors were almost in agreement with classroom teachers on these issues; but other university faculty members were even more liberal than the interns. Approximately three fourths of these faculty members endorsed the first and second actions, and over one half endorsed the right of interns to campaign for politicians.

As the sphere of authority claimed by the Teacher Corps became wider, the Corps was more likely to encounter opposition from vested interests. Accordingly, interns were severely criticized when they became involved in civil rights and similar sensitive areas. The federal guidelines simply stated: "Members of Teacher Corps are no more restricted in their political activities than are regular teachers in their school district. However, those Corps members who engage in political activities—local or otherwise—must do so as individuals rather than as groups representing the Teacher Corps. Other Corps members may not share their views." Some programs found it necessary to play down the community component altogether. Others established rules against certain types of activities. One interviewer, after visiting a Southern program, commented:

Some of the white interns here are trying desperately to get to know and to understand and help the people in the black community. But apparently persons in power positions, both inside and outside the Teacher Corps program here, are doing all they can to stop the interns from having any meaningful contact with the black community.

Still other programs apparently hoped to satisfy Washington guidelines by requiring interns to make nominal visits to local agencies. In other cases, projects seemed to be designed as public relations showpieces instead of programs that would directly benefit the children.

Because of its susceptibility to politicalization, this phase of the program tended to be treated perfunctorily, and only because the national office insisted on it. In general, no group in any program was strongly committed to community activity, with the exception of a few universities that offered courses requiring community involvement. A group that reviewed proposals for fourth-cycle programs wrote to the national Teacher Corps office in January 1969:

We are very concerned about this question of genuine commitment, after reviewing the fourth cycle proposals. We felt that most of the proposals *failed* to show any serious understanding of the significance and value of community involvement for either the intern, or for the institutions and program itself. Repeatedly there were contradictions between what the concept paper said the local program applicant anticipated doing—usually "bridging the gap," etc. —and the rest of the proposal, where, as it was set out, the program just could not possibly accomplish its stated objectives. Too often, proposals didn't even go through the *motions*. That this tendency was observable in so many continuing programs concerned us *even more*, as to the value and significance that *Teacher Corps/Washington* places in community involvement.

A third type of problem arose because, in most instances, there was no way of following through to guarantee the continuity of a project, once it was established. Corps members had to look to parents (who were only marginally involved) to maintain the projects, or to busy teachers who resented having other duties imposed on them by interns. They could not depend on subsequent cycles of interns to follow through, because each cycle preferred to design its own projects.

Finally, community activities suffered from poor coordination among schools, universities, and community representatives. Since faculty members had very little knowledge of, or control over, interns' off-campus experiences, these experiences seldom were systematically used to amplify university course work. Some professors suspected that interns were not well prepared for community work or were not supervised sufficiently to benefit from the work. Many interns felt that the university faculty members were not sufficiently interested or qualified to provide them with the kind of preparation and supervision that they needed.

Partly in recognition of these problems, university instruction on school sites and the use of schoolteachers as adjunct professors in university instruction were incorporated into later guidelines. By 1970, universities and districts were given joint responsibility for the community phase, and a staff person primarily responsible for this phase of the program was required. In addition, a committee that evaluated the community phase of a recent group of proposals from universities recommended that an advisory group of community representatives (that is, both parents and agency-organizations serving the area) should be involved in the Teacher Corps program from the inception of the planning stage.

The Rural South

The problems surrounding the community phase assumed different proportions in the rural Southern regions. The differences reflected partly the fact that the community component evolved from a Northern urban-ghetto model, which could not be easily applied in the Southern and rural small-town situations where out-of-staters often were regarded with suspicion. Interns in Southern rural communities were sometimes accused of teaching evolution and communism. Their racially mixed friendships, also, were the subject of gossip. In one Southern county it was said that whites controlled the elections by counting the votes of people long since dead, by buying the votes of blacks by sending them money and instructions in the mail, by refusing to place the names of blacks on the ballots, and by threatening the eviction of black tenants who voted the wrong way. An interviewer commented, "If the power structure in this area really knew what the Teacher Corps was all about—innovation, new ideas and all of that—I don't believe they would have allowed the Corps to come in here." The university located in this county added two local white citizens as team leaders, scaled back community involvement to conventional after-school, extracurricular activities, discouraged interns from fraternizing with blacks or living in the black community, and prohibited civil rights activities. Other Southern programs deliberately tried to recruit interns from the immediate region in order to mitigate some of these problems.

Despite the problems in these communities, the program had some impact. Community activities sometimes had the most visible impact because there was so much to be done—and the communities were not otherwise inundated with competing agencies, as is often the case in urban communities. In the rural areas, interns had been able to establish successfully, for the first time, PTA's, school newspapers, and the like.

In a particular rural program in the Southwest, the schools were almost totally isolated, socially, from the surrounding Spanish-speaking community. The teachers (most of whom spoke no Spanish) viewed their task as being one of preparing Indian and Mexican-American children for assimilation into the white community. Most of the teachers felt that the parents did not want them in their homes and conceded that the parents did not feel comfortable at school. By comparison, the interns appeared to be enthusiastic about the potentials of these children and were conscientiously concerned about their welfare. They had introduced films, audiovisual aids, booklets, and other reading material. They established the first school newspaper, physical-fitness and adult-education programs, a library, a school band, and athletic teams. However, they did not work in the community or make home visits. Some principals had deliberately selected only the interns who would fit into their school, and there was a real question about how much the interns actually could ever learn about the subculture with which they were involved.

SUMMARY

The program characteristically attempted to introduce change from the top down, to introduce innovations by adding to existing programs (rather than reallocating resources and revising priorities) or by making superficial adaptations to what already existed. Thus, idealistic, liberal interns, who expected reform in education, were often introduced into settings in which only relatively modest changes were taking place. These interns criticized the university, especially the competence of their professors and the curriculum. This criticism was encouraged by the university's tolerance and its lack of control over the interns. But the criticism also reflected the disillusionment of interns, who had expected more of their professors than of the schoolteachers and who were disappointed to learn that their professors did not know how to teach children from impoverished backgrounds.

Compared to their university work, interns were more satisfied with their internship experiences in the schools. In the schools they gained a more direct experience with children in actual school settings, a better understanding of disadvantaged children, and a better understanding of the communities in which they lived. Teachers, nevertheless, complained that interns had not learned how to maintain control over their classes and were unrealistic about the changes that could be accomplished within the system. A major difference between teachers and interns as that interns tended to encourage more student participation and to conduct more permissive, noisy classrooms than regular teachers.

In view of the diffuse and changing objectives of the program, role conflicts developed over how much stress should be given to teaching skills as opposed to helping potential teachers establish rapport with the impoverished children. There was also conflict over the amount of assistance that should be given to local schools as opposed to the introduction of innovation.

Interns were being socialized for roles that often did not yet exist, and they had the additional task of helping to develop these roles. But when the interns tried to assume a little authority in the process, teachers and professors were threatened. Teachers considered interns as additional manpower, functioning in the conventional role of an apprentice, although interns considered themselves as agents of change and as autonomous colleagues of regular classroom teachers. Interns felt that they had the authority and responsibility for introducing innovations and acting as catalysts. Actually, however, they were in low-ranking, marginal roles that offered little power.

The interns had to rely on the team leader to exercise influence on behalf of the team as a whole. This was not entirely effective because team leaders were used by principals to co-opt the program and otherwise to control it. But the team leaders also played a crucial intermediary role. Although they compromised the interns' proposals, they also helped to elicit the cooperation of the other teachers in the proposals on which the team finally agreed. In practice the team leader was a go-between, not a model teacher. Teaching teams seldom actually functioned as effective groups in the classroom. The interns' experience was this: individuals working with cooperating teachers within self-contained classrooms. There were, however, two situations in which teams did function as teams: where they were given complete responsibility for implementing a program and where they worked together on community projects. The latter situation occurred infrequently because community activities tended to be crowded out by pressures to complete college work and to assist in the classroom.

In concept, community work was one of the most innovative aspects of the Teacher Corps but, in practice, it was one of the most difficult, varied, and controversial phases of the program. Community activities that were observed were adaptations of traditional after-school, extracurricular activities with the children, such as arts and crafts, clubs, and sports. Generally, insufficient time had been allotted to this phase of the program and, since it was not well incorporated into the daily routine, it was the first activity to be slighted. There was disagreement over the amount of encouragement that should be given to social action as opposed to social service and over the amount of encouragement that should be given to communitywide activities as opposed to activities directly related to classroom teaching. Also, teachers preferred for interns to assist in the classroom instead of to work in the community without supervision.

CONCLUSIONS

The Teacher Corps has highlighted a fundamental problem that confronts all types of training programs in a changing, dynamic society: whether it is possible to design a program that prepares professionals (1) for an unknown future and nonexistent roles, and (2) to serve a wide variety of clientele. Training programs usually prepare the novice to work only with the clientele that is customarily served by the occupation and to adapt himself to the existing situations. These programs are poorly equipped to prepare the trainees for new clientele or for radically different situations. Nonetheless, because training programs represent one of the few available mechanisms that permit occupations to adapt smoothly to the future, they must cope with these problems. The Teacher Corps' answer to the dilemma was a coalition of institutions and groups, each having a different degree of commitment to the existing public school system —the schools, colleges of education, and liberal aspirants to the profession; and a federal agency admirably suited to the task of mediating the diverse groups because it, too, was subject to shifting political ties and crosscurrents from sectors of the public that had varying investments in the status quo.

The interns, with no commitment to the present system, functioned as advocates of change. They were a source of challenge and of irritation. Interns were seldom successful in introducing particular changes but, through sheer presence, often succeeded in prodding teachers and professors to rethink their assumptions and teaching practices. The conflict that occurred was a natural by-product of the uneasy coalition of groups involved, and it reflected legitimate differences of opinion between the interns and the classroom teachers over the feasibility of particular innovations and the need for strict classroom discipline, for example.

The university professors, whose own goals were not directly tied to the existing public school structure and who would gain in esteem by exercising leadership for change in public education, were to provide the guidance for interns. A great deal depended on their reform ideals and commitment to the program, on their knowledge of low-income schools, and on their ability to work with these schools. They were sufficiently secure to withstand the interns' criticisms and, perhaps, even to make adjustments to their criticisms and pressures.

The professors' primary link with the schools was the team leaders, who were to act as mediators among faculty members, interns, teachers, and administrators. The team leaders had a keen sense of the level of tolerance in the system, as well as its points of greatest vulnerability; if the leaders also were members of the minority group served and resided in the local community, they were able to counsel interns about the community's receptiveness to new proposals. Generally, they were regarded as reasonably competent teachers. Since they were selected by the principal from within the system, they added a dimension of legitimacy to and support for the team that it otherwise would not have had; they helped to link the team with the ongoing system better than an outsider could have done.

This loose affiliation of groups was cemented in the concept of team training. "Teams" provided a focal point around which a nucleus of new teachers could organize and work together; they helped to build a peer group in which interns could learn from one another; and they provided a senior teacher to consult and guide new teachers. Finally, the team provided an *expanded* change-agent mechanism by extending the range of necessary skills and talents beyond what an individual usually possesses.

However, there were too many structural weaknesses in this system for it to have been really effective. First, the federal agency's strength was also its major weakness: because it was subject to political currents, it could not provide clear and consistent direction for the local programs.

Second, because of the decentralized control structure at the local level, the interns had no reliable source of outside support. They were trapped between the overlapping authority of the universities that controlled their academic advancement and local school administrators who determined the conditions for their continued employment. Although university professors sometimes encouraged the interns to think of themselves as change agents, the professors were too remote and showed little inclination or ability to protect the interns while they were at the schools.

Third, the full potential of the team structure was seldom realized, either as a training group or as a change-agent mechanism. One of the major impediments stemmed from the haphazard way that most teams were composed. Typically, team members were arbitrarily assigned to teams with little sense of objective or task. They were never organized by the people involved on the basis of a common interest in a well-defined set of activities and tasks. The cooperating teachers, who were marginal to the main concept of the team but who monopolized the self-contained classrooms, were another major obstacle because in practice they stood between the interns and the team leaders, usurping the team leader's authority and providing most of the instruction for the interns. Teams therefore were co-opted by cooperating teachers who used the interns as their personal assistants. The practice of assigning interns to work with cooperating teachers in the individual self-contained classrooms was part of a bargain that was necessary to gain the classroom teachers' cooperation but that effectively sabotaged any potential for cooperation among the team as a whole.

Fourth, although the team leaders represented a reasonable compromise, precisely because they were a compromise, the interns frequently did not accept their legitimacy. They often felt that they could not trust the team leader to represent their interests and believed that his sole loyalty was to the principal who assigned him.

Finally, *the experience of the Teacher Corps inadvertently illuminated the woeful unpreparedness of many professors in teacher-training programs to deal with the poor.* Although the *interns* were often accurately criticized as being naïve and impractical (and often they admitted it), the key to the problem was that they found little guidance from either the college curriculum or the professors. With the exception of methods courses at a few universities, the curriculum generally was not directly tied to the interns' experiences in the schools, and it therefore could not be a realistic source of direction for them. While the colleges' social distance from the schools helped them to maintain a perspective, they actually seemed too distant to provide realistic alternatives. Even when experimental teaching methods were suggested in courses, they were seldom demonstrated; it was left to the interns to "try out" the ideas themselves at the school. Furthermore, the interns were not given systematic or specific information about the minority groups with which they were working, or the history, ecology, and values of the local community. More important, although the interns were led by publicity to view themselves as change agents (with the exception of a few largely irrelevant "sensitivity group training sessions") there was no attempt in any program to systematically expose interns to the literature on organizational change or to experiment with different tactics for introducing innovation into the schools and colleges.

Moreover, while the professors were sufficiently detached from the school system to allow them to be imaginative about it, the creative impulses of the majority seemed to have been suppressed by an equally stifling academic system. Many professors appeared to be so academic in their approach and perhaps so remote from the problems in the schools that they sometimes could not acknowledge that the problems in low-income schools might require special attention or that there was a pressing need for major reform. Most of the professors who did acknowledge special problems were admittedly uninformed about the poor and about minority subcultures who lived in the ghettos and rural areas. Moreover, the professors interviewed often were openly contemptuous of the youth who had come to them looking for leadership. This desperate situation frequently seemed to have a devastating effect on the creative impulses of the impatient and impetuous new teachers in the program. Many of these teachers became disillusioned—some were radicalized, some were alienated, and some simply were defeated. It was to the professors' credit, perhaps, that they often recognized that they were unprepared to furnish solutions even where they admitted the need for change.

At most universities, however, there were a few exceptionally knowledgeable, sensitive, reform-minded professors who could provide effective leadership and guidance for the interns. Even a few creative, competent professors could make a substantial improvement in the climate of an entire program. Moreover, in fairness, it must be recognized that the interns expected a great deal from their professors, partly because they did hold them in high regard as learned people. And the interns also were more impetuous and pragmatic than their professors; that is, they often seemed to be reacting more directly to the professors' intellectual, reasoned approach to problems and their lack of radical zeal than to their indifference and lack of technical competence. Nevertheless, the fact remains that professors were frequently accused of being unimaginative teachers, out of touch with both the schools and their own fields, steeped in tradition, and entrapped by expectations of local school boards, on the one hand, and academic prestige, on the other. Therefore, the charges cannot be easily dismissed.

The few social scientists marginally connected with the program were not much more effective. The program was not able to establish effective interdisciplinary linkages. Since the social scientists were preoccupied with the academic prestige system, they not only were disinclined to work with students and teachers in local schools but they seldom seemed willing (or able) to translate their abstract intellectual concerns into pragmatic proposals for the improvement of teaching. There was a conspicuous need for a "hybrid" professor who could bridge the gap between the academic social sciences and the realities of the local schools. But despite the fact that the necessary incentives had not been provided, an optimistic note of the study was some evidence that this hybrid might be developing in a few colleges of education.

This knowledge vacuum was compounded by two other factors, already mentioned: (1) since the team leaders seldom served as a teaching model for the interns, the interns were deprived of an opportunity to see these reputedly competent and skillful teachers in action; (2) *many of the interns brought to the colleges an unhealthy contempt for the intellectual approach to the problems of poverty.* The interns undoubtedly were correct in feeling that cognitive information is not nearly enough and that a good teacher must have firsthand knowledge and must develop a sense of compassion, rapport, and empathy with students. But in an age in which all citizens are confronted with a highly abstract world, denoted by the principles of travel and space, by atomic energy, and by bizarre economic programs, this disparagement of the scholarly approach only served as another barrier to the development of the kind of knowledge foundation needed in this field. A certain proportion of college course work for prospective teachers should continue to stress simply intellectual concerns, even if direct applicability of the knowledge cannot be immediately demonstrated.

In final analysis, the program attempted to attack the problems on two fronts and was not entirely effective on either. It tried alternatively to rely on (1) the *authority* of technical experts and (2) on the influence and power exerted by "change agents." The fact that different programs placed somewhat different emphases on these two strategies produced different program profiles but, generally, the two strategies were involved to some degree in all programs, with differing degrees of success. Each alternative is considered below.

First, the program attempted to promote change by capitalizing on *competence* of experts: the professors and the master-teacher team leaders. If they had been able to demonstrate the necessary technical competence in this field, the professors and team leaders could have used their authority to persuade teachers to adopt new ideas peaceably. However, the disagreements over the goals and the lack of necessary information undermined the professors' legitimacy in the eyes of teachers as well as interns. The professors not only were unable to provide the necessary intellectual leadership but they were placed in a poor position to win support for the ideas that the interns were trying out.

Since the program could not rely on technical competence, some members tried a second tact. They sought an essentially *political* solution by attempting to force change through the use of influence and power. There was some justification in this: because so little was known about the special problems involved in educating low-income children, there could be room for everyone in the program, including the interns, to make a contribution. Indeed, *perhaps the reason the political tensions of this program seemed*

*so important was partly because of the paucity of technical knowledge
needed to resolve the problems.* But, conversely, it must be acknowledged
that technical know-how might have been more fully developed and applied more effectively if the political dimensions had not been so intrusive.

In any event, the political solution was not entirely adequate either,
since the interns were in a very precarious position. They were generally
viewed as precursors of change but, actually, they were impotent because
of the lack of structural support that had been provided for them. Their
image only succeeded in threatening the sensitive, entrenched classroom
teachers and professors who thought the interns were trying to shake the
very roots of the professional roles and to alter traditional relationships
within and between schools and colleges.

If this power strategy is to be effective in the future, new forms of structural support and, ultimately, new structures must be built. One recourse
would be to reactivate the concept of laboratory or model schools. If these
schools were established and run jointly by universities and parents, they
might provide a supportive setting in which new roles could be developed.
But that would not suffice, either, because the training program must
somehow eventually be linked to a career, that is, to innovative schools
prepared to hire the graduates. This task of career building must accom-
pany and perhaps even precede effective educational reform. Perhaps this
type of career can only be established in *competitive* school systems outside
of the public sphere. The challenge of the 1970s is to find ways to effectively weld a more adequate knowledge base to influence structures and
thereby to harness the creative discontent of large numbers of young
people toward constructive careers.

NOTES

1. There was a wide range of variation in the level of interns' satisfaction with the
    faculties of the different programs. The proportion of interns classified as highly
    satisfied ranges from 61 percent (in site 8) to 10 percent (in site 10). The distri-
    bution of interns' scores on the nine-item scale measuring satisfaction with the
    faculty (see Appendix 1) was divided into three parts on the basis of the theoreti-
    cal (or possible) distribution. For the five sites combined, an average of one third
    of the interns are classified as highly satisfied, and 15 percent are in the bottom
    end of the distribution.

    Generally, professors rated the university support for the program as relatively good:
    27 percent rated support as excellent, although 13 percent rated it as unsatisfactory.
    The proportion who rated it as unsatisfactory varied from 12 to 50 percent. Never-
    theless, many university faculty members also were critical. Some of them felt that
    the program was being used by the college primarily for its propaganda value; some,

who were associated with the program, were skeptical about the administration's interest in it and doubted whether the university would continue to support the program if it lost its outside funding; some of those not involved in the Teacher Corps seemed to resent the extra money and publicity that the program bestowed on some of their colleagues in the program; others were defensive about any implications of invidious comparisons of the Teacher Corps with other programs in the college.

2. There was little evidence that interns were using the program to avoid the draft, but one out of three interns agreed that one of the primary reasons that interns join the program was to get an M.A. degree.

3. A Teacher Corps memo states: "Interns should learn consistently from other teachers, but bring them new materials and ideas, especially from the university. Although the team leader is the primary guide to the study of the teaching process, interns should begin to see the (their) philosophy and methods as but one means of approaching teaching; interns should become colleague(s) with the team leaders; interns should be able to continue the learning process alongside the team leader, especially during the joint planning of team teaching."

4. For example, an intern was observed conducting a "slave auction" as part of a history unit. At several points during the hour, the children became extremely noisy, running about the room, shouting with excitement. From the back of the room the regular teacher found it necessary to remind the intern to halt the proceedings until the children quieted down so that the teachers down the hall would not be disturbed. Although these events are usually confined to special classroom projects or sessions and are not done on a day-to-day basis, they reflect a similar approach to teaching used by interns across the country, which can be characterized, according to Amidon-Flanders, as exerting "indirect influence"; this includes questioning and supportive teacher behavior, awareness of feeling content, and much freer student participation, as opposed to extensive lecturing or frequent critical or disciplining behaviors.

5. According to Teacher Corps statistics, three fourths of the interns who have graduated from the Teacher Corps have accepted a position in education (which includes teaching) and have reported that they became involved in school and community work during the first year. Two thirds of them felt that, to some degree, they were effective change agents in school systems in which they were presently working, but only 52 percent were satisfied with the jobs they were able to do.

6. Fifty-nine percent of the first-cycle interns in Cort's study also said that this aspect of the program was not well planned and needed clearer definition, especially with respect to how community work relates to teaching; changes in the community aspect was the needed change mentioned second most frequently by interns.

III

What Happened

CHAPTER 5

Value Change in College

While the new programs seek to bring about political and social change, evalu-ators generally approach them as though they were standard efforts to produce educational change (achievement).

COHEN, 1970, p. 216

With this brief profile drawn, let us consider the effects of the program on the people involved and on the participating schools and colleges. This chapter discusses the manner in which the interns changed as a result of their experience. The following chapters deal with the impact of this change on the institutions.

PREVIOUS RESEARCH

Unfortunately, there is little previous research. Although there is a multitude of youth opinion surveys, very little is known about either the "natural" process of change in the values and career commitment of students as a result of college experiences or the capacity of a training program to deliberately shape them. Jacob's (1957) controversial report on American college students concluded that their values tend to remain constant throughout college and that, although the college may socialize, it does not liberalize the student. The fact that students seemed to hold homogeneous values and opinions, regardless of the college they attended, suggested that different colleges have little influence on student attitudes. However, these findings have been criticized by Barton (1959) and by

163

Rose (1963), who found greater variations among colleges. There were the strongest pressures on students to change who attended the small residential colleges and the quality private colleges, such as one studied by Newcomb and his colleagues (1967).

Yamamoto (1968) concluded that, as students proceed through college, they seem to become increasingly tolerant of people who differ in race, color, and creed, and of other people's views. Also, students become more interested in intellectual and cultural matters; more women than men change in this respect (p. 384). Other studies reported that students become politically more liberal as they proceed through the university, that the extent of change is greater in private than in public institutions, and that it varies considerably with the students' major subject (Selvin and Hagstrom, 1960).

Although a study of National Merit Scholars confirms that some students become more liberal during college, the study revealed that students of very similar ability may change attitudes in opposite directions (Webster, Freedman, and Heist, 1967). For example, in answering the question, "Should the government provide medical and dental care for citizens who cannot afford such services?" engineering students showed a significant shift from positive to negative; but, for humanities and mathematics majors, the significant change was in the opposite direction. Crotty's (1967) data also indicated that the better students' originally high commitment to liberalism declined during college, although this was more than offset by the increased acceptance of the liberal values by the average and below average students. Little is known about the particular conditions responsible for this varied reaction.

One question is whether students' values are influenced more by the formal curriculum or by the informal milieu of the college. Undoubtedly, one reason that students change in different directions, even within the same institution, is that every campus provides a variety of formal and informal settings and subcultures that different students belong to. There is evidence that students' values are influenced in different directions, depending on their membership in and degree of commitment to different subcultures (Gottlieb and Hodgkins, 1963) and to different living arrangements (Vreeland and Bidwell, 1965). From his analysis of the Cornell survey of college students, Suchman (1957) concluded that much of what students learn takes place outside the classroom. According to one study, by the end of the senior year in high school the peer-group status system of the school was more closely related to the college plans of students than was their parents' education (McDill et al., 1967). Another study arrived at somewhat different conclusions (Kandel and Lesser, 1969), although the investigation found that the academic standards enforced by the school were important. Wallace (1966) documented how college subcultures influence the way students perceive the importance of grades and their educational aspirations. Other writers point to the "structural" effects" of the peer culture. For example, a study of Argentine university students demonstrated that those who were located in academic departments where there was more sentiment in favor of students having a voice in university government were far more likely to vote leftist, regardless of family background and their personal attitudes toward student governments (Nasatir, 1968). Comparable studies of student activism have reached similar conclusions (Meyer, 1971).

In addition to the question of whether the formal or informal aspects of college have more influence on student values, it is not clear to what extent the changes that take place can be attributed to the personal *predispositions* to change as opposed to characteristics of the college environment. Some writers deny that the college's formal or informal aspects are important in comparison to the type of students recruited. They stress that what appear to be "college effects" are actually due to differences in the types of students recruited. Commenting on the capacity of colleges to produce scientists and scholars, Holland (1957) concluded that "differential student populations among colleges appear as a more probable explanation of differences in productivity than the special qualities of individual institutions." Various studies indicate that a small increase in the selectivity of an organization often results in a large decrease in the effort required to "socialize" its members. Conversely, it can be expected that the less stringent the standards of recruitment, the more emphasis must be placed on socialization; furthermore, the more the socialization, the higher the dropout rate. Finally, to the extent that neither recruitment nor socialization is emphasized, there can be expected a greater displacement of goals in the training institution.

Postgraduate Change

There are few studies devoted to the persistence of the values and attitudes of college graduates (Pace, 1941; Havemann and West, 1952). However, from one study, a follow-up of Bennington College graduates 25 years after graduation, Newcomb and his colleagues (1967) concluded that women who, as students in the 1930s, had moved away from the conservatism of their families retained the liberalism they had reached during college. Compared to the attitudes of other women of the same age, they retained a more liberal orientation toward the underprivileged, war, and race relations, and they remained socially and politically active, even while fulfilling traditional homemaking roles.

In another setting a study of medical students reported that during their training they developed cynical feelings specifically directed at the medical-school experience. However, they did not seem to lose their original idealism about the practice of medicine. At the end of their schooling a more general idealism about medicine reasserted itself, but it was within the framework of more realistic alternatives (Becker and Geer, 1958). Studies of other professional training programs have been less optimistic about the resiliency of idealism. Lortie (1959) reported that the exotic and dramatized image of law, held by law students, was gradually replaced by routine and pedestrian elements. And a study of first-year nursing students found that, by the third year, many ideals of these students had given way to the conviction that nursing is just a job (Ingmire, 1952).

The first systematic contact with clients is often a time of disillusionment. Students who may have entered a profession with the expectation of helping others may soon find that the clients are not so willing to be helped (or so grateful) as perhaps the students had expected. One study of nurses, based on the respondents' preference for pictures, concluded that beginning students in all types of schools were motivated by a desire to nurse patients, unaided at the bedside; by the second year of schooling the unaided patient relationship had lost most of its attraction, and in the final year of schooling it was no longer the majority response (Meyer, 1960). For understandable reasons students prefer clients who conform to their expectations of the "ideal" (Berkowitz and Berkowitz, 1960).

Roberts' (1969) comparative study of an experimental teachers college and two traditional colleges showed that trainees in all three institutions, between their freshman and senior years, became less favorable toward teaching in urban problem areas. Although trainees in the experimental college expressed less change in some attitudes than trainees in the two comparative colleges, these trainees showed a marked tendency to prefer the fast-learning student over the slum child and the suburban school over the inner-city school. However, when the trainees who placed priority on knowledge as a teaching objective were omitted from the analysis, the remaining students in the experimental college developed more favorable attitudes. There was little evidence that the social backgrounds of the students influenced the direction of change. Although freshmen from blue-collar homes and blacks were initially more favorable toward slum schools, when they reached their senior year their backgrounds made no difference. This indicated that the college experience itself was having a negative influence. If this is typical of other teacher education programs, it suggests that the patterns of socialization into teaching may follow the patterns of other occupations.

Another point of disillusionment occurs during the transition from school to work. Again, a study of student and graduate nurses showed that favorableness toward nursing and, especially, job satisfaction were greater for students than for employed graduates. The greatest differences occurred between students and employed nurses who had been judged most successful by their superiors (Corwin, Taves, and Haas, 1961). The "reality shock" after graduation seems to be produced by the discontinuity between the institutional perspectives stressed in the training program and the actual job requirements. Until the graduate assumes a full-time position, he cannot be fully aware of the array of professional, humanitarian, business, employee, and other norms that are imposed on him. *These norms are not always entirely congruent with the institutional ideals,* which must be compromised in the course of daily routines.

Teacher-training programs are not designed or equipped to give a completely realistic picture of the job of teaching. Professors preach an idealized version and, in their concern to improve teaching, they probably will overlook many of the less desirable *employment* characteristics of the profession. This idealism is not the result of a naïve ignorance of complex realities; it is an assessment of what is theoretically important—that is, the common institutional characteristics of teaching as an occupation (Corwin, 1961). The variety of employment conditions, differential salary scales, supervisory practices, and administrative chores are simply regarded as less important and thus are given less consideration. The question is whether the gap between the ideal and the actual teaching conditions can be closed and whether disillusionment can be minimized through the internship incorporated in the Teacher Corps program.

Studies of the Teacher Corps

Previous studies of the Teacher Corps tell us very little because most of them were psychological and were confined to local programs. Goldman (1966) studied 19 Teacher Corps interns, in comparison to noninterns, during their first year of service. On the Edwards' personal-preference scale used in that study, interns exhibited a greater need for personal achievement, autonomy, dominance, change, and heterosexuality; they had lower scores of deference, order, exhibition, affiliation, succorance, abasement, nurturance, and endurance. Although the interns' initial Minnesota Teacher Attitude Inventory (MTAI) scores were no different from the scores of graduate students in introductory courses in education, their scores changed significantly over the year and became more teacher-centered. Their IQ scores revealed high intelligence levels that were not reflected in their GRE scores.

Another study compared 15 Teacher Corps interns, 15 first-year teachers in a special program to prepare teachers for low-income schools, and 15 other teachers. It showed that the interns and first-year teachers scored differently from the other teachers on their MTAI scores but that they did not differ among themselves.

Hunt (1967) also found favorable change in the MTAI' scores of 26 Teacher Corps trainees over a 10-week summer program at Syracuse University. Trainees became more liberal, more accepting of different viewpoints, and more understanding of individual differences. From the analysis of behavioral task scores, improvement was also noticed in the trainees' ability to control classroom behavior and to respond sensitively to the learners' frame of reference.

Perhaps if the novices are sufficiently different initially, they will have the internal strength to withstand the training experience and the reality shock at the time of their first job. In these cases it is conceivable that the original liberalism and optimism will blend into a new hybrid unlike either the novice or the experienced teachers described in Chapter 3.

CHANGES IN INTERNS' OPINIONS

How did members of the Teacher Corps change during the program? Did their experiences affect them? If so, in what ways? Let us identify the specific program characteristics that might have been responsible for the changes that occurred.

Cross-sectional Patterns

The tables and other detailed analyses computed in connection with Chapter 3 were inspected in order to detect uniform patterns among the four groups that had been exposed to teaching for varying lengths of time; new teachers, experienced teachers, second-cycle interns, and third-cycle interns. The data indicated systematic differences (see Appendix 3). Assuming that these groups represented different points in the career line, the differences could reflect changes occurring during the career. Of course, changes also might result from differences in the people recruited at different periods of time or from differences among the programs in each cycle. Nevertheless, let us speculate on the implications of the data for careers.

The patterns, over the course of the career, suggested that the teachers in the sample had become assimilated into the system. For example, at each career stage there was a uniform decline in client orientation, initiative, and liberalism; this was accompanied by increased loyalty to the administration and to the rules and procedures, and by increased emphasis on pupil control. There was also a decline in commitment to teaching among the new and experienced interns, suggesting that disillusionment began to set in early; the reversal of the trend among employed teachers probably can be explained by the tendency for the least committed teachers to drop out after the first few years. Finally, it was observed that between the first and second year of graduate school, when commitment was declining, the alienation of the interns was increasing. But again, alienation scores were lower for first-year teachers than for second-year students, perhaps because of dropout. From that point they declined still further over the career, again partly because of dropout and partly because of psychological resignation.

Longitudinal Changes During the Program

A second source of data comes from comparisons in the scale scores of third-cycle interns between the time they first entered the program and the time they graduated from it. Each of the opinion scales discussed in Chapter 3 was subjected to reanalysis for each of the 72 interns in the third-cycle programs who completed all scales twice.[1] The evidence generally supports other studies, which suggest that training for a profession is a liberalizing and disillusioning experience. However, the data also reveal complex countertrends that are masked in the overall averages (see Table 5–1).

POLITICAL-SOCIAL LIBERALISM. We found that experience in the Teacher Corps tended to liberalize this already liberal group of interns. Over half of them (54 percent) became more liberal. However, there was some degree of polarization; some interns shifted to opposite directions, toward or away from liberalism. Marked variations also occurred from program to program. Whereas substantial liberalization occurred at three of the sites, at two other sites the majority of interns (62 percent in one site and 75 percent in the other) became more conservative. In fact, the *extent* of change was more substantial when it occurred in the conservative direction than in the liberal direction. The scores of interns who became more liberal increased on an average of 3.7 points, while the scores of interns who became more conservative declined 5.9 points.

Table 5-1 Change in the attitudes and role conceptions of 72 interns in five programs over a two-year period

Direction of change in attitudes and role conceptions[a]

	Percent
1. Political liberalism	
More liberal	53.52
Less liberal	39.03
No change	8.45
Mean difference	2.34
Difference in means	- .34
2. Initiative	
With more initiative	29.81
With less initiative	44.23
No change	25.96
Mean difference	- .41
Difference in means	- .47
3. Alienation from the Teacher Corps	
More alienated	72.46
Less alienated	15.94
No change	11.59
Mean difference	.11
Difference in means	1.37
4. Alienation from the school	
More alienated	47.76
Less alienated	34.32
No change	16.42
Mean difference	.69
Difference in means	.53

Direction of change in attitudes and role conceptions[a]

	Percent
5. Professional orientation	
More professionally oriented	29.58
Less professionally oriented	63.38
No change	7.04
Mean difference	-1.06
Difference in means	-4.37
6. Orientation to teacher colleagues	
More oriented to teachers	37.14
Less oriented to teachers	47.14
No change	15.71
Mean difference	-1.25
Difference in means	- .86
7. Monopoly of knowledge	
For whom knowledge is more important	26.15
For whom knowledge is less important	64.62
No change	9.23
Mean difference	- .45
Difference in means	-1.46
8. Decision-making of teachers	
Who want more authority for teachers	21.88
Who want less authority for teachers	65.63
No change	12.50
Mean difference	- .81
Difference in means	-1.18

9. Commitment to teaching

	Percent
More committed to teaching	20.00
Less committed to teaching	72.86
No change	7.14
Mean difference	-1.75
Difference in means	-1.11

10. Orientation to students

	Percent
More oriented to students	46.38
Less oriented to students	39.13
No change	14.49
Mean difference	.08
Difference in means	.26

11. Pupil control

	Percent
Who place more emphasis on discipline	24.29
Who place less emphasis on discipline	61.43
No change	14.29
Mean difference	-.20
Difference in means	-1.26

12. Loyalty to the administration

	Percent
More loyal	38.57
Less loyal	48.57
No change	12.86
Mean difference	-.19
Difference in means	-.25

13. Commitment to rules

	Percent
Who place more emphasis on rules	31.89
Who place less emphasis on rules	59.42
No change	8.69
Mean difference	-1.00
Difference in means	-1.58

14. Endorcement of racial integration

	Percent
More supportive of racial integration	44.44
Less supportive of racial integration	40.28
No change	15.28
Mean difference	.27
Difference in means	.24

a The number fluctuates slightly from scale to scale.

When interns were asked, in another question, to identify their political point of view, the proportion who chose "very liberal or radical" increased from 27 to 55 percent over the two-year period, with a comparable decline in the proportion who selected the "fairly liberal" label (from 61 to 34 percent). There was little change in the self-identification of team leaders and teachers.

Finally, when the interns were asked to identify the most effective remedy for poverty, they had become less convinced that the answer was greater job opportunity and more convinced that the remedy required changes in the basic structure of society. The proportion favoring the first response changed from 55 to 30 percent, with an identical shift in favor of the second alternative (from 31 to 55 percent). Some team leaders had become more convinced that the primary answer was an increased sense of self-respect among the poor.

INITIATIVE AND COMPLIANCE. Although the interns were becoming more liberal in their attitudes, their responses indicated that they were less predisposed to exercise initiative and that they were more cautious in their conduct. Almost half of the interns (44 percent) indicated less predisposition to take initiative, and only 30 percent expressed more inclination to take initiative.

ALIENATION. The majority of interns (72 percent) also became more alienated from the Teacher Corps in the process; a mean change in the different programs ranged from 0.5 to 2.7 (on a 10-point scale). Nearly half of the interns also expressed more alienation from their schools, while one third expressed less alienation by this measure.

PROGRAM OBJECTIVES. Possibly one reason for the interns' alienation was their changed perceptions of the program objectives. During the program, interns became more and more convinced that the actual objective (whether primary or secondary) was to "provide poverty area schools with much needed assistance" (not in Table 5–1). In the beginning, one fourth of the interns chose this alternative but, by the end of the program, one half of them selected it. A majority also felt that the program provided interns with certain effective teaching skills and classroom techniques, while only one in four believed that the purpose of the program was to allow interns to try out their ideas about teaching. There was little shift in the latter categories. By contrast, teachers and team leaders became more convinced that the program's purpose was to help interns try out their ideas; they became less convinced that the purpose was to better acquaint the intern with the type of child found in poverty-area schools. The proportion of team leaders and teachers who chose the first alternative doubled (from 26 to 56 percent and from 30 to 60 percent).

PROFESSIONAL ORIENTATION. A majority of the interns (63 percent) also became more disillusioned with the profession and with their colleagues (47 percent), although the extent varied among the programs. In two programs, shifts in professional orientation occurred in both positive and negative directions, while in three others the shift was overwhelmingly negative. As few as one third became disillusioned with colleagues in some programs, but in others as many as two thirds to three fourths became less favorable. Also, nearly two thirds of the interns (representing a majority in four programs) became less convinced that teachers deserve to have more decision-making authority. This perhaps reflects their growing lack of confidence in teachers.

COMMITMENT TO TEACHING. Probably the most telling aspect of the interns' disillusionment was that, during their two-year program, almost three fourths of them became less committed to teaching; only one in five expressed more commitment to teach in poverty schools. In each of the five programs there was a (mean) decline of from 1 to 3 points (on a 12-point scale); the mean for interns whose commitment declined was 3.3 points; for those whose commitment increased, the increase averaged 2.1 points. Whereas 38 percent were classified "high" on this index at the beginning of the program, by the end only 13 percent could be so classified.

In another analysis, nearly half (48 percent) of the interns initially planned to stay in teaching until retirement but, by the end of the program, only 16 percent intended to do so. However, only five of those who changed their minds planned to enter another vocation, and some of them (17 percent) were women who decided to become homemakers and to leave teaching. Most of the rest expected to continue in education but to shift from classroom teaching to some other aspect.

ORIENTATION TO STUDENTS. A large proportion of the interns became less committed to the students (39 percent). But considering their general disillusionment it is perhaps remarkable that the percentage was not higher. It is even more remarkable that nearly half (46 percent) of the interns increased their orientation to the children despite their disillusionment in other respects. In two programs a majority became more positive on this measure; in one program the majority shifted in the other direction.

PUPIL CONTROL. The resiliency of the interns' concern for the students was reflected in the interns' unwillingness to adopt a strict attitude toward discipline, despite pressures from the teachers. On the contrary, during the program a majority (61 percent) placed less emphasis on discipline than they placed at the beginning. This figure, however, ranged from a high of 92 percent in one program to 31 percent in another. In only one program, a majority or near majority became more convinced of a need for more discipline in the classroom.

LOYALTY TO THE ADMINISTRATION. Although almost half of the interns (49 percent) lost confidence in their school administrators during the program, this proportion was nearly canceled out by the proportion (39 percent) who became more favorable toward their administrators. More of them (59 percent) became disillusioned with their school's rules and procedures; still, one third valued rules and procedures more highly at the end of the program than in the beginning.

RACIAL INTEGRATION. A similar countercurrent occurred with the endorsement of racial integration. The proportion of interns who became more supportive of racial integration (44 percent) was canceled out by those who endorsed it less than before (40 percent).

Dropouts

Another source of information concerning the effect of the program on the interns comes from the dropouts. Dropouts often are the ones who most clearly perceive the discontinuity between college and future career demands. When this perception is coupled with a frustrating sense of alienation, the dropout rate will be especially high.

According to statistics collected by the national Teacher Corps office, the attrition rate of the first-cycle interns during the program was 51 percent; it was 27 and 9 percent for the second- and third-cycle interns. A sampling of the dropouts indicated that over half of them (57 percent) went into teaching. In the present sample, approximately one in four of the 125 interns who entered the five third-cycle programs dropped out before the end of the program. This proportion varied from 15 to 41 percent in the various programs. Even though the numbers involved were small and the differences were not necessarily statistically significant, the available cases will illuminate some differences.

A disproportionate number of the dropouts were women (60 percent, compared to 32 percent of the graduates). Social science majors also were slightly overrepresented among dropouts (44 versus 33 percent); persons with prior Peace Corps or VISTA experience were underrepresented (6 versus 33 percent).

There was a striking two-to-one tendency for dropouts to have been attracted to teaching through the Teacher Corps. Indeed, over one half of the dropouts (52 percent) said they would not have entered teaching without the Teacher Corps, compared to about one fourth (23 percent) of the graduates who made that claim.

The dropouts, compared to graduates, had relatively low administrative orientation scores ($\overline{X}$ difference $= 2.0$) and expressed greater concern with students' welfare (client orientation) ($\overline{X}$ difference $= 1.4$). Dropouts were somewhat alienated from the Teacher Corps at the beginning of the program, and they had higher initiative scores than the graduates. Whereas dropouts began the program with a higher professional orientation than the graduates, they underwent more disillusionment with the profession and became less oriented to the administration and less committed to teaching. Although they did not have different political attitudes initially, the dropouts became more liberal than the graduates.

CORRELATES OF OPINION CHANGE

In view of the variety of interns in the program and the extreme differences in the way the program affected them, let us examine some of the factors that accounted for interns' opinions and opinion change during the program. I shall deal with only one type of opinion for analysis: social and political liberalism. Previous studies of the effects that colleges have on students yielded inconsistent and contradictory findings. This was partly because these studies usually have not tried to identify the specific college characteristics associated with different types of change. Different characteristics of the same college can produce opposite effects that cancel out each other. One way to proceed is to examine one characteristic at a time and to standardize them. Various personal and structural characteristics are discussed in the following analysis.

Initial Liberalism

SOCIAL BACKGROUNDS. The initial liberalism of interns cannot be explained by their personal status characteristics. A series of regression correlations indicated that six personal characteristics accounted for only 7 percent of the variance in their liberalism scores (not in the tables). The positive correlations with their fathers' education ($B = .16$)* and with their sex

---

* B refers to the "Beta Weight."

(that is, females slightly more liberal than males) $(B = .12)$ were all small, and the relationship to race, age, and quality of undergraduate college were even more negligible. Although ascribed characteristics seemed to be slightly more important than achieved characteristics, an individual's political liberalism (according to the scale used here) could not be predicted from social backgrounds.

PROGRAM CHARACTERISTICS. Table 5–2A indicates that an individual's liberalism can be more accurately predicted from characteristics of the program that he joins.[2] Specifically, liberal interns tended to join programs in which the other students were also liberal $(B = .31)$; that is, the liberals tended to congregate in certain programs. These more liberal interns were also likely to be dissatisfied with their professors $(B = -.21)$. However, the explanatory power of these factors is not impressive. Even with these two factors included, the total set of program characteristics and personal characteristics accounted for only one third of the variance.

PRIOR EXPERIENCE. Table 5–2B reveals a small correlation between interns' liberalism, their prior experience, and their conceptions of the program. Interns who viewed the primary goal for the program as assisting schools (instead of as innovation), interns who already had teaching certificates, and interns who would join the Teacher Corps again were all less liberal $(B = -.35; -.30; -.13)$. There was a slight tendency for the more liberal interns to say that they would have gone into teaching even if the Teacher Corps had not been available to them $(B = .21)$; there was also a tendency for them to have had prior experience in the Peace Corps or VISTA $(B = .14)$. This set of variables, although it explains only 28 percent of the variance, provided a better set of predictors of liberalism than the interns' personal backgrounds.

Increase in Liberalism

The individuals who had become more liberal during the program had a tendency to express more initiative toward the administration $(r = .20)$, a tendency to change their self-image toward the image of a more liberal or radical person $(r = .17)$, and a tendency to express more alienation from the Teacher Corps $(r = .18)$. Can these changes be partially explained by the characteristics of the interns, the characteristics of their peer groups, and the characteristics of the program? Let us explore this question.

SOCIAL BACKGROUNDS. The interns' personal backgrounds, which were not good predictors of their initial liberalism, were not highly correlated with changes in their opinions during the program (Table 5–3A). There was a tendency for black interns to become more conservative ($B = -.43$) and for social science majors and humanities majors to become less liberal ($B = .15$). However, these two factors accounted for only 20 percent of the variance and, with five other factors added, only 23 percent of the variance could be explained.

PEER-GROUP CHARACTERISTICS. The variable examined that was most highly correlated with an individual becoming more liberal was his initial liberalism; that is, the more liberal an individual was when he came into the program, the more likely he was to have been radicalized by the experience ($B = .54$) (Table 5–3B). Therefore, this variable was statistically held constant ("controlled") while considering five characteristics of the individual's peer group.

The characteristics of an individual's fellow students seemed to have an influence on the way his opinions changed. Specifically, in schools with more interns who held a liberal arts major ($B = .27$), with more interns from outside of the region ($B = .28$), and with more interns from better undergraduate colleges ($B = .14$), an individual tended to become more liberal. The proportion of interns with prior Peace Corps or VISTA experience and the average liberalism of interns in a program had only negligible additional effects. These five context variables contributed 14 percent of the variance explained; the total set accounted for 47 percent of the variance.

PROGRAM CHARACTERISTICS. It is significant that, of the program characteristics considered, the most important one was the negative correlation with the extent of technological innovation that occurred in the schools ($B = -.41$); even after the individual's liberalism was controlled, this variable added 10 percent to the variance explained (Table 5–3C). The table also shows that interns who were assigned to schools that were receptive to experimentation and that were flexible tended to become more liberal ($B = .37$).

Thus, flexible, innovative environments seem to foster liberal opinions. But when expected changes fail to materialize, the individuals involved in the changes tend to become radicalized. However, there is an alternate interpretation: change is not likely to materialize in flexible environments until the change agents have tempered their liberalism. Perhaps both elements are involved: (1) the failure of interns to implement change may have disillusioned them with the system; but (2) teachers may have become less defensive and more open to change to the degree that the interns did learn to work within the system.

Table 5-2A Characteristics of interns and of their social contexts associated with their initial political and social liberalism scores (N = 249)

Characteristics of interns and of their social context	r	R^2	R^2 added	Final partial	Final T value	Final beta weight	F
Mean political liberalism of interns	.48	.235	--	.293	4.74	.310	75.91
Interns' satisfaction with university faculty	-.42	.278	.043	-.198	3.12	-.212	14.70
Interns' fathers' education	.19	.317	.039	.179	2.81	.155	13.95
Proportion who are male	.16	.340	.023	.127	1.98	.121	8.31
Proportion who have liberal arts major	.44	.350	.010	.118	1.83	.128	3.87
Proportion who are black	.11	.352	.002	.043	.67	.040	.62
Interns' undergraduate major	-.11	.353	.001	-.047	.72	-.045	.25
Quality of undergraduate college	-.01	.354	.001	.037	.58	.036	.14

Table 5-2B Goals and prior experience of interns associated with their initial political and social liberalism scores (N = 249)

Goals and prior experience of interns	r	R^2	R^2 added	Final partial	Final T value	Final beta weight	F
Proportion of interns who emphasize the goal of assistance	-.34	.117	--	-.301	4.90	-.352	32.83
Proportion who hold teaching certificates	-.33	.200	.083	-.276	4.46	-.299	25.57
Proportion who would have entered teaching without the Teacher Corps	.14	.257	.057	.196	3.11	.205	18.62
Proportion who would join Teacher Corps again	-.16	.266	.009	-.121	1.89	-.127	3.18
Proportion who have had prior experience with Peace Corps or VISTA	.04	.277	.011	.130	2.03	.141	3.45

Table 5-3A Increase in interns' liberalism associated with their social background characteristics (N = 72)

Social background characteristics	r	R^2	R^2 added	Final partial	Final T value	Final beta weight	F
Proportion who are black	-.40	.163	---	-.403	3.52	-.430	13.64
Interns' undergraduate major	.23	.203	.040	.151	1.22	.151	3.51
Type of undergraduate college	.08	.217	.014	.099	.80	.106	1.19
Age of interns	.02	.229	.012	.125	1.01	.121	1.05
Quality of undergraduate college	.16	.234	.005	.078	.62	.091	.38
Interns' fathers' education	-.03	.234	.000	.022	.17	.021	.03
Proportion who are male	-.12	.234	.000	-.001	.01	-.001	.00

Table 5-3B Increase in interns' liberalism associated with characteristics of their peer groups (N = 72)

Peer group characteristics	r	R^2	R^2 added	Final partial	Final T value	Final beta weight	F
Individual political liberalism of interns	.58	.334	--	.537	5.10	.543	35.17
Proportion who have liberal arts major	.22	.414	.080	.194	1.58	.266	9.41
Proportion interns from outside region	.20	.440	.026	.266	2.21	.279	3.08
Quality of undergraduate college	.24	.463	.023	.128	1.03	.135	2.93
Proportion who have had prior Peace Corps or VISTA experience	.05	.472	.009	.117	.94	.112	1.11
Mean political liberalism of interns	.28	.473	.001	.061	.49	.062	.14

181

Table 5-3C Increase in interns' liberalism associated with program characteristics (N = 72)

Program characteristics	r	R^2	R^2 added	Final partial	Final T value	Final beta weight	F
Introduction of new techniques into school	-.43	.185	--	-.173	1.36	-.406	15.93
Flexibility of the school	.23	.279	.094	.184	1.45	.369	8.93
Quality of the school	.11	.297	.018	-.210	1.66	-.323	1.81
Proportion of teachers with M.A. degrees	.16	.313	.016	.146	1.14	.215	1.57
Proportion of team leaders who consider themselves politically "very liberal"	.06	.324	.011	-.026	.20	-.074	1.08
Teachers' loyalty to the administration	-.21	.327	.003	-.086	.67	-.121	.20
Quality of teachers' undergraduate college	-.24	.328	.001	.050	.38	.111	.12
Interns' satisfaction with university faculty	.08	.330	.002	-.087	.68	-.211	.23
Competence of the principal as rated by teachers and interns	.28	.332	.002	.048	.37	.085	.19
Competence of the team leader as rated by interns	.29	.333	.001	.036	.28	.061	.09

Table 5-3D Increase in interns' liberalism associated with personal, peer, and program characteristics (N = 72)

Personal, peer, and program characteristics	r	R^2	R^2 added	Final partial	Final T value	Final beta weight	F
Individual interns' political and social liberalism	.58	.334	--	.599	5.13	.487	35.17
Introduction of new techniques into the school	-.43	.424	.090	-.227	1.82	-.244	10.80
Quality of undergraduate college	.16	.457	.033	-.359	3.00	.283	4.14
Flexibility of the school	.23	.481	.024	.387	3.28	.362	2.98
Proportion with liberal arts major	-.22	.512	.031	-.230	1.85	-.208	9.26
Quality of teachers' undergraduate college	.16	.528	.016	-.091	1.71	-.080	2.14
Interns' fathers' education	-.03	.544	.016	.201	1.60	.156	2.32
Proportion of teachers with M.A. degree	.16	.554	.010	.257	2.08	.263	1.43
Quality of the school	.11	.577	.023	-.242	1.95	-.263	3.39

Several indicators of school and program quality, listed in Table 5–3C, were also positively associated with increases in liberalism, but their combined effect was negligible. The total set of variables accounted for only one third of the variance.

ALL FACTORS COMBINED. Table 5–3D shows the relative contribution of the various types of variables considered together. Seven variables account for 54 percent of the variance in change in liberalism: the individual's initial liberalism $(B = .49)$, the amount of technological innovation in the schools $(B = -.24)$, the average quality of the interns' undergraduate college $(B = .28)$, the flexibility of the school $(B = .36)$, the proportion of interns with liberal arts majors $(B = -.21)$, the quality of the teachers' undergraduate college $(B = -.08)$, and the fathers' education $(B = .16)$. The additional contribution of two other variables, also listed in the table, was negligible; however, the betas indicate a respectable correlation in both cases. This set of variables can be portrayed in the form of a pathlike diagram (Figures 5–1).

Initial Commitment to Teaching

A comparable series of analyses was computed for interns' initial commitment to teaching. It was not possible to predict initial commitment to teaching from the interns' personal backgrounds or the characteristics of their social contexts that were considered. There was only a slight tendency for interns from higher status homes (based on father's education) $(B = .17)$ and from nonwhite families $(B = .11)$ to express more commitment to teaching in low-income schools; males tended to be slightly more committed to teaching than females $(B = -.14)$. Eight characteristics combined, however, accounted for less than 4 percent of the variance. Program characteristics had even less effect.

Higher quality programs tended to attract slightly less committed interns $(B = -.17)$.

Change in Commitment to Teaching

PERSONAL BACKGROUND CHARACTERISTICS. Change in commitment to teaching could not be predicted from the personal background characteristics of individuals. During the program there was a slight tendency for women and middle-class interns to lose interest in teaching in low-income areas and for older, nonwhite interns and interns from better undergraduate colleges to increase their interest. But all of these characteristics combined accounted for less than 5 percent of the variance.

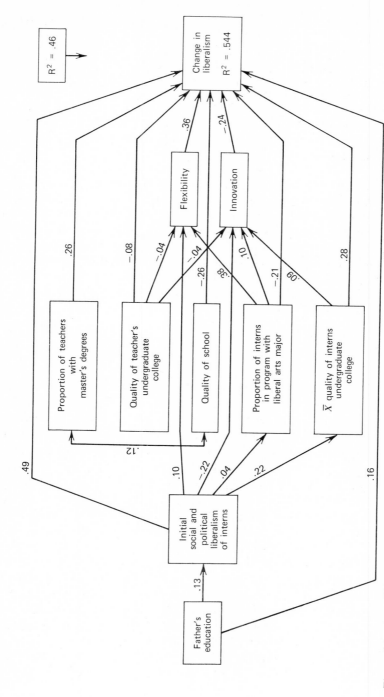

Figure 5-1 A pathlike model of change in interns' social and political liberalism during the program.

185

CHARACTERISTICS OF PEERS AND PROGRAMS. There was a tendency for an individual's commitment to teaching to increase as the average commitment of his peers increased ($r = .30$). Ten program characteristics, however, accounted for only 14 percent of the variance. These were consistently negative correlations with all program characteristics considered, including quality and flexibility of the schools and indicators of the competence of the personnel. A possible explanation is: interns find that the best that public education has to offer is still not good enough.

PERSONAL AND PEER-GROUP CHARACTERISTICS COMBINED. Not more than 16 percent of the variance could be explained with a combination of six personal and peer-group characteristics. The more liberal interns ($B = -.24$), who had become alienated ($r = -.32$), and interns with already high commitment to teaching ($B = -.20$) lost interest in teaching; interns from better undergraduate colleges ($B = .17$) and in programs with a high proportion of individuals with liberal arts degrees from good colleges ($B = .19$), and whose peers were committed to teaching ($r = .29$), tended to increase their interest.

CONCLUSIONS

As other studies have shown, the more liberal students came from families with well-educated fathers. But in contrast to some studies, the women attracted to the program were slightly more liberal than the men; this factor, together with the preponderance of men in the program, indicates that these men and women were not typical elementary school teachers. The more liberal interns did not endorse the use of the program to provide assistance to the schools; they were more likely to have had experience in other liberal, service-oriented programs such as Peace Corps and VISTA. They were less likely than the less liberal students to hold teaching certificates. These are the very types of people that the program attempted to attract.

Yet, ironically, the more liberal an intern was, the more likely it was that he would have gone into teaching even without the program. He was less likely to join the program again if he had it to do over. In other words, the program seems to have acted as a route for the liberals who were at or beyond the teaching threshold, but it did not necessarily attract them into the profession. The program seemed to be more effective in attracting a moderately liberal, somewhat committed person who might otherwise have entered another career; although this type was not *ex-*

tremely different from the typical teacher, there was probably a notable difference.

There seemed to be a dialectic operating in the program, based on the principle of natural selection. At the first stage of the program, many of the most unique new teachers were eliminated (or eliminated themselves). Of approximately one in four of the 125 interns in the five third-cycle programs who had dropped out before the end of the program, a disproportionately large number were social science majors who closely identified with the students. They appeared to be neither compliant nor loyal to the school administration, and they had been alienated from the program from the beginning. These interns, logically, were the leaders of educational reform. But as a result of their experiences in the program, they had apparently been radicalized and had lost interest in teaching. The very ones that the program was trying to attract became quickly discouraged and disillusioned with the professional teaching role. Consequently, the interns who were most bent on changing the system and who might have provided the greatest thrust for change had no influence at all because they were unwilling to compromise and were unable to work within the system.

Then, at the second stage, a parallel dialectic occurred among the vast majority of interns who had not been filtered in at the first stage. At the one extreme there was evidence of forces that probably would eventually temper their incentive for change. In this connection, patterns among a cross section of the sample who had been exposed to teaching for different lengths of time suggested that, over the course of their careers, teachers had become assimilated into the system, and perhaps the interns were doomed to the same destiny. There was a uniform decline at each of the four career stages in client orientation, initiative, and liberalism. This was accompanied by an increased loyalty to the administration, to the rules and procedures, and an increased emphasis on pupil control. An initial decline in commitment to teaching and an increase in alienation between the new and experienced interns also suggested early disillusionment; although the trend was reversed among employed teachers, it was probably because the least committed, most alienated teachers had dropped out after the first few years. Thus many of those who stayed with the program probably would become conformists.

At the other extreme, just as the majority of interns had stuck with the program while others dropped out, many of the ones who stayed were able to maintain their liberalism despite their general discontent. And again, among these liberals, many seemed to be going through a transformation comparable to that experienced by the dropouts. Thus, over the period of the program, many interns became progressively radicalized and disillusioned with teaching. In this respect, the data supported other studies in finding that professional training is often liberalizing and disillusioning. Probably both processes were triggered by the same mechanism —the difference between what the interns expected of the profession and what they actually encountered. Their high expectations of the profession and of the professors were often reinforced by their peers because of the distinct tendency for the more liberal interns to congregate in certain programs in which they could find mutual support.

This is probably what happened: the less change the interns observed taking place, the more convinced they became of the need for basic change. Many of the interns who were liberalized during the program had liberal predispositions to begin with; usually they had come from the social sciences and from good liberal arts colleges. Nevertheless, even with this predisposition toward radicalism on the part of certain types of people, *there was a marked tendency for the interns who became radicalized to be located in the programs where the* least *change had occurred.* Conversely, perhaps the change that did occur caused more interns to become conservative. There was probably a reciprocal relationship here. It reflected a tendency for interns who had expected change to become disillusioned with the system when it did not occur. It also reflected a tendency for the change to take place after interns had toned down their liberal commitments.

In any event, one of the latent effects of the program may have been to radicalize liberal interns, even though in other cases the program seemed to have helped some interns reconcile themselves to working within the system. The program inadvertently had convened several of the conditions commonly associated with radicalism, including:

1. A group of newcomers who, as sociological "strangers," acted as "men without history" (as Simmel expressed it), lacking in experience with the occupation and oriented to external standards of reference that were anchored in a generational revolt and middle-class-based romantic idealism.

2. A marked disparity between the low, vulnerable status of these marginal men and the status of veteran team leaders, teachers, and professors who insisted on placing them in the conventional subordinate roles of apprentice assistants.

3. High standards advocated for the profession, reinforced by the "revolution of rising expectations" that were supported by visible gains made by low-income racial and ethnic groups and fanned by the political rhetoric

of the times, that is, the war on poverty, the black power movement, and the student unrest of the late 1960s.

Intern's political radicalization also was reflected in a more permissive educational philosophy and relaxation of classroom discipline. The more aware they became of the way the program was actually being used— to provide assistance to the schools instead of to promote innovation—the more convinced they were that the change they wanted would not be realized through the Teacher Corps. Having lost faith in the one program designed to bring about change, they lost hope for the profession as a whole. Consequently, the interns who initially had been more liberal and more committed to teaching tended to lose interest in teaching during the program. The change that an *individual* experienced in his commitment to teaching was accentuated by the way his peers changed. But there was a slight tendency for interns from better undergraduate colleges to express more commitment to teaching during the program and for women to lose interest in teaching.

As the interns turned away from teaching, a significant number of them turned away from the children, although the shift from the children was not as complete as the shift from teaching. Perhaps this happened because initially the interns were more committed to the children than to a teaching career. As they lost faith in teaching and in the children, many of them realized that integrating the schools without improving them in other ways and without motivating children to get an education was not the final answer either.

The clearer the problems became to them, the more powerless they probably felt. They gave up their incentive to lead change in the system, and many began to "mark time."

Also they became disillusioned with the school bureaucracy and, to a lesser extent, with their school administrators. But ironically, many interns became more sympathetic with administrators, perhaps because they had come to appreciate their problems.

Thus the process by which typical newcomers are assimilated into a profession appears to be a complicated one that involves more than the terms "selection" and "accommodation" imply. A leavening process was taking place. Through a series of dialectics, the extremes were being successively eliminated at each stage of the career cycle. The individuals who remained either accommodated or automatically gravitated to the margin of the profession where they became the likely candidates to drop out at the next career stage. Nevertheless, despite these dual accommodation and elimination processes, if the initial differences between the newcomers and veterans are sufficiently great, the ones who survive the process might still be a unique breed of professional. The fact that the vast majority stayed with the program, despite their widespread disillusionment and the tendency to be radicalized is indicative that the filtering process was not entirely one sided. Moreover, the fact that the men, most of whom were teaching in elementary schools traditionally staffed by women, did not have an exceptionally high dropout rate suggests that they might eventually provide a new pool of liberal leadership in teaching. The question is whether the dropout ratios will remain constant at each career stage.

To summarize: the data confirm other studies showing that trainees for a professional occupation tend to become more liberal during the training program but also become simultaneously disillusioned with the occupation. Up to a point, both of these processes will tend to promote change (1) because the liberals will be supportive of change and (2) because their disillusionment will cause them to see the need for improvement. However, there is probably a point of diminishing return after which the newcomer, if he becomes sufficiently radicalized and disillusioned, will give up on the system entirely. He might continue to press for change through revolutionary actions, or he might withdraw entirely.

The problem is to identify the conditions under which these varied responses will occur. Again, the data provide some clues about who is most likely to undergo these changes and how the change takes place. Radicalization seems most likely to occur among the individuals who are already liberal, especially when they have the support of a liberal peer group. Thus there is apparently a tendency for individuals, in order to fulfill their initial predispositions, to go to the extreme nearest to their original position. The process will be accelerated if they have been led to expect change and then find that change is not forthcoming. The process described here is perhaps the same process by which the "marginal man" and role hybrids are produced; that is, the transitional professionals who represent a *blend* of commitment and discontent, of past and future. These are the people who will help to lead the profession through the transformations that undoubtedly will be demanded in the years ahead.

NOTES

1. It is possible that performance on such tests tends to change with the *age* of the respondents irrespective of their experiences. Since data on a comparative group are not available, there is no way to rule out this possibility.
2. The following will assist the reader in interpreting the regression tables in this and subsequent chapters:

Most people are aware of the hazards of drawing inferences from a simple correlation between two variables; for example, between a person's age and his political liberalism. The correlation could reflect an unidentified third variable correlated with both variables, or it could otherwise be influenced by other "uncontrolled" variables. One advantage of regression analysis is that the relationship between two variables can be examined while statistically matching them on other contaminating variables.

We have assumed that something as complex as change in a person's political opinions or in the rate of innovation is produced by a combination of several variables. The objective is to identify the variables most central to the process, those that "explain most of the variance." The variance refers to the variability in change in belief or in teaching techniques; some people or some organizations change more than others. The power of a variable is expressed as the proportion of this variance that can be explained by the variable alone, that is, how much help this variable would be in predicting the outcome (such as change in political liberalism) from a knowledge of the one variable? The error can be reduced by considering several variables simultaneously in order to account for a larger share of the variance.

In this study, a computer program was used to consider many variables and select the best predictor, that is, the one that would explain most of the variance. It then explored the remaining variables to identify the one that would add most to the explanation, controlling for the first variable entered. This step-by-step procedure culminated in the selected combination of variables that jointly explain a large part of the variance. The combination is the most parsimonious set of variables needed to predict the outcome, not necessarily the most theoretically significant.

In the tables: (a) the "r" column is the simple correlation, without taking into account other variables; (b) the "R^2" column reports the cumulative variance explained at each step of the process; (c) the "R^2 added" column reports the contribution of each variable to the amount of variance explained; (d) the "Final Partial" column is the relationship between two variables controlling for all others in the set; (e) the "Final t Value" refers to a test of statistical significance of the final beta weight for each variable, step by step; (f) the "Final Beta Weight" is the partial standardized for the differences in the scaling among the variables and is therefore a better comparative measure than the partial; and the "F" refers to a test of statistical significance for the entrance of each. When the F is below 3.84, the predictive power of the variable is not statistically significant. In some cases we have reported the nonsignificant variables because it is sometimes illuminating to know which variables did *not* add to the explanation, especially if there was some reason to believe that the variables might have made a significant addition.

When the explanatory variables are highly correlated, the regression technique can provide a misleading impression of their relative importance. This is because the "pooled" variance shared by both variables could be arbitrarily assigned to either variable. Once it has been assigned, the other variable will show up as relatively less important than it actually is. If the variables used to control are highly correlated with the variables being adjusted, the effects of the latter will be largely removed. For example, if the political liberalism of a university faculty is highly correlated with their competence ratings, the decision to enter the first variable into the equation before the second is entered will usually have the result of reducing the apparent effect of competence. However, the regression values are not affected by the order in which the variables are added. Therefore, the primary problem occurs if variables with high beta weights are eliminated from the analysis altogether, which seldom occurred. In any event, attention should be given to the beta weights in addition to the order in which they are entered.

Clearly, then, the procedure cannot be used mechanically. But there is no good answer to this problem when theory is not sufficiently mature to provide concrete guidelines. As a precaution, we have at times "forced" certain variables into the equation so they can act as controls.

Two step-by-step regression programs have been used: a program developed by the Biomedical Department, UCLA (BMD), and a program developed by Jon Cunnyngham, of the Ohio State University Economics Department. It is possible with the BMD program to control for (or partition on) specific variables by forcing them into the regression before other variables have been entered.

CHAPTER 6

An Inventory of Program Outcomes

The great questions of government have to do not with what will work, but with what does work. All that is needed is a rough, but hopefully constantly refined, set of understandings about what is associated with what.

MOYNIHAN, 1969, p. 194

It is not easy to describe the effects of the Teacher Corps program on the organizations involved, the curricula and procedures, and the teaching style and classroom atmospheres. Such a multiple-purpose, broad-scoped program must be appraised on several dimensions. Therefore, a variety of outcomes are considered here and in subsequent chapters.

In addition to the several explicitly stated objectives, latent and unintended consequences must be taken into account. The task of inventorying the outcomes is further confused when superficial changes pass for (or mask) more basic structural change. As already mentioned, such programs cannot be accurately measured against an absolute standard. Even if such a standard did exist, it almost certainly would not take into account the obstacles that the programs must overcome: limited and uncertain funding, local resistance to change, and variable rates of change already in progress in the separate institutions.

Ideally, an appraisal of outcomes should be comparative, and comparative analysis of the Teacher Corps might contrast its positive and negative outcomes with the outcomes of alternative programs that have similar objectives and use comparable resources. However, this is not a comparative study in that sense; the comparisons will be made among subparts of

193

the program. Internal variability in inputs and program quality will provide clues about the conditions associated with different types and amounts of institutional change. In this chapter these internal variations will be mentioned in the most crucial instances. In subsequent chapters they will be the major focus of analysis.

Several dimensions will be considered and, although they are not inclusive, they reveal the major contours of the program. Some of the data discussed here were mentioned in the summary of Chapter 4. Now I shall summarize the outcomes more systematically.

GENERAL REACTIONS

Persons who participated in the program had a somewhat favorable impression of it, but there was evidence of underlying ambivalence and, in some cases, despair. The vast majority of participants (85 percent) believed that their respective school or college should continue participating in the Teacher Corps program after completion of the present cycle; 80 percent said they would join the Teacher Corps again. However, additional probing in the interviews revealed underlying discontent that was masked in these figures. One in five teachers, principals, and coordinators were either negative or not sure about the advisability of their schools continuing; and even more telling, when probed, nearly half of the teachers (40 percent) and one fifth of the team leaders admitted that they would not join again.

A parallel ambivalence was reflected in another set of responses. One half or more of the team leaders, principals, coordinators, university faculty, program directors, and schoolteachers who responded rated the support of the Teacher Corps program by the university and by the school district as "excellent." But interns were less optimistic; between one fourth and one third in nearly every program considered the level of support to be "unsatisfactory" and, in several programs, the figure was higher. Large numbers of interns were uncertain about whether the college or school administration would back them if they got into trouble in the performance of worthwhile Teacher Corps activities. Over one third of them were undecided about the college's support, and only 40 percent felt assured of the school administration's support.

These general impressions, then, present a favorable but ambivalent picture of the program. The complexity of the program undoubtedly accounts for some of the mixed reactions. Therefore, a better understanding can be obtained by considering, separately, the different dimensions of the program.

CHANGES IN COLLEGE PROGRAMS

Nearly half of the college faculty members interviewed agreed (but only 14 percent "strongly agreed") that the Teacher Corps had a lasting effect on their colleges. The proportion varied from 20 to over 70 percent in different programs. A similar proportion of them agreed that the Teacher Corps had some effect on other service programs at the college, but again there was considerable variation. In every program, someone—the program director, coordinator, or some of the college faculty—was able to identify changes that had occurred in the college. However, 40 percent of the faculty members polled said that they had seen no significant program-related changes at their university.

New Courses

Two thirds of the college faculty members and program directors were aware of new courses that had been introduced into the college curriculum as a result of the program (Table 6–1, item 1); one in four had introduced such a course. The majority in all programs specifically reported new courses: courses focusing on the disadvantaged, courses in social studies, or courses that were more relevant to the community. In some cases they covered the sociology and history of minority groups, with interdisciplinary involvement, while in other cases the focus was on "human development." Generally the actual participation of members from social-science departments was minimal and, in the few cases where interns were required to take courses in these departments, the professors had little or no awareness of the program. However, in four of the five second-cycle programs, courses developed for the Teacher Corps were being offered by other departments in the university.

In addition to the new courses, over two thirds of the faculty members said they had modified the content of their courses or their approaches to teaching as a result of participation in the Teacher Corps. Most of them said they were giving more attention to teaching impoverished children or to understanding children from different racial and economic backgrounds, and many of them thought the content of the courses had become more relevant and concrete (Table 6–1, items 3 and 4).

Most faculty members who reported these changes believed that the new materials were useful. However, a strong minority of those interviewed had reservations about the amount of change that actually had occurred. Nearly half of the interns denied knowing of new courses, and one third

Table 6-1 Percent of participants who judged the program responsible for specific changes

		Position										
Type of change	Interns N = 173		Team leaders N = 37		Classroom teachers N = 571		Teachers who have worked with interns N = 60		Principals and coordinators N = 62		Faculty and program directors N = 62	
	Yes	No[a]	Yes	No[a]	Yes	No[a]	Yes	No[a]	Yes	No[a]	Yes	No[a]
I. Change in the college program												
1. The introduction of new courses into the college curriculum?	.32	.41	.50	.11	.09	.17	.12	.10	.36	.05	.68	.16
2. The introduction of new procedures or techniques for training future teachers?	.39	.36	.50	.19	.20	.06	.16	.10	.42	.05	.75	.16
3. Basic modifications of existing college courses resulting in more attention to educating the impoverished?	.38	.30	.61	.11	.30	.08	.25	.10	.41	.03	.67	.13
4. More course work in social studies related to understanding children from different racial and economic backgrounds?	.34	.29	.58	.14	.33	.06	.26	.09	.42	.08	.52	.23
5. More effective cooperation between the local school and the teacher-training program in the college or university?	.16	.50	.62	.16	.16	.14	.17	.20	.38	.24	.53	.15

II. Change in the schools

Item													No Res.
6. The introduction into at least one local school of new techniques for teaching the impoverished?	.57	.21	.64	.17	.30	.12	.28	.19	.54	.17	.63	.02	
7. Far more attention on the part of local school people to problems of educating the impoverished?	.26	.34	.53	.22	.33	.16	.31	.22	.35	.33	.43	.12	
8. More individual attention for children with special learning problems?	.91	.07	.97	.03	.73	.06	.71	.08	.97	.00	.87	.02	
9. More time for regular teachers teachers to work with students?	.67	.27	.78	.16	.66	.10	.70	.11	.88	.05	.66	.05	
10. More teaching personnel now available for regular or substitute classroom instruction?	.41	.20	.65	.17	.31	.20	.15	.12	.30	.12	.39	.07	
11. Smaller class size?	.44	.26	.30	.50	.26	.31	.11	.33	.27	.16	.27	.13	
12. The Teacher Corps provides one of the few means by which poor districts can have special education classes?	.40	.27	.46	.41	.40	.18	.25	.09	.36	.40	.56	.33	
13. The projects started by interns have been effective, useful, and have furthered the goals of education for the impoverished child.	.40	.04	.33	.18	.31	.11	.21	.07	.61	.01	.50	.50	
14. My attitudes toward working with impoverished children have improved since I joined the Teacher Corps.	.65	.20	.60	.41	.38	.12	.25	.25	No Res.		No Res.		No Res.

197

Table 6-1 (Continued)

15.	It is likely that six months after the Teacher Corps leaves this school things will have settled back the way they were before.	.70	.16	.46	.27	.30	.26	.39	.24	.39	.34	.0	.0
16.	The Teacher Corps has had a lasting effect on this school.	.19	.42	.46	.22	.34	.18	.37	.19	.33	.24	.0	.0

III. Problems

17.	More problems among teachers in the schools with Teacher Corps members?	.22	.58	.14	.78	.11	.55	.12	.52	.22	.62	.26	.29
18.	More problems with the local community of the schools with Teacher Corps interns?	.09	.73	.11	.76	.02	.55	.05	.58	.06	.77	.13	.46
19.	Increased the regular teachers' work load?	.10	.83	.05	.95	.09	.56	.08	.59	.18	.73	.0	.0
20.	More involvement on the part of the school in local community projects?	.30	.52	.51	.27	.37	.24	.42	.26	.43	.36	.58	.10
21.	If yes, has this involvement been effective?	.80	.19	.62	.32	.74	.26	.32	.13	.77	.23	.78	.21
22.	Have any teachers not in the Teacher Corps shown more interest in community projects due to the T.C. presence in the school system?	.50	.50	.56	.45	.49	.53	.14	.36	.62	.40	.57	.43
23.	More frequent communication between the school and parents,												

including parents not in-
volved in the school's program?

24. If yes, are there any indications that teachers not in
the T.C. are communicating
more frequently with parents
since the introduction of T.C.
in this school system? .42 .40 .60 .24 .31 .26 .35 .30 .56 .19 .56 .03

IV. Pupil outcomes

25. Less need for regular
teachers to spend time on
disciplinary problems? .40 .60 .38 .61 .31 .69 .13 .33 .16 .35 .78 .22

26. If yes, would you say that
there are fewer disciplin-
ary problems in the school? .34 .41 .48 .36 .27 .38 .27 .42 .45 .26 .35 .08

27. Improved academic achievement
on the part of at least some
children? .34 .43 .32 .45 .31 .42 .31 .46 .34 .46 .56 .19

28. Better relationships between
teachers and their students? .89 .02 .84 .08 .63 .34 .60 .04 .91 .0 .0 .0

    .58 .14 .59 .11 .31 .25 .30 .37 .52 .19 .0 .0

29. Improved attitudes of pupils
toward the school? .44 .20 .49 .22 .36 .16 .38 .19 .63 .16 .0 .0

---

[a] The remainder are "not sure."

199

of them denied that more attention was being given to the impoverished children. More important, in three programs the faculty almost unanimously denied that the Teacher Corps was *responsible* for any of the new courses, and there were only four programs in which the changes that had occurred were attributed *primarily* to the Teacher Corps.

New Approaches

Three fourths of the university faculty members and program directors reported that new approaches for training future teachers had been introduced by the program (Table 6–1, item 2). The most frequently reported procedures were role-playing, sensitivity training, microteaching, and the use of games. Slightly less frequently they reported more field work relevant to the community, greater involvement of university faculty members in the community, more use of interaction analysis, and more independent study.

Again, however, there were important exceptions. Although program directors uniformly reported that new teaching techniques were being used by the faculty of their colleges, in half of the programs many faculty members denied this, and in only one program did the faculty attribute these changes primarily to the Teacher Corps.

Teaching Style and Attitudes

Behind these overt changes, other subtle but fundamental changes were taking place in the demeanor and attitudes of some faculty members. Over one half believed that, as a result of the Teacher Corps, their university had become more interested in the problems of the disadvantaged and that all faculty members had become more knowledgeable about the realities of the problems in the local schools.

Also, over 70 percent of the interns and over half of the university faculty members (a majority of interns in every program and a majority of faculty members in all programs except one) believed that, as a result of the presence of interns in the college classrooms, there had been an increase in the dialogue between professors and students. There were occasional reports of a professor who, for the first time, was reading materials on the disadvantaged, on microteaching, or on interaction-analysis techniques, which he might have considered beyond his sphere of interest only a few years ago. In a few cases, confrontations with interns and other student pressures were forcing professors to read more widely, to expect and to encourage more discussion in class, and to expect penetrating questions from interns. Other professors reportedly had become more defensive and closed-minded after these confrontations.

University Relations with Schools

Three fourths of the faculty members said they visited the local schools occasionally, in most cases observing interns and sometimes consulting. However, only half of them (53 percent) agreed that the Teacher Corps had promoted more effective cooperation between the college and local schools (Table 6–1, item 5). Although a majority of the team leaders concurred (62 percent), only 38 percent of the principals and coordinators and even fewer cooperating teachers (17 percent) saw improvement. In several programs, teachers from the local schools had held nominal part-time appointments on the college faculty. But *in none of the programs were university faculty members conducting classes on the site.*

CHANGE IN SCHOOLS

When asked to anticipate whether the Teacher Corps would make a major "contribution" to the local schools, the majority of respondents were optimistic (83 percent). However, the program directors qualified their assessments, pointing out that any changes made by interns would be limited to classroom teaching methods, techniques or, occasionally, to the curriculum. Generally, school personnel and team personnel agreed that the Teacher Corps would not have very many long-range effects on the school. The interns were the most pessimistic; only 20 percent had any hope of long-range effects, and 70 percent believed that the schools would return to "normal" six months after the interns were gone (Table 6–1, item 15).

Assistance to Teachers

Most of the participants who had observed contributions from the program considered the assistance to teachers that the program had provided. Over half of the participants mentioned factors that would assist teachers: improved teacher-student ratios, other forms of relief for the teacher's workload, and more assistance for individual instruction. Only from one fifth to one fourth anticipated the incorporation of new ideas, methods, or materials; and only 15 percent expected changes in organizational structure of school-community relations. By comparison, the majority of those who felt they were familiar with the program reported that the Teacher Corps was at least partially responsible for providing more time for regular teachers to work with students and more individual attention to children with special learning problems (Table 6–1, items 8 and 9). The majority of interns, team leaders, faculty members, and program directors attributed the latter change mainly to the Teacher Corps. Many interns indicated that smaller classes were a result of the Teacher Corps, but only one fourth of the principals and teachers agreed (Table 6–1, item 11). Also many interns, team leaders, and principals believed more teaching personnel were now available for regular or substitute teaching in the classroom. Again, teachers (and others) disagreed or were not sure (item 10). Many of the teachers who were not directly involved in the program probably were not aware of the assistance that interns were providing to a few of their colleagues. But many teachers probably were expressing their dissatisfaction that even more of this assistance was not being provided by the program.

Large proportions of all groups also felt that the Teacher Corps provided one of the few means by which poor districts could have special education classes, but many others disagreed (item 12).

Alongside the advantages, only a few respondents (including one in four principals) reported that the Teacher Corps had created more problems in the school. There were even fewer reports of more problems in the community or increases in the teachers' workloads (items 17–19).

In short, the presence of interns supplemented the normal activities of the schools and permitted teachers to do things they normally could not do without additional manpower. The question is: Did anything more fundamental take place?

New Techniques

The majority of university faculty members agreed that the Teacher Corps was successful in achieving a more appropriate curriculum for local schools. A majority of all groups, except teachers, said that the Corps had been at least partially responsible for introducing new techniques for teaching poor children (Table 6–1, item 6). Most people interviewed also reported that they had observed Teacher Corps teams using innovative approaches to education (58 percent). The vast majority of interns (89 percent) and team leaders (85 percent) and two thirds of the principals made this observation. There was general agreement that audiovisual technology was being used more frequently (mentioned by 45 percent of those interviewed). Ten to 20 percent of the respondents mentioned games, small-group instruction, individual study, programmed reading, new math, greater informality in the classroom, various types of projects, various ways of presenting subject matter, individual tutoring, specialized teaching, and more relevant and better planned curricula.

However, since less than one in three teachers had personally observed new techniques being introduced and since less than half of the teachers (42 percent) had witnessed teams using innovative approaches, a question was raised about the type of changes that were actually taking place. Moreover, when pressed to identify specific new approaches, only 45 percent of the respondents were able to answer. Of course, the fact that many new approaches did not have names may have made it difficult for the informants to identify them. Nevertheless, there was widespread disagreement about whether real improvement had occurred. One third of the faculty members interviewed disagreed that the curriculum had improved. This figure included as many as three quarters of the faculty members in one program. Few people said that they had witnessed changes in the relationships among the teachers or in the way that teachers performed their jobs (15 percent). Over half of the teachers who said that their jobs had been affected were referring to the fact that the presence of interns gave them more time to cover their subjects. A majority of the informants (61 percent) said that they had not observed major changes in the school's curriculum, teaching techniques, or administrative practices.

Respondents also were equivocal about whether the projects started by interns had been effective, useful, and contributed to educational goals (Table 6-1, item 13). A majority of principals and coordinators and half of the university faculty members and program directors felt that the interns' projects had been effective. But fewer than half of the interns, team leaders, and teachers agreed. However, the fact that interns were more favorable toward second-cycle programs, which had been in operation for several years, than toward the newer third-cycle programs indicates that, with time, the interns might have become more effective.

Seven of 10 respondents who had observed an innovation commented on how well it was working. Nearly half of them believed that it was "working" very satisfactorily (this meant that they had observed improvement in student motivation and attitudes toward school). Twenty-three percent believed students' grades had improved. Half of those interviewed volunteered that they had also witnessed increased self-confidence and fewer disciplinary problems in a small number of children.

School-Community Relations

Although a majority of faculty members, program directors, and team leaders reported that the participating schools had become more involved in local community projects, only one fourth of them observed actual improvement in the school's relationship to the community (Table 6–1, item 20). Interns and cooperating teachers were divided on this question. So were principals and coordinators. The majority of those who observed more community involvement agreed that the experience had been useful, although substantial proportions of all groups—including 46 percent of the principals and coordinators and 43 percent of the faculty members and program directors—did not see much use in it. Opinion was divided about whether the Teacher Corps had prompted teachers who were not in the program to take more interest in community activities (item 22). Responses differed by position and between those in the second and in the third cycles. Opinion was also split about whether school personnel were communicating more frequently with parents. A bare majority of the team leaders, principals, and coordinators felt that there was more communication with parents, but fewer than half of the interns and teachers concurred (item 24). The majority of interns, team leaders, and teachers doubted whether increased communication extended beyond the participants in the program.

Changed Opinions and Roles

There seemed to be subtle, underlying changes in the opinions of the participants and in the way they performed their roles that were not observable to the outsider, but that the participants maintained were taking place. For example, more than half of the team leaders believed their schools were paying more attention to the problems of educating the impoverished as a result of the program; although, significantly, only one third of the teachers and principals agreed (Table 6–1, item 7). There was clearer agreement among team leaders and interns (also teachers working directly with interns, but it is not shown in the table) that their own attitudes toward working with impoverished children had been improved by working in the Teacher Corps (item 14). In interviews, one in three teachers mentioned that they had gained new ideas from the program or had been inspired to work harder.

Student Achievement

Nearly all interns, team leaders, principals and coordinators, and a majority of the teachers noticed improved academic achievement in some children as a result of the program (Table 6–1, item 27). The teachers said this improvement was limited to the pupils with whom the interns worked directly; but most of the principals and coordinators said that the impact extended to other children.

A slight majority of the interns, team leaders, and principals observed better relationships between teachers and their students, although only about one in three of the teachers concurred (item 28). The majority of principals and nearly half of the team leaders thought the pupils' attitudes toward school had improved; more than one in three teachers and less than half of the interns (44 percent) agreed with them (item 29).

Finally, the respondents disagreed whether there were fewer disciplinary problems as a result of the program. Although about half of the team leaders and principals thought so, most interns and teachers did not (item 25).

CONCLUSIONS

The program was intended to accomplish basic modifications in educational practice. It appears that it did not fully succeed. Nevertheless, we can say that, in the wake of resistance in many places, the program was partially responsible for changes of this kind:

- New courses in most colleges.
- New procedures for training teachers, including an extensive internship in local schools and, in a few cases, role playing, sensitivity training, microteaching, and the use of games.
- Subtle, yet basic types of changes in at least a few professors in most programs, including a reexamination of assumptions and usual procedures on the part of some professors, greater responsiveness to students, and more class discussion.
- More attention in the college to educating the impoverished, including efforts to acquaint interns with poverty conditions and more course work in the social studies aimed at teaching understanding about children from different racial and economic backgrounds.
- New techniques for teaching the impoverished, introduced into some local schools, and more attention on the part of some teachers given to problems of educating the impoverished.
- More time available for regular teachers to work with students and more individual attention given to children with special learning problems.
- More special projects started by interns, generally regarded as effective and useful in furthering the goals of education.
- In some cases, slightly more involvement of the school with the community.

• Improved academic achievement and reduction in absenteeism on the part of some children, especially those with whom the interns worked directly.

There was less agreement about whether the Teacher Corps had accomplished the following:

• Provided interns with the teaching skills and competencies necessary for teaching in poverty schools.
• Promoted more effective cooperation between colleges and local schools, promoted joint staff appointments between schools and colleges, induced colleges to hire new types of professors, or effectively capitalized on the team approach.
• Created basic changes in the school-community relationships or stimulated interest on the part of teachers not in the program in community projects.
• Encouraged regular teachers to define their jobs differently.
• Relieved teachers from discipline problems.
• Created more than superficial changes in the content and structure of university curricula.
• Created long-term changes in the school or the university.

This chapter has enumerated the varied outcomes of the program as perceived by the participants. In most cases, there was a degree of consensus. In some cases, the respondents were polarized.

The interns were polarized about problems in the schools: whether teachers not in the Corps had shown more interest in community projects because of the presence of the program; whether more frequent communication` had occurred between school and parents. (On these two items, the teachers questioned were also divided in their opinion.)

Interns were divided over the need for regular teachers to spend time on disciplinary problems and whether there were fewer disciplinary problems because of the program. Again, both team leaders and classroom teachers were divided. The interns were polarized about whether more attention had been placed on the education of the impoverished by the local schools. Principals and teachers who had worked with interns were almost evenly divided on this matter. Only the interns were more negative than positive about the issue.

This polarized pattern is significant. It suggests that the changes that occurred were far from overwhelming (they seemed to represent only subtle, small shifts in direction rather than basic educational reform). Also, in some cases, the lack of consensus reflects differences in the perceptions of the respondents which undoubtedly were colored by their own objectives for the program, their vested interests, and their values. In final analysis, however, much of the divided opinion very likely resulted from actual variability in outcomes in the different programs and in various components within programs. Thus it is necessary to utilize techniques of analysis that take this variability into account. Partly for this reason, the next chapter deals with two extreme cases, and subsequent chapters employ multivariate techniques.

CHAPTER 7

The Teacher Corps Story: Tales of Two Programs

The term broad-aim program is intended to describe programs which hope to achieve non-specific forms of change-for-the-better and which also, because of their ambition and magnitude, involve unstandardized, large-scale interventions and are evaluated in only a few sites.

WEISS AND REIN, 1970, p. 97

The two extreme types of programs described here will illuminate the nature of some of the variations in the program's impact among the different local programs, previously discussed. Whereas the observations and statistical data reported in other chapters provide a cross section of the program—its structural features, personnel, value climate, and the obstacles encountered in innovation—these data, alone, cannot tell a meaningful story. To round out the picture, I have blended observation with statistical and clinical methods to describe what happened in these two programs. My conclusions were reached from the impressions I obtained during several years of field work, and they cannot be fully documented. Moreover, the cases selected are unique in many respects. Considered by themselves, they might give a distorted view of the total situation. Nevertheless, they provide a sense of unity, a concreteness, a sequence of events, and drama, which cannot be accomplished in any other way.

PROGRAM I: *THE SAGA OF SOUTHERN UNIVERSITY*

Of the 10 programs in the sample, the first case most clearly illuminates the prevailing and deep-seated *obstacles* to innovation within educational institutions. I did not select it because it is representative but because it shows the structural barriers to change. Nevertheless, this program has certain features that are found, in varying degrees, in all programs.

The Setting

Southern University, with a full-time enrollment of 1500, was the smallest of the 10 universities studied. Formerly a teachers college, it was one of the oldest institutions in its state, and has continued to be dominated by the College of Education. The Southern town in which the university is located was the smallest town in the sample (population 4500)—outwardly serene and calm, almost bucolic. The state was the least economically and socially developed of the 10 in the sample, ranking forty-second among the 48 continental states on the index of modernization developed by Herriott and Hodgkins (1969). The economy was still based essentially on land and was controlled by a few millionaires who could trace their wealth and lineage to plantation days. The county had an active Ku Klux Klan as well as NAACP headquarters and, because of the integration issue, several FBI agents had been active in the area. Covert racial tensions had been high during the few years prior to the study because the desegregation issue had come to a head. Many of the whites were suspicious of federal programs such as the Teacher Corps. They considered them as programs imposed on them by Northerners.

There was only one other teacher-training program at the college. By usual standards the university ranked low academically.[1] Most of the 10 faculty members in the College of Education were originally from the South, having attended Southern Mississippi, the University of Alabama, the University of Tennessee, and other Southern universities. Two faculty members had been with the university for 15 years, although five had been there less than 3 years. Most of these professors were proud of being known on the campus as a good teacher and, to a lesser extent, of exercising leadership within the college or within their own departments. Only one of them expressed a secondary interest in becoming a nationally known scholar. None of them was interested in exercising leadership within the region or in their national professional associations.

The faculty was socially and economically conservative. Nearly half of

them considered themselves as being conservative; this was disproportionately more than in the other universities in the study; not one considered
himself as being "very liberal" or "radical." In sharp contrast to every
other university studied, in which nearly all of the faculty members believed that it was appropriate for interns to become involved in unpopular
causes, only one professor endorsed this view.[2]

The three local schools that were cooperating with the Teacher Corps
program were three-year high schools, located in different communities
and school districts surrounding the college. School enrollments varied
from 750 to 1050, with student-teacher ratios ranging from 1:33 to 1:41.
School A, the smallest and the one with the lowest student-teacher ratio,
was located in a district in which nearly one fourth of the families were
on welfare. The student dropout rate in this school was a low 8 percent,
compared to 42 percent in School B. School B, with the highest student-
teacher ratio, was located in a district in which 80 percent of the families
were on welfare. Half of the students in that school were doing academic
work below their age level. The third school—C—ranked between the other
two on these criteria.

By contrast to the college (with a 96 percent white student body),
85 to 100 percent of the high school students and nearly all teachers in
the cooperating local public schools were black. But the county superintendents and several of the principals were white. These schools were also
financially depressed, of low academic quality, conservative, and authoritarian.[3] On our measures, the teachers expressed a strong adherence to
procedure, a conservatism about procedure, and an emphasis on discipline.
And they were pessimistic about the intellectual capacities of their pupils.[4]
According to an index of centralization (based on the estimates of teachers
concerning where a variety of specific kinds of decisions are made), these
schools were among the most decentralized in the study. The principals,
whom interns generally regarded as authoritarian, ranked ninth among the 10
programs when teachers were asked to assess their principals' competence.
The principals were also relatively cautious about their public relations.
One principal was adamantly opposed to a student council that interns
had attempted to initiate, reportedly because he feared that it might become linked with an explosive black militancy that was rising in the
community.

Instituting the New Program

A Teacher Corps program was introduced into this setting in the late
1960s. It was a relatively inexpensive program, with a total federal cost

of $4780 per intern, ranking it ninth of the 10 programs studied and well below the median of $6900. A Washington staff member wrote of the program in the early weeks, "The promise is great. The university is ready for change and to serve blacks in the area." Several weeks later another staff member wrote, "It has potential, but it is a powder keg and could blow." Weaknesses, noticed at that time, included the uncertain leadership ability of the high school principals, the lack of realistic university instruction, and an improbability that the university staff would respond to interns' demands for change.

This prophecy proved to be correct. There had been trouble from the beginning. The first program director—the only Northerner in the college and reputedly one of the few faculty members who was well liked by the interns—quit after the first summer because of frustration. His replacement was an insider who assumed responsibility for the Teacher Corps as an addition to his other administrative duties.

The program was initiated and largely controlled by the university. According to the director, the college applied for the Teacher Corps because a progressive faculty had wanted to act as change agents to improve traditional educational training programs for blacks in the area, and the Teacher Corps was to serve as a model teacher-education program for the college. But he did not hide the fact that this financiallly strapped college needed federal money, and lamented, "It isn't a matter of what we want, but what we can get from Washington." Other professors reiterated that the university had applied for the Teacher Corps primarily because of a desire for federal money. Although two thirds of the interns rated the university's support for the program at least "average," other indications were that the interns were not satisfied with the university's level of commitment to the program objectives. The interns were, by comparison, much less satisfied with the level of support from the school principals and teachers, which nearly half of the interns judged to be inadequate or nonexistent. Most of the interns also said that the support from the parents was just as inadequate and nonexistent.

INITIATING THE PROPOSAL. The proposal was prepared entirely by a few administrators in the College of Education. Although the program had the support of a few top administrators, the dean of the Liberal Arts College said that his faculty had been reluctant to participate in the program, once it was under way, because they had not been included in the planning. And many of the faculty members in the College of Education had expressed little interest in the proposal.

Three county school superintendents had been persuaded to participate in the program after the proposal was submitted to Washington, D.C. One superintendent, who said that a university faculty member told him it "was a way to get free teachers," deplored the fact that he was not told that the interns were supposed to develop new teaching methods. Several of the principals also indicated they were specifically requested by the superintendent to participate in the program only after it had been funded. Some of them later attended seminars concerning the program but, even so, they complained that because they had not seen the proposal until the interns had arrived, they knew less about the program than the interns. Two years after the program began, they were not sure what the team leader's duties really were, and the teachers uniformly lamented that they still did not really understand the purpose of the program. It is understandable, then, that one intern wrote, "The school has not laid the proper groundwork for the Teacher Corps program. The public schools were never informed of its true purpose." Teachers in two of the three schools resented the fact that the Teacher Corps had been thrust on them and that they had no choice in whether to participate or in the way the team was to function. Moreover, many teachers denied the need for the program. One principal adamantly rejected a basic premise "that children in disadvantaged areas have a mind that works differently from that of other children."

ENTER THE INTERNS. Late funding for the program forced the university to rely on a national pool of interns, maintained by Washington, in order to have a full contingent of interns selected by the fall. Nearly half of the 27 interns (11) were drawn from this national pool; six of these were from the North. Most of the interns (80 percent) were white and male. Slightly over half of them had majored in the liberal arts, and one half of these had majored in the social sciences. Six of them had taken at least one course in education as undergraduates, but none was certified to teach. They came from higher-quality undergraduate colleges than the teachers in the local schools, judging from an index of school quality based on resources and selectivity. There were marked differences between interns and their team leaders, reflected in a status-consistency index combining racial background, sex, and level of education in this program; the index score was greater than in any of the other programs in the study.

Only one in five interns ranked high on the index of loyalty to the school administration and, although this was relatively high in comparison to interns in other programs (second), there was a large difference in comparison to the teachers, over one half of whom ranked high on this index. One half of the interns regarded themselves as only "fairly liberal" at the time they joined the program; but only one in four considered himself to be "liberal" or "radical" at that time, whereas over one half of the interns in the sample, as a whole, did so. It is revealing that three fourths of the interns, compared to only one fourth of the classroom teachers, considered it appropriate to become involved in demonstrating for unpopular causes. Moreover, the teachers ranked low on the liberalism index, and this was the lowest of the 10 programs on an index of teachers' endorsement of racial integration of the schools; only 21 percent of them scored high on this index.

Fewer than half of the interns planned to teach, and they scored low on the commitment to teaching index. The interns gave mixed reasons for joining the program. On the average, they estimated that approximately one third of their group had entered the program in order to teach; even fewer (one in four) had a high score on the commitment to teaching index. One third were thought to have entered in order to obtain an M.A. degree, and one third because of their interest in civil rights activities. Only four admitted to joining in order to avoid the draft. Every intern estimated that at least half of the interns he knew were professionally committed to public education, although not necessarily to classroom teaching. One of the interns had planned to work on a Ph.D. in philosophy but was attracted by a brochure. Another wanted to work on a Ph.D. in history but admitted he entered the program largely to avoid the draft. Still another intern had applied for a flight commission in the navy before deciding on the Teacher Corps. An intern from the immediate area continued to work as a preacher while attending the program.

Whatever their specific reasons, a relatively high proportion of the interns were dedicated to some kind of change in the society. As one of them expressed it, he had joined the Teacher Corps because, "Unless something is done in this country about the nation's poor, we will have massive unrest. I've come to realize how necessary it is to reach people down at the lower level before they drop out. Social revolution is a real possibility." However, a split developed between a "Northern Alliance"— interns from the North and those with sociology and related backgrounds —and interns from the South, many of whom had majored in education and educational subjects; most of the blacks were in this latter group. Many of the interns from the North came to "save the blacks from the whites," whereas the interns from the South and from nonsocial-science disciplines seemed primarily interested in getting an M.A. degree.

THE FIRST TRYING DAYS. The white community was suspicious of the interns from the beginning. These predominantly black counties had become politically active and were a real threat to the traditional white power structure. In one of the counties the blacks, having elected a predominantly black school board, were being threatened with a legal suit because they had tried to fire the white superintendent. In this tense situation, many whites and blacks alike feared that white liberals from outside the South would not be able to relate to the local situation without alienating the white community. Early in the program, therefore, steps had been taken to isolate the interns from the community. In fact, the university reputedly made an agreement with the local schools to suspend the "community" component of the program, and when a few university faculty members persisted in encouraging such activities, they were asked to resign from the program.

Nevertheless, several interns circumvented these precautions. Some embarrassed the university by attending black churches and cafés. In an attempt to start an after-school course in psychology, which included the topic of sex education, a few interns clashed with several white and black parents when black school girls began staying after school and working with white interns without supervision. Moreover, some black parents objected to "free thinking hippies" teaching sex education. Another group of interns wrote suggestions for the implementation of a court order to desegregate, but the principal refused to consider their plan. Other interns were told to avoid associating with one of the black teachers whose brother was a nationally known civil rights leader in the South. Finally, the fact that some interns had been active in a voter registration drive that helped to elect one of the few black school boards in the South was bitterly resented by some members of the white community.

The school and university took steps to curtail these activities. Several of the interns repeatedly wrote to the Washington office, first to urge that the university be required to restore the community phase of the program as promised in the proposal and, later, to recommend termination of the program. They charged that there was no real commitment on the part of the university, that the program had been ineffective and a waste of federal money, and that the university should be required to put into practice the proposals sent to Washington. Washington replied that any program in this area, even a curtailed one, would be better than none at all.

Seven of the original interns left the program during those first days. One black intern leveled a charge of contempt and racial discrimination against university faculty members and a team leader. An unmarried couple was asked to leave for living together, and another intern was asked to withdraw after his landlord expelled him, allegedly for embracing a black female intern in public. Two interns were judged by an outside clinical psychologist as being "maladjusted," one after he wrote to a government agency claiming that local officials were exploiting the poor blacks. Another left because of illness and excessive absences. Three of the four dropouts, for whom liberalism scores were available, had very high scores (40 out of a possible 45 points). One of the interns who was judged to have a personality problem had a very low liberalism score (20).

CONFRONTATION AT THE UNIVERSITY. The university faculty was not prepared to deal with these articulate and often aggressive Northern students. Although most of the faculty agreed that the experience had been intellectually rewarding, it also had been emotionally taxing. All of the interns and two thirds of the faculty members said that the faculty had perceived the program as being potentially disruptive because of the appearance and attitudes of the interns; the majority of the interns (80 percent) admitted that they had actually attempted to disrupt classrooms. Over half of the interns felt that the faculty members and the team leaders had penalized disagreement; only two of them said that disagreement had been accepted. However, the faculty members considered themselves to be more tolerant; over one half of them said that they had accepted disagreement (but only one said that he had encouraged it).

A two-day strike (a "mini-sit-in") was staged by the interns early in the program. They wanted less structured and more problem-oriented courses, more integration among the courses and separate units, and more individual reading at their own pace. They also unsuccessfully tried to eliminate the thesis requirement and to change the timing of the general exams. They wanted to be involved in planning for the courses.

Underlying these specific issues, there was a pervasive feeling on the part of interns and a few faculty members that the university faculty was incompetent, excessively traditional, and rigid in its thinking. The program ranked ninth among the 10 universities on a measure of interns' level of satisfaction with the faculty; only 3 of the 27 interns were "highly" satisfied. Every intern (and 60 percent of the professors) said he had encountered faculty members who were unwilling to depart from traditional methods of teacher training. Over one half of the interns felt that their professors were less academically qualified than the professors they had worked with in their area of specialization as undergraduates. The faculty was frequently charged with being antiquated and uninspired in its teaching. According to the interns, whatever they had learned was largely a result of their own personal reading and conversations with other interns. While similar criticisms occurred in other programs, nearly three quarters of the interns in this program said that these indictments applied to almost all of the faculty members. One of the interns commented, "The course titles are great, but you need professors who know what they are talking about." They estimated that about half of the faculty had no experience with the poor or that their experience was not current. Many interns believed that most of the professors viewed the Teacher Corps as a "handout"; the professors had little inclination to put much into it, and the ones who tried lacked the know-how. The interns especially resented faculty members who recited statistics about the disadvantaged but who had no personal knowledge of them.

Perhaps this factor was the crucial source of disillusionment: although the interns were prepared for the traditional school system, they had expected more creativity and competence from the university. Instead, they found the course work too abstract, and the professors were no better prepared to deal with the poor than they were. The faculty, they complained, never talked about *how* to implement theories. One intern, when asked if he had been prepared by the program, said, "I don't think that we are really trained in a scientific analysis of what is and what is not effective. We have enthusiasm and desire, but we are not really prepared." Another commented, "We know the theories—we know what's happening; but we don't work on *how* to effect change in the local area." Despite their complaints, many interns remained charitable. A black intern, giving the university credit for trying, said, "I'm not so sure that it's the university which is to blame. It may be a general problem. No one knows how to teach disadvantaged children."

STATUS THREAT IN THE SCHOOLS. Similar problems arose in the local schools, although they were less overt. One fourth of the classroom teachers interviewed said they had encountered problems because of the program. The ever present issue, barely beneath the surface, was: the Southern black teachers, from relatively poor universities, had been seriously threatened by the arrival of white liberals from the North who were better educated but who had not been clearly told what their purpose was. Many teachers feared that they might be replaced; they resented the interns' arrogance in presuming to be their colleagues without having gained firsthand experience. In one school the principal gave interns the responsibility for grading pupils. This had the effect of undercutting the teachers' leverage over their own pupils. The arrival of the Teacher Corps on the heels of student demonstrations also colored the teachers' attitudes. Team leaders openly complained that the interns believed they had all the answers, even though they had no experience with the disadvantaged. It was felt that the interns were too concerned with changing the Establishment and, particularly, with making "drastic" changes.

There was more conflict between teachers and other members of the Teacher Corps in this program than in any of the others. It ranked third in the proportion of teachers who reported that the program had created problems for them. Several of the interns reportedly had been abrasive and insulting to the principal and to some of the teachers. Some of the interns had openly refused to work with their cooperating teachers; they wanted to teach alone in the classroom without the teacher being present. There were reports of overt conflicts between some teachers and interns, in front of the pupils, concerning what should be taught and how it should be taught.

Many teachers reacted to the interns by sabotaging the program. Some requested the interns assigned to them to quit teaching because of their appearance and because they had challenged the teachers' methods and grading systems. Interns in every school said that at least four or five teachers had attempted to make life difficult for them. In one school nearly three out of four teachers were considered by the interns to be "uncooperative" and generally unreceptive to the ideas proposed by interns.

The degree of support given to the program by the principals ranged from opposition to mild neutrality. In view of their dependence on the white community in a racially tense situation, the principals were not in a secure position. At least one principal, although he supported some of the activities, lamented that the interns had come with a purpose in mind and were determined to carry it out regardless of local conditions.

On the other hand, in each school at least one or two teachers were cooperating with the interns, and all teachers were not entirely critical of them. More accurately, many teachers remained ambivalent. Despite the problems a few teachers were impressed by some of the work the interns were doing and generally regarded them as very competent and energetic individuals, if perhaps "misdirected." While the teachers did not believe that interns would make exceptional teachers, they felt that the interns would be better prepared by the school experience than most new teachers. Moreover, the interns did find support to the extent that they were able to relieve the teachers' workloads and were willing to play the role of part-time teacher aides (which was how teachers defined them). Thus, in one school staffed by interns who were from the South, teachers lauded the program, and the principal was very pleased with it. It had caused no problems; the teachers were elated over getting extra help; interns were being used to arrange schedules, to assist with slow pupils, and to tutor; interns had started a new art program, which the principal felt had a very good effect on the school; and cross-age tutoring was being used, in which retarded elementary students were being taught by high school students. At the beginning of the program only one intern felt that the primary objective of the program, as it actually operated, was to provide assistance to local schools but, by the end, half of the interns considered this as the goal.

SYSTEM DEFENSES

In trying to curtail the actions of the interns, teachers and professors used several types of strategies, including stigmatization, isolation, co-optation, and replacement of personnel.

STIGMATIZATION. Most teachers and many professors regarded the interns as naïve, irrational, and disrespectful trouble makers. Interns were often treated as "hippies" or as "outsiders." These diagnoses received official confirmation after a psychologist diagnosed some of the interns as being "maladjusted" upon learning of their letters to Washington, D.C., criticizing the program; some teachers construed "maladjusted" to mean "schizophrenic." Through this labeling process the teachers placed interns in a lower category; it was inappropriate for teachers to be compared with them, and it was unnecessary for teachers to give interns' opinions serious consideration.

ISOLATION. The teachers and the administration conspired to break up the teams in order to isolate the interns. Although a few interns had collaborated on a joint project or two, there were no group efforts, with one exception: a team reportedly worked for a week preparing an assembly commemorating Black History Week that was attended by some parents. The bulk of their time was spent working with a few pupils or teaching, individually, in self-contained classrooms. As one intern stated, "We don't operate as a team, and some of us even work independently of our own cooperating teacher; and even most of the work done with the cooperating teachers is actually carried out independently of them."

At the university or at the separate schools there was no reason for the interns to work as a team. At most, team leaders might hold occasional meetings with the interns and call in cooperating teachers only to discuss specific problems. One principal directly refused the interns' suggestions involving team activities and, instead, assigned them to clerical duties. Of course, time pressures and self-contained classrooms had precluded team work in most of the other programs as well. But in this particular program there was another factor involved, that is, a *deliberate* effort to isolate the interns from one another and from the teachers in the schools. In view of the interracial, male-female composition of some teams, and fearing further trouble, the administration sought to reduce the cohesiveness of the interns by forcing them to work as individuals. The white males in one team were segregated from two black women on the same team; they were assigned different tasks and were explicitly told by university officials not to visit one another's homes again. Other interns were barred from the classroom by the cooperating teacher and, instead, were assigned to work exclusively on one-to-one tutorials in the cafeteria. In one school the white team leader and interns ate lunch by themselves rather than with the other teachers, even though it was resented by the teachers. Partly as a result of this gap between the interns and teachers, the interns identified closely with the students and sometimes sided with the students against the teachers. Finally, the interns were also isolated at the university. Special courses had been designed for them that segregated them from the other students.

CO-OPTATION THROUGH TEAM LEADERS. Another strategy was to appoint team leaders who could control the interns. One team leader was replaced after the teachers, during a faculty meeting, rebelled against his "extremist" outlook, his apparent feeling that traditional forms of teaching were a failure and his innuendoes that Corpsmen were being brought in to replace the veteran teachers. He was replaced by a white teacher who was the only teacher at the school considered to be incompetent by one out of two interns. Interns charged that the team leaders' loyalties were mainly to the school, that their job was to keep the interns in line, and that white team leaders were afraid of black children and, because they knew little about the black community, did not want anyone else to learn about it, either. However, the principals viewed the white team leaders as being "strong enough in their convictions to guide the Corpsmen instead of being misdirected by the more radical elements among them."

The two white team leaders in the program identified themselves as being "fairly conservative," while the one black team leader considered himself as being "very liberal." One of the female team leaders, whose husband was a professional man in the local community, commented, "I'm a conservative about race. I've lived around blacks all my life, but I've never taught them before." She considered the goal of the program to be the establishment of rapport between the blacks and whites and the instruction of black teachers on the use of existing equipment.

REPLACEMENT OF PERSONNEL. Personnel who were most critical of the program were pushed out. Seven interns dropped out during the first year. Several of these were "radicals" who had been asked to leave (in at least two cases because of their community activities). In addition, eight university faculty members resigned because of a rift with the college administration over control of the program. The administration charged that these faculty members did not fit well into the progressive team-teaching procedures that were being fostered and wanted a degree of latitude that would have culminated in a haphazard program. The professors said that the administration was attempting to use team teaching as a method of forcing them to conform to conservative Southern biases and, in particular, to dispense with the community component of the program.

The policy of replacing persons who wanted change with loyalists was so critical to the schools and to the university that it was institutionalized. Two of the three principals in the study insisted they would participate in another cycle only if they could be involved in the selection of interns (as well as team leaders). There was a strong preference on the part of teachers and principals for selecting interns from among undergraduates who would "be more willing to work within the framework of the school to bring about change." Other respondents wanted more black interns; they felt that these interns could go into the community without arousing suspicion among the white power structure and that they would be more sensitive to the problems involved in community activities.

Comparisons of the third- and fourth-cycle interns revealed that these suggestions were later implemented. The fourth-cycle interns were from the Southeast; one half of them were black; and all of them were undergraduates, chosen because of their interest in teaching the disadvantaged and because they were from the local area. According to the program director, Washington, D.C. had advised him to apply for this type of intern because of the national office's concern that a large number of interns were not remaining in the area and because the recruitment of this type of student would upgrade the education of the local people.

As a consequence, according to the professors, the interns in the fourth-cycle had a lower academic standing than the typical education student at the university and were regarded as being intellectually dull, pedestrian, plodding students "with no dreams." It was conceded these interns probably would not be able to pass comprehensive examinations for an M.A. degree. One faculty member stated that the third cycle had included the best students he had ever taught, whereas the fourth cycle consisted of the worst students. Some professors felt that the low academic quality of the fourth-cycle interns would perpetuate the weaknesses in the children taught, but others felt that the interns might make marginal teachers.

Consequences

In light of the system's defensive reactions, what was produced?

EFFECTS ON THE SCHOOLS. Undoubtedly most of the interns were disappointed in their ability to effect basic structural change in these schools. One half of the teachers and principals, but only 10 percent of the interns, thought that the Teacher Corps would have a lasting effect on the schools. On an index of the number of new techniques introduced into the schools and the improvement of the motivation and performance of the children (which was based on the combined estimates of interns, teachers, and principals), the program ranked low—seventh out of 10. It ranked eighth on a similar index of school involvement in community projects. An intern commented, "This school has shown very little commitment to either the goals or guidelines of the Teacher Corps. It is spending a great deal of money for too little an effect." Only one intern felt that he had learned a great deal about teaching from his association with a team leader, and only one in five mildly agreed that he had learned anything from his cooperating teacher. This was a less favorable appraisal than was found in the other programs. Although these sentiments were widespread, a few interns viewed the situation philosophically. They were content that at least a few things had been accomplished, which was more than would have occurred without the program.

The teachers also were cautious in their appraisals of the contributions made by the interns. In the school staffed by interns from the South, the teachers felt that the interns had done a good job; that there had been changes in isolated children; that the children were coming to school more frequently because of the interns; that the children's interest in school had improved because of smaller classes; and that the interns had been useful and interesting to have around. But teachers in the other schools were more reserved. They sometimes conceded marginal and temporary changes in materials and approaches—some of which they considered helpful—and, in other instances, they reported favorable changes in the attitudes of some children. But, according to the principals, the only innovation brought about by the interns was the tutorial work that the additional manpower had permitted; in one case a poor reading student had become an enthusiastic sports writer for the school paper.

Yet it was clear that something was happening. The interns were trying out a few ideas on a small proportion of students in their tutorials, and they had created a new art program, had organized a PTA and a Boy Scout troop, had initiated more tutoring, had taken children on more trips, and had introduced a new grading system. Also the interns had made more use of audiovisual materials and supplementary books, and had encouraged the children to pressure the mayor to repair some of the roads. Furthermore, teachers were able to assign more written work because the interns were willing to grade the papers at night.

In one school a newspaper was started, a reading room was set up, an art program and literary club were initiated, and two students received university scholarships through the tutoring and other efforts of the interns. Although the teachers initially had been resistant toward the program, they apparently were learning to accept what originally appeared to be radical procedures, such as cross-age tutoring among students, free hours for students to engage in leisure reading, a course in black history and literature, and a dance troupe that performed African dances. Interns also were trying to coordinate independent courses in literature and history in order to reinforce what the children learned in different courses. Greater use was being made of films on black literature and history through a video machine borrowed from the university.

The majority of all the groups—even interns—agreed that the Teacher Corps had improved the attitudes and academic achievement of some of the children. Even the interns who were convinced that they had no impact on the system believed that they might have affected some individual students; some of these students felt that the classes taught by the interns were interesting and increased their ability to verbalize. Reportedly the interns helped slow students to improve their academic skills and encouraged bright students to aspire to college. Some teachers felt that the interns provided a needed positive male role in the classroom and that the interns were a favorable model for proper language uses and academic values. Also, since the interns did not use corporal punishment, they increased their rapport with the students.

Beyond this, the interns helped to pave the way toward an integrated situation by breaking down racial stereotypes for the children. The six white interns at one of the schools represented many more whites than the children had ever seen in the school before. Reportedly, some of the children not only were seeking help from interns but were talking more freely with white counselors who were not associated with the program. Some interns had taken black children to restaurants and other places where, formerly, the blacks thought they could not go. They took the children to basketball games and sat with them, cheering for their team.

Of course, the interns were severely criticized for these acts. The teachers felt that the interns were trying too hard "to get down to the level of the children." This threatened the prestige of the teachers and created the risk that the teachers would lose the children's respect. A black girl, who had been working with a white intern after school on tutorials, was reprimanded by a teacher and principal about her moral relationship with the intern. Nevertheless, one of the major effects of the program was to desegregate the faculty, regardless of all of the attendant problems in the South. In fact, some interns suspected that they were being deliberately used for token integration. Beyond the race issue, some of the principals felt that the teachers had been influenced by the broader background of the interns who had come from different geographical regions. Even a principal who resented the interns for looking down on the teachers was, nevertheless, in favor of Corpsmen from outside because of what he considered to be the "educational stagnation" of the area.

CHANGE AT THE UNIVERSITY. This program ranked only fifth among the 10 universities on an index of change in the university's procedures and on an index of cooperation between colleges and schools, based on the estimates of interns, faculty members, and the program directors. One fourth of the faculty members said they had observed no changes. Moreover, there were indications that some of the changes observed would not be permanent. The former program director concluded that, although new courses had been put into the curriculum to meet the Teacher Corps needs, he did not think they would remain. He concluded, "At first I looked at the Teacher Corps as a new way to prepare new teachers. Now I realize that these kids could not go into traditional schools." Actually, in many cases, only the titles of the courses had been changed. Many interns still felt that the content of the classes was not relevant. It was charged that the university faculty members were unaware of many differences that might be required in teaching in low-income areas and that they were inflexible about the available alternatives. Most of the faculty members were local people. Their husbands or wives were employed in the town, and they did not want social change.

Nevertheless, most of the university faculty members agreed that the Teacher Corps had a lasting effect on the college. Nearly half of the professors said that the university had become more interested in the problems of the disadvantaged as a result of the program; most of them felt they were more knowledgeable about problems in the local school.

There are several indications that the university was attempting to expand and otherwise alter its curriculum. The requirement of field experience in the local schools was unique for teacher education in this university. Moreover, two thirds of the professors said they had modified the content of (or their approaches to) the courses, although only two

professors had introduced new courses—one on black history and literature and a psychological course on teaching the disadvantaged. Also,
courses in sociology and reading were now required for people in the program, and a new minor was created in sociology, a subject that previously
had been neglected by education students. Modifications were made in existing courses, including the use of more reading, observation trips to the
local schools, and more discussion of controversial issues in the classroom.
There were reports of an increased use of a materials center, created for the
program, and of the faculty center at the university, which now had a
better supply and greater use of videotapes. Also, the arts and sciences
faculty started a national science program for high school teachers, largely
through the stimulus of the Teacher Corps.

Generally there was better cooperation between the university and the
schools, although it seemed to be limited mainly to the Teacher Corps
project, and there was little reason to believe that it would continue after
the project was concluded. Over half of the faculty members said they
were now visiting the local schools regularly, chiefly to observe interns and,
less frequently, as consultants. The Teacher Corps had paved the way
for the faculty to consult with the schools—particularly in cases in which
they had not felt welcome in the past.

But there was little structural change in this area. Although a few
teachers supposedly had college faculty appointments, none were teaching
university classes for credit; their duties were primarily to observe interns
in the schools. Moreover, the program was creating strains with the schools
that might preclude a continuing improvement. Many local townspeople
resented the increased numbers of black university students who were
being brought into the university by the program. The problem was aggravated by fraternization between black and white interns, which prompted
several phone calls to the college administration.

Perhaps the major change at the university was that, at least for a
time, it had to cope with a more aggressive and brighter type of student
than it was accustomed to. Even the angriest, most frustrated faculty
members saw some benefits. One professor commented that the interns
had acted as college students should act. Another considered the teaching
of interns as the most rewarding experience in his academic life. The
librarian said that the interns used the library more than all of the other
students combined. Professors from outside the College of Education were
particularly impressed with these less docile students.

Apparently it was unusual at this university for graduate students, who
typically enter education through traditional routes after being socialized
in undergraduate colleges of education, to challenge the ideas of their

professors. But the liberal arts graduates, particularly those from outside the region, did confront their professors, and the professors, by their own accounts, were less comfortable with their traditional ways as a result. At least five or six faculty members admitted that they were frustrated by the interns' lack of respect and impatience, and that they were threatened by the interns' assertiveness. They resented the fact that the most demanding interns were also the least experienced and the most radical in outlook. One professor, who considered herself to be a good teacher for the poor, rural, disadvantaged undergraduates was especially shaken by the experience. The interns baffled her so much that she said she could not teach. She commented, "It has been a radical education for me. I'll never be the same. They argued about any and every point. I represented the Establishment, and I guess they didn't like me . . . it was horrible."

As a result of these episodes the professors were more willing to listen to the interns' points of view. Even though the interns did not feel that their suggestions were being taken seriously, the faculty probably was more aware that changes were needed and was more sensitive to the issues than before. The experience had promoted more student-dominated discussion in classrooms, greater use of self-evaluation on the part of both students and faculty, and more independent study. Nearly all of the interns (84 percent) and faculty members (71 percent) agreed there had been an increase in dialogue between the faculty and the students as a result of the program. Most of the interns also felt there was more room for disagreement now than when they first arrived because they had "pushed" the faculty. One professor said that the interns raised more relevant questions and that he was using a different approach, even though the course content had not changed. Another admired the fact that "they always wanted to know how to apply the things that I talked about." According to another, "I suddenly understood that I was talking only about middle-class values in my course."

CAREER PLANS AND ATTITUDES. Although the program may have been a progressive step for the university and the schools, it did not meet the expectations of the interns. They expected more innovation and experimentation and, particularly, a community-centered curriculum that was more oriented toward local low-income black pupils. They had wanted to participate in change. But change had not happened—at least, not in the way they had anticipated—even though the program was a personal learning experience that they considered worthwhile. When asked whether the Teacher Corps had met his expectations, one intern said, "No. We really haven't done anything. I don't feel I've learned anything. I expected we would really get involved and really make some changes, and I expected to learn more from the courses I'm taking."

Consequently, many interns became pessimistic; they fought disillusionment and creeping cynicism. Many, reportedly, were also disillusioned with the children because they could not give them homework and because the children did not ask questions. By the end of the program nearly two thirds of the interns expressed a *slightly lower orientation* toward the students on the index developed for the study, while only one fourth had become more student oriented. Moreover, half of the interns became less convinced of the advantages of integrated schools.

For perhaps 50 percent of the interns who had originally planned to go into teaching, the Teacher Corps seemed to offer a greater incentive to stay in. Although other interns were reportedly dedicated while they were in the program, they really had no long-run intention to stay in the classroom teaching the disadvantaged; when the chips were down, the most idealistic of this group tended to give up. Several of the interns said they would like to have stayed in the school in which they gained their field experience, but they could not get a job offer, partly because of a job shortage and partly because the system did not want to hire liberal interns from the North.

Three fourths of the interns for whom data were available both times expressed a lower level of commitment to teaching at the end of the program than they had expressed during the first month and had changed their minds about staying in teaching. But one in four interns had become more committed to teaching over that same period.

By the end of the program nearly one half of the interns expressed slightly greater alienation from the schools, and more than half expressed a higher level of alienation from the Teacher Corps. All of the interns expressed less loyalty to the administration, and nearly three fourths were less committed to rules and procedures in the schools after the experience. A parallel shift occurred in their leniency toward student discipline; one half placed less stress than previously on the importance of discipline in the classroom, while almost one third thought that discipline was more important than before.

Eighty percent were less convinced that teachers should have more decision-making authority and were less oriented toward their teacher colleagues in general. But two thirds became more convinced of the importance of knowledge as a basis for the teachers' competence. Some of them also had changed their image of the ideal teacher. Whereas almost all interns who were questioned twice originally expressed a preference for the type of teacher who strives to make class interesting and who encourages creativity and independent thought, nearly half of them had switched to another alternative by the end of the program. A few of them also changed their original preference for schools composed equally of black and white children as opposed to predominantly white schools.

One professor stated that the interns were also learning to temper their "house-afire" attitudes with realism. Although the combined proportion of interns who considered themselves "very liberal" or "radical" did not change, nearly half of the ones who initially considered themselves to be "fairly liberal" switched to "fairly conservative" or "quite conservative." Whereas most of them ranked "high" on the liberalism scale in the beginning, only one in three could be classified as liberal at the end. By comparison, for the sample as a whole, over half of the interns showed increased liberalism.

While their classmates were accommodating, a few interns were being radicalized by the experience; one in four registered "more liberal" on the liberalism scale, and about half of those who initially identified as "very liberal" later considered themselves "radical." Although nearly half of them became more compliant in their attitudes toward the school administration, over one third showed an increased tendency to use initiative. One intern, who said he had joined the Corps because he wanted to put his idealism into action, said, "I used to believe in changing things from within the system. But I haven't seen anything changed here in two years. Now I don't believe anything can be changed within the system down here." The Northern liberals seemed to have pushed the traditional Southern interns toward a slightly more liberal posture, while the Southern interns tended to temper the militancy of some of the Northern liberal interns.

PROGRAM II: *THE SITUATION AT URBAN UNIVERSITY*[5]

I selected this second case because it was regarded by the national Teacher Corps office as a model program. Here, I shall use the name, "Urban University."

The Setting

Urban University was located in a major city on the Eastern seaboard, and it was situated in a deteriorating section of the inner city's core poverty area. It was the largest of the 10 universities studied. The College of Education was staffed by 38 faculty members, several of whom had received their advanced degrees from large, well-known universities. They expressed liberal social and political beliefs, and ranked second, of the 10 programs, on the proportion of faculty members who identified themselves as being "very liberal." The college had a reputation for competence and leadership in education, especially in working with ghetto schools. There were at least six other training programs in the college. However, the university as a whole was of average quality, judging from its score on the resource-prestige index; it ranked sixth of the 10 universities in the sample.

The local schools associated with the program were selected by a panel that consisted of the district supervisor, the district coordinator, the program director at the university, and the director of federal programs at the university. The three schools associated with Urban University were elementary schools with enrollments from 510 to 1380. Although the schools were not in close proximity to the university, they were in high-crime-rate ghetto areas. Most of the students in these schools were black (88 percent), and over half of them (58 percent) came from homes at the poverty level, although this estimate ranged from 40 to 58 percent among the different schools. Nearly all of the teachers in two of the schools and more than half of the teachers in the third school were black. Two of the three principals were white.

These schools ranked high on an index of school quality. Although on the index specifically measuring the quality of their undergraduate college, the teachers ranked only sixth among the 10 programs, a high proportion had M.A. degrees from good schools. Most were members of a teachers union. Both teachers and principals expressed moderately conservative political attitudes in comparison to teachers at the other sites studied. In addition, these teachers expressed high loyalty to the administration, showed strong adherence to rules and procedures, and strongly emphasized the importance of maintaining discipline in the classroom.

Of the school systems studied, this was one of the most decentralized. It ranked eighth of the 10 sites on the index of centralization of decision making. The interns viewed the principals as being flexible and technically competent but not exceptionally so. The principals were also rated by the interns as the most supportive principals of all of the 10 programs studied, and all three principals considered themselves to be strong supporters of the program; although they did not blindly support all aspects of it, they were very optimistic about its potential. The team leaders and teachers in two of the schools concurred about the enthusiasm of their principals for the program. In fact, at one school, some teachers thought that the principal was too supportive because he treated interns as regular members of the school faculty. But in the third school there was less agreement that the principal gave support to the program, apparently because he was uncertain about his own role and the role of the interns in his school; consequently, he tried to use the interns for what they called "baby-sitting" duty much of the time.

Instituting the New Program

The program was introduced in 1967 as one of the first programs funded. At the time of the study it was in its second cycle. It also was the most expensive of the 10 programs studied, with a federal cost of approximately $10,375 per intern. At the outset, the national office administrators were optimistic about the program's prospects; in fact, they considered it to be exemplary. There was a basis for their enthusiasm because the university staff was relatively competent and was devoting a serious, cohesive effort to the program.

Nevertheless, by the second cycle, reservations were expressed that perhaps the program was not working as well as had been hoped for. There seemed to be little agreement among the persons concerned with regard to the program's design and its immediate objectives. One intern observed, "Even the Teacher Corps staff can't seem to agree on the goals." Interns and the staff disagreed over the amount of flexibility that should be left to the teams and their right to experiment. At the university there were disagreements over which courses should be taught and how they should be conducted. There were difficulties in getting the commitment of social scientists and other professors outside of education, and there were severe conflicts over the degree of involvement and the amount of time the interns should spend in the community. Some faculty members were criticized by their colleagues and by teachers for not spending enough time with the local schools and for not gearing their courses more directly to what was going on in these schools. Many faculty members doubted whether the program would have any real cumulative impact on the community or on the schools because of the traditional content of the courses and the traditional teaching procedures that were used. Even where the university Teacher Corps staff agreed on how things were to be run, how the courses should be taught, and how the interns were to function in the schools, the staff's ideas were not always relayed to the interns, who persistently complained of a lack of communication between themselves and the university staff. Principals, team leaders, and teachers in the schools also noticed a lack of communication between the interns and the faculty.

INITIATING THE PROPOSAL. This Teacher Corps program was initiated and, to a great extent, controlled by several members of the university. Over half of the education faculty—but only one of the local school principals and none of the local teachers—had participated in the proposal for the program. However, in each of the cooperating schools, principals had been well informed about the program's purpose and, although the teachers were less informed, they were aware of its presence.

Originally, the majority of the cooperating teachers had reacted favorably to the prospect of having the Teacher Corps in their school. But when they were suddenly confronted with a group of interns with little advance preparation, they expressed confusion as to what the program was about, who the interns were, and just what their functions and roles were to be. The reception of the interns varied from school to school, of course, depending on the degree to which teachers had been prepared. At one school the principal had held no briefing session, and the interns did not have an opportunity to meet with the teachers beforehand. A teacher said, "An intern just walked into my room the other day and asked if he could stay, and I said yes." Many of the teachers stated that they were not given a clear definition of the goals of the program or of their role in it.

In other schools a few teachers were familiar with what they were supposed to do; they knew what was expected of them; and many of their doubts had been dispelled by their principals before the Teacher Corps team had arrived. One of the cooperating schools was definitely well prepared to receive this program and its ensuing problems, and experienced few serious personal antagonisms. In this school there was a general feeling that the Teacher Corps members had been well chosen, that they were of high caliber, and that they were well prepared to teach. This situation may have reflected the high opinion of the team leader, shared by interns and teachers; they considered him to be a superior teacher who had good rapport with the children and who was able to arouse their interest.

ENTER THE INTERNS. Only one other site had more interns from within its own region. Only 6 of the 20 interns came from outside the region; most of them were locally selected, but a few came from the national pool. In contrast to the other nine programs, this university had a relatively high percentage of black interns (25 percent) and one of the lowest percentages of male interns (40 percent).

The interns came from high-quality undergraduate colleges, ranking highest of the 10 programs on the measure of the prestige and resources used to rate their undergraduate colleges. By comparison, teachers in the local schools ranked only sixth among the 10 programs on a comparable index of the quality of their undergraduate colleges. However, a combined index that assessed the overall differences between teachers and interns, based on their racial backgrounds, sex, level of education, and quality of undergraduate college, revealed little status differences between the interns and teachers. Moreover, a comparable proportion of interns and teachers (50 percent) ranked high on loyalty to the school administration; teachers, in particular, ranked third on this index among the 10 programs studied. But the interns and teachers differed on the political liberal-conservative dimension. Even though the interns were not exceptionally liberal in comparison to other programs—they ranked fifth among the 10 programs—more of them than the teachers described themselves as "very liberal" or "radical" (50 versus 30 percent). This does not mean that the teachers were blindly conservative in all respects, however. The majority of the teachers agreed, for example, that it was appropriate for interns to become involved in demonstrating for unpopular causes. Also, the teachers were only slightly less favorable than the interns toward racial integration; 13 of the 20 interns had scored high on an index of racial integration, while none had scored low.

Interns gave varying reasons for joining the program. Of the 13 interviewed, five gave as a primary or secondary reason their desire to gain a master's degree. Five said that the Teacher Corps sounded interesting, that it would be a change of scene, or that it would perhaps give them a sense of direction in deciding on their future careers. Most interns thought the program would give them a feel for teaching—particularly in disadvantaged areas—before they actually made the commitment and would give them the needed preparation to be good teachers of the disadvantaged if they should decide to go into teaching. Two interns stated that they had become disillusioned with their previous occupations and hoped to find satisfaction in the Teacher Corps. In contrast to some other sites, none of the interns stated that they had joined the Teacher Corps to avoid the draft.

Many of the teachers felt that the interns were interested in obtaining good training for going into teaching and that they were devoted to the individual children in the program. But other teachers were not so flattering in their estimation of the interns' motives. A principal suggested that many of the interns had "less than ideal motives" for joining the Teacher Corps, including draft evasion and a free ride for a master's degree, and that they were not really committed to teaching in the inner city. Several teachers were dubious about the interns' sincerity. One teacher pointedly said, "The Teacher Corps program is really a good deal—with pay, a short working day, community work, and a free master's degree. I don't think they join out of love for the poor child, mainly because they are well-to-do. I resent them getting a free master's. I had to struggle to get the same thing." On an objective note, only one of the 20 interns rated high on the commitment to teaching index, but 15 showed a moderate commitment to teaching, and only three expressed a low commitment to teaching.

CONFRONTATION AT THE UNIVERSITY. The university faculty did not seem to expect (and often were not prepared for) the aggressive students who had been attracted by the program. They generally agreed that the interns were much more difficult and challenging to teach than other students in the college. The curriculum professors, particularly, found that their entire way of teaching was being questioned again and again by the interns. Interns often complained, "They stand up there and lecture to us about how not to lecture to the kids." Interns also criticized what they felt was a lack of opportunity to participate freely in the classroom, and faculty members were dismayed by what they considered to be the interns' utter tactlessness. A great many faculty members said they were under pressure from the interns to change their class presentations and to use some of the innovative approaches about which they were lecturing.

This situation was aggravated by the fact that the vast majority of the interns regarded only a few of the faculty members as superior teachers, although they conceded that the professors, in most cases, were competent. Perhaps it was because the interns had some confidence in the ability of the faculty (even though they were not considered to be ideal) that they were so persistent in pushing the faculty. Some interns admitted this. They believed their role was to challenge the professors to make courses more relevant for the teaching situation in which they found themselves. One intern said, "We do much to tax the teachers. Our standards are high. We don't give the teacher much leeway. We do not forgive." Although the majority of the professors accepted these challenges, over two thirds of the interns felt that the faculty members did not welcome disagreement and, actually, penalized it. The interns had recommended courses dealing with the language of the disadvantaged child, with social change in the inner city, and courses concerned with the actual teaching of the disadvantaged child. But they felt their suggestions had been resented.

On the positive side, a few interns felt that their suggestions had been accepted and that their criticisms had been encouraged by some instructors. Moreover, despite the disputes, interns were generally well satisfied with their faculty; their level of satisfaction was the highest of the 10 programs in the study. Interns repeatedly mentioned several university courses that were helpful: critical thinking, intergroup relations, children's literature, creative methods, black history, and the reading, math, and science-methods courses. All of the interns felt that the university course work was instructive in preparing them to teach. However, only three of the 13 interviewed thought it was the most important aspect of the program. The majority ranked it second in importance after teaching experience in schools, while one fourth felt it to be least important.

By far the most far-reaching and all-encompassing conflicts occurred over the community activities. The university Teacher Corps staff originally strongly supported this part of the program for several reasons. (1) A general feeling prevailed that change and innovation in the schools would come about only by integrating community work with the curriculum. (2) They believed that community involvement would give the teacher a better picture of the "underprivileged child." (3) Community involvement was a new area that afforded the university faculty members a chance to contribute to a new development and to gain recognition.

The original plans for the program required the interns to spend time in the individual schools, in the community, and in participation in university course work. But, by the second cycle, university faculty and school personnel were beginning to feel that the extent of community activity was overtaxing the interns. They complained that the interns were almost required to be social workers in addition to their other duties. The interns were especially concerned about too many demands on their time and energy. The university staff was accused of pushing them into irrelevant activities. Moreover, the interns were not always left to their own resources but were urged to participate in arranged activities. Generally, they felt that community work was not as important or valuable for training as work in the schools.

Although some principals recognized the advantages of community work, they insisted that the interns should concentrate on the immediate area of the school to become more familiar with their own pupils. The interns agreed. Team leaders were perhaps the strongest opponents of community activity; in some cases, because of personal disagreement resulting from their overlapping authority with the Teacher Corps community coordinator (this was mentioned by all three team leaders). One team leader reemphasized that his job was to train interns to be teachers, not social workers. Interns said that there was a heavy bias toward community work because three of the original staff at the university had no teaching experience.

Although the teachers knew little about the interns' work in the community, many felt that the need for it was overemphasized in comparison to the need for classroom experience during training. However, the interns provided teachers with assistance while they were in the classroom, and this probably accounted for the teachers' reluctance to support any outside activity. The one exception was when the interns worked with individual children after school or in the community. Otherwise, the teachers generally felt that community work and university work were just added loads that were not particularly relevant.

PROBLEMS AT THE SCHOOLS. There was little evidence in this program that the teachers were threatened by the interns. With the exception of the community work, teachers had encountered few problems. None of them reported having personal problems as a direct result of the presence of the Teacher Corps in their respective schools (even though many of them sensed that "other" teachers may have felt some resentment because the interns were in their classrooms or because they did not have interns to help them). They viewed the Teacher Corps as a boon; the interns were of great help to them in their classrooms. Their one criticism was that interns sometimes failed to perform as "student teachers," which was their role in the teachers' eyes. The teachers, in spite of their many reservations, also felt that the interns' experience in the community helped prepare them socially to work closely with the children. The teachers frequently mentioned home visits as being important in establishing rapport with parents. A teacher stated, "Parents fear the Teacher Corps people less than they fear regular teachers. It breaks down the idea that parents are used to thinking of teachers as being above them."

Because teachers were not defensive or highly critical of the interns, they were generally receptive to the new ideas that the interns brought with them. They did not seem to feel threatened by the presence of the interns. Although the teachers may have felt, in some cases, that the interns' altruism was naïve, they conceded that interns were hard-working, concerned individuals and so were very willing to cooperate.

Of course, some teachers had suggestions and hopes for improvement in the future: improvements by the university and by the interns in the school. Their major complaint was that the program was merely a "drop in the bucket," compared to the overall need for educational reform. They considered the program as being "too limited, with too few in it, and even fewer who will stay in the school system." They thought that interns would be better prepared if they were able to spend the entire day in the classroom; they were convinced that "interns are never trained in regular situations, never stay in the classroom long enough. They don't have the exposure to large classes, which is unrealistic in terms of everyday teaching."

Many teachers criticized their intern's inability to control his pupils. Indeed, they suspected that, at times, their own ability to control their classrooms was undermined by an intern's apparent disinterest in having well-behaved pupils. A methods course in "class control" was suggested by one teacher as a means of remedying what she felt was an undesirable situation. When teachers were criticized by interns for being too strict, the teachers said that the interns were simply being naïve and were overstepping their authority to criticize. However, despite their anxieties about interns' laissez-faire philosophy of discipline, the teachers frequently admitted that there were fewer discipline problems when the interns were in the classoom. They attributed this to the greater range of individualized attention permitted when there were two teachers in the classroom and to the fact that interns were not in a position of authority and therefore could afford to be friendlier and closer to the children. The friendliness of interns to the children was a source of resentment, however; some teachers felt that interns had more opportunity to become close to their pupils than they had. The principals generally respected the interns for their rapport with the children.

Consequences

EFFECTS ON THE SCHOOLS. In comparison to the other programs, this one was relatively successful in bringing about certain types of innovation. Although the cooperating schools ranked only sixth out of the 10 sites studied on an index of improvement in the motivation and performance of the children, it was second on an index of the number of new techniques introduced into the schools and on an index of the number of new community projects started. Moreover, while the interns had few illusions about their ability to make basic changes in the system of education, they were generally convinced that they had influenced the system in minor ways. Certainly, the changes they were able to make were largely procedural; they were able to introduce very few new major techniques. Although the teachers were generally pleased with the achievements, they often claimed that they had already tried the techniques, and they did not agree that the Teacher Corps had been primarily responsible for the innovations. Nevertheless, a number of practices observed (novel or not) were not being used in these schools before the teams came.

The change most often cited was a project designed to teach math as a game by using concrete objects; it was based on an open-ended technique. Another change attempted to relate reading and writing more closely to the child's personal experience, for example, by using "experience stories," written by the children, who then read them to the class. Favored by the teachers was the commonly used practice of grouping, in which small groups of children at different levels of achievement were given special work. The teachers were impressed by the ability of this simple procedure to increase the attention of the children and to provide a more individualized instruction. The teachers liked the "inquiry approach" to science and social studies, which was based on the children's questions and their own research instead of on a set lesson plan. There was evidence of increased willingness on the part of teachers to involve pupils in planning their course work wherever feasible, partly because of the urging of the interns. Both teachers and interns felt that this had a stimulating and motivating effect.

Another procedural change that pleased teachers was for interns to relieve them during the noon hour. Whereas teachers were normally required to spend at least part of their 45-minute lunch period with their students, they were now permitted to eat by themselves while the interns took over.

In certain schools, some teachers felt that their pupils had become more motivated and more interested in school as a result of the Teacher Corps. Thus there were fewer discipline problems. Some teachers also reported that absenteeism had noticeably decreased. Of course, the extent of improvement in these areas varied considerably from school to school and from classroom to classroom. Much of it was attributed by the teachers to the mere fact of having another person in the room. But many felt that, in addition to increasing individualized attention, the presence of the intern allowed children to see teachers interacting with one another, which may have helped to improve cooperation among the children themselves. The withdrawn children, particularly, reacted favorably to the presence of more than one teacher because of the increased attention and because of the generally cooperative situation that had been introduced. Teachers noticed an increased motivation, especially for independent research, and they felt that the interns had helped to give students confidence in dealing with materials. They felt that many children now were more eager to come to school because they were able to look forward to doing different things, and to experiment on their own with help from their "tutors." A few teachers reported that the interns were probably among the first groups of whites who seemed sincere to the black teachers and to the pupils. The self-image of the children seemed to have been improved by working informally with white teachers.

Notwithstanding the interns' complaints about community work, they were able to start a number of different activities in the community. After initial suspicion, they met little resistance from residents. The interns who seemed to be most interested in community work, also said that they had been allowed to use their own judgment and initiative in starting activities, although they sometimes followed suggestions of the Teacher Corps staff and their team leaders. Some interns were involved with a local housing group, which advised people on their housing rights and helped low-income residents to find new housing. Other interns worked with a United Veterans for Freedom group, which was founded to keep youth off the street and which maintained a center to help children make personal adjustments. Some interns worked at health centers, at established community centers, or became involved in the local Model Cities program (notably its areawide council, which helped to set up programs for the community). The team at one school helped to organize a buying club in the community, which provided food at wholesale prices to residents. The co-op, which was licensed by the state, seemed to flourish, but the interns had little hope of its survival after the Teacher Corps program left the area.

The university urged interns to go into the community and talk with the parents, especially to familiarize them with other community services available; most interns talked with several parents each week. They also recommended that the interns work for the YMCA and, if possible, attend Board of Education meetings.

Many of the interns wanted to encourage services other than those connected with the school. For example, they believed that all-night pharmacies, more doctors, and all-night public transportation were needed in these particular areas. The interns did much to help community-school relations by independently seeking out the children for such purposes as walking them to public libraries or dancing with them. They often took the children to the library after school, helped to organize a bookmobile for the community, and tutored in homes and at the YMCA. They helped to set up a sewing class in a predominantly Puerto Rican neighborhood and participated in adult-education classes at night. Their attendance at Board of Education meetings was also favorably noticed by the teachers.

However, the interns contributed some ideas that were not well received by teachers in some of the schools. When one team, for example, suggested that teachers should spend more time visiting the homes of the children, they were flatly refused on the grounds there was not sufficient time and that it was not the teacher's place to do this. The same team opposed the practice of using corporal punishment against the children and, in fact, succeeded in having a teacher removed for excessive use of corporal punishment. The interns' frequent attempts to improve individual relationships with the children sometimes brought them into conflict with the teachers, especially when there was reason to fear that the informal approaches used by interns would lead to noisy situations or discipline problems. The presence of a nonauthoritarian teacher figure seemed to have varying results from classroom to classroom. One teacher felt that the presence of the interns had simply caused overactive children to become wilder in a relatively undisciplined situation. But, even here, there were signs of change. In one school, interns felt that the teachers had become less resistant to their informality in the class, even though they still had not been successful in introducing specific ideas.

Another problem was that the teams did not always function as such on community projects; in two schools, each intern worked individually. Another source of discontent concerned the home visits. The interns were convinced that home visits were not sufficiently integrated into the program and that the full potential of this aspect of the program was not being realized. They were convinced that more could be done to help parents assist their children, and that the interns and teachers could learn much about the children and community problems from their association with parents.

CHANGE AT THE UNIVERSITY. There was more change at this university than in most of the others studied; only one other university had a higher rating. It also ranked first on an index measuring improved cooperation between the schools and the university. Most of the faculty verified that changes had taken place and predicted that the innovations would last as long as the Teacher Corps program was there. But many faculty members questioned how long the changes would persist, and some members doubted whether all changes were positive. Some of the faculty stated that they had made individual changes in their course presentations and curriculums. Several others felt that their individual attitudes had moderated; they had become more tolerant and more aware of what was happening "out there" because of contact with the interns.

Some of the faculty stated that new courses had been introduced as a result of the Teacher Corps, including a few courses that were being taught in regular teacher-preparation programs. These included a course in intergroup education and several workshops. Also, some courses designed for this program were being taught to all liberal arts majors at the university. Some of the Teacher Corps staff were taking part in other new projects, including the establishment of two individual schools staffed almost entirely with Teacher Corps interns and graduates. Some of the faculty members said that their experiences in the Teacher Corps had sharpened their qualifications and that they were in more demand as consultants outside and within the university, whereas previously they virtually had nothing to do with the local schools.

Of course, other faculty members were skeptical about the changes that had occurred. Two members, who had been given a rough time by the interns, found it very difficult or impossible to adjust to the interns' aggressiveness and, as a result, were negative toward the program. They believed that because the program had been disseminated through the university system, it had essentially no innovative impact on the schools. Also, dealing with aggressive interns in their classes had rattled them so much that they stated they would never teach Teacher Corps people again. But even the faculty members who were most skeptical about the program admitted they were reconsidering their teaching and were taking into account the interns' opinions in evaluating their teaching and in finding ways to improve it. Although this evaluation was not always solicited, some of the faculty members were beginning to ask the interns to work with them on improving their courses. Some conceded that they would not have felt sufficiently pushed by the typical student to reevaluate the courses themselves.

Opinions differed as to whether the changes would last. The director was confident the program would be retained even without federal support because it was so well incorporated into the university. "The various components will remain," he said; extension to the undergraduate level had already been planned. Courses also would remain. But he felt that the student financial-aid aspect might be dropped. The faculty was less optimistic. One member conjectured that nothing would be retained; another member thought that the program would be slowly "squeezed out." Others speculated that the Teacher Corps staff would be absorbed into Urban University's faculty so that everyone would benefit. The teachers and professors concurred that the interns initially had been more impatient for change but had "toned down" considerably, especially after a few of the most radical dropped out early in the program.

INFLUENCE ON THE INTERNS. The interns' commitment to teaching was a point that concerned many teachers and professors because the Teacher Corps did not require its graduates to teach in impoverished areas. Nevertheless, 70 percent of the interns maintained that they planned to teach in low-income schools. Generally, they felt adequately prepared for teaching the disadvantaged and better prepared than most graduate students. Many of them believed that they could function as agents of change after leaving the program.

However, none of 13 interns interviewed felt that the program had met his original expectations, although some of them conceded that they had probably expected too much. Although they felt their Corps training had been very valuable in preparing them for teaching, they were convinced that in some areas they were inadequately prepared for teaching in a low-income school. More concrete methods and teaching techniques were needed, they said, in ways to deal with problems of discipline. Some interns charged that they had not been trained well enough to teach children and that too much emphasis had been placed, instead, on working in the community.

CONCLUSIONS

The two cases described here represent extremes in several respects. They also exhibit some features in common. A certain amount of innovation occurred in both settings, but the resistance was greater and the rate was slower at Southern University than at Urban University. It is instructive to review the characteristics of these programs to understand better the forces that produced the patterns of change and resistance to change.

1. The programs were located in very different settings: one in a rural, small, traditional town, based on a backward economy in which there was a high level of suspicion of outsiders and of federal intervention; the other in a large, cosmopolitan, and dynamic metropolis. Although both communities served black ethnic minorities, in the rural program the blacks were extremely poor and were only beginning to overtly challenge a long tradition of suppression and subjugation; many whites and blacks alike questioned the need for educational reform and the wisdom of a special program for the black community. By comparison, in the urban program it was taken for granted that the black community, which had political power, deserved better schools. The program at Southern, therefore, had been thrust into a precarious, politically tense situation in which the objectives of the program found little support.

2. The respective colleges of education reflected these different social climates. The aggressive, cosmopolitan, and politically liberal faculty at Urban University was a sharp contrast to the locally oriented, conservative faculty at Southern. Southern University's need for outside financial resources was instrumental in its faculty's decision to apply for the program. By contrast, the wide range of training programs for low-income people already instituted at Urban University was evidence of greater commitment on the part of this university to improving education for the poor. Similarly, there was a qualitative difference in the schools cooperating with the universities. In both cases the school systems were decentralized and the administrations were relatively authoritarian; also,

the teachers in the schools associated with both programs were n
especially liberal, but the teachers at Southern were the more conservative.

3. In both cases the program was instituted by a few university faculty
members without widespread participation of the local school personnel.
However, at Urban there was more faculty participation; more concerted
effort was made to inform the participants in the schools about the nature
of the program. Moreover, the principals were regarded as more competent than those in Southern's program, and they were far more supportive.

4. A somewhat different type of intern had been attracted to each
program. Although the interns in both programs had come from far better
undergraduate colleges than the teachers in the local schools, the *disparity*
was probably greater at Southern. Moreover, at Southern there were more
very liberal, white, male, liberal arts graduates from outside the region
who were bent on social reform. The interns at Urban, on the other hand,
seemed to have a longer range commitment to teaching in low-income
schools.

5. In both programs there were confrontations between the interns
and the university faculty members who, in each case, were unprepared
for these aggressive, critical, and assertive students. In both programs the
interns considered it their role to act as gadflies, challenging the university
faculty to apply their skills more effectively and more fully to teaching in
low-income schools. In neither case did the interns find that the faculty
welcomed disagreement, but at Urban the interns had more confidence in
the ability and willingness of the faculty to improve. This confidence,
together with the fact that the interns were less radical than those at
Southern, accounts for fewer of the clashes being disruptive.

6. In both programs the most serious controversies arose over activities
in the community, but there were different sources of resistance. At
Southern, with its politically sensitive climate, powerful figures in the
community, together with the university administration, monitored,
throttled, and eventually eliminated most community activities. At Urban,
local community support ranged from passive to supportive, and the university was aggressively pushing activities. In this case the teachers and
interns resisted this phase of the program (with the exception of home
visits) largely because of its time-consuming nature and the ambiguous
objectives of most activities, and also because they were more committed
to teaching and believed that classroom experience would be more valuable. These differences probably reflect the previously noted difference
in the political orientation of both interns and faculty members in the two
programs as well as the higher commitment to teaching on the part of
interns at Urban.

7. Whereas the interns were a threat to the black classroom teachers at Southern, who had been prepared at low-quality undergraduate colleges in the South, they were less of a threat to the relatively well-trained and highly organized black teachers at Urban. A high degree of confidence and power on the part of teachers and team leaders at Urban, coupled with a less radical group of interns, produced fewer problems for the teachers and less conflict in the local schools. On the one hand, these conditions inclined the interns to accept a status subordinate to the teachers and the administration. On the other hand, because the teachers were not threatened and defensive, they were willing to entertain and sometimes support the interns' ideas—not as frequently as the interns would have liked, but frequently enough to give them a sense of accomplishment.

8. Finally, because of these different profiles, change in the two programs came about in different ways and the interns played different roles in the change process. At Urban, the changes that were implemented represented cooperative ventures between the university faculty, interns, and classroom teachers; whereas, at Southern, some of the changes occurred only because of the aggressive insistence on the part of the interns. At Urban, where the program was well supported by the administration, not only was there less need for pressure to be applied but the interns would have been no match for the competent, well-organized teachers; and besides, the interns' commitment to teaching made confrontation somewhat risky. At Southern, although there was strong resistance to change, the interns had some leverage, not only because they were less committed to teaching and thus willing to take the risk, but also because of their superior educational and social status and their outside point of reference.

Thus, in final analysis, the interns were probably more influential in precisely the situation that was less amenable to change from other sources. Conversely, more change occurred where there were more forces working with the interns in favor of change, even though in these situations the interns themselves were only one of many contributing factors. Some of these general observations about sources of variability in the program are examined in more detail in Chapters 8 and 9.

NOTES

1. The university ranked ninth of the 10 in the study on an index of quality based on its resources, such as the proportion of Ph.D.'s, number of books, student-teacher ratio, and the selectivity of its admission policy (Nash, 1969; Cass and Birnbaum, 1970).

2. One group of the faculty was behind a new private elementary school in the town, stating that their children could not obtain quality education in schools that were 80 percent black. But they were reluctant to subscribe to the other "red-neck" private schools in the area designed primarily to avert desegregation. Nevertheless, at least for the time being, the school would be de facto segregated.

3. Three fourths of the pupils came from homes at the poverty level, more than in any of the other systems in the study. The schools also ranked low (ninth out of the 10 programs) on an index of the quality of the school developed for the study (based on ratings by interns and teachers of the competence and attitudes of teachers and the quality of curriculum and decision-making procedures). Over three fourths of the interns and two of the three team leaders in this program expressed dissatisfaction with the level of competence of most of the teachers, with their attitudes toward students, and with the quality of curriculum. These teachers ranked eighth of the 10 programs on an index of the quality of their undergraduate colleges, based on their resources (e.g., percent of Ph.D.'s) and selectivity (Nash, 1969; Cass and Birnbaum, 1970). Teachers in this part of the United States also achieved the lowest "verbal ability" scores of any location in the country in the USOE *Equality of Educational Opportunity* survey (Coleman et al., 1966).

4. Nearly two thirds of them ranked high on a rules and procedures index used in the study (the highest proportion of any of the ten cities in the study) and over one half of them ranked high on an administrative orientation scale (the third highest in the sample). They were sixth on an initiative scale. None of the teachers in this town belonged to a union.

The schools ranked ninth out of the 10 in the study on an index of flexibility and readiness for change based primarily on the opinions of interns about their opportunity to engage in experimental and innovative activities; the interns also rated as low the administration's willingness to encourage teachers to engage in innovative activities (over one half were dissatisfied on both counts).

The teachers scored highest of the 10 programs on an index measuring the extent to which they emphasized discipline in the classroom. Only slightly more than half of them said they prefer the type of teacher who stresses making classes interesting and encourages independent thought and creativity among their students, which ranked them lowest in the sample on this index. Sixty percent of them agreed that there are some groups who cannot be taught, the highest program in the study; and fewer than 10 percent of them estimated that nearly all of their students were capable of graduating from high school, the lowest in the study.

5. This case study was prepared with the assistance of Kathy Hudson, who is a research assistant on the Teacher Corps study.

IV

Theoretical Implications for Organizational Structure and Change

CHAPTER 8

Technological Change in Organizations

A science moves from the possible to the plausible to the probable.

BORGATTA, 1966, p. xii

To give a more systematic, theoretical consideration to the relation of variable outcomes of the program and the circumstances under which it operated, this chapter focuses on the fundamental issue of how to deliberately change social organizations, drawing inferences from the data pertaining to this program. Here we attempt to systematically assess the consequences of introducing liberal newcomers into a profession in comparison to other alternative strategies. However, it is not possible to demonstrate, with the data at hand, what "causes" innovation to occur; we can only identify some of the myriad of conditions associated with change or the lack of it. Therefore, the interpretations and inferences about cause have been supplied ad hoc, and the reader should supplement the interpretations with his own insights.

Several alternative strategies for change will be identified from the literature. Then a set of indicators reflecting the various strategies, or combinations of them, will be selected. The relative explanatory power of each alternative will be compared through a statistical analysis of the extent of technological innovation that occurred in the 42 schools in the study. Finally, one type of variable—the regional and community setting of the program—will be analyzed in detail.

Some of the data will be analyzed through step-by-step regression-analysis procedures. At each step the computer programs used, select, from the available variables not yet entered in the equation, the one that accounts for the most variance (i.e., that adds the most to the R^2). This results in a cumulative, multiple correlation. The order in which each variable is added reflects its relative explanatory power, the important consideration being its relative contribution to the total correlation. However, when several variables are highly correlated, the order selected by the program is likely to be arbitrary. In that event it is necessary to control for certain variables by forcing them into the regression in an order based on prior knowledge or theory.

APPROACHES TO CHANGE

There have been few studies of *deliberate* efforts to change *organizations*. However, *unplanned, crescive, social* change has been a major preoccupation of the classical and modern theorists. Several distinct (sometimes overlapping) approaches can be identified that can serve as guidelines for approaches to organizational innovation.

The Diffusion Approach

The diffusion approach focuses on the combined effects of the personal characteristics of individual members and the structure of informal communication (Tarde, 1890; Kroeber, 1944; Berelson and Steiner, 1964; Rogers, 1962; Menzel, 1960; Riley and Riley, 1962). Most of the literature in this tradition bears the marks of Tarde's early conception of change as a process of mental influence, involving imitation and invention and occurring in three steps: repetition, opposition, and adaptation. Recent writers have stressed that certain personal characteristics of "gatekeepers," or boundary personnel, and other key members of the system have a critical influence on the rate and direction of change, such as their tenure in the system, their liberalism and support for innovation, and their technical, administrative competence.

The first members of a system to adopt are usually young, of high social status, and liberal and cosmopolitan (Berelson and Steiner, 1964; Rogers, 1962). It can be conjectured, then, that organizations comprised largely of persons of this kind will be more receptive to innovations than they would be if their members were older, more conservative, and locally oriented. This is especially true of the personnel in gatekeeping positions of authority where information is received and filtered in a two-step process

(Menzel, 1960; Riley and Riley, 1959). Their tenure in the organization, their liberalism, their support for the innovation, and their technical administrative competence are important forces for change.

The Socialization Approach

Classical and contemporary writers have been preoccupied with the assumption that a society is largely a product of the way it socializes its children; individuals are taught to adjust to their social surroundings (Cooley, 1922; Mead, 1934; Dewey, 1922; Baldwin, 1911; Giddings, 1897; Thomas and Znaniecki, 1918–1920). A prevailing strategy of innovation, therefore, is to modify the process through which the members are socialized into a system. The evidence regarding adult resocialization is equivocal, however, especially evidence bearing on the impact of college and professional schools on the attitudes and values of students that might make them more receptive to change (Jacob, 1957; Barton, 1968; Clausen, 1968; Rose, 1963).

Although there is evidence that the amount of professional training teachers have received is positively associated with their willingness to try new techniques (Ross, 1958), there is also evidence that students tend to become disillusioned (Becker and Geer, 1958; Lortie, 1959) and to lower their expectations during their training period and upon realization of their first job (Corwin, Taves, and Haas, 1961). It has been suggested that the closer the working relationship between the training program and the setting in which the profession is practiced, the greater is the program's potential to act as a stimulus for change in practice. Also, it is reasonable to expect that the incentive for change will increase with the competence of the socialization agents and the quality and flexibility of the institutions involved.

The Replacement Approach

Still assuming that the personal characteristics of the individuals involved provide a key to change, another alternative is to recruit new outsiders whose backgrounds and experiences differ from those of the typical member. Pareto (1968) argued that the receptivity of a social system to change depends on the outcome of perennial struggles between governing and nongoverning elites (the latter composed of capable people not in positions of power). Simmel (Wolff, 1950) called attention to the "objectivity" that the sociological "stranger" could bring to a situation. As a man without a sense of the history of the group and yet who is marginally committed to it, the stranger can be critical of the group's practices while bringing fresh perspectives and ideas that can spark a new direction. Conflict arising from differences between unconventional outsiders and members of the host system can be presumed to force compromise and, hence, change. This implies that the greater the difference between newcomers from the outside and the insiders, the more innovation there will be. There is evidence that recruitment at the administrative level is crucial (Gouldner, 1954; Carlson, 1962).

It has been maintained that administrative support is a necessary condition for the success of an innovation (Ginzberg and Reilly, 1957; Clark, 1970) and that it is easier for change to occur from the top down than from the bottom up (Griffiths, 1964). Instances have been described of failure of innovations, even when supported by subordinates, because of lack of necessary administrative action (Gross et al., 1968). Thus, it can be expected that the extent of change produced by an innovation will be directly associated with the amount of administrative support for it.

Some writers have argued that administrative support for change will be inversely related to the chief administrator's longevity in the organization. However, other writers have questioned whether recruiting new leadership necessarily promotes change (Guest, 1962). They have doubted whether the persons in control will always have the monopoly of power necessary to control change (Lipset et al., 1956; Selznick, 1949); whether these persons are as influential as is sometimes supposed; or whether they will support change in view of their responsibility for maintaining the continuity and stability of the system and their concern with boundary maintenance and hierarchy (Barnett, 1953).

Administrators can promote change only to the extent that their subordinates accept the intent of the new program and are willing to cooperate in it. Thus, some writers conclude that basic changes seldom come from the group in control (Berelson and Steiner, 1964; Carlson, 1962; Marris and Rein, 1967). In view of the power of the lower participants (Mechanic, 1962), deliberate recruitment of a critical mass of unconventional subordinates from nontraditional sources might be a better way to promote change (Clark, 1960). Also, when recruitment is not restricted to specific territorial boundaries, there is greater probability that the new recruits will hold conceptions divergent from those held by persons already in the system.

Organizational Differentiation

Although the debate about the importance of officials and subordinates in the change process has introduced a structural element, the preceding approaches do not give sufficient importance to structure. By contrast, drawing on the traditions of Marx, Weber. and Durkheim, several writers have proposed that unplanned social change is more likely to occur in large, heterogeneous, specialized, complex contexts than in smaller, homogeneous ones (Berelson and Steiner, 1964; Carroll, 1967; Aiken and Hage, 1968; Thompson, 1967); that specialization creates new spheres of autonomy, which contribute toward flexibility (Durkheim, 1933); that a large number of linkages in complex organizations require compromise (Loomis, 1959); and that a wide diffusion of uncertainty encourages adaptive behavior (Thompson, 1967). Burns and Stalker (1961) have argued that the existence of diverse types of professionals in an organization promotes innovation, but only if the division of labor is highly coordinated so that their tasks are integrated into a coherent program. Aiken and Hage (1970) and, earlier, Cillie (1940) identified several structural properties closely associated with the rate of program change in welfare agencies and in schools. However, even if innovations tend to be proposed more frequently in complex organizations, Wilson (1966) and Sapolsky (1967) have pointed out that there are more sources of resistance in such organizations, thus reducing the probability that a given innovation will actually be adopted in its original form. Of course, this does not preclude the possibility that, even when innovations do not succeed as planned, they can be adapted piecemeal (Evan, 1967); thus they may promote unplanned change (Clark, 1968).

In the organic model proposed by Burns and Stalker (1961) the decision-making structure assumes vital importance. In this model decision making is diffused throughout all levels. They contend that in innovative organizations authority tends to be spread among the members in a network fashion without rigid task definition. However, some observers have argued that innovation falling outside the province of any department will take place at the top levels of a federal type of organization (March and Simon, 1958; Carroll, 1967). The decision-making hierarchy also takes precedence in the "power equalization" model, which is based on the premise that subordinates are more likely to support an innovation when they have participated in decisions concerning it (Greiner, 1965). Participation is viewed as a way of minimizing alienation (Leavitt, 1965). Aiken and Hage (1968) reported that participation in decision making was the one variable most closely related to program change when other variables were controlled. This literature suggests that the amount of change produced by an innovation will be positively associated with the frequency of the organization members' participation in formulating the program.

In sum, the relevance of this stream of literature to deliberate change is its implicit suggestion that the success of an innovation can be influenced by the type of target system selected and the way it is introduced; that it will be more successful when introduced into large, decentralized, complex organizations than when introduced into smaller organizations.

Economic Surplus

In line with classical conflict theory, the economic basis of organization is often presumed to be the prime determinant of the rate and direction of change. In modern versions it is advocated that "organizational slack" or risk capital be provided to help organizations absorb the economic costs of innovation (Guetzkow, 1965). This implies that technological innovation is a direct function of the level of funding.

Status Maintenance

An important type of cost not directly reflected in economic calculations is the extent to which social status, power, esteem, and related rewards must be redistributed in order to accommodate the innovation (Thompson, 1967). It might be computed as the product of the *number* of persons whose prestige or influence is threatened by a proposed change and the *degree* of the threat. This implies that the greater the group's influence and status security—as reflected in factors such as its control over the innovation, the strength of the organization among its members, the level and quality of the formal training of its members, and their tenure in the organization—the less threatening the innovation will be and, hence, the more receptive the organization will be to it.

Environmental Contexts

Another approach to change stresses the importance of the organization's sociohistorical context. Some writers believe that the pressures to innovate derive largely from outside forces in the environment (Terreberry, 1968; Becker and Stafford, 1967; Evan and Black, 1967). The outside environment includes other organizations; change in one organization can affect the rate and direction of change in other organizations closely linked to it (Turk, 1970; Evan, 1965; Litwak and Hylton, 1962; Aiken and Hage, 1968). One of the major barriers to change in an organizational society is presumed to arise from the division of labor among organizations through which they separately exercise only segmental influence over complex problems. It follows that a coalition of organizations, which can bring to bear a range of skills, influence, and other resources, can be a force for change.

Wayland (1964) describes how the interorganizational networks in education have blocked change, whereas Clark (1965) describes a case in which a coalition of powerful organizations was instrumental in producing curriculum reform.

The success of an innovation will be a function of both the degree of incompatibility between two systems and their rate of interaction; for a given level of incompatibility, the probability of an innovation being successful seems likely to increase with the rate of interaction. Two primary types of relationships can be distinguished under which one organization may act as an incentive for change in another: competitive and symbiotic. In the first case, change in the structure of one organization can be induced by introducing a competitive structure either within the organization or in its environment; each organization is forced to make adjustments in order to remain competitive with the other. In the second case, two types of mutually beneficial symbiotic relationships among dissimilar systems can be identified: a confederative organizational setting and role-blending, or "hybridization" produced by overlapping memberships (Ben-David, 1966). In either case, conceivably, organizations dependent on other organizations that themselves are undergoing change will be forced by exigencies of survival to make rapid adjustments and thus to be receptive to innovation. Following the same reasoning, it might be expected that an innovation will be more successful if it is introduced in an organization that has a history of innovation than if it is introduced into one that has not been innovative in other respects (Putney and Putney, 1962).

Also, the general cultural demographic context must be taken into account. Organizations are not shaped simply by their internal structures and processes. They are *open* systems, subject to the pressures unique to the region and community in which they are located, thus taking on the color of their immediate surroundings. Some of the research on the modernization of nations has demonstrated that organizations have different forms in the developing and advanced nations (Farward, 1970). There is also evidence that school systems in the United States exhibit differing degrees of professionalization and effectiveness, depending on the level of economic development of the region in which they are located (Herriott and Hodgkins, 1969). Indeed, there are many striking parallels between the process by which organizational innovations are adopted and the process of political and economic modernization in total societies. In both cases the system evolves highly differentiated structures to deal with an increasing range of problems (witness the wide variety of schools that comprise the system of education). In neither case is evolution continuous or linear; instead, changes occur at different rates in various segments of the system, producing lags between the more and less modern segments (Eisenstadt, 1964). And, as in the case of modernized societies, it appears that some segments of even moderately complex institutions are able to preserve traditional forms by developing autonomy and finding special "niches," or by developing a symbiotic relationship with higher systems (Parsons, 1964) (as exemplified by some rural schools). Prompted by what Parsons calls "fundamentalism," or the resistance to change anchored in traditional value systems, organizations (like societies) usually guard their boundaries from outside control. Accordingly, they attempt to limit changes to purely technical matters that can be easily adapted within the present framework, and they avoid innovations that require basic changes in the organization itself.

Since modernization occurs within and between societies (Eisenstadt, 1964), studies of particular nations, in which internal variations will be magnified, can help to identify the role that various organizational structures play in the innovation process. Although separate principles eventually may have to be used to explain change in advanced societies and in those still at the outset of modernization, a case study of an advanced nation can be illuminating. By confining the analysis to one nation, it is possible to limit the number of variables involved at any one time, and case methods can help to identify the most sensitive variables which, if they explain limited ranges of variance within a nation, will also provide clues for cross-national research.

Toward a Synthesis of Different Theories

This abstract enumeration of different strategies, of course, does not do justice to the complexity of the actual experimental programs, which are likely to employ several strategies either simultaneously or from one time to another. Conceivably, the effects of a strategy will vary depending on (1) how it is combined with certain other strategies, (2) the level of the system where it is first introduced, and (3) the type of change desired. For example, a strategy that combines an environmental dimension (such as changed interorganizational relationships) with an internal dimension (such as the reduction of status threat) might be more effective than a strategy that combines several strategies that deal with the internal dimension or with only the external dimension. Also, some strategies (such as reducing status threat) would be more effective with subordinate levels of organization, while others (such as the diffusion and replacement approaches) would be more successful with higher levels of administration. Finally, different strategies might be more or less effective with different types of change. It is possible, for example, that an attempt to introduce new methods of reading would be less threatening to teachers than a plan to use cross-age teaching methods, making the status-reduction strategy more appropriate in one case than in the other. Although the analyses here do not simultaneously take into account all of these facets of the problem, they should be kept in mind. Factor analysis procedures are at least helpful in dealing with the first type of problem, that is, the effects of combining different approaches.

With these reservations in mind, the above discussion suggests that an organization can be more easily changed:

- If it is invaded by liberal, creative, and unconventional outsiders with a fresh perspective.
- If the outsiders are exposed to creative, competent, flexible socialization agents.
- If it is staffed by young, flexible, supportive, and competent boundary personnel ("gatekeepers").
- If it is structurally complex and decentralized.
- If it has the outside funds to provide the "organizational slack" that is necessary to lessen the cost of innovation.
- If its members have positions that are sufficiently secure and are protected from the status risks involved in change.
- If it is located in a changing, modern, urbanized setting and is in close cooperation with a coalition of other cosmopolitan organizations that can supplement its skills and resources.

The antecedents of the preceding approaches can be traced to several macro theories of change identified by Moore (1963), Hagen (1962), Smelser (1967), Applebaum (1970), and others, although the linkages are imperfect and often overlap. For example, socialization and diffusion are the peaceful mechanisms of natural adaptation underlying various forms of equilibrium theory; evolutionary and neoevolutionary theories give priority to structural differentiation and the sociohistorical and environmental context; replacement and status maintenance, to the extent that they imply an unstable balance of power and pressure for redistributions of power, are ingredients of conflict theory. However, there are no rigid boundaries between these intellectual traditions. Thus, conflict theory, in both its classical and modern forms, also stresses structural differentiation as a prime basis of the distribution of power; replacement is also an implicit part of the rise and fall theories; diffusion is an aspect of some versions of evolutionary theory; and status maintenance is a critical process within equilibrium theories as well as conflict theory.

The major difference between these explanations of crescive change and the main concern of this book—deliberate change—is that many aspects of the classical theories deny causative factors (as in the case of functionalism, evolutionary theory, rise and fall theories, and classical conflict theory). The potential for human intervention is somewhat greater in the modern conflict and diffusion theories. However, all these theories contain some components that are amenable to deliberate manipulation, such as the ones identified above. Of course, the theories overlap and are too abstract to permit us to derive mutually exclusive indicators. But they have been useful as sensitizing perspectives to identify a range of indicators that, with further analysis, could tap the salient factors underlying these perspectives. Now we examine the data for clues about the way these approaches were combined in this program and the relative effectiveness of each approach.

PROCEDURES[1]

Indicators and Measures

Thirty-seven indicators were used to guide the collection of data bearing on the several explanatory perspectives outlined earlier. In effect, these indicators represent the independent variables in this analysis. However, there were persistent and complex problems involved in relating concepts to indicators due to the looseness of fit between the two in the social sciences (Torgerson, 1958).[2] The 37 variables were assumed to be proxies for more complex phenomena. They were operationalized in terms of measures described in Chapter 2 and Appendix 1.

The dependent variable is technological change in schools. Each school was given a score based on all reported or observed intended and unintended changes, weighted for the "innovativeness" of each change (rated by two judges). Each innovation was scored on a five-point scale on each of five dimensions: new classroom methods, new materials, changed relationships with clientele, the addition of implementing personnel, and extracurricular activities. The weighting was based on the assumption that changes requiring altered or new social relationships and changes affecting the basic curriculum are of greater importance than additive changes or changes in extracurricular or other peripheral activities. Thus, team teaching, the introduction of black history, mixed-age grouping, and the use of indigenous laymen received higher weights than the use of films or the establishment of a photography club, for example. A similar procedure was used for weighting secondary changes which, in addition to the above dimensions, included reports of improved attitudes on the part of students, professors, or teachers. A school's score, then, is a product of the number of planned and unplanned innovations multiplied by the weights assigned to each dimension of change that applied to that innovation.[3]

Intended, or primary, changes were the innovations introduced and implemented within the school that were attributed to the Teacher Corps by the respondents. Unintended, or secondary, changes were more generally attitudinal or relational changes not associated with any specific innovation. Many of the unintended changes might have been the outcomes, or by-products, of specific primary changes, but the data do not permit this distinction to be made. The two types of change were therefore treated separately. Also, the analysis does not control for the many intervening factors such as the stability or innovativeness of the school context, although a crude adjustment for such factors seemed to be operating through respondents' differential perceptions of what constituted change. In cases in which a reported activity was judged by the respondent *not* to constitute any new or innovative practice, such activities were not considered to be "changes" in the analysis. In this way the "innovativeness" of the school operated as a frame of reference for the respondents as they identified changes that occurred.

ANALYSIS*

The analysis of data was organized around three steps.

1. The degree and direction of association among the dependent and independent variables was computed. In addition to examining the relationship between the dependent variable and each of the independent ones, this step was undertaken to reduce the number of independent variables by eliminating any variables found to be correlating highly with others.

2. The 37 independent variables were submitted to factor analysis. As pointed out earlier, the explanatory perspectives that were used to isolate the various indicators overlapped considerably among themselves, and the indicators were selected and grouped primarily on face validity. It was decided to use a factor analysis to determine whether we could inductively identify some common themes underlying the 37 independent variables.

* This section is adapted from the author's paper, "Strategies for Organizational Innovation: An Empirical Comparison," *American Sociological Review*, 37, August 1972, pp. 441–454.

Table 8-1 Component loadings of seven factors yielded by an oblique factor analysis

---

1. Quality and modernization of context[a]
    Size of university (-.79) (r = .32)
    Quality of university (-.90 (r = -.17)
    Modernization of region (-.91) (r = .13)
    Number of other training programs (-.69) (r = .02)
    Federal funds allocated per intern (-.63) (r = .39)
    Size of city (-.94) (r = .19)

2. Professionalism and social liberalism of staff
    Professional orientation--teachers (.83) (r = -.05)
    Administrative orientation--teachers (-.42) (r = .28)
    Liberalism--teachers (.43) (r = -.12)
    Client orientation--teachers (.86) (r = -.05)
    Liberalism of the team leader (.57) (r = .43)

3. Organizational control by the schools
    Teachers' emphasis on pupil control (.81) (r = -.11)
    Rules and procedures orientation--teachers (.43) (r = .04)
    Centralization of decision making (.75) (r = .33)
    Proportion of program funds locally controlled (.63) (r = -.33)
    Size of the school (-.65) (r = -.09)

4. Competence of the administration
    Principals' support for program (-.72) (r = -.05)
    Competence of the principal (-.86) (r = -.15)
    Quality of the school (-.75) (r = -.07)
    Tenure of the principal (.22) (r = .02)

---

[a] The first number in parentheses refers to the factor component loading from the rotated matrix. The second number in parentheses refers to the correlation between each independent variable and the dependent variable, technological change.

The results were (a) to refine concepts by identifying constructs more closely fitting the indicators and measures, and (b) to clarify the explanation of organizational innovation by reducing the number of independent variables to a few salient and more abstract factors.

3. The amount of variance in the dependent variable explained by the emergent factors was examined individually and collectively. This was accomplished through regression analysis.[4]

Intercorrelation Among the Variables

The magnitude of correlations among the independent variables ranged from .00 to —.87 (see Appendix 2). But, in general, there was not a suffi-

5. Quality and interdependence of boundary personnel
    Interns' satisfaction with university faculty (.66) (r = .53)
    Proportion of university faculty who consider themselves very
        liberal politically (.37) (r = .66)
    Cooperation between school and college (.93) (r = .35)
    Competence of the team leader (.29) (r = -.01)

6. Competence and status of teaching staff
    Proportion of teachers with M.A. degree (-.91) (r = .10)
    Quality of teachers' undergraduate college (-.44) (r = .14)
    Proportion of teachers in the union (-.63) (r = .25)
    Proportion of teachers who participated in proposal   (-.52)
        (r = -.26)

7. Uniqueness of outsiders
    Political liberalism of interns (-.62) (r = -.32)
    Proportion of interns with liberal arts major (-.92) (r = -.19)
    Interns' emphasis on pupil control (.57) (r = .20)
    Difference in political liberalism between teachers and interns
        (-.46) (r = -.16)
    Quality of interns' undergraduate college (-.73) (r = .12)
    Difference in status of teachers and interns based on education,
        race, and sex (-.56) (r = -.32)

ciently high correlation among a significant number of the variables to warrant using some variables as substitutes for others.

The Independent Factors

All variables were submitted, ungrouped, to an oblique factor analysis. This procedure yielded seven dimensions (see Table 8–1). The intercorrelations among the seven factors were relatively low; only 3 of the 21 correlations in the matrix exceeded .30: 2 with 6, $r = .58$, 2 with 7, $r = .42$, 1 with 5, $r = .37$ (not reported in the table). The question that now must be considered is how the factors in Table 8–1 relate to the original concepts and their indicators listed in the key for the table (Appendix 2). At least one factor ("uniqueness of outsiders") corresponds to the original concept (the replacement strategy). Other factors represent combinations of two or more strategies; in other words, different ways of organizing the concepts and different emphases among them. Thus the factor, "competence and status of teaching staff," combines elements of two dimensions—status security and competence of the socialization agents; "professionalism and social liberalism of the staff" is a product of the status security and diffusion explanation; the "organizational control" factor incorporates variables associated with organizational and decision-making structure; "competence of the administration" combines the variables associated with the diffusion and socialization strategies; and "quality and modernization of context" includes organizational structure and other institutional characteristics as well as other aspects of the environmental context. In some cases the factors expose fallacies in the original groupings. For example, it is now clear that "participation of teachers in the decision-making process" logically and empirically could have been included with their status characteristics instead of with the decision-making structure; and "quality of the institutions" need not have been considered as an aspect of the socialization agents' competence. Finally, at least one factor, "quality and interdependence of boundary personnel," seems to be an emergent concept that at best was only implicit in the explanations reviewed above, consisting of a unique combination of elements associated with the competence, diffusion, and environmental dimensions. But in general, although these alterations modify the original theory, they do not invalidate it. On the contrary, concepts that were defined only narratively in the literature now have been refined through an inductive process and have assumed new meanings that extend their utility.

Explaining the Variance in Organizational Innovation

The seven factors account for 51 percent of the variance (Table 8–2). Three factors account for most of the explained variance (48 percent): (1) "quality and interdependence of the boundary personnel," which refers to characteristics of the university faculty and team leaders, including the cooperation between them $(B = .59)$; (2) "organizational control exercised by the school system" $(B = -.23)$; and (3) "uniqueness of the outside change agents" $(B = -.39)$. "Competence of teaching staff" $(B = -.10)$, "quality and modernization of context" $(B = .16)$, "competence of the administration" $(B = .11)$, and "professionalism and social liberalism of staff" $(B = .01)$ make little additional contribution to the explanation, once the first three factors have been taken into consideration.

Table 8-2 Seven factors correlated with the introduction of new technologies into schools: oblique stepwise regression analysis (N = 43)

Number	Factors (Title)	r	R^2	R^2 added	Partial	T-value	Beta weight	F
5	Quality and interdependence of boundary personnel	.64	.405	---	.600	4.37	.588	27.22
3	Organizational control exercised by the schools	-.26	.445	.040	-.301	1.84	-.228	2.79
7	Uniqueness of outside change agents	-.13	.475	.030	-.304	1.86	-.388	2.18
6	Competence of teaching staff	.07	.493	.018	-.095	.56	-.095	1.34
1	Quality and modernization of context	.17	.503	.010	.155	.91	.161	.69
4	Competence of administration	.08	.507	.004	.093	.55	.109	.31
2	Professionalism and social liberalism of staff	-.10	.507	.000	.019	.11	.014	.01

DISCUSSION OF THE FACTOR ANALYSIS

Relationship to the University

The most salient factor is the quality and interdependence of the boundary personnel, which consists of four variables: competence of the university faculty members (as rated by the interns); faculty members' political liberalism (based on their own self-identity); the extent of cooperation between the school and the university (assessed from a content analysis of the interviews); and the competence of the experienced teacher-supervisors, the team leaders (based on the combined ratings of teachers and interns). In this connection it was found that interns' ratings of the faculty members' competence ($r = .53$) and the faculty's political liberalism ($r = .66$) are probably more important than either the university's prestige or its resources. Perhaps the better universities are too socially remote and too well integrated into the academic system to have developed the interest or competence for this kind of problem. [Also, the better colleges tend to attract more liberal arts majors ($r = .61$) from better undergraduate colleges ($r = .70$)—factors that were found to be negatively associated with innovation (not reported in tables).]

The overriding importance of the university faculty supports the contention of some writers that organizations change primarily in response to an outside stimulus. But more specifically, it reinforces the generally acknowledged significance of interorganizational relationships and underscores the crucial role played by boundary personnel in particular, in this case represented by the team leaders from the school and the university faculty members. In this sense the findings support the diffusion approach with its emphasis on the importance of the openness of boundary personnel to change. While the technical competence of the occupants of both boundary roles appears to be important, the attitude climate set by the university faculty seems to be even more important.[5]

The dominating role of the university can be attributed to several sources. In comparison to schools, universities are more cosmopolitan. They rely on regional or national financial and recruiting bases, and distribute their products throughout the nation and the world. In addition to this institutional base, faculty members tend to be more professionalized than teachers and are less tied into the local political structure. Moreover, they have less investment in the existing technology of the schools (as opposed to their investment in their own institutions). Finally, the fact that universities are the prime contractors for this program (the program director being a faculty member) enhances their influence. However, this leverage for change, no matter how great, cannot be applied unless there is a channel through which the university can exert its influence, that is, a working relationship between the universities and schools. Competent and receptive team leaders are a necessary component of such a channel.

Comparison with Other Environmental Conditions

Stated another way, the major dimension of the environment contributing to innovation is the amount of cooperation between the school and the university. With that factor controlled, modernization of the state makes only a small contribution. There was some support for the contention that innovation can be promoted by adding outside resources [in this case the volume of total funds is less important ($r_p = .11$) than the relative level of funding provided for each new trainee ($r_p = .40$)], and there is slightly more change in schools associated with larger universities ($r = .32$); but these variables are relatively unimportant compared to other factors examined. Since the number of training programs at the university is inversely associated with program change ($r_p = -.40$), there is a need for reconsideration of the proposition that change occurs more readily in otherwise changing environments (above figures are not reported in tables). Perhaps some allowance should be made for a ceiling effect, that is, the fact that it is also more difficult for a given program to make additional changes when there is already a high rate of change.[6]

ORGANIZATIONAL CONTROL. The second critical factor is the extent of internal control exercised by schools, consisting of four variables: centralization of the school system's decision-making structure; stress that classroom teachers and administrators place on rules and procedures; emphasis that teachers place on pupil control (that is, strict discipline); and the proportion of program funds controlled by the schools.

This factor reflects the opposite side of the relationship: the capacity of the cooperating host organization to filter and shape the changes proposed by the cooperating outside organization. The first two variables form a "containment dimension" through which an organization (school system) develops the capacity to control its members and that determines how effectively it can regulate its members' reactions to proposed changes. However, these two variables operate in opposite directions, and the positive correlation between the centralization of the decision-making structure and technological change ($r = .33$) is at variance with the widely held assumption that decentralized organizations are more adaptable. The higher school system administration was usually responsible for introducing the Teacher Corps program to the schools. Under these conditions, the more power that is concentrated at the top, the more effective the program will be (Griffiths, 1964). In other words, a centralized organization (school system) does not for that reason necessarily resist change; instead, centralization gives it the capacity to select and enforce innovations as well as to resist them. Also, where teachers emphasize classroom discipline, it probably reflects and reinforces strong administrative control.

The tendency for innovations to decline as the proportion of funds controlled by the local schools increases ($r = -.33$) reflects the conflict in goals between schools and universities. Control over the funds provides a leverage for co-opting the program. Schools attempted to use funds to supplement their existing programs rather than for innovation. There may have been a slight tendency for the more competent principals to gain more control over program funds ($r = .22$; not reported in table). While it is probably true that educational decisions are moving up and out, placing initiative outside the local system (Clark, 1965), local school boards often maintain final veto power over changes that they do not want.

THE ROLE OF DISSONANT CHANGE AGENTS. The third factor reflects the amount of dissonance between the change agents and the members of the host organization. But contrary to the theory, the correlation is negative. Independent field observations and interviews also confirmed that interns were often a source of friction and tension in the local schools, and that schools tended to react defensively when even a few of these critical, liberal, change-oriented newcomers were introduced.[7]

Perhaps the resulting conflict was not entirely counterproductive, however. There were small positive correlations between innovation and (a) the amount of conflict between interns and other members of the program ($r = .26$), and (b) the number of teachers reporting that the program had created problems for them ($r = .22$; figures are not reported in tables). These correlations support the notion that conflict often accompanies change. But the fact that the correlations are not higher also suggests that conflict does not necessarily produce extensive change under certain circumstances.

PROFESSIONAL COMPETENCE. Despite the theoretical importance that could be attributed to variables relating to professionalism and competence of the administrators and teachers, these variables were less important than the characteristics of other boundary personnel who were more directly associated with the program. Teachers' participation in the proposal is the other side of administrative centralization discussed above and is related to the dimension of teachers' competence. Their participation had only a minor (statistically insignificant) effect and, contrary to usual expectations and findings from other studies (Aiken and Hage, 1970), the small effect that appears is negative ($r = -.26$). The power-equalization model presumes that changes are produced from the consent of the parties involved. However, some innovations are forced into a system, which arouses suspicion or opposition of the incumbents. This was frequently true in this program. When subordinates fail to agree on the objectives or strategies of these proposed changes but are relatively professionalized, their participation in the decisions places them in a better position to sabotage the innovation (Mulder, 1971); and under conditions in which their participation is only nominal, the strategy can backfire by producing unrealistic expectations (Lefton, Dinitz, and Pasamanick, 1959). Thus, this strategy can inhibit as well as promote innovation, depending on the initial balance of power, the degree of consensus, and the status threat involved.

The fact that the competence of the teaching staff is negatively correlated with change and has a low negative correlation with their professionalism and liberalism questions the assumption that status security and professionalism necessarily promote change. More important: in view of the theoretical significance often attributed to the more generic social context, the characteristics that made up the quality and the modernization of the school context did not contribute much to the explanation. Again, the more immediate organization context, reflected in cooperation with the university, appeared to take precedence over these more general context variables.

These latter findings may have implications for the current decentralization issue concerning demands for community control that are being made by residents of ghettos in the large cities. On the one hand, the data support the contention of many critics that the professionalism and technical competence of teachers in itself provides no assurance that efforts will be made to improve the schools. On the other hand, central administrators would have less capacity to impose change from the top down in decentralized school systems. Perhaps the whole controversy over the schools' relationship with their communities has eclipsed an equally important relationship—the relationship of the schools with innovative universities.

REGIONAL AND COMMUNITY CONTEXTS

Generally, the pattern of statistical evidence reported thus far was reinforced by my own informal observations and interviews. However, there was a major exception. It was my impression that the regional and community contexts played a more important role in innovation than was reflected in the factor analysis. The case studies reported in Chapter 7 suggested this, too. Obviously, with only 10 programs, these data could have acted erratically in the regression, and subtle but important differences sometimes cannot be easily detected with multivariate statistical techniques. Moreover, the measurements I used were probably not as precisely calibrated, nor as linear, as they should be for multiple regression. For these reasons, two contextual variables were singled out for more intensive analysis using less statistically sophisticated techniques. I must emphasize that the data throughout this chapter, and especially in this section, are introduced only for illustrative purposes to add plausibility to the thesis that the way an educational system is organized can influence a nation's receptivity to educational change and to suggest some larger issues. I do not imply that these data confirm a theory.

City Size, Modernization, and Organizational Change

Indicators of (1) the size of city and (2) the level of modernization of the states in which the 10 programs were located are modestly associated with the index of technological change in the 42 schools ($t_p = .27, .11$) (Table 8–3, part I).[8] The coefficient of concordance among the three variables is $W = .67$. The two independent variables are correlated ($t = .67$; not reported in tables); city size accounts for more of the variance ($t_p = .27$) than modernization ($t_p = .11$).

The joint effects are reflected in a different form in Table 8–4. Although based on a small number of cases (42 schools, but only 10 programs), the first part of the table suggests that schools located in the larger cities in modernized states show the most change; schools in smaller cities in less modernized regions show the least change ($\overline{X} = 372$ versus 279).

Cooperation between schools and colleges also improves with urbanization ($t_p = .52$) and with modernization ($t_p = .56$; Table 8–3, part I). Modernization requires new forms of cooperation among organizations that monopolize different resources. Community activity increases only slightly with urbanization and modernization (Table 8–3, part I). Although community activities are less pronounced in less urban and modernized areas, judging from the proportion of teachers who want to reduce community projects, there is more resistance to community activities in such settings ($t = -.36$; not reported in tables). The community power structure in small towns provides a secondary line of defense, insulating schools from national pressures and throttling the activities that schools and colleges may have tolerated. Moreover, teachers in these areas are likely to have been recruited locally and are likely to subscribe to local traditions. They are less likely to possess the level of expertise that might buffer them from local pressures.

The index of change in the college curriculum seems to be largely independent of either urbanization or modernization. As relatively cosmopolitan institutions, universities rely on regional and national sources for recruiting and placement of the students and are not supported or controlled directly from the home community; therefore, they should be among the first institutions to be freed from territorial controls as modernization occurs.[9]

The remainder of the analysis concentrates on the measure of technological change in the schools.

Impact of Recruits from the Liberal Arts

Before discussing the implications of the above patterns, I must comment briefly on my previous conclusion that the strategy of attempting to promote change by recruiting change-oriented newcomers from liberal arts backgrounds seems to have boomeranged. After reexamining this dimension, I shall consider the implications of the general problem of modernization in light of the findings.

The proportion of liberal arts interns in a program is negatively associated with the rate of technological change in schools, as well as with the other three types of change (Table 8-3, part V).[10] The average political-liberalism scores of interns, the proportion with prior Peace Corps or VISTA experience, and the quality of their undergraduate college also are negatively correlated with this index of change. And, as already noted, the proportion of teachers who reported that the program had created problems for them increases with the proportion of interns with liberal arts majors ($t = .33$), while an index of flexibility of the school (based on judgments of teachers and interns in the program) declines ($t = .23$; not reported in table).

Liberal Newcomers in Less Modern Rural Systems

In contrast to the general pattern, however, in the less modernized rural areas there is a *positive* relationship between the presence of liberal newcomers and technological change. Thus, when the correlations between

Table 8-3 Indices of program innovation and other program characteristics: rank-order correlations among 10 Teacher Corps programs.

	Urbanization	
Program characteristics	Tau	Partial tau[a]
Part I--Program innovation		
The number and innovativeness of new techniques introduced into the schools (7-d)	.29	.27
The number and innovativeness of activities in the community	.33	.19
Rate of increase of school-college coop-eration (7d-1)	.38	.52
Number of changes reported in the college curriculum	-.02	-.08
Part II--Characteristics of colleges		
Level of interns' satisfaction with the com-petence of the university faculty	.20	.19
Quality of colleges in the program	.20	.02
Total amount of funds allocated for the program	.38	.0
Amount of funds allocated per intern	.16	.0
Political liberalism of the university faculty	.80	.85
Part III--Characteristics of schools		
Proportion of teachers in the union	.47	.44
Number of pupils enrolled in the school	.38	.15
Principals' support for the program	.18	.32
Tenure of the principal	.0	-.28
Proportion of classroom teachers who participated in the program proposal	-.30	-.81
Proportion of funds controlled by local school	-.29	.02
Flexibility of the school	.20	.15
Centralization of the school system	.24	.36
Rate of turnover among teachers	.70	.39
Part IV--Characteristics of the teachers		
Verbal facility of teachers (by region)	.51	.22
Proportion of teachers who attended predominantly white undergraduate colleges (by region)	.16	.04
Administrative orientation of the classroom teachers	-.05	-.19
Rules orientation of the classroom teachers	-.32	-.33
Proportion of teachers in the school with an M.A. degree	.02	.26

268

| Modernization | | Technological change in schools | | | Proportion of interns with liberal arts major | | |
| | | | Partial tau | | | Partial tau | |
Tau	Partial tau[b]	Tau 7d	a	b	Tau 7d	a	b
.16	.11	1.00	--	--	-.52	-.53	-.57
.27	.09	.70	.66	.69	-.43	-.23	-.34
.14	.56	.56	.50	.55	-.29	-.61	-.54
.05	.08	.24	.26	.24	-.16	-.15	-.20
.07	-.07	.38	.34	.37	-.38	-.42	-.48
.25	.19	.56	.53	.54	-.29	-.33	-.49
.52	.42	.38	.30	.35	-.02	-.09	-.37
.20	.16	.60	.59	.59	-.33	-.37	-.51
-.11	.32	.20	.35	.21	.0	.0	.11
.25	.14	.29	.18	.26	.16	.10	.06
.43	.22	-.07	-.20	-.14	.24	.20	.07
.0	.27	.28	.32	.37	-.55	-.66	-.66
-.28	-.30	-.33	-.29	-.33	.49	.43	.38
-.23	-.41	-.42	-.23	-.31	.80	.85	.29
-.02	-.03	-.33	-.02	-.02	.11	.11	.13
.16	.0	.73	.72	.73	-.38	-.42	-.51
.07	.10	-.33	-.21	-.10	-.30	-.38	.0
.64	.46	.43	.33	.43	.20	.13	-.14
.56	.31	.24	.30	.27	.38	.35	.17
.20	.10	.24	.21	.22	.02	.0	-.07
-.18	.08	.41	.42	.42	-.54	-.56	-.55
-.46	-.32	-.18	-.06	-.10	-.45	-.45	-.33
-.20	-.33	.20	.20	.25	-.20	-.21	-.11

Table 8-3 (Continued)

Proportion of teachers who want team leaders selected exclusively from the region	-.11	.0
Part V--Characteristics of the interns		
Proportion of interns with liberal arts majors	.16	.25
Quality of interns' undergraduate college	.51	.09
Political liberalism of the interns	.32	.11
Proportion of the interns with prior Peace Corps or VISTA experience	.18	-.08
Proportion of the interns from outside the region	-.56	-.46
Difference in the political liberalism of teachers and interns	-.41	-.24
Status differences between teachers and interns (race, sex, and education)	-.36	-.05

[a] Controlling for modernization.
[b] Controlling for urbanization.

technological change and both urbanization and modernization were partialled against the proportion of interns in the program with liberal arts majors, both correlations increased (from $t = .29$ to $t_p = .39$ and from $t = .16$ to $t_p = .41$; not in Table 8–3).* Similarly, when the proportion of liberal arts majors is added to a multiple correlation among modernization, urbanization, and technological change, the coefficient of concordance drops from $W = .67$ to $W = .47$. This suggests that the presence of liberal interns is depressing the rate of change in schools in urban, modernized regions or, conversely, accelerating it in the less modern, rural regions.

The fact that the presence of liberal arts graduates in the less modernized rural regions is positively associated with the introduction of new techniques is also reflected by Table 8–5. Although these programs recruit disproportionately fewer interns from the better liberal arts colleges, they tend to attract more interns from outside of the region. Because teachers in these regions are not as well trained as their counterparts in modernized areas, there is a greater difference in the political liberalism and status characteristics of teachers and interns. The sudden presence of even moderately liberal interns in these areas, therefore, is often such a notable event that it has an effect on the community.

---

* The correlations in Table 8–3 show the relationships partialing for urbanization and modernization but *not partialing* for liberal arts graduates.

−.09	−.08	−.44	.44	.44	.39	.45	.49
.47	.47	−.52	−.53	−.57	1.00	--	--
.65	.53	−.02	−.21	−.18	.20	.14	−.18
.33	.17	.09	.03	.07	.28	.22	.12
.36	.32	−.18	−.23	−.23	.63	.59	.53
−.20	.02	−.33	.06	−.06	.07	.13	.18
.36	−.09	.41	−.31	−.36	.05	.09	.21
−.50	−.35	−.23	−.10	−.15	−.41	−.40	−.25

Table 8–5 can be interpreted in two ways. Reading across, it shows that variations in the proportion of interns with liberal arts backgrounds seem to have the most effect on schools in large cities of the more modernized regions; that is, in these contexts a *high* proportion of liberal arts majors is associated with *less* change than when fewer of these alien types of teachers have been introduced (211 versus 437). Conversely, the proportion of liberal arts majors added to a school seems to make little difference for the rate of change in the smaller cities and less modernized regions.

But Table 8–5 also suggests the answer to a different and more important question: Under what conditions *does* the introduction of more liberal arts majors produce change? Viewing the table from this perspective, and reading down column 1, it is in the smaller cities, compared to the larger ones, where variations in the proportion of liberal arts majors appear to be more closely associated with change (211 versus 328); and, to a lesser extent, it is in the less modernized states, compared to the modernized ones (288 versus 310). In other words, liberal newcomers appear to have more of a positive stimulus for change in the smaller cities of the less modernized areas.

These patterns suggest two implications: (1) the program may have stimulated more innovation in the more urbanized, modernized context than in the less urban and rural areas; and (2) the strategy of introducing interns from liberal arts backgrounds appears to have been more effective in the smaller cities of the less modernized states. Assuming that this is partially true, two fundamental questions arise. What accounts for the

Table 8-4 Technological change in schools, by type of city and region, proportion of interns from the liberal arts, and structural characteristics of the schools

	Change index score
A. Type of city and region	
Modernized regions	
Large city	372
Small city	307
Less modernized regions	
Large city	360
Small city	279
B. Proportion of liberal arts major--high	
% classroom teachers in union--high	366
% classroom teachers in union--low	301
Centralization--high	261
Centralization--low	328
% classroom teachers with masters degree--high	376
% classroom teachers with masters degree--low	287
Classroom teachers verbal ability--high	327
Classroom teachers verbal ability--low	252
C. Proportion of classroom teachers in union--high	
% liberal arts majors--high	366
% liberal arts majors--low	388
D. Centralization--high	
% liberal arts majors--high	261
% liberal arts majors--low	402
E. Proportion of classroom teachers with masters degree--high	
% liberal arts major--high	360
% liberal arts major--low	376
F. Classroom teachers verbal ability--high	
% liberal arts major--high	327
% liberal arts major--low	496

Table 8-5 Technological change in schools, by type of city and region, and proportion of interns assigned from liberal arts backgrounds

Type of city and region	Proportion of interns with liberal arts major in program		
	High	Low	Score difference
A. Large city	211	437	226
Small city	328	340	12
Score difference	117	97	
B. Modernized	288	533	245
Unmodernized	310	346	36
Score difference	32	187	

apparent ability of schools in the smaller cities of the less modernized areas to resist change? Why does the introduction of liberal arts outsiders seem to be more effective in precisely these regions in comparison to the more modernized urban ones?

SOURCES OF DEFENSE. Table 8–3 reports several program characteristics that are inversely associated with urbanization and modernization (and thus typical of schools in the smaller, less modernized areas) and that are also negatively associated with indices of technological change. These characteristics can be viewed as potential sources of these schools' defense against external pressures for change. The direction of the coefficients in the table suggests that:

1. Schools in smaller, less modernized regions can count on school principals to provide less support for the program (Table 8–3, part III). The principals' relatively longer tenure and the fact that they are part of relatively decentralized school systems perhaps also places them in a better position to influence the program. And, in view of a critical shortage of resources in these schools, principals will tend to support the program only to the extent that it provides supplementary assistance for the normal program. Thus, their support correlates with the emphasis that teachers in the program place on this assistance factor ($t = .33$), but it is not correlated with whatever inclination teachers might have to help interns try out new ideas ($t = .05$; figures not reported in table).

2. Schools in these regions have teaching faculties that are exceptionally

loyal to the school administration, that are supportive of the existing system of rules and procedures, and that are more stable (have lower rates of turnover) (Table 8–3, part IV).

3. These schools are in a position to exercise local control, as reflected by both the proportion of program funds controlled by the local schools (as opposed to the college) and the proportion of teachers who have participated in the proposal.

4. These schools are judged by both teachers and interns in the program to be less flexible. The tendency of these systems to react defensively to the threat of alien external forces is reflected by the fact that either or both organizational flexibility and support from the principal are inversely correlated with variables of this kind: the proportion of interns from outside the system; the proportion of interns with liberal arts degrees and who have not had education courses; the quality of interns' undergraduate college; political liberalism of interns; and the difference between teachers' and interns' political liberalism and social status (based on an index of education, race, and sex).

Most of the above characteristics are inversely correlated with the rate of technological change.

Schools in rural regions are less likely than schools in urbanized, modernized areas to be confronted with strong external sources of pressure for change. For example, the colleges have fewer resources and lower standards of admission, and their faculties' competence is judged by the interns to be relatively low. Furthermore, these schools are more independent of the college (as reflected by the index of school-college cooperation). Also, the fact that schools associated with lower quality programs receive fewer funds from Washington (both in dollars and in relation to the funds allocated per trainee) is probably a reflection of the way they are judged by the national office, that is, of lower quality than other programs.[11] It also might reflect the fact that these programs are more socially and geographically remote from Washington's influence. Because they are willing to operate programs for less money, perhaps less is expected of them. Although their remoteness and low-quality image may place them in a poor bargaining position from one standpoint, these same factors help to insulate them from external pressures.

Sources of Vulnerability

In light of these defenses, what accounts for the apparently greater effectiveness of liberal arts majors in promoting innovation in the most rural systems? Suggestions about the vulnerable points of these schools' defenses are also contained in Table 8-3:

1. A weaker administrative system.
2. A weaker teacher organization.
3. Less competent teachers.

Table 8-3 identifies several internal characteristics of schools. Each characteristic is positively associated with technological change—decentralization, the proportion of teachers in the union, and the level of education and verbal ability of teachers. When each of these factors is reinforced by the presence of liberal arts graduates, which represents an external force for change, rates of change are relatively high. Thus, *schools that have been assigned a high proportion of liberal arts graduates* and that are (a) unionized, (b) decentralized, or (c) staffed with better educated and more articulate teaching faculties have higher change scores than when an equally high proportion of liberal arts graduates is assigned to schools with the opposite characteristics.

But these relationships also can be viewed in another way. Considering only *the schools that are high on any one of the structural characteristics mentioned,* there is a crude inverse correlation between the proportion of liberal arts majors assigned and technological change (Table 8-4, parts C through F). This suggests that the more unionized, centralized, expert schools may have been able to more effectively control liberalizing influences than the less centralized, less unionized schools with less expert faculties.

In other words, the same features of organizations that under some conditions serve as internal stimuli for change, under other conditions act as structural defenses against pressures from outside the system. Although the higher administrators in more centralized school systems (compared to those in the less centralized systems) are in a better position to exert pressure on principals and teachers to accept innovations that they support, they are also in a better position to control alien influences. Unionization and specialized training reinforce teachers' status security which, under some conditions, makes them more open to change; but both are also sources of power to resist unwelcome pressures for change.[12]

It is precisely these structural forms that are less available to rural schools in less modernized regions. The fact that they have less protection from centralized administrations, strong teacher organizations, and expert faculties makes them more vulnerable to the often useful ideas advocated by enthusiastic and better educated interns from good undergraduate colleges; and even if they choose to resist, they do not have a strong administration and teachers' union to fall back on. The primary defenses available to them fall into the category of "fundamentalism"—the conservative attitudes of principals and their loyal teachers.

SUMMARY AND DISCUSSION

The findings should be interpreted with caution in view of the necessarily inadequate way in which some of the complex concepts were measured. But a comparative analysis of alternative explanations, regardless of its tentativeness, offers the advantage of pointing the way to more systematic models of organizational innovation. Toward this end, by drawing on the assumptions advanced by other writers (Gouldner, 1970; Gerard, 1957; Clark, 1968) and by extrapolating from the tentative findings reported here, I have formulated four general propositions.

1. *The way an innovation is conceived and implemented is a product of a combination of forces inside and outside the organization.* Organizations exist in an environment of constraint and, therefore, the success or failure of an innovation will vary with the context in which it is introduced. This might include characteristics such as the quality of the institutions involved and modernization of the region but, in this case, the data indicated that the characteristics of the general organizational network were the most salient aspects of the environment. Specifically, they indicated that technological innovation was a product of a balance of power between strong but interdependent organizations. The necessary ingredients include (a) a dominant outside organization staffed by competent and liberal members; (b) competent, receptive boundary personnel in the host organization; and (c) functional interdependence and channels for cooperation to take place. These conditions can be reformulated to apply to characteristics of the organizational set itself; that is, there will be more technological change in organizational networks in which there is unequal balance of power but a high degree of interdependence and in which boundary roles are staffed by cosmopolitan, liberal, and professionally competent members.

2. *Characteristics of both occupation and organization must be taken into account in order to explain innovation.* The outcomes of attempts to change an occupation are conditioned by characteristics of its organizational context, such as centralization of decision-making structure and standardization; whereas organizational innovations are influenced by characteristics of the occupational group, such as, in this instance, the teachers'

emphasis on pupil control. However, in this study, the competence, professionalism, and social liberalism of the rank-and-file professionals in the host organization were less important than either the comparable characteristics of the boundary personnel or the characteristics of the organizational structure.

3. *The more structural controls that are available to a group, the less likely that the group will be threatened by a particular innovation or innovative strategy; but, once threatened, the group will have a greater capacity to* either *support or successfully subvert new activities and arrangements.* Where teachers and administrators had power, their support assured the success of change efforts. But the same power gave them a measure of discretion to choose what they would and would not support; therefore, change efforts could easily be blocked in such systems. Unionization and technical competence provided teachers with the power to redirect change efforts of which they disapproved and, similarly, centralization gave administrators a degree of control over systemwide activities that they could not fall back on in decentralized systems. This structural power base seemed to be more potent than conservative attitudes, administrative loyalty, and system stability, which constituted the primary defenses of schools located in rural, less modernized areas.

Reciprocity, which is a key to any stable social system, depends on the existence of a stable set of personal relationships anchored in the status system. It is in the rural, less modern sectors of the society—where loyalty to the local institution tends to be reinforced by personal sanctions and where relationships are less contractual and more directly based on interpersonal relationships—that change in the traditional status relationships is most threatening (Thompson, 1964). It is precisely the existing status relationships that were challenged by these change-oriented, well-educated outsiders, especially since they were marginal to the present system. The fundamentalism, which seems to have been relatively effective against the intrusions of impersonal nationalizing influences and often remote government pressures, proved to be less effective against these outsiders working within the system.

4. *A split develops between the established leaders of the profession and a new generation.* The new generation is identified with outside leaders who stand to gain from new roles that promise to open new channels of success and to circumvent the status monopoly controlled by traditionalists. Conversely, since the proposed changes would redistribute existing tasks that formerly were the responsibility of other units, the newcomers are resisted; a dialectic develops in which the traditional, conservative pro-

cedures are reasserted or slightly adapted in order to compete with new procedures.

This last point deserves further comment. An attempt to influence the change process by introducing change agents as an independent force can be effective only under limited conditions, which were not present in this case. Even with the two most influential factors controlled, the more liberal the interns were in a school, the less innovation there was. This fact indicates that the interns' ineffectiveness was not simply a product of institutional balance of power; it was inherent in the strategy of this program. The tactics used in this program, of course, provide an extreme test of the replacement approach. The attempt to unite the change-agent roles with the apprenticeship system placed the interns in a precarious position between two powerful organizations. They were representatives of the outside organization in the schools but could count on little direct support from remote university professors; also they were directly supervised by defensive teachers. Sensing this resistance to them, and often finding the schools conservative toward change, a vocal minority of interns in most programs resorted to confrontation tactics. However, the conflict theory of change presumes a balance of power that did not exist in this case. As inexperienced newcomers to the profession, still in training and temporarily assigned to schools under direct supervision of experienced teachers, the interns could not gain leverage within the schools—even though, ironically, these very characteristics enabled them to maintain the autonomy that encouraged them to take the risks involved in promoting change. Nor did the interns constitute a sufficiently critical mass in any of the schools to provide power from numbers or to promote the development of a strong peer group. They were so outnumbered and overwhelmed by the structural defenses available to administrators and teachers that the schools were able to neutralize their efforts. Indeed, the interns' militancy gave the teachers little latitude to compromise without jeopardizing their authority, which created a win–lose situation. Teachers retaliated by completely withdrawing their support for interns' proposals. Thus, while some change accompanied conflict, the fact that interns had little leverage with which to wage a successful conflict explains the negative correlation between technological change and the proportion of liberal arts interns in the program.

This suggests that two additional conditions must be present—which were not, in this case: (1) the change agents must be introduced in sufficiently large numbers; and (2) they must be introduced at more than one echelon in the hierarchy. The impact might have been modified by assigning a higher ratio of interns to each school or by recruiting interns into the administrative ranks. In any event, the experience in this program suggests that caution should be exercised in employing the replacement strategy for purposes of innovation without further examination of the conditions under which it can be successful.

In conclusion, explanation of technological innovation requires a *combination* of several distinct theoretical approaches. The pattern of variables identified here has moved us beyond the framework that initially guided the study design. As is often the case when theory is confronted with evidence, not one, but a mixture of the components of several theories is necessary. It appears there is a great deal of truth and fiction in the various streams of thought that served as the original guideline to identify approaches to deliberate organizational change. But sociologists often have served as advocates for separate streams of thought and, like the blind men with the elephant, various theorists have illuminated a small part of the total process while exaggerating the importance, autonomy, and coherence of different traditions. In the empirical world, each set of variables seems to play a supplementary and, to some extent, interchangeable or even contradictory role. Although the advocacy role is probably functional for originating new ideas and bringing them to the attention of scholars, theory must be integrated in new ways through research.

Even in combination, the variables explored here explain only part of the total variance. Some strategies may be more effective than others, but the crucial element seems to be the way they interact. The conditions under which any given strategy is applied (that is, the situation into which an innovation is introduced) seems to be as critical as the strategy itself. Perhaps the fundamental dimension considered here is the way local organizations are insulated from, or integrated into, the larger context. Thus, decentralization gives local interests leverage over unwanted changes, while centralization more closely links the organizations to the broader system, as do institutional cooperation and liberal and competent boundary personnel. Future research must give more attention to the conditions that enable organizations to maintain functional autonomy within an increasingly interdependent, changing society (Gouldner, 1959; Katz, 1968).

Reminder: the data have not been presented as a means of confirming these conclusions but, instead, to illustrate the plausibility of the general thesis that characteristics of organizations play an important role in the processes of organizational innovation and modernization.

NOTES

1. For assistance in interpreting the regression analysis technique, see footnote 1, Chapter 5.

2. Specific comments will be helpful. First, in the preliminary analysis the ratio of interns to teaching staff was considered as an index of the replacement approach but, because of several circumstances, there was actually little variance on that measure; thus it made little contribution to the variance explained when included in a regression analysis. For that reason it was deleted in favor of the characteristics of the interns that clearly differentiated them from teachers. Second, although the "diffusion" label in some sense was applicable to the program as a whole as it was *conceived*, in practice there was considerable variability in the way the program was implemented, which made it feasible to consider the indicators associated with diffusion as variables. Third, the term "socialization" is used here advisedly because the extent to which the staff actually were able to indoctrinate interns was not measured directly and therefore remains a matter of conjecture inferred from the "competence" of the staff. This is a reputational measure based on the esteem accorded by other members of the program; it is not implied that these judgments are equivalent to objective criteria that neutral third parties might have used (although there is a strong relationship between the interns' satisfaction with university faculty members and the quality of the graduate schools that professors attended, based on a resource index; also between the quality of the local school and the quality of the teacher's undergraduate college, based on indices of resources and selectivity of the student body).

3. Elizabeth Hanna supervised this phase of the coding. The term *innovation* has been used in a variety of ways (Hage and Dewar, 1971; Becker and Whisler, 1967). It is viewed here as a variable pertaining primarily to a deliberate change in structural relationships and procedures in a particular organization that could lead secondarily to changed outputs. Carroll (1967) used a comparable procedure to rate the innovativeness of curriculum changes in a medical school in terms of the extent of restructuring of relationships among the faculty and students required by the change. Another procedure was used by Evan and Black (1967), who asked respondents to describe one proposal that had been implemented and one that had been rejected by management. Most other investigators have used checklists to indicate the presence or absence of specific types of innovations (Becker and Stafford, 1967) or have asked executives to list the number of new programs and services implemented (Hage and Aiken, 1967; Hage and Dewar, 1971). The latter investigators used follow-up questions to distinguish an expansion of existing services from new programs.

4. Because of the crude measures, small sample size, and an unavoidable multicollinearity among some of the variables, these data do not conform perfectly to the assumptions of the regression model. Nevertheless, if interpreted cautiously, this is probably one of the best available means for answering the kinds of questions posed in this chapter. Although the small sample size is not necessarily very reliable, the data can be viewed as a multicase study. What is important here is not the magnitude of a particular correlation but the *patterns* in the data that can suggest *clues* or propositions that warrant further tests. Moreover, although we do not have equal interval measures, Labovitz (1967) has argued extensively that data that are only partially interval can be used with more sophisticated models. His argument is based on the grounds that an approximation to equal distances between adjacent scores is preferable to the knowledge that one is greater than the other.

5. Even with the proportion of interns having liberal arts degrees and the amount of

cooperation between the school and college controlled, liberalism of the university faculty continues to contribute .50 to the R^2, whereas once these three variables have been controlled, faculty members' competence adds little more (R^2 added = .02).

6. The number of other training programs ranged from one (at one university) to six (at two others); the typical college of education had between three and four separate training programs.

7. The fact that the presence of unconventional, change-oriented newcomers created problems in the schools is reflected in three other analyses. The characteristics of interns contributed to the explanation of (1) the number of conflict incidents reported among members of the program, and (2) the proportion of teachers reporting that the program had created problems for them. The difference in the liberalism of the interns and teachers and the proportion of liberal arts majors were correlated with each variable. The defensiveness of schools in the face of this conflict is also revealed in (3) parallel effects that the presence of liberal newcomers appears to have had in promoting organizational inflexibility; five characteristics of the interns explain more than half of the variance ($R^2 = .55$).

8. Also, in the less modernized areas many changes observed were relatively minor compared to changes that had already occurred in modernized areas. In the former regions, even the introduction of audiovisual aids could represent a substantial innovation for that particular context, which would be discounted in major urban areas.

9. This national reference of colleges should make them particularly responsive to federal funds. The rank-order correlation between the index of change in college and level of funding per intern is $t = .30$. Controlling for urbanization and modernization does not change the correlation, indicating that colleges in the less modern rural areas are neither more nor less responsive to funds than colleges in the modernized areas. However, the colleges that already have relatively substantial resources and competent faculties receive more funds per intern; the rank-order correlation between funds per intern and quality of the college is $t = .38$, and with interns' satisfaction with the faculty it is .52; change in college increases with both indices of college quality ($t = .33$ in both cases). The rate of change in colleges diminishes as the proportion of funds controlled by the local schools increases ($t = -.51$); control by the schools diminishes with both indices of college quality ($t = -.20, t = -.29$).

10. In all cases it is recognized that causal inferences are being made from correlational data. The data are being used as a source of conjecture and clearly do not provide confirming evidence for the inferences made.

11. The funds allocated to the program per intern increase with two indices of quality of the college: the index of resources and selectivity ($t = .38$), and satisfaction with the faculty as evaluated by interns ($t = .52$).

12. A slightly different interpretation is also possible. Perhaps the schools that seem to have stronger defenses against the liberal arts graduates also have a history of being more innovative. If so, there would be less opportunity for variation in *newly introduced* changes in these schools to show up, resulting in lower correlation with the liberal arts graduate variable. Conversely, the less innovative the school, the greater the chance that an external change force would have a measurable effect.

CHAPTER 9

Patterns of Organizational Change, Flexibility, and Conflict

Social change can come through a process of influence, but it can also come as a developmental outgrowth of societal processes.

GAMSON, 1968, p. 188

Having considered one dimension of organizational change—technological innovation in schools—let us examine the change process, other dimensions of change, and the associated phenomena of flexibility and conflict.

INNOVATIONS IN UNIVERSITY PROGRAMS

A parallel analysis of the number of innovations reported in the training programs at the 10 universities revealed two salient characteristics: (1) the proportion of college faculty members who identify themselves as politically "very liberal," which is positively associated with this type of change ($B = .52$); and (2) the proportion of program funds controlled by the local schools, which is negatively correlated with change at the college ($B = -.46$) (Table 9–1).[1] These two variables account for three fourths of the variance, but notice the small number of cases.[2] Several other variables also seem to make a contribution: the proportion of interns with liberal arts majors ($B = .20$); quality of the college ($B = -.36$); and the number of training programs at the college ($B = .30$). These five variables account for over 88 percent of the variance.

282

Table 9-1 Program characteristics associated with innovation in university programs

Program characteristics	r	R^2	R^2 added	Final partial	Final T value	Final beta weight	F
Proportion of university faculty who consider themselves politically "very liberal"	.79	.629	--	.719	5.93	.521	67.50
Proportion of funds controlled by the local schools	-.61	.756	.127	-.728	6.09	-.464	60.51
Proportion of interns with liberal arts majors	.23	.811	.055	.453	2.92	.203	54.53
Quality of the Teacher Corps college	.005	.843	.032	-.530	3.59	-.358	49.65
Number of training programs at the college	.39	.884	.041	.425	2.69	.301	54.90
Proportion of interns from outside the region	.15	.888	.004	.172	1.00	.067	46.14
Predisposition of interns to take initiative	.04	.888	.000	-.062	.36	-.023	38.55
Quality of interns' undergraduate college	.43	.888	.000	.061	.35	.050	32.88

When the liberalism of the college faculty was excluded from consideration, the proportion of funds controlled by the local school ($B = -.51$), the number of programs at the college ($B = .56$), and the quality of the college ($B = -.60$) still accounted for 70 percent of the variance. The competence of the university faculty, as rated by the interns ($B = .48$), the proportion of interns with liberal arts majors ($B = .47$), and the quality of their undergraduate college ($B = .28$) also made small contributions (the three variables adding 16 percent to the variance explained). When the variable, funds allocated to the program per intern, was added in another analysis, it made little additional contribution to the explanation. (Figures above not in table.)

Finally, two separate analyses were made to determine the relative contribution of the faculty's liberalism and their competence (as evaluated by the interns). These analyses indicated that while liberalism may have been, relatively, the more important variable, both variables made independent contributions. When liberalism was controlled (by forcing it into the regression first), *competence continued to make an independent contribution.* It entered as the fourth variable as follows: (a) faculty liberalism ($R^2 = .10$), (b) percent of funds controlled by the school (R^2 added = .30), (c) percent of interns from outside the region (R^2 added = .05), (d) intern satisfaction with the faculty (R^2 added = .05). When the faculty competence was controlled first, *their liberalism also continued to make an independent contribution.* It entered as the fourth variable, as follows: (a) intern satisfaction with the faculty ($R^2 = .05$), (b) percent of funds controlled by the schools (R^2 added = .33), (c) number of training programs (R^2 added = .07), and (d) liberalism of the faculty (R^2 added = .10).

These data, at best, can only be suggestive in view of the few cases involved and, as is true of any case study, at least some of the relationships could be unreliable if extrapolated to a larger universe. Nevertheless, the patterns in the data make sense, intuitively and theoretically. The extent of change that took place in these particular colleges appears to have been determined by the way they were integrated into the larger social and political structure, and by the way they were integrated into the academic system. Thus, more attempt was made to adapt the training program to conditions found in poverty schools if the faculty members were relatively sympathetic to the need for broader social and political change, especially if these sympathies were reinforced by the presence of liberal interns. In other words, the value climate of the college, established by the faculty and to a lesser extent by the interns, provided a bridge for translating into

specific program changes the social pressures for change that impin,
on the college. Stated conversely, conservative faculties served as a bound.
defense against such pressures. The importance of this diffuse type of linkage to events in the broader society parallels the critically important relationships with the schools in the task environment reported in the preceding
chapter. In both cases the college faculty members played a crucial role. The
relative autonomy of the university professors probably accentuated their
importance in comparison to other instructional or administrative factors.

Examining the other side of the college's situation, the higher its position in the academic system (as reflected in the quality of its resources
and students), the less effort it made to adapt to the requirements of low-
income schools.[3] There could be a number of reasons for this. As pointed
out in Chapter 4, the fact that the Teacher Corps was in several respects
a marginal program gave the national office less leverage over the higher-
quality colleges than over the lower-quality colleges. The failure of a
college to change does not indicate how well adapted the program might
have been before the Teacher Corps. It is possible, in other words, that
the higher-quality institutions were already so superior in this field that
they could not make further improvements with the small increments
provided by this program. And judging from the correlation between the
quality of the college and the number of training programs it was operating ($r = .57$), there is probably some validity in this interpretation.[4] However, the reverse could be true. The academic structure might have imposed
a ceiling on the amount of adjustment that high-status institutions were
willing to make to the type of clientele served by this program. For, not
only were higher-quality colleges of education more likely to have more
rigid standards but they also were perhaps more socially remote from the
schools and more insulated from the liberalizing forces within the university
and the community that might better prepare them for dealing with problems of people living in poverty.

But irrespective of the college's social position, it was unlikely to have
made an effort to change while the schools were receiving the lion's share
of the funds. Again, several factors probably were involved.[5] There likely
was an economic dimension; that is, colleges needed slack funds to implement the changes they desired to make. But the fact that the total
volume of funds awarded to a program made little difference in the amount
of change that took place in the college suggests that it was not entirely
a matter of money. Also, a political dimension was probably involved.
That is, the proportion of funds controlled by the local schools probably
reflected their relative control over the program, in which case it appears

that colleges must be in a controlling position if a program of this kind is to make an impact on them. This, together with the fact that schools also changed less when they controlled the funds (reported in the previous chapter), suggests that colleges had more leverage over the schools than the schools had over the colleges (as mentioned in the last chapter); it further suggests that with additional funds the colleges could more easily trigger change because they were more predisposed to change than were the schools. Of course, it is also possible that the way funds were distributed within a program for some reason reflected a preexisting incentive to innovate on the part of the colleges. To that extent it does not necessarily follow that increasing a college's proportion of these funds will necessarily promote innovation there. Nevertheless, there was a strong possibility that colleges would not be inclined to push innovation unless they were in control of a relatively large proportion of the funds.

Finally, interns (in contrast to their role in the schools) not only seemed to play a less important role at the college but, paradoxically, the amount of influence they did have was positive (with the possible exception of a small negative correlation with their initiative predispositions). Their less important role in the colleges probably indicates that they were far less visible on a large campus than in the tightly controlled small schools that employed them; their main contacts with the professors were in a few classrooms for a couple of hours a day.[6] Most of the time they were not even on campus. However, the fact that they made a small positive contribution to the college under these conditions is notable in itself. Perhaps their contribution can be attributed to this factor: the university faculty members were better trained, had more autonomy than the classroom teacher, and therefore reacted less defensively toward liberal students, even when these students were from good undergraduate colleges. This conjecture corresponds with my previous observation that, as a result of the interns' prodding, many professors were developing more interest in the problems of educating the disadvantaged.

These findings again emphasize the importance of the quality of colleges selected to participate in Teacher Corps programs. The most change occurred in the mediocre colleges that had competent faculties and liberal social climates. These are the institutions that were most vulnerable to the type of outside influence that a program such as this could produce through the infusion of marginal funds and liberal trainees from good undergraduate colleges—even if they probably were among the least influential institutions in the higher education stratification system. This finding supports Caplow's (1964) conjecture that organizations of intermediate prestige are more receptive to change than organizations that rank high or low.

Improved Cooperation Between Schools and Colleges

A parallel set of analyses was undertaken to identify the characteristics of the program that might have contributed toward improved cooperation between schools and colleges.

The seven dimensions of the program, identified by factor-analysis procedures in Chapter 8, were entered in a regression analysis, with school-college cooperation as the dependent variable (Table 9–2).

Again, the quality of the boundary personnel is the critical ingredient for good relationships between these two institutions. This factor alone accounts for 30 percent of the variance. (For the purposes of this analysis, one variable—cooperation between school and college—was deleted from this factor because the procedures used to compute it were very similar to those used to compute the dependent variable.) With this aspect controlled, the competence and status of the teaching staff also makes a small but statistically significant contribution as does the organizational control exercised by the schools. These three factors account for 41 percent of the variance.

Notice that the second and third factors listed in the table signify how important it is for a school to have a secure status and to be in a position of control in order to cooperate effectively with institutions of higher education. Without these status guarantees, involvement with a college can be intimidating because of the disparities of status and influence between the two institutions. Also observe that once the first three factors listed have been controlled, the social context, professionalism, and liberalism of the staff, the characteristics of the interns, and the competence of the administration make little additional difference. In other words, although the interns' characteristics are associated with cooperation, they probably are not a very influential factor compared to the structural characteristics of the schools and colleges. The interns' presence was more likely to be felt *within* small elementary schools.

As a crude way of estimating the relative importance of the two institutions involved—(a) the school and (b) the college—and of the primary ingredient added to the program—(c) the interns—three separate regression analyses were undertaken. Each regression included only the indicators associated with one of the three elements of the program.

Several different characteristics of the interns were associated with the cooperation that took place between colleges and local schools. The underlying dimension appeared to be the interns' compatibility with the teachers' political and educational philosophy and personal backgrounds. This was reflected in several ways. The most important specific characteristic seemed

Table 9-2 Seven factors correlated with the extent of cooperation between schools and colleges: oblique stepwise regression analysis (N = 42)

Number	Factors[a] (Title)	r	R^2	R^2 added	Partial	T-value	Beta weight	F
5[b]	Quality and interdependence of boundary personnel	.55	.30	--	.35	13.4	.40	17.30
6	Competence of teaching staff	.09	.36	.06	.29	1.97	.21	11.17
3	Organizational control exercised by the schools	.05	.41	.05	.20	2.05	.18	8.96
1	Quality and modernization of context	-.14	.44	.03	-.15	1.87	-.15	7.03
2	Professionalism and social liberalism of staff	-.14	.44	.00	-.15	.43	-.08	1.78
7	Uniqueness of outside change agents	-.06	.44	.00	-.10	.18	.04	.37
4	Competence of administration	.10	.44	.00	.03	.15	.06	.29

a For the variable components that make up each factor, see Table 8-2.
b The variable, "Cooperation between school and college," was deleted from factor 5 because of similarity in scoring used for that variable and the dependent variable.

to be the extent to which interns subscribed to strict discipline in the class-room: the more they emphasized pupil control, the more improvement there was in the cooperation between schools and colleges $(B = .74)$. Conversely, cooperation declined according to the extent to which interns were likely to have posed status threats to the teacher—specifically, the proportion of interns with liberal arts majors $(B = -.68)$, their status dif-ferences $(B = -.40)$, and the quality of their undergraduate colleges $(B = -.31)$. These four variables accounted for 56 percent of the variance. The proportion of interns from outside the region, the difference between their liberalism and that of teachers, and the proportion who were male had minor additional negative effects. The total set of variables explained 60 percent of the variance.

By comparison to the characteristics of the interns, college character-istics appeared to be even better predictors of the extent of cooperation with schools.[7] Only four college characteristics accounted for more than three fourths of the variance. Two variables had a positive influence: interns' ratings of the college faculty $(B = .89)$ and number of training programs $(B = .95)$. Two others appeared to interfere with cooperation: the quality of the college $(B = -.68)$ and the liberalism of the college faculty members $(B = -.36)$.[8] In other words, once again the data point to the crucial role that faculty members play in the change process. But notice that their liberalism may have played a very different role in this case than in the other types of change already considered. Improved co-operation seemed to stem from the faculty's *competence*; or at least, interns perhaps saw their cooperation as a mark of competence. When the faculty's liberalism was controlled first, their competence continued to contribute .32 to the R^2, whereas when competence was controlled, their liberalism made very little further contribution to the R^2 (.005). Not only did liberalism apparently have a less important influence, but it actually appeared to have hindered cooperation. In view of the precarious position that many schools in the sample had within politically volatile communities, teachers and principals were reluctant to take the risk that liberal faculty members might cause the schools to become involved in sensitive or explosive situations. Even though liberal university faculty members could cooperate with comparably liberal team leaders, it appears that the professors were not widely accepted by the other teachers. Thus, the university faculty members' commitment to broad social and political change and their attempts to *push through* specific technological changes might have had an adverse effect on longer-range, broad-based, cooperative efforts between the two institutions.

Although the political climate was less important in this area, the insti-

tutional characteristics appeared to be relatively more important. Even
though the college's prior commitment to improving teacher training (as
evidenced in the existence of simultaneous programs) did not necessarily
guarantee that more technological innovation would be introduced into
the classroom, the amount of prior experience the college had with schools
through other training programs perhaps did help to pave the way for the
Teacher Corps. Not only had the problems associated with such programs
already been confronted and some elementary understandings and procedures worked out but, in a few cases, there had been past favors and a
mutual dependency had developed that encouraged local institutions to
overlook each other's transgressions. In other words, improved cooperation
appears to have been the joint effect of a relatively competent university
faculty in less prestigious institutions that had prior experience in cooperative training programs and that did not have excessively activist
orientations.

The characteristics of the schools explained less of the variance than did
either of the other two groupings of variables. However, the higher the
proportion of classroom teachers who participated in the proposal ($r_p =$
$-.46$), the less improvement occurred in relationships between the school
and the college. Cooperation also declined as the quality of the school
($B = -.40$) improved and as the proportion of teachers having M.A.
degrees ($B = -.25$) and the tenure of the principal ($B = -.25$) increased. Probably for reasons similar to those advanced concerning a
parallel relationship with the introduction of technological change in
schools, the social distance between the two institutions appeared to have
increased with the status and autonomy of the school just as it increased
with the quality of the college. Funded and controlled from separate
sources, schools and colleges tend to function somewhat autonomously;
perhaps the greater the resources and prestige of each institution, the less
willing each was to make the necessary compromises to cooperate with one
another in this type of program. In any event, it is especially difficult to
maintain cooperation between two prestigious institutions. However, cooperation seemed to improve slightly with the longevity of the teachers
in the school ($B = .21$) and the quality of their undergraduate colleges
($B = .20$), perhaps because these factors helped them to identify with the
college and helped to alleviate whatever degree of status insecurity there
might have been. There is much in this pattern, then, to suggest that less
cooperation will take place when schools are in a position to co-opt the
program.

Finally, a multiple correlation regression was computed for the 13 most
salient variables selected from the above groupings. A set of seven vari-

ables emerged as the single best set of predictors, accounting for 94 percent of the variance:

Satisfaction with the faculty, $R^2 = .36$.
Number of training programs, $r_p = .42$, R^2 added $= .12$.
Quality of the interns' undergraduate college, $r_p = -.76$, R^2 added $= .30$.
Quality of the Teacher Corps college, $r_p = -.49$, R^2 added $= .05$.
Quality of the school, $r_p = -.38$, R^2 added $= .02$.
Percent of interns with a liberal arts degree, $r_p = -.35$, R^2 added $= .02$.
Proportion of teachers with an M.A. degree, $r_p = -.31$, R^2 added $= .01$.

Once these particular characteristics were controlled, many of the other variables that correlated with the amount of cooperation that took place between the school and college added very little to the explanation, including the liberalism of the faculty, status difference between interns and teachers, tenure of the principal, proportion of teachers who participated in the proposal, and interns' pupil-control ideology.

Thus a *combination* of characteristics of all the groups and institutions represented—the faculty in the college, the interns, the school, and the teachers—is needed to fully account for the amount of cooperation that took place between the schools and the colleges in this program.

NUMBER OF ACTIVITIES IN THE COMMUNITY

Another dimension of change considered was the number of new activities the interns initiated in the local community. Again, the seven summary factors described in Chapter 8 were examined as possible explanations for the number of community activities (Table 9–3). And again, the quality and interdependence of the boundary personnel ($B = .55$) was by far the most important factor, although in this case it accounted for only 35 percent of the variance; and the amount of control exercised by the schools made a small positive contribution ($B = .55$). However, the other factors made no additional contribution to the explanation. The total set of factors accounted for less than half of the variance (42 percent). In other words, to the extent that community activities could be accounted for by these variables, they were largely the product of the competence of and cooperation between the faculty and the team leaders. The teachers had little faith in community activities and, because the schools were generally defensive, the college faculty's efforts were more likely to be successful where the schools were in a position to maintain some control over this sensitive type of activity. Since the initiative for and control over commun-

Table 9-3 Seven factors correlated with the number of community activities: oblique stepwise regression analysis (N = 42)

Number	Factors[a] (Title)	r	R^2	R^2 added	Partial	T-value	Beta weight	F
5	Quality and interdependence of boundary personnel	.60	.35	--	.58	3.09	.55	16.20
3	Organizational control exercised by the schools	.13	.39	.04	.27	2.46	.23	2.30
4	Competence of administration	.02	.41	.02	.12	.52	.08	1.80
7	Uniqueness of outside change agents	.14	.41	.00	.08	.89	.05	.80
1	Quality and modernization of context	.20	.42	.01	-.07	.83	-.03	.30
6	Competence of teaching staff	-.18	.42	.00	-.07	.17	-.05	.40
2	Professionalism and social liberalism of staff	-.03	.42	.00	-.02	.15	-.01	.20

[a] For the variable components that make up each factor, see Table 8-2.

ity activities was largely in the hands of the faculty, other elements, including the characteristics of the interns, made little additional difference.

Three separate regressions were also computed again, one for each group of the characteristics associated with the schools, colleges, and interns. Seven characteristics of the interns accounted for 36 percent of the variance. In particular, when there was greater status difference between teachers and interns ($B = -.66$) and when there were more interns in the program with liberal arts majors ($B = -.58$), there were fewer community activities promulgated by the program. Also, contrary to what might have been expected, there was less activity in the community in the programs having higher proportions of interns who had prior experience with the Peace Corps or VISTA ($B = -.24$). Interviews and site visits indicated that the interns with this type of background were often more inclined to become involved in politically oriented and controversial types of activities, which schools and colleges tried to discourage. Again, it appears that the unique types of individuals the program sought to attract turned out to be least effective in producing change, perhaps because of the status defensiveness on the part of the teachers, although as already pointed out, the interns probably were not the critical factor.

Four characteristics of colleges accounted for 37 percent of the variance. Again, the liberalism of the faculty seemed to be the single most important factor ($B = .32$), but their competence also seemed to help ($B = .38$; R^2 added $= .11$). (This *relatively* greater influence played by liberalism held true when competence was controlled first, although both variables continued to make independent contributions.) But by comparison to the faculty members' characteristics, the structural characteristics of the college made little additional difference. Since community activity was entirely at the discretion of the faculty, their personal commitment to social and educational reform was the determining factor.

Eight characteristics of the schools accounted for 44 percent of the variance. Participation in the proposal by more teachers caused fewer community activities to be initiated ($B = -.41$). Teachers' defensiveness about interns getting involved in controversial community activities perhaps was a major factor; perhaps, for that reason, activities in the community increased very slightly with increases in the teachers' professional and organizational status, that is, with their formal education ($B = .19$) and with the quality of their undergraduate college ($B = .13$).

Finally, a multiple correlation regression was computed for the 10 most salient variables selected from the above groupings. A set of five of these variables emerged as the single best set of predictors, accounting for 48 percent of the variance:

Liberalism of the faculty, $R^2 = .26$.
Interns' satisfaction with the faculty, $r_p = .38$, R^2 added $= .11$.
Proportion of interns with a liberal arts major, $r_p = -.21$, R^2 added $= .05$.
Proportion of teachers with an M.A. degree, $r_p = .25$, R^2 added $= .04$.
Pupil-control ideology of the interns, $r_p = -.24$, R^2 added $= .03$.

Once these variables were controlled, five other variables contributed only an additional 1 percent to the variance explained: proportion of teachers who participated in the proposal; the status difference between interns and teachers; the liberalism of the team leaders; the proportion of interns with prior Peace Corps or VISTA experience; and the quality of the interns' undergraduate college.

In other words, the characteristics of the university faculty and of the interns were the major factors in the number of community activities that took place in this program. The only characteristics of the schools or of the teachers that seemed to make a major difference was the level of education of the classroom teachers (and their participation in the proposal).

In view of the important linkage role played by team leaders, it is perhaps surprising that their liberalism was not more instrumental in the amount of community activity that took place. But there is a good reason for their relatively low influence in this area: being experienced employees of the local schools, they were committed to the traditional classroom role of the teacher and were reluctant to take interns out of the classroom. By comparison, the university faculty members were more progressive in this respect.

ORGANIZATIONAL FLEXIBILITY

Thus far we have been searching for the characteristics of schools and colleges in the Teacher Corps program that might have contributed to (or minimized) various types of technological and organizational change that materialized. Clearly, change was more likely to occur in certain types of organizational climates than in others; that is, some organizations were more receptive to change than others. This, of course, did not mean that change would materialize, because many other factors were involved. Nevertheless, the setting was a compelling intervening ingredient. Therefore, we should examine the conditions that produced organizational flexibility and defensiveness. This dimension was tapped in the index of organizational flexibility developed for the study and reported in Appendix 1.[9]

As in the other analyses, the seven summary factors described in Chapter 8 were analyzed in relation to organizational flexibility. However, since the items in the flexibility index (see Appendix 1) were logically comparable to, and often empirically correlated with, several of the factor components, the analysis reveals more about the validity of this index than about the independent sources of flexibility. The factors correlated in the following manner with flexibility:

The competence of the administration, $r = .26$.
Organizational control, $r = -.18$.
Quality and modernization of the context, $r = .15$.
Quality and interdependence of the boundary personnel, $r = .25$.
Uniqueness of the outsiders, $r = -.05$.
Professionalism and social liberalism of the staff, $r = .02$.

It is more revealing in this case to examine how the individual variables are associated with flexibility. Table 9–4 (part I) reinforces what has already been suggested: schools tend to become rigid and defensive when threatened by aggressive interns with unique backgrounds. Organizational flexibility declines with the predispositions of the interns to take initiative in opposition to the administration ($B = -.40$), with the proportion who are males ($B = -.33$), the proportion who have liberal arts majors ($B = -.27$), their political liberalism ($B = -.36$), the proportion who stress creativity in teaching ($B = -.22$), the quality of their undergraduate college ($B = -.20$), and the proportion who have had prior Peace Corps and VISTA experience ($B = -.16$). These seven characteristics account for 59 percent of the variance.

Another analysis indicated that the quality of the Teacher Corps college also was negatively correlated with the flexibility of the schools ($r_p = -.47$, controlling for the proportion of interns who are predisposed to take initiative against the administration and the proportion with liberal arts majors; R^2 added $= .12$), which suggests that the schools' defensiveness reflected the presence of other high-status organizations in addition to the presence of interns. Perhaps the teachers were intimidated by the fact that many interns were considered to be associated with, and perhaps backed by, prestigious and resourceful colleges.

Another finding reflected that the inflexibility of schools was partly a response to threat. The more conflict that occurred in a school over a program, the less flexible the school became ($r = -.55$). Of course, it also seems likely that rigid schools were not able to accommodate the program without creating conflicts, but it is plausible to assume that, once threatened, they became even more rigid. This interpretation was also

Table 9–4 Characteristics of interns and schools correlated with the organizational flexibility of schools

Characteristics	r	R^2	R^2 added	Final partial	Final T value	Final beta weight	F
I. Interns							
Predisposition of interns to take initiative against administrators	-.54	.296	--	-.488	3.26	-.402	16.84
Proportion of interns who are male	-.37	.381	.085	-.398	2.53	-.325	12.03
Proportion of interns with liberal arts undergraduate majors	-.23	.449	.068	-.328	2.03	-.273	10.32
Mean political liberalism of interns	.06	.485	.036	-.409	2.61	-.358	8.72
Proportion of interns who emphasize creativity as the most important aspect of the teaching role	-.46	.539	.054	-.278	1.66	-.217	8.41
Quality of interns' undergraduate college	-.17	.567	.026	-.252	1.52	-.202	7.64
Proportion of interns with prior Peace Corps or VISTA experience	-.18	.588	.021	-.219	1.31	-.162	6.93
II. School							
Proportion of teachers who have M.A. degree	.32	.106	--	.446	2.86	.449	4.72
Teachers' length of service	-.32	.195	.089	-.408	2.57	-.398	4.31
Proportion of funds controlled by the local school	.08	.253	.058	.328	1.99	.311	2.94
Competence of the principal as rated by teachers and interns	.19	.291	.038	.282	1.69	.241	2.00
Centralization of decision-making in the schools	-.04	.324	.033	.267	1.59	.247	1.78
Proportion of teachers in a union	-.04	.357	.033	-.245	1.46	-.220	1.78
Quality of teachers' undergraduate college	.19	.366	.009	.110	.63	.100	.48

supported by an inverse correlation between the number of problems the program had created for teachers and organizational flexibility ($r = -.52$, controlling for the proportion of interns with liberal arts majors and the quality of their undergraduate college).

From this pattern of evidence it can be inferred that outside intervention can sometimes have the effect of minimizing an organization's *receptivity* to change. But this does not imply that it is impossible to force *innovation* on unreceptive or inflexible organizations. Flexibility may help to contribute to innovation, but it is not always a necessary condition. This explains why organizational flexibility was not correlated with the introduction of new techniques into the schools ($r = .04$).

However, the extent of actual threat to a teaching faculty seems to depend on the faculty's own characteristics, particularly the ones that reflect a measure of status security. Seven school characteristics account for 37 percent of the variance in the flexibility measure (Table 9–4, part II) (only the first four are statistically significant on a one tail test). Some signify a degree of competence and status on the part of teachers that perhaps gives them a sense of control over a changing situation. For example, the proportion of teachers with an M.A. degree ($B = .45$) and, especially, the proportion from better colleges ($B = .10$) can be interpreted as indices of the teachers' competence, or at least their status. Faculties with more education are perhaps less threatened by change because of their status; similarly, they are more likely to trust a principal during a period of change when they rate him as competent ($B = .24$). In the same vein, schools are more liberal toward change when they control a higher proportion of the funds ($B = .31$). A centralized administration ($r_p = .27$) can be interpreted in the same way, that is, as having more control and therefore less reason to be threatened by the program. Centralized systems tend to be powerful ones, even though teachers may feel subordinated within them; as pointed out in the previous chapter, they can be more easily protected from outside influence by centralized systems. Teachers in this situation can afford to be tolerant toward change, since they have leverage and personal and structural protections to keep the innovation from getting out of hand.

Negative correlations with the longevity of teachers ($r_p = -.41$) and with unionism ($r_p = -.25$) are not as easily explained, but they are consistent with the concept of status security. A status based on longevity is tenuously dependent on the stability of the existing system because it stems from experience in and success with that system. The value of success and experience can be threatened by new departures. Thus, although length of service in the system may provide teachers with a sense of security in a *stable* situation, it has the reverse effect in a changing situation in which experience becomes irrelevant and a handicap. Moreover, the longer a teacher has been in the profession, the more vulnerable he is to the charge of having become technically obsolete and the greater the disparity is likely to be between the deference he expects and the deference accorded him by younger, often better-trained colleagues. Furthermore, teachers who have been in the school longer perhaps have a measure of influence with the administration, which only increases the relative deprivation when they are not accorded respect from their peers. The fact that someone has deemed that innovation in teaching is necessary and the fact that young outsiders are leading it call into question the competence and authority of teachers who are now in charge and who presumably are responsible for the situation that needs changing.

The negative correlation with unionism (although not statistically significant) might be similarly explained. Although unionism conceivably would provide teachers with a sense of corrective protection and, hence, status security, the fact that teachers have unionized is, in itself, probably indicative of an underlying sense of vulnerability on the part of teachers and of tension with the administration. Therefore, unions, having been formed to protect teachers from the threat of change that they do not control, contribute to organizational rigidity.

Table 9–5 indicates that a combination of nine characteristics, of both interns and schools, accounts for much of the variance in the measure of flexibility ($R^2 = .65$). However, the fact that school characteristics account for only 8 percent of this figure is indicative of the overwhelming influence that introducing interns into schools had on organizational flexibility. The three most important variables were all intern characteristics: their predisposition to take initiative; the proportion who are male; and the proportion with liberal arts majors. Together, these three variables account for 45 percent of the variance. Even with the four most significant school variables controlled, these same three intern characteristics account for 22 percent of the variance explained.

CONFLICT AMONG PARTICIPANTS

I have stated that the schools seemed to have become inflexible in their reaction to the overt conflict associated with the Teacher Corps program and to the general status threat posed by the new teachers from the liberal arts. To determine whether the interns were responsible for any of the conflict, the respondents were asked in interviews to describe the types of

Table 9-5 Characteristics of interns and schools correlated with the organizational flexibility of schools

Characteristics of interns and schools	r	R^2	R^2 added	Final partial	Final T value	Final beta weight	F
Predisposition of interns to take initiative	-.54	.296	--	-.476	3.07	-.361	16.84
Proportion of interns who are male	-.37	.381	.085	-.375	2.29	-.288	5.38
Proportion of interns with liberal arts major	-.23	.449	.068	-.327	1.96	-.259	4.65
Teachers' length of service	-.32	.495	.046	-.316	1.88	-.216	3.35
Proportion of interns who consider themselves politically "very liberal"	.06	.527	.032	.422	2.63	.342	2.45
Proportion of interns who stress creativity in teaching	-.46	.570	.043	-.109	.62	-.087	3.56
Proportion of interns with prior Peace Corps or VISTA experience	-.18	.602	.032	-.325	1.94	-.234	2.74
Quality of interns' undergraduate college	-.17	.624	.022	-.327	1.96	-.274	1.90
Proportion of teachers who have M.A. degree	.32	.652	.028	.273	1.61	.211	2.58

overt arguments and disagreements that had occurred among participants in the program. Most of the disputes were between team leaders and either principals or teachers, although interns frequently were indirectly involved. Each of the 42 schools was assigned a score reflecting the number of different incidents reported.

The seven summary factors described in Chapter 8 were examined for possible explanations of conflict (Table 9–6). The highest rates of conflict are associated with the smaller, poorer quality institutions located in less urbanized, modernized regions (factor 1) ($r_p = -.45$); where the college faculty is relatively liberal, competent, and in touch with the schools ($r_p = .46$); where the teachers are less professionally oriented and relatively conservative (factor 2) ($r_p = -.43$); and where the schools have less control over the program (factor 3) ($r_p = -.29$). These four factors account for slightly over half of the variance.

A clearer picture can be obtained by examining the factor components separately. The one program characteristic that was most highly correlated with this index was the mean difference in the political liberalism scores of teachers and interns ($r = .60$); this simple (zero order) correlation, however, is lower ($r_p = .36$) when partialled against two other variables— quality of the cooperating college ($r = -.56$) and the proportion of program funds controlled by the local schools ($r = -.41$) (see Table 9–7). Also, even with this and the two other variables controlled, the proportion of interns with liberal arts majors ($r_p = .50$) makes a statistically significant contribution (R^2 added $= .10$). These four factors account for nearly three fourths of the variance.[10]

In short, the conflict seems to have been minimized by the two program characteristics, quality of the college and control by local schools. I shall now consider each in turn.

Quality of the College

It is not clear why there is less conflict in programs associated with higher-quality colleges, especially since this latter variable is associated with the proportion of interns with liberal arts degrees ($r = .61$) and with the mean quality scores of the interns' undergraduate college ($r = .70$), both of which are positively associated with conflict and with inflexibility ($r_p = -.47$). But it is true that in the better colleges there is less difference between teachers' and interns' status index ($r = -.87$) or their political liberalism ($r = -.26$). This can be attributed to the fact that better universities are located in the larger cities ($r = .71$) of the modernized areas ($r = .80$) in which the classroom teachers hold liberal political views

Table 9-6 Seven factors correlated with the rate of conflict among participants in the program: oblique stepwise regression analysis (N = 42)

Number	Factors[a] (Title)	r	R^2	R^2 added	Partial	T-value	Beta weight	F
1	Quality and modernization of context	-.45	.20	--	-.45	2.90	-.41	10.29
5	Quality and interdependence of boundary personnel	.22	.37	.17	.46	3.06	.43	11.69
2	Professionalism and social liberalism of staff	-.13	.49	.12	-.43	2.10	-.39	12.11
3	Organizational control by the schools	-.24	.53	.04	-.29	2.10	-.31	10.55
7	Uniqueness of outsiders	.09	.54	.01	.10	1.15	.09	8.37
6	Competence and status of teaching staff	-.06	.54	.00	-.02	.30	-.01	6.79
4	Competence of the administration	.08	.54	.00	.02	.00	.01	5.66

[a] For variable components that make up each factor, see Table 8-2.

301

Table 9-7   Program characteristics and rate of conflict in the
program

Program characteristics	r	R^2	R^2 added	Final partial	F
Difference in the political liberalism of interns and teachers	.60	.356	--	.36	22.18
Quality of the college	-.56	.530	.174	-.52	21.99
Proportion of funds controlled by local schools	-.41	.621	.091	-.44	20.75
Proportion of interns with liberal arts major	.35	.716	.095	.50	23.33

$(r = .52)$. Moreover, since there was less technological innovation in schools associated with higher-quality colleges, there may have been less activity taking place and less reason for conflict to develop. However, this is not the total explanation; in another analysis, quality of the college continued to make a small but independent negative contribution to the conflict rate, even with most of the above variables controlled. A possible explanation is that the resources, prestige, and influence of these institutions may have provided them with sufficient legitimacy and autonomy to buffer them from overt resistance.

In addition to the quality of the college, several other characteristics of the university and program are positively correlated with the conflict rate in the schools. (1) The more university faculty members who participated in the proposal, the greater the rate of conflict $(r = .49)$. (2) The greater the university's support for the program, the higher the conflict rate $(r = .51)$. (3) There is a slight tendency for the university with a more liberal faculty to be associated with high conflict rate in the schools $(r = .24)$.[11] In general, the college's support for the program (including its backing for interns) seems to have aggravated the conflict. This finding can be regarded as a by-product of the fact, previously noted, that the colleges often exerted pressure on resistant schools.

Control by the Local Schools

Conflict also depends on the involvement of the local schools. The proportion of funds controlled by the local schools explains more of the variance ($r_p = -.66$) than total cost of the program ($r_p = -.33$) or cost figures on the ratio of dollars per intern ($r_p = -.51$). After these latter two variables have been controlled, the proportion of available funds controlled by the local school still makes a contribution (R^2 added $= .34$); these three variables explain 57 percent of the variance.[12] In another analysis, with three other variables controlled—the proportion of interns with liberal arts degrees, quality of the interns' undergraduate college, and their political liberalism—the proportion of funds controlled by the local schools added .275 to the R^2 ($r_p = -.59$). These four variables explain 50 percent of the variance.

The proportion of funds controlled by a school probably reflects its ability to maintain control over the interns. Not only do programs that control more of the funds select interns whose backgrounds are closely matched to the backgrounds of the classroom teachers ($r = -.45$) but, more important, universities are less supportive of the programs in which local schools control more of the funds ($r = -.41$). Moreover, where schools have more control over the funds, fewer teachers ($r = -.41$) and university faculty members ($r = -.35$) identify themselves as "liberals." In short, there seems to be no major source pressuring for change in such programs and, hence, little cause for conflict.

The picture that emerges, then, is that conflict is produced when these ingredients are present: (1) broad-based support for the program on the part of a competent and liberal faculty located in a mediocre university that controls a substantial proportion of the program funds and that attempts to push change; (2) cooperation with conservative, reluctant schools; (3) assigned interns who have graduated from the liberal arts and who are substantially more liberal politically and socially than the classroom teachers. It can be conjectured that the interns are encouraged to push their ideas in the schools when they feel they have support from an involved and liberal faculty at the university.

SUMMARY

We have examined the program characteristics that contribute to several types of innovation: (1) change in college programs; (2) improved cooperation between colleges and schools; and (3) initiation of projects in the local community. We have also identified factors contributing to (a) organizational flexibility, and (b) conflict among the participants.

Changes in College Programs

The small positive influence suggests that the replacement strategy is more effective in colleges, especially those ready for change, than in the schools. However, while the proportion of interns with liberal arts majors was related to changes in the college, interns' characteristics appeared to be less important than the competence and liberalism of the college faculty and the proportion of funds controlled by the college. Other significant determinants were the number of training programs at the college and negative relationships with the quality factor. The direction of this negative relationship again signifies the importance of the type of institution recruited into the program and the difficulty of inducing change from the outside in prestigious organizations.

School-College Cooperation

Interns generally had little effect on cooperation, but those with liberal arts backgrounds and whose status differed markedly from teachers seemed to affect it adversely; cooperation was better in systems in which interns endorsed an ideology of close control over pupils. Among the characteristics of the college and the school that seemed to have a positive effect, competence of the university faculty, as rated by interns, and the liberalism of the team leader were important. However, the more liberal the professors and the greater the difference in liberalism between teachers and interns and the higher the quality of the college, the less cooperative is the relationship.

The quality of the boundary personnel was the most important determinant in the amount of cooperation that took place between the two institutions. The competence and status of the teaching staff and the organizational control exercised by the schools had a small positive effect. Relative to these three factors, the characteristics of the interns and other characteristics of the schools made little difference. In other words, in the absence of a tradition, a structure, or an official incentive system to promote cooperation, the major initiative had to come from concerned and competent faculty members who, as members of the dominant institution, were the determining factors. However, for cooperation to occur, it was essential for the faculty members not to be too radical and to find a receptive, competent school staff. In this case, it was necessary to have competent team leaders but, since cooperation required a wider base of support, it also helped if the entire teaching faculty was sufficiently competent and exer-

cised enough control that they would not be intimidated by member
the college.

Community Projects

Although the number of new activities in the community was not closely
correlated with any specific characteristics of the interns, the pattern
parallels other change dimensions in this respect: fewer activities were
reported in programs with more interns from high-quality liberal arts colleges and with prior Peace Corps or VISTA experience, and more projects
were reported in which the interns emphasized pupil control. The findings
suggest that the policy of assigning change-oriented newcomers to traditional schools, as practiced in this program, was not beneficial and may
have been self-defeating insofar as producing this type of change was
concerned. At best, intern characteristics seemed to play a minimal part in
innovation in community projects.

The single most important variable identified was the proportion of
college faculty who considered themselves liberal. The number of training
programs at the college also was related to change, as was the competence
of the professors and teachers and the proportion of classroom teachers
having M.A. degrees. The participation of more teachers in the proposal,
however, resulted in fewer innovative community projects. Also, the higher
the proportion of teachers who belonged to a union, the less change there
was.

Again, the number of community activities was largely a product of the
liberalism and competence of the university faculty members, the team
leaders' competence, and the amount of cooperation between these two
positions. Usually, few people in the program outside of a few faculty
members had any interest in promoting community activities. Therefore,
their characteristics were the determining factor. But because the community activities were sometimes politically sensitive, the schools were
very cautious and more likely to lend their support if they had some
control over the situation. Even then, the teachers curbed these activities
where they were given a voice.

Organizational Flexibility

An index of organizational flexibility of the schools indicated that the
more aggressive the interns were, the more defensive the school became.
More of the variance in organizational flexibility was accounted for

by the threatening characteristics of interns than characteristics of school personnel. Flexibility declined with interns' predisposition to take initiative, the proportion who were males, the proportion with liberal arts majors, and their political liberalism. The more stress interns placed on creativity in teaching and the higher the proportion of interns who had Peace Corps or VISTA experience, the less flexible the organization was. Finally, the higher the quality of interns' undergraduate colleges, the greater the inflexibility of the organization.

Conflict and Problems

There was an inverse correlation between flexibility and *staff conflict* and the *problems* that the program created for the teachers. Both variables were highly correlated with the difference in liberalism between interns and teachers. Also, the proportion of interns with liberal arts majors was related to the rate of conflict and to problems.

The conflict that arises when newcomers are given a mandate to help improve the traditional system is perhaps inevitable. The question is whether the personal characteristics of new people alone can be relied on to change a profession when there are features within its structure that support or inhibit attempts to introduce innovation. The answer in this program is that there also must be outside support and influence.

CONCLUSIONS

In the discussion of a range of related dependent variables, several characteristics associated with schools, universities, and interns in the program repeatedly emerged as salient, independent factors that seem to underlie the different dimensions of change, and the phenomena associated with it, that were considered. Let me identify some of these variables more explicitly.

One of the most important of these independent variables was the social and political liberalism of the university faculty and, to a lesser extent, their competence. Perhaps the decentralized nature of the decision-making structure in the colleges accentuated the importance of the role of the university faculty in this program. The faculty established the critical value climate and played important boundary-spanning roles. Their liberal attitudes not only seemed to reflect the university's general integration into the network of relevant organizations and identification with the broad

social reforms being proposed on behalf of the low-income people, ι
they seemed predisposed to work with their counterparts in the schoc
and on their own in the community to accomplish change. They were
especially effective when they were able to cooperate with liberal team
leaders in the schools or to work directly with interns in the community
where they did not need the cooperation of the classroom teachers. However, their liberal attitudes and actions seemed to prevent them from
developing a broad base of cooperation and support within the schools. By
comparison, the university faculty members whom interns judged as being
competent seemed to have had more success in establishing cooperative
relationships with the schools.

A variable that sometimes seemed to be of parallel (but lesser) importance
was the way the college was integrated into the academic system, as reflected in the quality of its resources and students. Fewer changes
uniformly occurred, and there was less conflict in the programs associated
with high-quality colleges, even though the schools associated with these
institutions appeared to be somewhat intimidated and defensive toward
them. A variety of reasons for this has been discussed—their prior superior-
ity in this field, the impotent effects that a small program could have on
them, and their autonomy and social distance from the problems of low-
income schools. However, the fact that the higher quality public schools
also had difficulty cooperating with the universities suggests that status
differences between the two institutions may have been the critical factor.
The fact that the schools seemed to be defensive suggests that they might
have believed the universities were in a position to exercise influence over
them if they had wished to do so.

There is, of course, more to a college's quality than the competence of
its faculty and its other resources. The number of training programs
sponsored by the university, for example, could be considered as a reflection
of its commitment to teacher training. This measure was associated with
improved relationships between colleges and schools, with changes in the
college and, to a lesser extent, with activities in the community, although
it was not necessarily associated with the introduction of new techniques in
the schools, perhaps because the colleges had already reached a ceiling on
what they could do. In other words, whereas the measure of institutional
quality was indicative of the college's social distance from the schools, commitment to teacher training had the effect of closing this gap. Because the
quality of the college was positively associated with the number of training
programs, the final outcome was sometimes indeterminable. But *despite* the
fact that the better institutions had more training programs, they still did

not register much change. This indicates that something else, perhaps the status of the institution, was counteracting the effect of the training programs.

Finally, the interns' evaluations of the college faculty's competence might be considered as another indicator of the college's quality. This measure consistently was an important positive factor. Indeed, because there was a high correlation between the political and social liberalism of the faculty and their competence ratings, it was sometimes difficult to determine which had priority, even though in the regression analyses the former variable usually obscured the latter. But clearly, the index of faculty competence measured something quite different from what was measured by the institutional resource index. The difference between the two measures is perhaps analogous to the difference between teaching and research criteria or between local and cosmopolitan standards of prestige. In other words, perhaps the interns' satisfaction with the college faculty reflected the faculty's commitment to teaching, not only teaching in the college but also the improvement of teaching in the public schools. Thus, whereas the index of university quality was negatively associated with most types of change, the competence of the faculty, as rated by the interns, had a positive influence in most cases, especially with respect to improved school-community relationships.

Another type of independent variable that was consistently important was the liberalism of the interns, especially the difference between their attitudes and status and those of the classroom teachers. Different indicators of this dimension showed up in different analyses, but generally, the more liberal the interns, the greater their impact (even though in most cases it was a negative impact). The more liberal the interns, the fewer technological innovations and community activities that were introduced, and the lower the level of cooperation between the school and the university. Moreover, there was more defensiveness on the part of the schools and more conflict within the program.

Yet, the interns were not an entirely negative influence. In addition to their contribution to technological innovations of rural programs, where they represented one of the few positive forces for change, they seemed to play a positive (if only supplementary) role in promoting change in the colleges. Moreover, to the extent that they subscribed to a conservative political and social ideology and to a conservative philosophy of teaching, especially one that stressed discipline, they had a positive effect.

The interjection of interns into these schools illuminated some of the dynamics of organizational responses to stress. The findings in this connection are stated in the form of a miniature propositional theory:

1. The greater the status threat posed by newcomers to an organization, the more conflict that will occur.

2. The more conflict that occurs, the more defensive and inflexible the organization becomes.

A third proposition follows from the above:

3. Schools tend to become inflexible and defensive against status threats posed by aggressive, liberal interns.

The defensiveness on the part of schools increased when the university backed the program and it seemed to be mitigated when teachers were in a secure status situation, either because of the quality and length of their own training or because of a centralized decision-making structure; however, the effects were relatively small. Generally, the better educated teachers were more responsive to change, those with longer service were less responsive. However, there seemed to be less cooperation with the university where a higher proportion of the teachers had an M.A. degree, perhaps because they were able to remain independent of the university's influence, just as the high-quality schools generally were able to do.

Another type of variable, reflected in a number of different indices, was the extent of control the schools exercised over the program. Generally, the more control the schools had, the more change and the less conflict there was, and the less defensiveness the schools exhibited. This pattern was reflected in different ways with respect to the proportion of program funds controlled by the schools and perhaps with the tenure of the principal. But, the more classroom teachers who participated in the proposal, the less change there was, although this form of control was also associated with higher rates of conflict, probably because it had to be shared with other groups. Also, unionization had an equivocal effect. The union gave the teachers more control. Thus, unionized schools were less flexible, but they evidenced more technological change. As discussed previously, well-organized teachers were probably in a position to accept the changes they had endorsed but to reject others, which would account for an indeterminable outcome.

I have discussed the impact of the Teacher Corps program on the participating institutions and, specifically, on the changes that occurred in the local schools and colleges and their relationships to each other and to the community. A number of variables were identified which, taken together, constitute a profile of a local program that was receptive to change. This profile, however, is necessarily incomplete because it does not take into account the broad social and political forces that were impinging on the local institutions. The next chapter takes into account the pressures on the national program.

NOTES

1. The various types of change referred to in this chaper were measured in ways comparable to those used for technological innovation. See Appendix 1.

2. Since there are essentially only 10 different cases aggregated across the 42 schools, the results from this (or any other procedure) will not necessarily be reliable, and extreme care should be used in generalizing to a larger universe. What is important here are the patterns in the data.

3. Even controlling for the proportion of funds controlled by the schools, the cost per intern, and the modernization of the region, the quality of the university ($r_p = .71$) has a substantial negative effect on the number of innovations (R^2 added $= .17$, total $R^2 = .85$).

4. In view of the low negative correlation between the university's resource scores and interns' ratings of the faculty competence, it is clear that these two indices are measuring different aspects of the academic system. Interns' ratings of faculty members clearly were colored by their liberalism ($r = .46$) as well as by the faculty's own liberalism ($r = .39$). However, since these two factors did not entirely account for the ratings, the possibility remains that the faculty's professional competence, as reflected by this measure, contributed to change, which would indicate that the academic system is not entirely detrimental to change. The nature of the difference between these two measures is discussed further in the conclusion to this chapter.

5. Another analysis indicated that even with the proportion of liberal arts majors and their satisfaction with the faculty controlled, the proportion of funds controlled by the local schools makes a negative contribution (R^2 added $= .15$, total $R^2 = .70$); this latter factor is more important than the funds allocated per intern, although that, too, makes a small contribution, even after the other variables have been controlled (R^2 added $= .05$).

6. Even with the proportion of funds controlled by the local schools, the interns' satisfaction with the university faculty's competence, and the quality of the university all controlled, one analysis indicated that the quality of the interns' undergraduate college ($r_p = .62$) and the proportion of interns with liberal arts majors ($r_p = .67$) both made contributions to the variance explained. (R^2 added $= .06$ and $.03$; $R^2 = .82$). The proportion of interns from the outside ($r_p = .15$) also made a negligible positive contribution, and the initiative predisposition of interns ($r_p = .17$) made a negligible contribution (R^2 added in both cases $= .005$).

7. The method of grouping the variables in separate regressions can provide only a crude picture of the relative power of different types of explanations, however. The results are not strictly comparable because different numbers of indicators are involved in each set, because there is some multicollinearity (Blalock, 1963), and because of the partialling fallacy (Gordon, 1968).

8. Notice, too, that the larger universities seemed to be more cooperative ($r = .44$), but the size of the program, as reflected by its total cost, is negatively correlated

with this index $(r = -.62)$. My visits suggested that in the larger faculties there was more chance that at least one or two professors would show some interest in the local schools, whereas when a program receives a relatively large grant, it creates more coordination problems and greater conflict in policy and competition for control between the schools and universities.

9. This index is based on the combined ratings of interns and teachers concerning the restriction placed on their activities, their opportunity to engage in experimental and innovative activities that depart from the routine, the flexibility permitted in the curriculum, the extent to which the administration encourages teachers to exercise initiative and innovation in the teaching program, and the backing that the administration will give an intern in the event he gets into trouble with other teachers in the course of worthwhile Teacher Corps activities (see Appendix 1).

10. In another analysis, when the indices of the quality of the college and quality of the schools were simultaneously controlled, the proportion of interns in the program with liberal arts degrees $(r_p = -.58)$ contributed more (R^2 added $= .226$) than did either quality of the intern's undergraduate college (R^2 added $= .056$, $r_p = .35$) or the difference between teachers' and interns' liberalism (R^2 added $= .021$, $r_p = .23$). Controlling for the proportion of funds controlled by the local school did not substantially alter the situation.

    The difference in liberalism between the interns and teachers also correlates more highly than any of the other variables considered with the *proportion of teachers in each school who indicated* (in response to a questionnaire item) *that the program had created problems for them* and/or increased their work load $(r = .54)$. The quality of the interns' undergraduate college $(r_p = .73)$ also adds to the variance explained. These two variables explain 67 percent of the variance. In addition, the proportion of teachers who participated in the proposal $(r_p = .53)$, the proportion of interns with liberal arts majors $(r_p = .38)$, the proportion of male interns $(r_p = .22)$, and the proportion of funds controlled by the local schools $(r_p = -.24)$ all make minor contributions. These six variables explain 82 percent of the variance.

11. There is also a tendency for the *problems* that the program created for teachers to increase with the proportion of university faculty members who have participated in the proposal $(r = .46)$, with their liberalism $(r = .46)$, and with the university's support for the program $(r = .44)$.

12. Also, teachers report fewer problems within the program where the schools controlled more of the funds.

CHAPTER 10

Strategies of Survival: Adaptation to the National Society

Evaluators of social action programs often complain that the programs lack any clear and concise statement of aims. . . . Their response generally has been to bemoan the imprecision and fuzzymindedness of the politicians and administrators who establish the programs. . . . I propose to stand this on its head and question the . . . fuzzy single-mindedness of much educational evaluation. It generally has not grasped the diverse and conflicting nature of social program aims.

COHEN, 1970, p. 231

This chapter examines the national program and devotes special attention to the role of the Teacher Corps office in Washington, D.C. Judgments are based on the analysis of documents, interviews with informants, secondary-data sources, and the data systematically collected on local programs. These data were used not to confirm hypotheses but to inform my observations and to develop tentative interpretations.

THE SOCIAL CONTEXT

The Teacher Corps program reflects the milieu in which it was spawned. Rapidly changing technological societies, continuously faced with large reservoirs of laborers and professional workers whose skills have become obsolete, must find self-renewal mechanisms; they must learn to accom-

312

modate traditional patterns of stratification to revitalized social ideals and to new realities of power; and, torn by a high degree of differentiation in the face of growing interdependence, they must search for new ways to coordinate the efforts of the powerful organizations that comprise them. Nowhere are these problems more evident than in the field of education.

Rehabilitation

Traditionally it was assumed that the individual was responsible for his own fate. But this comfortable assumption is giving way in the face of widespread poverty, unemployment, and derivative social problems. A post-industrial "welfare state" has emerged and has assumed the primary responsibility for managing the economy, imposing its own market controls. The informal controls and custodial measures traditionally used to cope with the "unproductive"—the unemployed and the poor—are being supplemented by formal training programs designed to reshape the persons involved. As the principal agents of socialization over which the government has some control, schools must assume a major part of this burden; and because the universities are responsible for training the teachers and other professionals, they are expected to lead the way. When the problems are not quickly alleviated, the profession itself comes under a broad frontal attack. Thus the teaching profession has been confronted with a crisis of major proportions as it has become more and more evident that schools cannot cope effectively with the needs of many low-income children. A generation ago these children would have dropped out of high school, but now they are being forced by conditions of the labor market and job discrimination to remain. In view of criticism of the profession, the training institutions are being forced to reexamine their conventional assumptions about the teachers' authority and role in society.

Social Conscience

Public attacks on professional autonomy have taken place within broader waves of hope and humanism, of frustration and alienation, among large numbers of college students attempting to cope with a dramatically polarized society. Revivals of the romantic social consciousness have worked their way into the political arena, partly through a confluence of two forces: the rising power and expectations of lower-class people and the growing numbers of youth from that mushrooming segment of the population who do not make their living directly from commerce—those preparing for careers in universities, publishing, the helping professions, public service, the arts, and mass media. Clustered in universities in which social criticism is tolerated and encouraged, these students are sufficiently educated yet marginal enough to the economy to be aware of the need for structural change, and they are sufficiently secure and wealthy to take the risks involved. Not only does this group supply the manpower for change, but politicians were quick to realize that unless outlets were provided for their altruism within the system, they would turn against it. Thus, new careers were developed to appeal to idealistic youth in an effort to channel their humanism into practical directions. New roles have been fashioned within established occupations, and the emergence of entire new professions is imminent. The Teacher Corps, the Peace Corps, and VISTA are only a few of the many programs created to serve the culture of poverty.

Organizational Autonomy and Public Opposition

The initiation of these programs by the federal government constitutes an implicit challenge to the effectiveness of the local level, and their content represents an attack on middle-class privilege and on traditional assumptions underlying the helping professions. Francis Keppel's reorganization of the U.S. Office of Education and the establishment of regional educational laboratories, designed to bypass the authority of state departments of education, signaled a broader effort of the Kennedy administration to wrest public institutions from the established professions—in this case, from the school administrators, teachers organizations, college professors, and others who traditionally had controlled education in this country. The programs did not stop at efforts to undermine the control of professions but sought to deprofessionalize and otherwise change them. Therefore, it is not surprising that they have encountered formidable opposition, despite the coalition of forces behind them. The conflict and defensiveness produced by these circumstances are obstacles to improved cooperation among members of different organizations from various sectors of the society.

CONSTRAINTS ON THE PROGRAM

The Teacher Corps program did not arise from a position of strength and authority but from compromise and vulnerability. It was designed to reform from within the system, a position which provided a sense of legitimacy for its proposals; but its limited *power* minimized the scope of change that could be contemplated. Problems were to be resolved by adding resources to the present system and by making minor adjustments to it.

Political and Legislative Constraints

Programs such as the Teacher Corps are handicapped from the beginning by long-standing and pervasive anxieties among the people. Many people feared that the Corps would be another wedge to breach local control and politicize schools and colleges. These fears were intensified by the innovative features of the program, especially the use of federal funds to recruit nontraditional change agents. In response to the growing public concern, shortly after the program started Congress modified the initial legislation in an attempt to assure local autonomy:

Members of the Teacher Corps shall be under the direct supervision of the appropriate officials of the local education agencies to which they are assigned . . . such agencies shall retain the authority to (1) assign such members within their systems; (2) make transfers within their systems; (3) determine the subject matter to be taught; (4) determine the terms and continuance of the assignment of such members within their systems.[1]

Apparently this language still was not sufficiently strong. After the first year of operation, Congress deleted the term "National" from the original program title. It shifted responsibility from the Commissioner of Education to local education agencies and institutions of higher education. It provided for team leaders to be selected from the local schools and for interns to be recruited by local systems, instead of being assigned by Washington from a national pool. The national director, in order to minimize jealousies and costs, requested a reduction in interns' salaries to make them noncompetitive with other first-year teachers.

Financial Constraints

Because of congressional ambivalence, only a small portion ($10 to $37.5 million) of the $100 million per year authorized in the legislation, has been awarded during a single year. The federal share of the cost for the 10 programs in the study sample ranged from only $124,000 to $565,000, averaging $4369 to $10,375 per intern. These funds were split between the school systems and the universities involved; the universities usually received one sixth to one third of the amount. Congressional ambivalence was also expressed in deadly funding delays. Because of these conditions, the program, of necessity, was marginal in many of the universities and was in a poor position to compete with other funded programs.

Program Structure

Other constraints arose from properties of the program itself. First, as a federation of cooperating agencies, final control remained at the local or unit level (Warren, 1967). The national office was given specific and limited authority over the schools and universities. Any organization in the program could sabotage provisions that might have intruded on its autonomy.

Second, the program used a combination of *temporary systems* and *broad-front* strategies (Bessent and Moore, 1967). Funding was temporary and, as a matter of policy, interns and team leaders held temporary appointments. There was also a high rate of turnover among program directors.[2] Related to this was the fact that the program had little protection. Although a special team structure and special courses at the university might have helped to insulate Corps members from the day-to-day pressures of the ongoing system, the program actually had to confront opposition and red tape from the beginning because it had to be fitted within the existing structure of universities and schools.

Finally, the program was internally complex, consisting of several distinct parts, including a preservice workshop, college study, on-the-job work experience, and community involvement. The schools and universities did not have to decide simply to accept or reject the program as a whole but could bargain to accept some parts while rejecting others.

Local Constraints

The national office, operating within constraints of policy, financial, and program structure that increased the vulnerability of the program, had to work through local school systems and colleges while implementing a program that, in its basic premise, implied that the problems of lower income schools resulted from faulty teaching and teacher training. Numerous local schools were making persistent efforts to co-opt the program. In addition, educators resented the fact that a federal agency was trying to assume a position of power and leadership over local institutions.

The program was, therefore, subject to additional constraints arising from the local level; and members of the program, as the agents of change, were often the subject of suspicion and conflict.

University Factors

A specific constraint operating within the local university was the competition from other training programs that the Washington model had to confront.

The majority of people interviewed judged these other training programs to be as effective as the Teacher Corps. Deans at eight prestigious colleges of education had not applied to the Teacher Corps because they presumed the guidelines would be too rigid and would require the college to sacrifice control, or because they were already committed to their own programs.

Multiple training programs were found in the larger cities and in modernized regions (Table 10–1); these programs attracted the most liberal interns who were very critical of local faculty members (Chapter 9). The threat that they posed could be another reason for the observed resistance in institutions with multiple training programs.

The number of training programs at the university had some effect on the amount of cooperation between that institution and the local schools, and the rate of community activity (Table 10–1).

Local School Factors

Within the local schools, attitudes and action required of school-system personnel to introduce and implement the program further constrained and defined the parameters and conditions within which the program operated.

The local programs typically were introduced to teachers from the top down by a few university professors in collaboration with a superintendent of schools. Teachers and principals, having seldom participated in the proposal, tended to be skeptical of the program, and their suspicions were often confirmed by a few disrespectful, liberal interns committed to educational reform; frequently they became involved in controversial political activities in the community. Teachers and principals used various means to undermine the power of the interns, including stigmatizing them, isolating them within individual projects outside the classroom, co-opting the program through team leaders appointed by the school administrators, and replacing staff members who were sympathetic with the change objectives of the program.

Teachers and professors subscribed to two ideologies that in effect underscored the teachers' competence and authority: the importance of expertise and cognitive skills as a basis for teaching, and of providing more assistance to low-income schools. By contrast, the interns regarded the ability of a teacher to establish rapport with children as more important than technical competence and, instead of being used as assistants, they wanted more opportunity to introduce creative teaching innovations. As one means of defense, members of local school systems redefined the objectives of the program to coincide with their own desires. This produced a displacement of goals.

Table 10-1 Cost of program, program funds allocated to schools, and number of other training programs correlated with program characteristics

Program characteristics	Federal funds granted per intern	
	tau[a]	partial
I. Indices of organizational change		
Introduction of new techniques	.64 (.39)	.66
Change in college	.21 (.22)	.20
School-college cooperation	.32 (.14)	.35
Community projects	.64 (.32)	.68
II. Type and setting of schools and universities		
Modernization of region	.46 (.46)	.20
Size of city	.16 (.69)	.12
Size of university (enrollment)	.45 (.66)	.44
Quality of college	.11 (.37)	--
Interns' satisfaction with university faculty	.51 (.70)	.52
Proportion of university faculty who consider themselves politically "very liberal"	.43 (.42)	.39
III. Characteristics of interns		
Proportion with liberal arts degrees	-.57 (-.67)	-.59
Quality of undergraduate college	.49 (.49)	.17
Proportion who are male	-.47 (-.32)	-.51
Proportion with Peace Corps or VISTA experience	-.18 (-.35)	-.27
Proportion who are black	-.18 (-.25)	-.27
IV. Characteristics of teachers		
Proportion of teachers and principals who participated in Teacher Corps proposal	-.48 (-.45)	-.44
Rate of conflict between teachers, team leaders, and principals in the program	-.24 (-.48)	-.22
Proportion who have experienced problems because of the Teacher Corps	.02 (.03)	.01

[a] Numbers in parentheses refer to linear correlation.
t_p^1 controlling for quality of college;
t_p^2 controlling for cost per intern.

318

tau-1	tau	partial tau-1	tau	partial tau-2
		Proportion of funds to local schools		
			Number of other training programs	

tau-1	tau	partial tau-1	tau	partial tau-2
	−.24 (−.33)	−.25	.02 (−.02)	−.07
	−.43 (−.62)	−.43	.07 (.38)	.05
	0.0 (.08)	−.01	.35 (.18)	.33
	−.07 (−.16)	−.08	.22 (.10)	.18
	0.0 (.03)	.06	.64 (.80)	.63
	−.02 (−.29)	.01	.75 (.45)	.75
	−.23 (−.32)	−.22	.64 (.62)	.66
	−.07 (−.16)	−−	.51 (.03)	.50
	−.29 (−.21)	−.29	.07 (−.25)	.01
	−.29 (−.34)	−.31	.13 (.44)	.11
	−.02 (−.13)	−.02	.43 (.56)	.23
	−.16 (−.26)	−.15	.61 (.77)	.60
	.16 (.11)	.15	−.61 (−.37)	−.62
	.14 (.41)	.19	.44 (.36)	.47
	.05 (.04)	.09	.59 (.20)	.62
	.07 (.18)	0.0	−.08 (.16)	−.07
	−.15 (−.41)	−.21	−.37 (−.17)	−.35
	−.24 (−.53)	−.24	−.17 (.15)	−.17

For example, when asked to formulate the objectives in their own words, one half of the people interviewed on the first visit said that the aim of the program was to train teachers specifically to work with disadvantaged children. But over one fourth of them had in mind primarily the benefits that accrue to the public schools through special programs—to upgrade the education of disadvantaged children and to aid the classroom teachers and lighten their load (the latter mentioned third in frequency by classroom teachers and principals). Only 15 percent mentioned the advantage of recruiting more or better trained people into teaching through the program.

In spite of the national office's view of the program as an agent of change, therefore, only 12 percent of those interviewed (primarily program directors and team leaders) mentioned developing and disseminating innovative approaches to teachers as one of the primary goals; serving as an innovative force in the community was mentioned by only 9 percent of interviewees.

The lack of consensus on goals was, as mentioned in a previous chapter, accompanied by confusion of roles among the members of the program. In the five second-cycle (established) programs, 40 percent of the principals and 15 percent of the classroom teachers reported disagreement over their roles; the confusion was greater for the classroom teachers who were working most directly with the interns. Very frequently these disputes centered around the efforts of interns to use innovative approaches in the classroom, types of interns recruited into the program, and the involvement of interns in community activities. This role definition problem was crucial because, without an alternative structure to protect the team members from becoming enmeshed in preexisting routines and authority systems, there was little likelihood they could effect any redistribution of power, which was necessary to implement sustained change.

TACTICS OF INNOVATION

In view of these constraints, how did the program manage to survive? Several coping tactics that the program administrators used are discussed below. In the course of discussing these, it will be necessary at some points to review some data comparable to that already presented in another form. Notice that when this occurs the data are being viewed from a different perspective.

Goal Transformations

The goals of the program evolved from transactions with other groups in the environment. Confronting opposition in a precarious environment, the program proliferated goals in order to satisfy diverse audiences. These are reflected in the guidelines and the official ideology.

GUIDELINE MODIFICATIONS. The three program goals embodied in the legislation were expanded by the national office into nine objectives with unspecified priorities (Table 10–2): to expand the manpower pool concerned with educating the disadvantaged; to encourage cooperation between schools and colleges; to provide a practical, experience-based internship for new teachers; to encourage and disseminate innovation in procedures for training teachers; to create understanding of training goals; to stimulate learning in disadvantaged children; to implement innovative curriculum and instruction in schools; to provide service to low-income schools; and to improve the links between home and community. As is true of most organizations, there was no goal-setting machinery within the program to guarantee that priorities would be carefully worked out and preserved. Thus, innovation became only one of many competing objectives. In the original guidelines issued by the national office, a paragraph was added (almost as an afterthought) to a long list of criteria to be considered for funding programs, stating that "strong preference" also would be given to "innovative proposals which test new approaches . . ." and that the university in-service training program should provide innovative and creative approaches to the relationships of universities, schools, and communities. However, over the course of a few years innovation emerged as the one objective that was most emphasized in the guidelines. A shift in priority from service in local schools to implementing change is apparent when the first-year guidelines are compared with those issued in 1970. The goal statement in the first year repeated verbatim the legislation and emphasized in the first paragraph that interns were local, not federal, employees and were under the supervision and control of the local educational agencies. Programs were to be selected on the basis of the schools' need for the services of Corps members. But by 1970, Corps members were being described as "catalysts" for organizing community groups (although it was still emphasized that they were subordinate to the community leadership). The change objective was now an explicit part of the description of purposes: "The Teacher Corps is intended to encourage and assist changes within the institutions which educate children and prepare teachers."

In recent years, guidelines have been adapted in still other ways. The program now was to lend support to locally designed programs of change. It has been stipulated that regular teachers and principals, as well as interns and team leaders, must be involved in the planning, and a specific form of school structure is being advocated—the "portal" or "multiunit" model school, and flexible, individualy paced and personalized models of teacher

Table 10-2 Objectives of the Teacher Corps program

I. Broaden programs of teacher preparation

Recruitment and retention
: To expand the manpower pool for education of disadvantaged children by recruiting, training, and retaining qualified persons who might not otherwise have entered the education profession.

School-college coordination
: To encourage colleges and universities, schools, and state departments of education to work together in providing for effective training and use of teachers.

Functional internship
: To generate more relevant preparation for teachers of the disadvantaged through an internship of coordinated study and practical experience in schools and community.

Teacher training innovation
: To encourage institutional change resulting in the development, acceptance, and implementation of effective techniques for teacher training.

Dissemination of training results
: To create broader professional and public understanding of teacher-training goals and how the Teacher Corps is meeting them.

II. Strengthen educational opportunity for children of low-income families

Educational opportunity
: To stimulate learning in disadvantaged children.

Innovative curriculum and instruction
: To advance institutional development, acceptance, and implementation of effective curriculum and instructional innovation for the disadvantaged.

Service to disadvantaged
: To provide service to schools having concentrations of children from low-income families by furnishing supplementary teaching teams to work with and assist children and faculty.

Community-school partnership
: To establish or expand links among school, home, and community through activities that heighten Corpsmen's understanding and identification with the community and children he is attempting to reach and enrich educational experiences of the children themselves.

training. "Contracts" between college teachers and students are also being advocated that specify a sequence of experiences that the student must master; this is supposed to alter their traditional hierarchical relationship. Contracts for performance between the university and Washington are also being considered.

SHIFT IN OFFICIAL IDEOLOGY. As the program achieved security with respect to Congress and in the Washington bureaucracy, the national office became more insistent about the objective of innovation. In September 1967, former Teacher Corps Director, Richard Graham, wrote a paper with the revealing title, "Teacher Corps: More Help in the Classroom" (Graham, 1967), in which he stressed that the Corpsmen "augmented the regular teaching staffs in these schools, using special techniques designed to assist disadvantaged children in the learning process." In congressional testimony in March 1967, he stated that the Corps was a series of local programs, that the team leaders were appointed from their school systems, and that the Corpsmen were hired, fired, and reassigned by the school administrators. Only in the closing remarks did he allude to a "national commitment to improve education" and to "helping to raise the sights and status of dedicated teachers who are already working with the disadvantaged."

But, within a year, Graham (March, 1968) was speaking to another audience more directly about the objective of facilitating change, although reference was primarily to the changes that had been first proposed by local universities and schools. The role of the program was to provide a structure for assisting local institutions with *their* plans for change. It was denied that Washington had some national plan for change. Later, he made a more explicit reference to the innovative objectives of the program, challenging the effectiveness of the existing system of education (Graham, October 1968). Quoting a high school principal, he observed that the seeds of innovation and change have been missing in both new and old teachers who have been afraid or reluctant to try new things in education. He acknowledged that the schools may not be ready for the interns and conceded that many veteran teachers have sympathy for the disadvantaged children, but he charged that many of them "don't know how to get to these kids or how to help them learn." The term "revolution" was used in reference to the colleges:

It's in the ivory tower that the greatest revolution has taken place. All courses still may not be "relevant" to what's going on in the schools, but Corps members have made sure that their professors, deans, and Teacher Corps Washington are very aware of that fact.

In February 1970, Graham published an article called "Educational Change and the Teacher Corps." The opening paragraph referred to educational reform and "change in our educational institutions." Acknowledging two purposes of the Teacher Corps—to strengthen educational opportunities for children from low-income families, and to encourage colleges and universities to broaden their programs of teacher preparation—he emphasized that it is the latter that assumes priority. A 1970 publicity brochure, seeking to attract interns into the program, states:

> The old ways are resistant to change, but changes that will provide a good education for all of America's children are demanded now. . . . As you study and teach, you will be asked to help develop and test new ways of doing things.

Structural Change

Although the innovation objective was becoming more explicit in the leadership's ideology, the program's structure was subtly changing in an entirely different direction—toward greater emphasis on local control and, hence, service to the local schools. The effect of structural change was to preclude widespread innovation even as the ideology of change gained momentum.

GUIDELINE MODIFICATIONS. In recent years clauses have been added stipulating that interns hold only provisional' status in the program during the preservice component; that they are to be selected by the participating school districts and may be dismissed at any time "for good cause"; and that "all interns accepted for in-service should be persons the district feels will develop into teachers whom they wish to hire." Presumably, these changes would lend legitimacy to the interns who were selected and assure that their proposals would be taken seriously. It was assumed by the national office that interns could be sympathetic with the existing system even while being dissatisfied with it. Local programs also were now permitted to enroll persons with undergraduate work in education and/or teaching experience, which represents a fundamental change in the character of the program. In 1970, guidelines provided that school districts and universities could be a prime contractor for the basic programs.

AUXILIARY PROGRAMS. The changes described above were paralleled by a proliferation of at least five alternative versions of the basic model within the Teacher Corps: the Extern Program, the Undergraduate program, the Urban Corps, Veterans in Public Service, and Volunteer Tutors (Table 10–3). The official view was that these programs represented *variations* of the basic model. However, in certain respects they were actually *competing* alternatives. In 1970 the combined projected budgets of these programs exceeded the cost of the basic program. More important, the programs reflected a shift in priorities: (1) assistance to schools was to be increased, with a corresponding reduction in the training component; (2) local schools were to be given full responsibility for the funds, a shift in power base that seemed likely to minimize the school-college partnership dimension (of Extern, Urban Corps, and Tutors); and (3) priority on recruiting liberal arts graduates was supplanted by students in education (Undergraduate and VIPS) and by lay persons (Tutors).

INSTITUTIONALIZATION OF THE NATIONAL OFFICE. This program had features in common with comparable poverty programs throughout the government that were making appeals to idealistic youth. From the beginning, Washington administrators had sought to link the program to the Peace Corps and VISTA.[4] But these programs were becoming the subject of controversy, and bureaucrats in Washington and local school administrators were applying pressures to harness the Teacher Corps to the routine administrative structure of the Office of Education. Perhaps in deference to these pressures, by 1968, Graham began to backpedal the Peace Corps analogy: "Originally, I suspect it was seen as a kind of 'domestic Peace Corps,' or teacher training program. But that was not the intent of the creators." He concluded that these "programs of good works" have produced little change and have satisfied no one. However, it was doubtful that Graham ever questioned the underlying brotherhood among these poverty programs.

Because of its location within the federal hierarchy and its entanglement in civil-service regulations, the national office was unable to gain the necessary discretionary status. Its efforts to gain control of its own affairs were resisted by higher-echelon administrators responsible for coordinating the activities of this agency with other agencies. The national office was not able to obtain sufficient funds to adequately monitor local programs because it did not conform to the formula used in making staff allocations, which was tied to the *volume* of funds administered by an agency. While this might have been a reasonable basis of allocation for traditional grant programs, the criteria used do not fit innovative programs that depend on people who can maintain constant feedback from the field. Although the program budget tripled in size, the number of professional staff in the national office decreased, and there was little travel money available to visit local programs. Ironically, even though the agency's ability to exercise direct supervision over local programs was thereby minimized, the local programs were left with fewer channels through which they could exert influence on national policy.

Table 10-3 Alternative Teacher Corps programs

1. Extern program
   The extern design permits second-year interns who have earned their certification to carry approximately a two-thirds teaching load and to be teachers of record. The university load is reduced to compensate for increased responsibilities in the school. The local education agency then pays them two-thirds of a teacher's beginning salary, thus relieving the Teacher Corps of the $75-per-week stipend. This type of arrangement cuts the cost of the second year by roughly 60 percent, while providing the local school with full-time employees.

2. Undergraduate program
   Teacher Corps legislation was amended in 1968 to permit the enrollment of undergraduates at the junior level. The resulting undergraduate program follows a similar design to the graduate program, except that a bachelor's rather than a master's degree is earned during the two years and the interns are recruited into colleges of education early in their training. Depending on the university and state requirements, a few programs award certification and a degree in less than 24 months.

3. Urban corps
   The Teacher Corps recently designed a one-year internship model to provide more impact in large cities. It provided the interns with teacher certification but only two-thirds of the credits needed for a master's. The funding procedures enable the cities to almost triple the size of

their programs with no additional cost to the Teacher Corps and no cost for the cities. Approximately 90 percent of a $75-per-week stipend for 100 interns is covered in each program by the school system through the use of salary funds that would normally be used to hire 50 new teachers. The Teacher Corps pays the remaining part of the stipend, the academic costs, and the administrative costs. The total cost to the Teacher Corps equals the average cost for the first year of a regular Teacher Corps program for forty interns.

4. Veterans in Public Service (VIPS)

VIPS was initiated to attract minority group veterans returning from Vietnam to the education profession. Veterans who are high school graduates can volunteer their services in the same fashion as Teacher Corps interns. They receive two years of training at the university level that could lead to an Associate of Arts degree. Office of Education funds cover the basic stipend of $75 per week; the G.I. Bill covers the university tuition, and the existing Teacher Corps programs provide the administrative structure in the university, the local education agency, and the school. VIPS programs of approximately 25 interns are currently operating in seven cities.

5. Volunteer tutors

In 1969 legislation was amended to permit the program to compensate part-time or full-time adult and adolescent volunteer tutors and instructional assistants for certain services. The act also permits the Corps to train high school and junior high school students as tutors at government expense, under the supervision of experienced team leaders.

327

The national office's control was chipped away in other ways. Public relations, program evaluation and, eventually, grant management itself—the major leverage over local programs—were centralized within the U.S. Office of Education out of direct control of Teacher Corps administrators. As the program's discretionary status was undercut, its distinctive mission became blurred.

Graham was apparently reassigned as a result of bureaucratic in-fighting. The program's fate is still being debated, but it appears to have lost all hope for a discretionary status and special constituents and has become another line agency in the federal bureaucracy. However, this might not be entirely detrimental because bureaucratic rules can help to insulate maverick programs from political pressures.

CO-OPTATION THROUGH SELECTION
OF MEMBER ORGANIZATIONS

It appears that the innovative image the national office tried to project might have been part of a broader strategy intended to attract a preferred type of member organization. In light of the program's federative structure, understaffing, and limited travel funds, its most crucial leverage was at the point where new member organizations entered the program. The national office reserved its limited resources for the institutions that were likely to be most compatible with its objectives and most vulnerable to its influence.

But it was not a simple policy of seeking out the weakest universities. There was a dilemma: the institutions most willing to give up their autonomy and comply with demanding guidelines were not the ones that could best serve as national models for teacher education. The institutions most in need of resources would be willing to bargain for the marginal funds available in Washington; but, if these criteria were blindly applied, the program would end up with only the least resourceful and least prestigious institutions. It is safe to assume that the leadership was acutely aware of the stratification among institutions of higher education and was aware that some institutions are more influential than others. In practice, therefore, the institution's prestige apparently was weighed against its vulnerability, and both extremes were excluded—some relatively powerful and prestigious universities were excluded because they had other sources of funds and were jealous of their autonomy, and other, less powerful universities were excluded because their prestige was below the level of acceptability.

Table 10-4   Quality of resources of Teacher Corps universities compared to a national sample of universities

	Level of quality of university resources				
	Low (5–19)	Low middle (20–29)	Upper middle (30–39)	High (40–50)	Total
National population[a]	239 (21%)	459 (40%)	292 (25.5%)	154 (13.5%)	1144
Teacher Corps universities	21 (24.7%)	30 (35.3%)	23 (27.1%)	11 (12.9%)	85

[a] Columbia University, Bureau of Applied Social Research, College Data Rank Code Book.

Chi square is not significant.

Resource Rating

A standard college resources index was computed for universities in the second and third cycles of the program.[5] For the 85 universities with Teacher Corps programs in 1969, the mean score (26.7) was slightly lower than the national average of all universities (28). None of the Teacher Corps universities (the highest score was 46) reached the maximum national score (50). In two cycles the dropout institutions scored higher than the national mean, and the colleges that requested but were not awarded third-cycle programs had higher scores (30.9) than the programs selected. However, the difference should not be exaggerated. A chi square analysis indicated that average distributions *approximate* the national distribution (Table 10–4). The differences reached or approached statistical significance in only two of the five cycles.

Selectivity

But the selectivity index (measuring the quality of students in the university) leaves little doubt that lower status colleges were attracted to the program. Over two thirds (69 percent) of the Teacher Corps institutions were among the *least* selective, compared to less than one half (44 percent) of the nation's institutions of higher education that fall into that

Table 10-5 Selectivity of admission policies of Teacher Corps
universities compared to a national sample of universities

	Selectivity of university admission policies[a]			
	Least selective	Selective	Most selective	Total
National population	194 (44.3%)	163 (37.2%)	81 (18.5%)	438
Teacher Corps universities	31 (68.9%)	11 (24.4%)	3 (6.7%)	45

[a] Based on Comparative Guide to American Colleges (Cass and Birnbaum, 1970).

$x^2 = 10.35$ 2 df $p < .005$

category (Table 10–5). At the other extreme, only 7 percent of the
Teacher Corps institutions rate among the most selective; that figure
would have to be nearly three times higher (19 percent) if the Teacher
Corps programs had matched the national distribution. There was little
variation among the different cycles.

Region and Selectivity

Washington's latitude over selection, however, was limited by a Congressional mandate to distribute programs regionally. What influence did this
policy have on the type of institutions recruited? Considering all Teacher
Corps programs, each of the five regions of the nation (Nash, 1969) were
proportionately represented (Table 10–6). But this overall pattern masks
some important differences. In the fifth cycle, colleges in the Northeast
(12 percent) and Midwest (8 percent) were underrepresented, while those
in the Far West (26 percent) (and to some extent in the Plains states,
32 percent) were overrepresented ($p < .07$). Moreover, during each of the
first four cycles, the South was consistently overrepresented and the Northeast was consistently underrepresented. Since institutions in the South
scored relatively low ($\overline{X} = 27.1$) on the resource index, the effect was to
pull down the average quality of the universities in the program. Indeed,
even if the South had been represented only *proportionately*, the effect
would have been the same.

Table 10-6 Distribution of Teacher Crops programs in five regions of the country, compared to a national sample of institutions

	Region					
	Northeast	South	Midwest	Plains	West	Total
National sample of colleges[b]	(28.9)[a] 253 26.8%	(27.1) 247 26.1%	(29.1) 155 16.4%	(26.9) 191 20.2%	(29.7) 99 10.5%	945
Teacher Corps programs	17 20.0%	25 29.4%	12 14.1%	17 20.0%	14 16.4%	85

$X^2 = 4.54$, 4 df not statistically significant.

[a] The figures in parentheses refer to the mean resource index scores for colleges in the region.
[b] From Nash, 1969.

Teacher Production

If the emphasis was not on quality, was it on quantity? Perhaps the program's thrust was to revitalize the critical institutions that train the bulk of the teachers. To answer the question, the 25 largest producers of teachers were considered. Only 7 of the 25 (28 percent) have participated in at least one cycle. They constitute a negligible proportion of all programs funded for the past five years. Only three of the seven (or 12 percent of the total) have participated in more than one cycle.

Implications and Consequences

It is conceivable that funds could have been used most effectively if they had been used to upgrade the colleges that had the least resources. It is equally plausible that if the program had subsidized the high-prestige institutions, which act as pacesetters and models for other institutions, it would have had broader repercussions. The Teacher Corps appears to have followed neither course. Although it did not concentrate on upgrading the poorer institutions, it attracted a disproportionately high number of these institutions with the least selective admission policies. What were the effects of a selection policy that favored the lower status institutions? Three types are identified.

Table 10-7 Proportion of interns with liberal arts majors and from outside the region, and quality of the Teacher Corps college correlated with organizational change and other program characteristics

Program characteristics	Proportion of interns with liberal arts major tau^a	Proportion of interns from outside the region tau^a	Quality of college tau^a
I. Indices of organizational change			
Introduction of new techniques into schools	-.52 (-.30)	-.02 (.12)	-.07 (-.17)
Community projects	-.51 (-.16)	-.29 (.17)	-.16 (-.03)
School-college cooperation	-.37 (-.37)	-.37 (-.05)	-.14 (-.29)
Change in the college	.21 (.37)	.11 (.17)	.07 (.005)
II. Characteristics of interns			
Proportion with liberal arts major	1.00 (1.00)	.07 (.07)	.02 (.61)
Proportion with B.A. degree	.48 (.59)	.39 (.02)	.11 (.16)
Quality of interns' undergraduate college	.20 (.36)	-.02 (-.36)	.64 (.70)
Initiative-compliance	.23 (-.13)	.09 (.07)	.27 (-.08)
Political and social liberalism of interns	.28 (.49)	.05 (-.24)	.28 (.18)
Proportion who are black	.18 (-.20)	-.23 (-.16)	.45 (.21)
Proportion of interns with prior Peace Corps or VISTA experience	.63 (.22)	-.05 (.05)	.45 (.12)
Proportion who are male	.07 (.0002)	.47 (.35)	-.56 (-.32)
Proportion of interns who consider themselves politically "very liberal"	.32 (.39)	.23 (.31)	.23 (.09)
Proportion from outside the region	.07 (.07)	1.00 (1.00)	-.11 (-.34)

Difference in the political and social liberalism of teachers and interns	.32 (.51)	.58 (.22)	-.18 (-.26)
III. Characteristics of the university			
Size of university (enrollment)	-.14 (-.005)	-.32 (-.33)	.36 (.56)
Interns' satisfaction with university faculty	-.38 (-.52)	.02 (.04)	-.02 (-.13)
Number of other teacher training programs	.15 (.45)	-.19 (-.33)	.48 (.56)
University's support for the Teacher Corps program	.20 (.44)	-.20 (-.18)	.11 (.33)
IV. Characteristics of the school			
Quality of the school	.02 (.06)	.07 (-.04)	.11 (.11)
Flexibility of the school	-.38 (-.23)	-.33 (-.25)	-.11 (-.25)
Principal's support for the Teacher Corps program	-.55 (-.20)	-.14 (-.21)	-.09 (-.25)
Competence of the principal as rated by team leaders, interns, and teachers	-.12 (.003)	.26 (-.26)	.07 (.26)
V. Characteristics of teachers			
Quality of teachers' undergraduate college	.29 (.28)	-.20 (-.10)	.11 (.36)
Competence of team leader as rated by interns	.05 (.12)	-.32 (-.07)	.49 (.33)
VI. Context			
Ratio of federal funds allocated per intern	-.33 (-.25)	-.20 (-.19)	.11 (.36)
Total federal funds granted to program	-.02 (.02)	-.42 (.15)	.24 (-.32)
Size of city	.16 (.25)	-.33 (-.34)	.42 (.70)
Modernization of area	.45 (.65)	-.18 (-.23)	.58 (.78)
Proportion of program funds controlled by the local school	.11 (.08)	.16 (.16)	-.07 (-.17)

a Numbers in parentheses refer to linear correlations.

1. *Types of Students.* There was a tendency for the better universities in the sample to attract interns from better undergraduate colleges (tau = .63) (Table 10–7, part II). The mean resource index of their undergraduate college was associated with the proportion of interns who considered themselves to be politically liberal ($t_p = .45$, controlling for federal dollars granted).[7]

2. *Level of Funding.* There was a modest but positive linear correlation between a university's prestige ("quality") and its level of funding (per intern in the program) ($r = .36$; $t = .11$) (Table 10–7, part VI). The favorable bargaining power of the more prestigious universities (perhaps together with their sophistication in writing research proposals) might have provided enough leverage so that they could claim a disproportionate share of funds.

3. *Organizational Change.* Did the status of prestigious universities give them the security needed for bold experimentation? Or did their status make them so remote from the problems of schools that they were unwilling to make the necessary compromises? Prestigious universities were not necessarily more effective than the less prestigious ones if technological change in schools is taken as an index,[8] and they might have been slightly less effective ($r = -.17$) (Table 10–7, part I).

A policy that attempts to distribute programs to the less well-developed regions of the country also increase the odds against the program. As pointed out previously, modernization of the state in which a program was located was positively correlated with the introduction of new techniques into the schools (tau = .29), the number of community activities (tau = .20), and change in college (tau = .16).[9] But modernization did not seem to be related to school-college cooperation (tau = .09).

ROTATION AND DISPERSION

Rotation among programs was a counterpart of a strategy that sought to influence vulnerable institutions with marginal funds. As a means of spreading the impact, there was a deliberate policy to provide only short-term funding with the hope that the local colleges and schools would cover a larger portion of the cost each year. Theoretically, they would cover the full cost by the fifth cycle. Because the starting costs were necessarily higher than the continuing costs due to the expense of curriculum development and staffing, an effort was made to use the funds as "risk capital" by underwriting the initial costs. However, there is little indication that the schools were financially able or sufficiently committed to the program to participate in this arrangement. Another variation was to fund only alternate cycles at a university; for example, to fund a two-year cycle, skip a two-year cycle, and fund the next cycle. Richard Graham (1970) commented, "The Teacher Corps was never supposed to be a sustaining program. It was to provoke change, then move on."

Three fourths of the universities that participated in the Teacher Corps dropped out, and most were not readmitted—only one in four reentered the program. Only 20 percent of the first-cycle programs were still being funded in the fifth cycle, while more than half of the programs in the fifth cycle were being funded for the first time. Moreover, only 25 percent of the programs funded were supported for three or more cycles, and only 20 percent were funded for four or more cycles. The program dropout rate between the cycles was as follows.

Percent Dropout (Between Cycles)	Percent New (Never Funded Before)
1 and 2—42	cycle 2— 0
2 and 3—24	cycle 3—38
3 and 4—33	cycle 4—38
4 and 5—42	cycle 5—53

Directors of seven programs that dropped out of the Teacher Corps were contacted about their experiences with the program. Five of the seven were directing other programs in colleges of education. Six had applied for renewal and were turned down. They cited a variety of reasons for not being refunded: lack of commitment on the part of the local school system; failure to conform to Washington's image of the program; the political structure of the Office of Education and lack of political support in Congress; and Washington's policy of rotating programs. Most of the programs had met serious obstacles. The Teacher Corps was almost unnoticed in large universities and school systems; tensions arose over hiring personnel at the university who were not "qualified" by usual criteria used by academic departments; team leaders were not regarded as qualified instructors; deans sometimes failed to take the program seriously; there had been a lack of cooperation from the business office because of the uncertainty of funds; turnover among directors created discontinuities; red tape in the schools created delays; teachers resented the efforts of interns to become involved in planning the curriculum; and many principals had discouraged community work.

Frequent rotation also provided a means to stretch limited funds across a large number of programs to increase the visibility and influence of the national program and to continually weed out incompetent or uncooperative programs that slipped through the initial screening process. In other words, rotation maintained the primary objective of innovation and prevented goal displacement or co-optation because of recalcitrant member organizations. But the practice also minimized the possibility of concentrating a sufficient number of resources in a particular place for a long enough period to provide the sustained "critical mass" needed for a multigoal program to have an impact.

CO-OPTATION THROUGH THE LOCAL BALANCE OF POWER

In addition to selection and rotation, Washington was occasionally able to increase its leverage slightly by favoring either the schools or the university in local programs. The university faculty members usually seemed more cosmopolitan and more committed than schoolteachers to the need for educational reform, perhaps because they are financed by and responsible to a broader political base, because their graduates compete in a national market, and because they usually are better professionally trained and more mobile. Moreover, autonomous organizations will be more eager to change one another than to change themselves.

Universities were given some leverage in contracting arrangements. They were the prime contracting agents and the host institution, and the program director was usually recruited from the university faculty. In view of these considerations, if the local balance of power was favorable to a university, it should have served as a power stimulus for change in the cooperating schools. But in practice, universities seldom had decisive control over the program. Professors were no match for the political connections of large city school-board members, and the program director was in a precarious position. Although he was legally responsible for monitoring the school district's use of funds and personnel policies, his effectiveness depended on the cooperation of the same institutions. Moreover, the dominant part of the national Teacher Corps office (the program branch) monopolized most of the available travel funds and was staffed by personnel with public school backgrounds who seemed inclined to favor schools over universities in controversies. Four of the six former program directors who were contacted believed that the specialists from the Washington office were more partial to problems of the local schools than to problems of the university. They felt that Washington was inclined to pacify the schools, repeatedly overruling the university by making exceptions to published guidelines that would have upheld the university's authority.

Nevertheless, even slight increases in the university's share of funds seemed to have a disproportionately favorable effect on the magnitude of change that took place. On the basis of this limited sample, as the proportion of funds going to local schools increased, changes in the college and in the number of new techniques introduced into the schools diminished (tau = −.43 and tau = −.24).

THE PRINCIPLE OF MARGINAL LEVERAGE

One of the overriding strategies of this program was to deploy its marginal funds strategically so as to trigger change within a system (Graham, 1970). Outside funds sometimes provided the venture capital and "organizational slack" needed to absorb the costs of innovation (Guetzkow, 1965). Even relatively small increments of funds influenced the rate of innovation. The federal cost of the program (figured as a ratio of cost per intern) was positively associated with three measures of innovation: the introduction of new techniques into classrooms (tau = .64), increased community activity (tau = .64),[10] and change in college (tau = .21; Table 10–1, part I).

RECRUITMENT THROUGH UNCONVENTIONAL CHANNELS

The national office, chartered to operate within the established organizations and laboring under serious political constraints, placed heavy reliance on newcomers to the field as a means of changing the profession. Thus, the fulcrum of the national program was a concerted effort to attract into teaching altruistic graduates from the liberal arts and members of minority groups. A humanistic transfusion for education was expected that would produce a new hybrid teacher, sympathetic but critical of current practice, and searching for practical alternatives. At an early stage, the National Advisory Council on the Education of Disadvantaged Children viewed the Teacher Corps program as being "an unusual group of young people who, but for the Corps, would never have been drawn to the teaching profession . . ." (Wilson, 1967).

Two provisions in the initial legislation helped to open the door: (1) recruitment of liberal arts graduates and members of minority groups not trained as teachers, and (2) national distribution of interns and team leaders from a central pool of personnel maintained in Washington. In practice these objectives were only partially realized. Only 63 percent of the interns in the present study had not taken courses in education as undergraduates; 13 percent were graduates of a college of education or a teachers college and had teaching certificates (between 10 and 47 percent of the interns in different programs). The number of undergraduates increased appreciably in subsequent cycles, which brought in even more interns from among students already in colleges of education. Relatively few were members of minority groups, although subsequent cycles were far more successful in this respect. But many of the minority-group interns were already certified teachers. The second provision was effectively reversed in 1967 by legislation withdrawing the Commissioner of Education's authority to assign members to local programs from the national pool. Many school administrators complained that, from their point of view, it was not useful to bring interns from other parts of the country because they were essentially transients who were not willing to take jobs in the local system when they graduated. Furthermore, the outsiders were particularly vulnerable to the charge of being naïve about local minority groups and conditions in the local community. Therefore, some subsequent programs began to recruit from the immediate region—partially to appeal to the indigenous minority groups but, primarily (probably), to pacify local educators by selecting compatible interns.

The interns were not well defined as teachers, and their personal values were largely unacceptable to the host colleges and schools. As new teachers, they were the least potent forces in the system. Although their temporary and marginal connections with schools gave them a measure of autonomy, their physical and social isolation from the college professors undermined their efforts. Moreover, numbering only four to six per school, they did not form a critical mass within a school or school system. Finally, their change-agent role was subordinated to an apprenticeship supervised by experienced teachers who viewed the interns as additional manpower. Interns frequently complained that they were being used as substitutes and were assigned to routine auxiliary roles. Thus estranged, they often identified closely with their pupils, sometimes supporting the pupils against regular teachers.

Consequences

As previously noted, recruiting from nontraditional sources created conflict and problems and did not necessarily produce the technological changes that were intended. It must be conceded that some change occurred, but it was not easily identifiable.

PROBLEMS. To review the data, presented in a slightly different form, the proportions of interns with liberal arts majors and from outside the region were positively related to the *difference* between teachers' and interns' political liberalism (tau = .32, tau = .58) (Table 10–7, part II). This helps to explain the fact, revealed in an additional analysis (not in the table), that the more of these interns in the program, the more problems created for the teachers (tau = .36, tau = .42). Both characteristics—the difference in liberalism and the number of problems created—were also positively correlated with the rate of conflict reported among program personnel (tau = .36, and tau = .27); this latter variable, however, was more highly correlated with the proportion who were male (tau = .72). The proportion of teachers who wanted to reduce the level of interns' involvement in community activities, in particular, increased with the proportion with liberal arts degrees (tau = .54) and the proportion from outside the region (tau = .37). The principals' support for the program, as rated by the interns, also declined with the proportion with liberal arts degrees (tau = —.55).

INSTITUTIONAL CHANGE. The introduction of new techniques into schools, the number of community activities, and the cooperation between the school and community all *declined* as the proportion of interns with liberal arts backgrounds increased (tau = —.52, tau = —.51, and tau = —.37). But change in college showed a slight increase with the proportion of liberal arts interns (tau = .21). This pattern suggests that, insofar as the schools were concerned, the strategy seemed to have backfired. However, it may have had a more positive effect on the colleges, where it was observed that some professors were more open to criticism, new ideas, and discussion and were more concerned about the problems of teaching in disadvantaged schools as a result of their experience in the program, particularly their encounters with interns.

SUMMARY AND CONCLUSIONS

Because the Teacher Corps was a complex, variable program with multiple goals operating in a politically volatile climate, it was subject to repeated transformations of goals and structure. Politically, major legislative changes and guideline modifications helped to protect local control; organizationally, the program was plagued by uncertainty, temporary status, and a deficiency of funds that had to be shared among colleges and several participating schools. The program, understandably, was in a marginal position in the local institutions, and in Washington it was in a poor position to compete for congressional appropriations with more established programs.

The Teacher Corps has continued to change since this study was concluded; therefore, caution must be used in applying the findings reported here to its present operation. Nevertheless, the program is likely to remain a product of its history and its environment. I believe that the program can expose principles that go beyond its particular circumstances. For example, the way it operated can illuminate the neglected problem of how organizations are recruited into larger organizational networks. Because of the bargaining process involved in recruitment, a distinctive type of member organization was recruited that ranked lower than the population of universities on a resources index and that was considerably less selective of students than are typical universities; many lesser known colleges were participating in the program while many colleges that in the past have served as models of educational reform were not. As a result, less able students were attracted (than if more prestigious universities had been involved), and the local programs had less leverage to bargain for the necessary resources.

The national office also used other strategies that have a more general relevance. For example, it used its funds as venture capital; it concentrated marginal funds in the institutions most likely to be receptive (or vulnerable) to outside pressure for change; it stretched funds by rotating member organizations; it created competing, alternative objectives and programs to satisfy different publics and to meet changing situations; and it recruited new members to the profession from liberal, unconventional backgrounds. In view of these general principles, let us examine other patterns underlying these events that can guide further study of a wider range of organizations.

1. Since the national office carried the primary responsibility for the program's political survival, and it could not rely on the momentum of tradition of strong outside support, the director's commitment to its continuation and expansion was a necessary condition for its survival. The director also could set outside limits on the amount of goal adaptation that would be tolerated as a condition of survival. There is little doubt about his determination to press for educational reform within the limits of the legislation. This does not mean, however, that charismatic leadership was sufficient

in itself. On the contrary, there were direct links between the dire office and Capitol Hill, which helped to buffer the program fro critics and gave it leverage within the Washington bureaucracy.

2. These cases illustrate that, even under seriously adverse circumstances, organizations do not passively adapt and relinquish their original objectives without a struggle. Despite the goal proliferation and structural adaptations that occurred, the Washington administrators steadfastly maintained their original vision of the program as an agent of educational reform. Indeed, to some extent, the adaptations and alternatives devised provided a smoke screen that helped to protect the basic model from pressures to make similar transformations. Blocked in several directions, the administrators searched for alternative ways to fulfill the objectives, ways to go around the obstacles when they could not be surmounted. The question is whether, in the long run, these alternatives will give local organizations enough leverage to completely co-opt the rest of the program.

3. Official ideologies were strategically used to protect the innovative objectives. The national office, initially faced with combined opposition from local school districts and a few Congressmen, and yet without a secure administrative berth, emphasized the program's symbiotic, auxiliary relationships to existing programs and minimized its competitive, innovative, and displacement functions. The organizational structure was adapted at the points of greatest pressure: the authority of the national office over local organizations. Local programs were given more control, and auxiliary programs were proliferated, which had the effect of partially transforming the Teacher Corps into a service agency. But the corollary is that as the program gained more administrative security in Washington, the innovative objectives could be reasserted and other ways could be devised to approach them.

The meaning of these ideological shifts is not entirely clear. On the one hand, it appears that program administrators could afford to be more explicit about the change objective precisely because local control had been assured; in other words, the change ideology served as a smoke screen to disguise and compensate for the fact that extensive change was not occurring. This interpretation suggests an element of "cognitive dissonance" in the situation: the rhetoric of change grew more vocal as a means of denying that the program had become co-opted by established institutions. As program managers in Washington became more aware of the disparity between the announced innovative purposes of the program and the way it was actually being used at the local level (as added manpower to supplement traditional practices), they sought to reduce the disparity by reiterating their beliefs, thus denying the existence of the disparity. On the other hand, this interpretation at best can be only partially correct because the innovative program image evolved from a search for more effective means to implement change, and it was being projected by Washington as part of a broader strategy to attract institutions that were highly committed to its concept of change.

4. Despite the valiant defense of the program's objectives, another point is also clear. Organizations—particularly those spawned by the political system—often remain prisoners of the coalition of conflicting forces that created them. The number and diffuseness of official objectives of the program was as much a reflection of the political cross-pressures as professional considerations. However, this does not mean that the program was completely straitjacketed by the political forces.

The range of the program's objectives probably helped to broaden its base of support, which permitted it to pursue alternative courses of action; the national office could maneuver in response to its critics simply by making subtle shifts in priorities among already announced goals. Nor did the conflicting goals and political constraints, in themselves, prevent innovation. Goal conflict has been identified as a major source of change (Moore, 1963; Wilson, 1966), and even when a program does not completely succeed in producing the changes as originally planned, unplanned change often results (Clark, 1968). But the point is: the changes that did occur in this way were difficult to identify. It is inaccurate to say that the program had little or no effect. Instead, its efforts were so dissipated that its effects were diluted and often were hardly visible.

5. As the program lost some of its political character and became institutionalized within the line bureaucracy, the charismatic and politically sensitive leadership was replaced by career bureaucrats. The romantic idealism that had focused on the culture of poverty began to recede in favor of a more utilitarian, task-oriented image of the program, based on career opportunities, a greater stress on partnership with the local system, and incorporation into the local system. Concomitantly, a shift occurred in the priority given to the liberal arts specialists as opposed to the training of technical specialists.

6. The central administration, constrained to work within the existing system, relied heavily on its ability to select vulnerable and compatible member organizations to maintain its leverage over the objectives. Although the national office portrayed the program as a series of local institutions receiving federal assistance for their own innovations, it actually attempted to select the programs whose conceptions of change were compatible with its own. The selection process is summarized in the following propositions.

1. The greater the resources of an institution, the greater its autonomy and the less responsive it will be to outside funds.

2. The willingness of high-quality institutions to participate in a particular program will decline with the number and stringency of the conditions necessary for being accepted into that program.

3. The higher-quality institutions will be in a better position to maintain their autonomy and will be less inclined to participate than the lower-quality institutions.

4. Among the organizations that are willing to give up their autonomy, preference will be given to the ones that have the highest prestige; thus, member organizations tend to have somewhat middling prestige and autonomy.

7. Rather than concentrating its efforts on a few programs, the national office, constrained by limited resources, sought to extend the scope of its influence through a policy of extensive participation. This policy had a dual advantage. First, in view of its political vulnerability, an extensive funding policy helped the program to solicit a broad base of support from the many organizations through which funds had trickled; even modest attempts within a few programs to establish one or two intensively funded model Teacher Corps schools were strongly resisted by teachers and administrators who wanted to share the benefits of the program. Second, by keeping the individual size of programs to a minimum, the national office did not tie its fate to the outcomes; therefore, it reduced its dependence on particular programs. The effect of this funding policy, however, was to create an extensive network of small, dispersed, and largely autonomous organizations with little coordination or sense of brotherhood and mission among them.

The scope of the Teacher Corps was further extended through a policy of rotating programs. This also increased Washington's leverage because programs that already had been funded had to remain competitive and acceptable to Washington, and programs that had not been funded could continue to hope for consideration in subsequent cycles if they were willing to meet the conditions. But in the final analysis the Washington office was bargaining away the possibility of creating a dramatic and visible effect in order to secure its very survival.

8. The principle of marginal leverage, used by the central office, required it to favor one or more types of organizations over others in a particular set. By co-opting an influential local institution that could influence other local institutions, the national office could hope to extend its own hold over all of the organizations in the set. Also, the discretion

of the national office to exert this kind of influence was actually limited by its internal composition—it was staffed by personnel who often favored the more conservative school systems—and by a delicate relationship between universities and schools that precluded either organization from completely dominating the other.

9. The central administration, faced with resilient, traditional organizational structures, had to rely heavily on cosmopolitan individuals, who were to be recruited from outside of traditional channels, in order to pressure for change. Although this approach was perhaps less threatening than a direct assault on the *structures* of schools and universities, there were implications (from the perspective of many local educators) that schools and universities had failed and that newcomers could lead the way to change; liberal imagination would take precedence over professional competence and experience. These implications did not escape defensive classroom teachers and university professors who had powerful organizational defenses at their disposal. And since the interns had not been recruited en masse and were controlled by the local institutions, their efforts easily could be thwarted. Yet, within these limits, their presence was often felt, if only to challenge the basic assumptions of the system.

10. The case demonstrates the way that working for change from within a system results in negotiation and compromise. The extent and direction of change will be partially a function of the difference between the existing system and the proposal. In this case, because *outsiders*, who had less to lose from change, were to implement the proposal, they sometimes went to extremes. The presence of outside forces (the national office and the interns) probably provided more *impetus* for change in local schools than would have been produced by schools without this stimulus. In this sense the proposition that internal change occurs largely in response to outside forces has credence (Terreberry, 1965). But it does not follow that an outside stimulus will necessarily produce change. The amount of change depends on the leverage of the outside force, which in this case was minimal.

This process can be summarized this way (Gouldner, 1970): the supplying organizations (schools and universities) are pressured by consumers (for example, politicians) to improve their performance. They search for new techniques, which are assigned as specialized functions to new or established units (on one level, the national office; on another level, the Teacher Corps team, composed of interns and team leaders). But because these new functions were created by redistributing tasks that were formerly the responsibility of other existing units (the local school boards and classroom teachers), the loss of functions and authority to the new unit is resisted.

11. The brief history of this program underscores the folly of attempting to evaluate an organization's "effectiveness" apart from its history and social context. Indeed, when forced upon a program that already has been severely compromised by political opponents, evaluation becomes a political tool. Before deciding on a program's effectiveness, it is necessary to recognize the constraints that it labors under and, generally, to take into account how organizations cope with serious external constraints in order to explain how they manage to survive at all.

Finally, viewed at a higher level of abstraction, the theme of compromise that runs through this program illuminates a critical tension in modern society: the drive for autonomy on the part of separate organizations versus a pressure for reintegration at higher levels. The growing power of government organizations might suggest that there is a trend toward oligarchy among *sets* of independent organizations that parallels the oligarchical decision-making process characteristic of individual organizations. However, there was no evidence from this program that federal control over education is an imminent or inevitable threat. The ability of the local organizations to protect their autonomy makes this specter of a complete oligarchy a dubious prospect. At most, the federal agency acted as a countervailing force, exerting a modest influence. Although the initiative for social problems has perhaps shifted from local to national levels (Clark, 1965), the local level continues to exercise a veto power over the changes that it does not want. The result is a system of checks and balances that assures a measure of compromise between these extremes. While this balance of power produces tension, the fact that there is a negotiation process assures every organization that it will derive some benefit from the arrangement, which in the long run produces a stabilizing effect.

This chapter has sketched the dimensions of the national program in order to supplement and extend the discussion of the local programs. We have completed the analysis of data. As the findings have accumulated, a picture of the program has unfolded. I have tried to interpret, selectively, the more salient patterns. However, the task of placing the program and the main findings of this study in a larger framework remains. The final chapter conjectures about the broader implications of the study.

NOTES

1. Congresswoman Edith Green of Oregon initially feared that the Teacher Corps would bring untrained and unqualified people into the teaching profession and that the fringe benefits—bonuses to master teachers for supervising interns,

tuition-free graduate study for interns, and lighter teaching loads—would give the Corpsmen advantages over regular teachers. Congressman Albert H. Quie of Minnesota had voiced strong opposition to the program because of his concern that the use of federal money to hire and pay the salary of local employees would give the federal government undue influence over public education.

2. Sixty-two percent of the universities that participated in three or more cycles have changed directors at least once, and one in four has had three directors. For all universities that have participated in more than *one* cycle, the turnover in directors ranges from 43 to 63 percent.

3. Tau is a measure of association among ordinal measures. In this case the 10 universities or the 42 schools in the sample were rank-ordered on the variables indicated.

4. A former director of the Peace Corps in Tunisia, Graham described the Teacher Corps as a "domestic version of the Peace Corps." Brochures in which the Teacher Corps was advertised along with the Peace Corps and VISTA were mailed across the country.

5. The 85 colleges and universities that have had Teacher Corps programs were rated on a combination of two measures: (a) a *college resources index* constructed for 1144 accredited colleges and universities by Columbia University Bureau of Applied Social Research (Nash, 1969); and (b) a *selectivity index* of their admission policies reported in Cass and Birnbaum (1970).

6. According to the American Association of Colleges for Teacher Education publication, *Teacher Productivity*, 1967, the volume most applicable to the sample at the beginning of the study.

7. t_p refers to a partial rank-order correlation (tau) using three variables.

8. Schools were rated on the number and innovativeness of technological changes that had been introduced, and on the number of community activities, based on a content analysis of the interviews.

9. Modernization was measured by the index developed by Herriott and Hodgkins. When the programs were dichotomized on the basis of this index, the mean prestige score for universities in the more modern areas is $\overline{X} = 35.8$, and for those in the less modernized areas it is $\overline{X} = 25.2$. Conversely, dichotomizing the university prestige scores, the mean modernization score for the high-prestige universities is $\overline{X} = 13.6$, and for the low-prestige universities it is $\overline{X} = -10.7$. Including the less modern regions in the program, then, depresses the prestige level of the universities in the program.

10. However, it is possible that the change was because the Washington office may have recognized the potential for change in its initial selection. The better endowed programs tended to be in larger $(t = .45)$, higher quality universities $(r = .37)$ and were located in the more modernized regions of the country $(t = .46)$. The size of the grant also correlated with the favorableness of the interns' evaluation of university faculty $(t = .51)$. The more money granted, the less likely the program was to attract interns with undergraduate degrees or majors in the liberal arts $(t = -.57, t = -.46)$, although they were more likely to come from relatively good undergraduate colleges $(t = .49)$. There was also a tendency for the better funded programs to attract fewer males and blacks, and fewer interns with prior experience in the Peace Corps or VISTA.

V

Reflections

CHAPTER 11

A Sociological View of Social Reform:
Toward A Theoretical Interpretation

The qualitative approach to evaluation permits the social scientist to evaluate programs without having either to act solely as a technician or alternatively to give up his commitment to careful empirical work as a basis for his judgments.

WEISS AND REIN, 1970, p. 108

These focal questions were raised in Chapter 1: How can organizations be deliberately changed? How and in what respects can the teaching profession be improved? What role can the federal government most effectively play in this process? Although these questions have not been, and cannot be, answered in a definitive way, I shall present a tentative framework that will help to interpret the events that shaped the program and that suggests areas for further study.

First, we shall consider how social reform is shaped by organizational principles and, in particular, by the compromising "political" nature of organizations. Then a model will be proposed, consisting of several key sociological dimensions of organization that will be a framework for the remainder of the chapter.

349

POLITICAL ASPECTS OF ORGANIZATION: A PARADIGM

Let us broaden our perspective on the nature of reform programs as a general class of events. Perhaps we should first view the Teacher Corps itself from a larger perspective. Whereas previous discussion concentrated on limited aspects of change—the technological changes and new patterns of interorganizational relationships that emerged from the program—perhaps the specific changes that occurred were, in final analysis, only peripheral to the main contribution of the program (noted at the outset of this study): the program provided the incentive and opportunity for more collaboration to occur among a variety of groups and organizations concerned with education; it sought to expand and cement the interorganizational network that is rapidly evolving among educational institutions in this country. For the schools and for many of the colleges, *participation in the program* was the critical innovation. Irrespective of the immediate success and failures in local programs, the fact that the Teacher Corps deliberately attempted to establish a nationwide collaborative framework among organizations to attack an educational problem is the program's real significance. On this basis it can claim a position of historical importance in education.

The Teacher Corps program, then, must be viewed primarily as a concerted, national effort to forge a coalition of subunits within a network of larger organizations—schools, colleges, and government agencies. It was designed to effect systematic change in the functions, performance, and objectives of the host organizations. Because the program was a complex social structure, it was subject to all the forces and constraints that shape any organization. Ironically, *whereas the program was intended to effect change, it became modified by the same principles and processes that had shaped the organizations it was trying to alter.* The organizational character of this change agent—and the change-agent character of the Teacher Corps organizations—produced status dilemmas, conflicts in goals and roles, political constraints, local resistance, co-optation strategies, and the other problems noted.

This emphasizes the need to take organizational principles and processes into account in trying to understand the reform process. Clearly, the strategies used to introduce innovation, and indeed the idea that it is possible to change organizations at all, are based on *implicit* assumptions about the nature of organizations. But a major problem is that reform programs seldom have been derived from, or geared to, an explicit, plausible model of organization. The assumptions that are made tend to be simplistic or totally misleading. Organizations seem to be regarded by leaders of reform and persons who evaluate the effectiveness of reform programs as being rational, potent instruments for implementing policy decisions, with a capacity to accomplish any assigned task. So great and prevailing is this faith that failures are usually blamed on certain individuals or on a minor procedural flaw. But it is seldom taken into consideration that it may be *impossible* to fully implement a controversial, complex, or inconcise plan in the manner that it was originally conceived. Reform programs are expected to perform in accordance with this rational image and will be held accountable for what they fail to do or cannot do—while their major contributions go largely ignored. However, the fundamental role that status, role structure, scarcity of resources, and power play in many complex organizations makes it clear that there are definite limits to what can be accomplished by a reform program.

The thesis here is that, because social reform must be implemented through organizations in modern organizational societies, it will be subject to and shaped by the forces and the constraints that govern any complex social organization. The reform process is multidimensional but there are five orders of variables that any analysis should take into account: (1) the task structure of the organizations involved, which includes their goals, role structure, and incentives used; (2) their status system and the status identities of their members, including their social backgrounds, positions of authority, technical competence, and values; (3) the economic resources available to the organizations and the way they are allocated; (4) the distribution of power and the internal processes used to resolve conflict; and (5) the occupational setting. Power is the most critical dimension because, frequently, power struggles determine the relative priorities among the other dimensions and determine the nature of the goals and role structure and the distribution of status and economic resources. The way specific innovations are received and implemented will also be subject to these power struggles and related "political" processes such as bargaining and compromise.[1] In view of the importance of power within organizations, let us consider the role it plays in more detail.

The Elements of Organization

Power must be understood as a means of integrating a social system. Any social system is bonded by one or more of three primary, integrative mechanisms: (1) *consensus,* or shared expectations among the members, which in turn establish authority; (2) *power,* which ranges from coercion (total power) to minor influence wielded by some members over others;

and (3) *reciprocity*, or the exchange of goods or services. Each mechanism is tied to different theoretical models of society—the functional model, the conflict model, and the exchange model. Different combinations of these mechanisms produce two different models of organization—the "rational" model, and the "political" or "natural system" model (Gouldner, 1959). There are several differences between these models, but there are also some points of similarity.

DIFFERENCES. The *rational model* presumes that organizations are goal-directed entities. Organizational goals dominate the decisions made by the official leaders. The rationality of these decisions increases with the number of alternative courses of action considered and the amount of planning. By comparison, the *political model* presumes that direction is determined by external constraints on the organization and by the commitments made by the members in the course of bargaining for resources; official goals are only one among many possible sources of commitment and are themselves subject to compromise. Unless an unusually high consensus on goals and priorities prevails throughout the organization, commitments and constraints not related to the goals take precedence in setting direction.

SIMILARITIES. These differences stem largely from differences in *priority* among the variables; the models are not necessarily comprised of different variables. Therefore, there are many elements that are implicitly or explicitly shared by both models, including the role structure, status and incentive systems, and the like. Perhaps the two models can be integrated by comparing them on these underlying components. At least three components seem to be essential: (1) the degree of consensus on stated objectives, status, and roles; (2) an integrated division of labor and rational planning for the organization as a whole; and (3) the power of each segment of the organization to achieve its commitment. Rationality can be considered as the *limited* case where there is (a) complete consistency on the stated objectives, (b) effective power and knowledge on the part of the central offices and subunits within the organizations to achieve commitments, and (c) extensive and integrated organization-wide long-range planning that takes into consideration many alternatives (Corwin, 1967).

If there were full consensus, the system would remain static in the absence of an outside force. But these conditions seldom can be achieved. However, at best, an *incomplete* consensus will prevail in most situations. Without full consensus, the amount of effective planning that can be done will be *inversely* related to the power of the subparts of the system. In other words, the more decentralized the power, the less likely that planning of a comprehensive nature can be implemented. Thus, even with extensive planning by a central office that considers several alternatives over an extended period of time, rational choice among the alternatives will tend to be subverted if subunits have autonomy to pursue their separate objectives or their differing versions of the overall goals. Therefore, the power relationships among subparts, as these affect the logic behind decisions, should be the analysts' primary concern.

There must be some consensus on basic principles before exchange can occur. Also, both parties must have some power and/or control scarce resources. But the priority given to consensus and power varies. This relative priority can be described in a profile of "equilibration." Certain patterns of equilibration, or disequilibration, are more conducive to change than others. Learning the precise effects of difficult balances is the first step to understanding the change process.

The "Political" Aspects of Organizations

Power often assumes an important role within organizations. The recurrent power struggles resemble political processes. The organization's actions are shaped by the outcomes of the power struggles, that is, the compromise that is inherent to all forms of politics. As a result, the organizational structure itself is seldom coherent but consists of *alternating* sets of norms and actions that are selected through a process of "role bargaining"—that is, negotiation, compromise, and conflict—that results in selective enforcement of conflicting norms and selective performance (Goode, 1960). Thus, an organization is a product of what Strauss calls "negotiated order"; it is in a continual process of being revoked, revised, and renewed.

The tension among the alternatives, then, is a source of dynamic energy and stability. Since the alternatives are mutually dependent, a change in the priority of one alternative provokes a counteraction in others that often produces change. This system of checks and balances acts as a constraint that may produce temporary stability and continuity. Inertia, in other words, is produced by the same process that accounts for change; the inertia often occurs when the organization is polarized by cross-pressures (Buckley, 1967), unless the balance is upset by an outside influence. But as power and resources are expended in the process of bargaining, shifts can occur in the power distribution, which require new forms of adaptation.

APPLICATION TO THE INNOVATION PROCESS

Innovations introduced into this framework necessarily become ensnared in the internal power struggles; the fact that the reform program studied here was organizationally complex merely compounded the political element. Viewed from the standpoint of the new program (innovation) the power structure establishes limits on the amount of control that can be exercised by any one group over how the program is to be implemented. This essentially "political" process leaves much room for maneuvering and compromise. From the viewpoint of the organization hosting the new program, the program structure can do no more than provide general rules or broad guidelines, while the cross-pressures will provide a basis for developing different alternatives; individuals can influence the process by throwing their weight on one side or the other of the balance of forces. Thus, when an alternative mode of organization is deliberately imposed on the dominant mode, in addition to compromising the dominant mode, the alternative itself is likely to become altered in the process. Let us examine the problem by applying a series of postulates.

Some Postulates About Innovation

It is axiomatic that a professional group's conduct is strongly influenced by its organizational setting. Therefore, *to explain change in a* profession *it is first necessary to take into account the effects of its organizational context and, in particular, to explain how* organizations *change.*

It follows that the responsiveness of professions to changing demands will be contingent upon external pressures and the nature of support from other organizations and groups in the environment. *Professional goals and practices become adapted to environmental constraints as a result of competition from powerful organizations and bargaining with other organizations for necessary resources.*

The key to any stable social system is reciprocity based on dependency relationships in which each party requires assistance from others in order to maintain his own position and perform his roles. Since structural change requires alteration of these relationships, it poses threats to existing status prerogatives. Hence, *an attempt to train people for new, emergent roles will be dysfunctional for existing roles* to the extent that they make incompatible demands on role incumbents, at least until the new roles become dominant or some other accommodation is made.

Some subgroups in an organization will benefit from change while others will stand to lose. The leaders in control of a profession tend to be supported by outsiders who benefit from the status quo. But the internal leaders' authority also will be challenged by aspirants. External incentives and pressures can shift this internal balance for power for or against change in a profession. In other words, *change in organizations and professions is a product of the* interplay *between the internal and external forces for and against change.*

At least three dimensions of change must be distinguished because each revolves around different principles: the *source* of the change; the *mode* of the change; the *form* of implementation.

SOURCE. A change may be produced by *deliberate* innovation or it may be the result of unintended *crescive* changes that accumulate from natural processes. Crescive change occurs through cyclical processes, evolution, or bargaining. As an example of crescive change, a school's goal priorities may shift in response to hiring younger male teachers or admitting new types of students (Selznick, 1949; Clark, 1956; Clark, 1960). Deliberate innovation, on the other hand, refers to planned efforts to change an aspect of a system in order to achieve a stated purpose, such as the effort of the Teacher Corps to introduce team teaching.

This is not a mutually exclusive dichotomy. There is always a crescive aspect in deliberate innovation because all actions are part of a bargaining process and all deliberate innovations set certain crescive processes in motion. In short, deliberate innovation does not take the place of normal, crescive processes of change. Instead, it may accentuate or counteract them.

MODE. According to Merton's (1957) typology, "innovators" subscribe to the cultural goals but, rejecting the means being used to achieve them, seek new, alternative means. Dubin's (1959) extension of the basic typology distinguishes between innovation in values and behavioral innovation, and distinguishes further among innovations at the normative, institutional, and operating levels. Considering first the *values* dimension, equal educational opportunity is largely an unquestioned cultural value (normative goal) in the United States to which most innovations in education are intended to contribute. The effectiveness of professional training organizations in preparing professionals to achieve this goal exemplify some of the *institutions* involved. The present curriculum and teaching practices are examples of the *operating level*. Rejection of both the cultural value of equality of educational opportunity and the existing practices designed to promote the equality would amount to "rebellion."

The more radical forms of *behavioral innovation*, which require substitution of new institutional roles, are exemplified in proposals to use indigenous, untrained lay teachers or college graduates without professional training. By contrast, the development of new practices at the technological level (such as new math and team teaching) do not challenge the assumptions underlying the institutional arrangements.

FORM. An innovation, in *any* mode, can assume one or more of several *more specific* forms (Chin, 1963): (1) making a minor alteration in what already exists; (2) making additions to what already exists; or (3) restructuring what already exists around new functions and roles. Although new additions might eventually require modifications in the rest of the system, it is also possible for symbiotic relationships to develop between the new and the old in such a way that the existing structure is not changed but actually is reinforced by the introduction of an innovation. For instance, new functions might be added to existing roles or new staff may be added without altering the work roles, but the authority of the persons performing the roles would be increased.

Returning to the general postulates, the kind of constraints placed on organizations will affect the success or failure of an innovation. Variable levels of resistance therefore must be taken into account in any effort to anticipate or assess outcomes (Scott, 1966). Comparable levels of performance will result in variable degrees of success under different circumstances. As a corollary, innovations tend to vary their form in the course of being applied to specific, local circumstances. In other words, *variable levels of resistance to an innovation must be taken into account in order to anticipate its outcomes and evaluate its effectiveness; an innovation can be understood only in terms of the conditions under which its variant forms do and do not survive and suceed.*

Finally, the fact that there is widespread disaffection between professionals and low-income clientele suggests that the relative inability of a given profession to serve low-income people cannot be explained entirely in terms of personal characteristics of the professionals. Instead, part of the disaffection must be seen as generic to the structure of professions and their organizational settings.

Innovation as Process

These postulates will form the basis for a more complex, dynamic view of the process of innovation. Although few writers have attempted to reconstruct the process of change systematically (Gouldner, 1970; Gerard, 1957; Clark, 1968), the work to date seems to assume that deliberate innovation is part of an orderly, dialectical process consisting of several stages, discussed below.

1. *Structural Lag.* During the first stage there is a change in the functional needs of a society, rendering structures originally designed to serve particular functions inadequate for the new demands now being placed on them. Improvement stimulates public expectations, leading some segments of the public to demand further change while others are satisfied with modest results. The more rigidly structured the organizational unit involved, the less sensitive it will be to the new ideas and the public demands to implement them (Gerard, 1957).

2. *Crisis.* The growing strain between the system used to deliver the services and public expectations may intensify to the point where a public mandate for change crystallizes. The pressure for change reaches a peak when a general social crisis develops that affects a large number of institutions. During such periods leaders, who in normal times are under conservative pressures, are expected to innovate; rules are suspended and new opportunities arise for exercising ingenuity (Putney and Putney, 1962).

3. *Outside Intervention.* Innovations are conceived and implemented through a combination of forces inside and outside the organization. New structures are proposed by concerned outsiders who are in a position to exercise personal leadership and have less investment in a given structure. When new fields of specialization, roles, and administrative units are created, tasks that formerly were the responsibility of other units must be redistributed. The new units will be resisted by the established leadership identified with the existent division of labor.

A dialectic develops through which the traditional, conservative procedures are reasserted or slightly adapted in order to forestall the introduction of new procedures. An internal split is produced between the established leaders and a new generation identified with the outside leaders. The latter stand to gain from new roles that promise to open new channels of success and to circumvent the status system controlled by traditionalists. The new proposal becomes more attractive to the younger professionals as the profession grows in size and becomes more competitive over the fixed number of status positions. This coalition of influential outsiders and a competitive leadership group within the profession may seriously challenge the resistance of established professionals by successfully identifying a new content area and reorganizing subject-matter fields and eventually the profession itself.

4. *Dialectic Process.* The solutions to one set of organizational problems will create new problems. A change in one part of an organization is likely to modify other parts, often in unforeseen ways. And certain modest

changes may be made deliberately to avoid or delay more fundamental changes.

5. *Variations and Adaptations.* No single innovation will be fully suitable in its original form for the variety of circumstances under which it must be implemented. Variant forms will evolve that have few features in common except a common administration and funding source. The original plan becomes one of many alternative forms. Most variants become extinct or so well adapted that they are indistinguishable from the existing forms. But through a process of natural selection and cross-fertilization of values and technique, new *hybrids* arise in some cases from an optimal match between the innovation and local conditions. "Survival" is a variable condition, which may range from an almost complete replication of the innovation, as conceived, to complete rejection.

6. *Routinization.* Once an innovation has been established, it becomes subject to the same institutionalizing forces that originally created the need for it. That is, it must conform to rules, regulations, and red tape. Routinization, increases in size and complexity, traditionalism, and the control of special interest groups contribute to the process by which an innovation becomes integrated into the society.

A MULTISTAGE MODEL OF THE INNOVATION PROCESS

Although power is of vital importance, there are other important elements within organizations that influence the results of an attempted reform program. We shall examine these other dimensions. The model must allow for the primary importance of political contingencies without obscuring a chain of related sociological variables that also intervene to alter and shape plans. It must also specify the mechanisms that regulate the process and identify the targets to be changed.

The Political Economy of Organizations

The term "political economy of organizations," which has been profitably used by Zald (1970) and by others, will serve as a point of departure.[2] This concept not only points to some promising lines of inquiry but also illustrates a number of conceptual ambiguities that must be clarified. Although the concept customarily has been applied to nations, Zald and others have applied it to organizational change. Writers who use it assume that the primary incentives and constraints that motivate and shape social systems are fundamentally political and economic in nature. It is supposed that the "political economy" generates the social energy that propels, deflects, and shapes organizational life.

Zald defines the "political economy" of an organization as the relationship of goals to the power and incentive systems. The economy includes the external demand for change, external supply of funds, and internal allocation of skills, resources, and technology. The polity encompasses the total system of legitimate and illegitimate influence and power, the amount and distribution of power, and normative limits on the use of power. While Zald used the concept to analyze a single national organization (the YMCA), it can be applied to organizational networks such as were involved in the Teacher Corps. However, the way the concept has been formulated weakens its utility. Although it is rich with implications, it is in many ways imprecise and is the source of potentially serious distortions in the way organizations function. At least three types of weakness can be identified.

1. *It Obscures Other Sociological Dimensions.* The term "political economy" obscures the importance of sociological dimensions that are indiscriminately mixed in under this rubric and whose independent contributions therefore are not easily recognized. It is apparent from the types of phenomena Zald included that the concept alludes to more than political and economic variables. Included are the value structure, technology, and the allocation of skills, to mention only a few others normally included as part of the organizational status system and task structure. In other words, this is a blanket concept so extensive in meaning that it is doomed to be imprecise.

2. *It Inflates the Importance of the Economic Factors.* Just as the term "political economy" causes the role of important sociological dimensions to be ignored, it tends to exaggerate the importance of economic factors. Again, there are other dimensions of equivalent importance, some of which have been mentioned already. It is misleading to single out the economic factors in the absence of compelling evidence that they completely eclipse other variables that an extended sociological literature suggests are important.

3. *It Confuses Organizational Power with Political Institutions.* The term "political," as applied to organizations, tends to confuse political institutional processes with the "internal politics" of organizations. There is, of course, certain merit in this analogy. As already pointed out, there are some convincing parallels between the power struggles and com-

promises that take place within organizations and *processes* in the political institutions. Moreover, there may be an extremely crude but discerning parallel between the democratic and authoritarian political *structures* and comparable structures in organizations. Also, in both cases power is couched within and regulated by deliberately created authority structures.

However, one must be careful to distinguish between the way internal power struggles affect an organization and the effects of political institutions on it. The Teacher Corps, for example, was created by Congress and was regulated by an agency of the federal government as well as by school boards and other local government agencies. The program was shaped partly by these institutions. Also, the schools and colleges had their own internal power structures that influenced the program. Clearly, the political institutions exerted an independent influence on the program, but they provided only one of many bases of the internal power structures within the schools and colleges.

An Expanded Framework

My brief comments on the concept of political economy are not intended to detract from its valuable aspects. My purpose is twofold: to point to ways of refining the concept, and to identify other, complementary dimensions that deserve to be elevated to comparable importance. With this in mind, I shall propose a typology consisting of five major concepts, each having an external dimension in the larger society and an internal dimension within the organization. Then we shall consider the way that the components fit together.

DIMENSIONS THAT EFFECT CHANGE

   I. *Power Structures*
      A. *External*
         1. An external mandate for change that provides both legitimacy for the program and, depending on the amount of dissent, sources of constraint and resistance.
         2. A deliberately controlled guidance system consisting of (Buckley, 1967):
            a. A *control center*—that establishes certain desired goal states and describes means by which they are to be attained.
            b. *Administrative bodies*—that transform goal decisions into action (output).

       c. A *feedback process*—through which information about the effects of the output are recorded and fed back into the control center.

       d. An *evaluation procedure*—that computes deviations from the original goals.

       e. *Regulating procedures*—that institute necessary corrective action taken by the control center.

  B. *Internal*

    1. Access to power and an effective distribution of power within and among network organizations.

II. *Resources*

  A. *External*

  Access to external resources.

  B. *Internal*

  An effective internal distribution of resources within the network.

III. *Task Structures*

  A. *External*

    1. A clear, rational division of labor among member organizations and mechanisms for coordinating their contributions.

    2. Effective mechanisms to promote collaboration among organizations in an organizational network.

  B. *Internal*

    1. A facilitative structure and required technologies available to individual member organizations.

    2. An internal consensus on organizational goals within the network and universal commitment to the need for change.

IV. *Status Characteristics of the Members*

  A. *External*

    1. Social status, including educational and social, ethnic backgrounds, age, and sex.

    2. Cultural values supported by the members.

  B. *Internal*

    1. Organizational status.

    2. Technical competence.

V. *Occupational Environment*

  A. *External*

    1. The professional component:

       a. The organization of new bodies of knowledge and ideologies.

       b. The development of new professional activities and new forms of collaboration.

      c. New institutions for teaching the innovation.

      d. Provision for a new professional reward system and new professional roles.

  B. *Internal*

    1. The bureaucratic component:

      a. Specialized roles.

      b. New, official full-time status and responsibility for implementing the innovation.

      c. Separate specialized subunits (such as departments) responsible for innovation.

RELATIONSHIP AMONG COMPONENTS OF THE MODEL. The dimensions identified above are the links in the complex innovation process chain. (A) The political institution, in conjunction with (or in opposition to) the internal "political" processes within organizations, provides the *energy source* for change or inertia, which is fueled by economic resources. (B) This force is controlled by a *goal-directed mechanism* that directs the innovative thrust, evaluates progress, and adjusts to unanticipated consequences. (C) The innovation is further shaped and deflected by the *status characteristics* of the people involved. (D) Finally, the thrust for change must be *targeted toward* what Clark (1968) identified as the *professional* and *bureaucratic components* of the profession.

Having posited this series of logical steps that must take place before an innovation is fully implemented, I must now add the qualification that, in practice, this process seldom occurs in only one direction. The number of linkages in this complex chain of events leaves much room for slippage, reversals and setbacks, sabotage, and selective attention between the conception of the innovation and its implementation.

As a general working hypothesis, then, it can be expected that a change in any one of these dimensions requires a prior change in one or more of the other dimensions; and once a dimension changes, there will be repercussions in one or more of the remaining dimensions. For example, a shift in the distribution of power could create a goal displacement, which could affect the division of labor. Or, if an increase in the external demand for change occurs, it can be expected that organizations will form new linkages with one another and with the environment.

In other words, in identifying the major dimensions of the innovation process, the model also helps to pinpoint where in the process problems can arise. Now let us examine the sources of some of these problems as they could be identified in the Teacher Corps. The three major sections that follow—sources of incentive and constraint in the Teacher Corps, the critical targets for change, and the national office as a guidance system—correspond approximately to the three questions asked at the beginning of the chapter.

SOURCES OF INCENTIVE AND CONSTRAINT IN THE TEACHER CORPS: *HOW CAN ORGANIZATIONS BE CHANGED?*

In this discussion it is presumed that the professional and bureaucratic principles of organization make somewhat different demands on teachers, professors, and students, and that each principle has a different implication for how schools and colleges ought to be organized. The profession and the bureaucracy are subject to differing amounts of pressure to change and will change at different rates and in different directions. Therefore, incompatibilities are bound to arise at points of overlap between the profession and the individual schools and colleges employing teachers and professors. This means that before professional reforms can be implemented, it is first necessary to adapt the education organizations concerned so that the reforms can be accommodated by them.

The Public Mandate for Change: *Value Consensus as a Source of Incentive and Constraint*

Generally, the environment into which an innovation is introduced determines how the innovation will be altered and adapted. The greater the consensus on the need for social reform, the more authority will accrue to the agency responsible for initiating the reform, thus maximizing the likelihood of the success of the innovation. The national Teacher Corps office was blessed with the authority attributed to any governmental body, but its governmental status also thrust the program more squarely into the political arena. The politically volatile climate in which the Teacher Corps was operating proved to be fateful. The very fact that the issues had become sufficiently political to require public legislation meant that the program would be subjected to compromise from the start. The lack of a consensus within the society on the need for change or the appropriate direction or vehicle for change compromised the program's legitimacy and integrity. The national office was blocked by controversies concerning the *need* for the reforms it advocated, the *legitimacy* of federal intervention in local institutions, and the *threat* that poverty programs posed to middle-class privilege, in general, and to professional autonomy, in particular. The agency was held in check by the cross-pressures of a wary public, opponents in Congress, competition from other agencies, control from higher echelons in the government bureaucracy, resistance from participating local member organizations, and the dissipation of its limited resources and energies in the attempt to satisfy different publics. At the same time, the fact that there was controversy gave the national office some latitude because it could always count on having supporters and opponents for any decision.

Consensus on Program Goals

As a corollary of the lack of consensus among the general public, there was little consensus among the constituent members of the program. Multiple goals and competing models resulted in a dissipation of effort and blurred the division of labor.

GOAL-SETTING AS STRATEGY. The national office was forced to compromise the innovative thrust of the program by establishing competing models designed to render service to school districts as currently structured. But this was not a simple case of "goal displacement," a term that implies that the dominant goal has been slighted in order to preserve an irrelevant structural form. What actually happened was that the adaptations in both the structure and the goal system of the program were made in an effort to protect the goal of innovation in the face of hostile forces. In other words, goals were proliferated and priorities were altered as part of a larger strategy. Alternative goals were advanced as a way of allaying opposition and deflecting criticism from the controversial goals and as a way of increasing the capacity of the national office to maneuver by subtly manipulating existing priorities without having to admit that anything fundamentally new or at variance with the model was taking place. In short, goals were used as bargaining resources; some goals were bargained in order to salvage others.

RHETORIC AS A PERSUASIVE FORM OF INFLUENCE. The innovative image of the program was kept alive through an aggressive rhetorical campaign reiterating the objective of innovation. Rhetoric was deployed as a way of preserving the official goals in the face of the actual compromises being made. By helping to preserve the illusion of consensus and concealing the political impotence of the program, the rhetoric probably enhanced the capacity of the national office to attract preferred member organizations.

Amount and Distribution of Resources

Without a clear public mandate, and confronted with internal opposition, the national office attempted to *bargain* for the changes it desired, but it did not have the resources needed to be fully effective; a divided Congress had appropriated only a small share of the authorized amount, which had to be shared between colleges and several participating schools; and the funding was always temporary and uncertain. Thus, while the rate of technological change in schools was proportionate to the amount of outside resources added to local programs, the total impact was relatively negligible.

Discretionary Operating Funds as a Source of Flexibility

The deficit in program funds was compounded by a chronic shortage of discretionary operating funds available to employ professional national office staff and for travel. In the absence of a discretionary status the national office became tied by the red tape and standardized controls that were designed for a traditional line agency, which were inappropriate for a reform program. For example, staff allocations for government agencies are normally geared to the volume of funds dispersed. However, since this was not simply a fund-granting agency, its workloads had little relationship to this criterion.

Faced with these limitations, the agency sought to optimize its bargaining power in four ways.

1. *The Principle of Resource Dispersal.* It was decided to maximize the program's visibility and to broaden its base of support by dispersing small amounts of funds over many local programs and by rotating the programs frequently. As a result, the program was marginal in two respects: it was temporary, and it constituted only a negligible percentage of the total college budgets. Not surprisingly, the program's impact became highly diffuse. The change agents (interns) were not sufficiently concentrated in local programs over a sufficiently long period of time to overcome powerful teachers organizations, tradition, centralized administrations, and professionally remote universities. Whatever visibility the program achieved was at the expense of whatever concerted effect the program might have had on a few local programs.

2. *The Principle of Marginal Utility.* Another strategy was to fund only the most volatile programs in which there was a balance of forces that could be easily tipped with marginal increments of dollars. Marginal utility could be increased by recruiting the less wealthy, academically mediocre institutions that were in a poor bargaining position and thus were vulnerable to federal influence. But the national office, in focusing on its leverage over local programs, ignored the national balance of power produced by the stratification system among colleges. For the reasons discussed in

connection with selective recruitment of the member institutions, the funding policy necessarily excluded the most visible prestigious universities, which might have served as regional models. Without sufficient authority, power, or resources to bargain effectively with the outstanding teacher-training institutions, the agency failed to influence the critical leadership within the network of higher education that might have triggered institutionwide change. Because of the types of institutions that were recruited, the program became committed to an isolated sector of the network. (More recently, preference also has been given to institutions already in the process of change, but this policy also obscures the program's unique contributions.)

3. *Recycling Funds Through Capital Investment.* The agency also tried to preserve its resources for what it considered the most critical points in the life cycle of innovations: the initial "start up" costs of the program. Once a local program was under way and the local institutions were committed to it, they were expected to gradually assume responsibility for the operating and maintenance costs in order to permit federal funds to be recycled into new programs in subsequent years. However, without sustained outside support and influence, the local institutions usually were unable to maintain the temporary momentum; or, if they did retain a program, it tended to evolve into variant forms that often had little resemblance to the parent programs.

4. *Maximizing Leverage Among Member Organizations.* The national office also could increase its own influence by allocating funds disproportionately to the schools or to the colleges, whichever was the more change-oriented institution. Each institution (that is, schools and colleges) was generally more committed to changing the other than to changing itself. But since colleges had more leverage over schools than schools had over colleges, even slight increases in college control over funds disproportionately increased the rate of technological change in the schools.

Distribution of Power Within the Network

Faced with dissent and a resource deficit, the agency had to rely on its *influence.* Even in the absence of consensus, change might have been forced on member organizations if power had been centralized in the national office. However, power was not sufficiently concentrated anywhere in the network to provide a sustained thrust for change. Although the initial legislation may have given the national office an edge over local institutions, once the program was in motion, dialectic counterpressures from local school districts (through their political influence and their ability to co-opt the program) shifted the balance in favor of local control.

The local organizations were more concerned with maintenance activities than with innovation, partly because they were preoccupied with day-to-day problems and partly because the tenuous and incendiary balance of forces in big-city ghettos and tradition-bound small communities increased the risk that any form of change might ignite conflict. Generally, organizations whose survival is threatened will turn their attention to "support goals," that is, activities needed to maintain the present status, as distinguished from "influence goals" designed to improve organizational status (Gross, 1958).

POWER DIFFUSION. School districts were able to expand their influence over the program, partly through the efforts of local politicians and partly by virtue of their control over the routine operations of the programs. They were in a position to stigmatize the interns (so they would not feel obligated to listen to the interns), to isolate members of teams in individual projects, to co-opt team leaders, and to replace personnel who were disloyal to the local institution. School districts received the bulk of the money; they gained final control over the selection and dismissal of personnel; they could serve as the prime contractors for some programs; and they eventually succeeded in "cooling out" the troublesome liberal arts graduates.

But to say that power was "decentralized" would be an oversimplification. Instead, power was *diffused* throughout various levels of this nationwide organizational network. This diffuseness produced a system of checks and balances that had two effects: (1) the national office was limited in the amount of control it could exercise over certain aspects of the program because of the resistance of member organizations; and (2) the national office retained veto power over certain important activities of the member organizations.

SELECTIVE RECRUITMENT OF MEMBER ORGANIZATIONS. The national office's prime source of control over the program resided in its authority to select the constituent member universities. Preference was understandably given to relatively vulnerable institutions that could be co-opted by the national office. The policy was partially effective; there was more change in local schools when the college backed the program. But, in view of the policy of dispersing the modest funds over many institutions, the agency was not in a position to bargain with the strongest universities that were most likely to act as national models. The decision was made to aim for a localized impact on mediocre institutions that trained relatively few teachers at the price of excluding the institutional leaders—a decision that was to limit the scope of the agency's impact. Teacher Corps programs

ranked a little lower than the population of universities on their academic
and intellectual resources, and they were considerably less selective of
students than typical universities.

PRESTIGE OF MEMBER INSTITUTIONS AS A BARGAINING RESOURCE AND SOURCE
OF CONSTRAINT. The prestige of the member organizations has an exchange
value as a resource that could either bestow influence or impose constraints
on the other members of an organizational network. The type of member
organizations that are recruited into the network, then, sets the level of
power and resources available and enmeshes the coordinating organization
and the entire network in a set of institutional incentives and constraints
that limit the options open to the coalition.

The Organizational Structure and Division of Labor

The power within individual *local* programs, that is, the school districts
and colleges, was distributed as diffusely as the power within the network
as a whole. Internal control and organizational structure are discussed
below.

INTERNAL CONTROL. A greater technological change took place in centralized school systems where more of the decisions were made by the superintendent's office, and less change occurred where individual schools (as
opposed to the universities) controlled more of the program's funds and
emphasized rules and procedures and strict discipline. These factors reflect
the capacity of the member organizations to control their operations and
to filter outside influences. Contrary to a widely held opinion, broad-based
participation in decision making did not assure that the program would
be successful. Where power was equalized, less technological change occurred, apparently because teachers were in a better position to co-opt the
program and to use it for their own purposes. Power equalization facilitates
change only if all parties involved agree that change is necessary or desirable. In the absence of consensus on the innovation's desirability, it can
be more effectively achieved if a centralized authority can force change
from the top. This does not mean, of course, that decentralized systems are
generally any less adaptable than centralized ones. On the contrary, precisely because decentralized systems are likely to be more adaptable, a
particular innovation might be subjected to more compromising pressures
if it is incompatible with the direction of the crescive changes in the system.
Ironically, then, it might be more difficult to implement a deliberate change
as planned in an otherwise adaptable environment than in a highly structured environment where the change is favored by the central authorities.

The national office seldom succeeded in securing the full commitment of the member institutions largely because it was possible for a few people in weak official positions to commit an entire school system or college to a program even though they did not have strong administrative support from the crucial bases of power within the organizations. Neither college deans nor school superintendents were required to demonstrate their personal commitment to the program as a condition of approval, whereas persons who *were* operationally in charge—the professors and school principals—seldom had command over the necessary resources to make this program a central focus of their organization's operations.

ORGANIZATIONAL STRUCTURE AS A SOURCE OF INFLEXIBILITY. The national office, being politically committed to work within the existing system, did not have the option of circumventing resistance by establishing alternative institutions, that is, new prototypes in the public and private sector to compete with existing local institutions. Competition from alternative institutions might have forced the member organizations to innovate on their own initiative. But, actually, the program interrupted normal routines and provoked resistance from the teachers and administrators who were being asked to shoulder new burdens and risks with little direct benefit. In fact, the existing structure was so impervious to the program that the only activities that could be introduced were the activities that would least affect it, and then only by adding them to the usual operations without changing existing priorities, which overloaded members of the system. However, two devices were used to try to force compromise in the existing structure.

1. *Promotion of a Latent Culture.* A deliberate effort was made to promote a "latent" or unofficial culture supportive of the idea of change. New teachers were recruited from liberal backgrounds and were encouraged to think of themselves as change agents with the hope that they would provide a stimulus to recalcitrant professors and defensive classroom teachers.

2. *Imposition of a Team Structure to Promote Structural Looseness.* An effort was made to redistribute internal power through a team structure. The team gave some support to the interns by conferring a special status on them and on the veteran teachers who, although they were far from radical, were more sympathetic to the interns than were their colleagues. The team also constituted a supplementary structure that transcended the individual classroom and sometimes encroached upon the teachers' monopoly over their classrooms. The team helped to rearrange the tradi-

tional fixed division of labor, to establish different lines of authority and, by providing new sources of loyalty, to blunt the vertical hierarchical pyramid. It substituted a flexible division of labor based on experience, interpersonal interests, skills, and training. Because the team was a *temporary* arrangement relatively insulated from the ongoing system, it was of minimal threat to the system. Teachers were able to tolerate the temporary redistribution of roles more than if the redistribution had been viewed as permanent.

In the final analysis, however, the team was a poor match for the self-contained classroom. It was imposed on the traditional organization but failed to replace it. Because the term was an insulated, temporary system, it had no real leverage, and it was plagued by contradictory roles and overlapping authority among team leaders, university faculty, and cooperating teachers. This pulled the team in several directions.

Interorganizational Relationships

A comparable, broad-gauged division of labor had been worked out among the member organizations. The universities were responsible for transmitting abstract knowledge and approving certification, and the schools were responsible for providing the operational setting for the experience-based internship.

INTERDEPENDENCE AS A STIMULUS FOR CHANGE. Because each of the organizations involved was specialized and controlled certain resources needed by the others, the organizations were forced to depend on one another, especially during periods of change when they were in greatest need of additional resources. Concerted action among the cooperating organizations was required to effect structural change, and this interdependence made it possible for one organization to act as the stimulus for change in the others. It is not surprising, therefore, that the major force for innovation in the schools in this study was the extent of cooperation between schools and universities.

AUTONOMY OF MEMBER ORGANIZATIONS. Nevertheless, in most cases, each institution controlled its own sphere of responsibility so well that it was impossible to fully mobilize the potential power within the network. At best, the relationship between colleges and schools could usually be described as one of antagonistic cooperation. Their autonomy and independence blocked the emergence of local centers of power and authority that might have improved coordination.

The institutions operated under different incompatible incentive systems and had independent publics and resources. The schoolteachers were precariously trying to maintain daily teaching schedules with inadequate resources, often in the face of challenges from both students and the community. They were not primarily responsible for training and resisted being used as laboratories unless they had been provided with assistance or other benefits. University professors were oriented to an academic status system and were insulated from the operational pressures of school teaching and from the unruly or dull classrooms. Therefore, they could not provide the practical guidance and leadership that interns needed. The interns were trapped between the university, which controlled their professional *certification* and the schools, which controlled their professional *experience.*

BOUNDARY PERSONNEL AS LINKAGES. These centrifugal tendencies, however, were counteracted to some extent when especially liberal-minded personnel occupied the key positions, especially the boundary-spanning positions responsible for the amount of cooperation that took place between colleges and schools. In the absence of a structure that required these institutions to cooperate, the personal qualities of the people in the boundary roles assumed disproportionate importance. Perhaps because of the professors' autonomy, their values and other personal characteristics seemed to be somewhat more influential than the personal characteristics of the teachers and even the team leaders, who were more subject to administrative controls. In any event, the critical factor that determined how much change took place seemed to depend on whether the university professors and the team leaders espoused liberal, flexible attitudes and were fully committed to the idea of change; a less critical but nonetheless persistent factor was whether they were regarded by the interns and the classroom teachers as being technically competent. It also helped when the team leaders' attitudes bridged the extremes expressed by the interns and by classroom teachers.

Status Characteristics of the Members

It was presumed that the interns, as newcomers to the profession from unique backgrounds, would bring fresh perspectives to the profession and that their very presence would produce change. They were encouraged in the recruiting publicity and by the national office to view themselves as "catalytic change agents," while it was implied that veteran educators were traditionalists obstructing needed change. Interns were to be the colleagues of veteran teachers; and socialization was to be a two-way process, with interns helping to resocialize their professors and veteran classroom teachers. Presumably, the greater the difference between these newcomers from the outside and the veteran teachers, the more innovation would take place.

However, it did not usually work that way. The more aggressive the interns were, the more defensive and inflexible the schools became. Their image only threatened teachers and irritated the professors. This produced confusing role reversals, compromised traditional teaching and learning roles, and paralyzed the innovative thrust of the program. Since the interns had been recruited and socialized for a status that did not yet exist in public education and since they were not given any real authority in the program, classroom teachers tried to force them into the available conventional student teacher roles. In reality, as novices in the profession, interns were the least potent forces in the entire educational system. Their presence was valued by the schools because it allowed the schools to do things they normally would not have had the manpower to do. The interns were not particularly valuable because of any new ideas they introduced.

Without legitimate status the interns resorted to power tactics in an effort to force their conceptions of needed experimentation on the schools and colleges. As their efforts gained velocity, however, there was a buildup of resistance and friction. They were outnumbered and, as representatives of the university, they were the subject of suspicion at the schools while they could not count on protection from the remote university professors. The number of technological innovations introduced into the schools and the amount of school-college cooperation declined with the proportion of liberal arts graduates in the program and with their political liberalism and change orientation. Many interns became alienated and others radicalized when introduced into settings in which little change was taking place—especially the more liberal interns, who belonged to liberal peer groups, and interns who were least satisfied with the competence of the university faculty members. Indeed, one of the unintended consequences of the program appears to have been the radicalization of a substantial number of reform-minded, optimistic young people who gave up hope on the system while they were in the program.

However, there were also benign consequences. Some interns successfully blended their change orientation with an increasingly realistic assessment of the possibilities. This suggests that the program occasionally succeeded in promoting new "role hybrids."

Moreover, there were some changes taking place in certain schools and colleges. For example, there was a positive correlation between the interns' presence and the rate of change at the *college*. Furthermore, even where technological innovations were not implemented in the schools, most of the teachers and team leaders, and many of the university faculty members working with the interns, said that some of their own attitudes toward working with poor children had improved considerably as a result of their experience in the program; a substantial portion said they had gained new ideas or had been influenced to work harder. The university faculty members also expressed more awareness of the problems of the disadvantaged. In fact, the interns often felt it was up to them to close the gap between the university and the school by bringing practical problems into more abstract classroom discussions. A few professors were reading more widely on poverty and were experimenting with new techniques; many professors were more receptive and sensitive to the views of interns, which resulted in more dialogue and more room for disagreement between professors and interns.

Finally, there were limited conditions under which interns were able to promote innovations in the schools, especially where classroom teachers were not well organized, had poor professional training, and were located in decentralized schools (where they could not rely on higher authorities for protection). But in spite of this, it is still doubtful whether personal characteristics of new people alone can change a profession as long as there are structural features that inhibit innovation.

There were two especially important aspects of the interns' status: the values they brought to the profession, and their level of technical competence. The implications of these characteristics can be understood more clearly within the context of the profession as a whole, discussed next.

THE CRITICAL TARGETS FOR CHANGE: *HOW CAN THE TEACHING PROFESSION BE IMPROVED?*

The Teacher Corps' objective was to improve the education of low-income children, indirectly, through organizational change and through reform of teacher education and, directly, by introducing innovations into the classrooms.

Thus far we have examined the ways to alter the organizational environment to help achieve these objectives, that is, changes in the schools and colleges that employ professional educators. Changes are required to permit professional reforms to be implemented. However, although schools and colleges are vital to the teaching profession, a profession extends beyond the individual organizations in which the profession is practiced. What actually took place, then, can be best understood in terms of how the program affected the principal components of the profession and the aspects of the bureaucratic framework that specifically impinge on professional work. Several components of the profession that must be changed in the course of professional reform were identified in the paradigm on pages 360 to 362.

Ideologies

Perhaps the main contributions of this program to the teaching profession were: (1) to provide a channel to attract reform-minded young people into education, (2) to provide a vehicle available to educators who wish to experiment, and (3) to publicize and perpetuate the general philosophy that teachers in low-income schools ought to become more sensitive to the special problems of their pupils. Its effectiveness, however, was contingent on the kind of ideologies that it supported and the competencies for which it provided.

The program succeeded in attracting a few new teachers who were more open to new ideas and who advocated a more humane and liberal philosophy of teaching than prevailed in the schools. Their compassionate social consciousness, their support for innovation and structural change, and their dedication to, respect for, and rapport with low-income children served as reminders of the need to find alternatives to better serve these youngsters. By insisting on more egalitarian and personal relationships with children, the interns challenged the traditional assumption held by university professors that cognitive knowledge is the basis of good classroom teaching, and they challenged the assumption held by teachers that "experience" and maintenance of discipline in the classroom are the critical ingredients of good teaching.

However, the humane and liberal ideologies were introduced at the expense of other scholarly and academic values. Thus the interns who were the most self-consciously personable, warm, and compassionate in their relationships with students also appeared to be the most hostile to scholarship; they not only discounted the importance of cognitive achievement in their own pupils but often regarded university course work as meaningless and irrelevant for themselves. Similarly, the interns who were the most dedicated to the need for educational reform often espoused a radical political dogma that undermined their ability either to present a balanced view of society in the classroom or to work toward reform effectively within the existing system. Perhaps the interns' marginal relationship to the society and to the profession accounts for their humane and liberal posture toward the teaching profession and also for their inability to fully accept the academic principles of reasoned scholarship and detached fairness. This does not imply that scholarship is inherently incompatible with compassion and liberal dogma; there are other traditions within academia that provide for a workable combination of these characteristics, but the interns were not committed to them, either. In light of this marginal relationship to both academe and the profession of teaching, their actions were largely influenced by their own personal predispositions, especially when their inclinations were reinforced by the peer-group climate.

But regardless of the reasons for the interns' radical and dogmatic approach to political and social problems, the interns posed a dilemma for the liberal professors and teachers in the study who were committed to social reform. On the one hand, the radicals alienated so many people that they were relatively ineffective; indeed, many of them dropped out of the program or withdrew entirely. On the other hand, the radicals upheld challenging standards for what could be done. Although doomed to frustration, they provided a thrust for change. But these questions arise: Is it possible to train people who are passionately committed to the need for reform *and* who are calculating and patient enough to work effectively within the system? Can they become *sophisticated* about the system without losing their zest for change? Can they learn to temper their *romanticism* without losing their *compassion* for and *optimism* concerning the children? In many instances these ingredients did not mix.

Nor was the interns' compassion for the children necessarily an unmixed blessing. The interns were discounting the importance of cognitive achievement for precisely the group of youngsters who most needed to improve their academic skills.

New Bodies of Knowledge

The program was probably more successful in supporting a philosophy in favor of improving teaching in low-income schools than in developing or applying the essential techniques. Although the professors seemed to be more cognizant of the problems and were reading more widely as a result of the program, the interns continued to complain that professors did not systematically incorporate the available information about the effects of ethnicity, class, race, and minority-group problems into their courses. This explains why the majority of interns, team leaders, and classroom teachers identified course work as the least relevant aspect of the program, and only a negligible number rated university-conducted preservice experiences as excellent. For example, where there was a serious language problem connected with the disadvantaged group, universities seldom provided courses in the second language that would have helped the teachers work more effectively with the students. Moreover, even when professors tried to employ special information, they tended to present it at such an abstract level that its relevance for the practical problems of teaching was seldom immediately apparent to the interns. This is one of the reasons why the interns were only slightly more satisfied with social science courses than with their other courses.

In addition to the tendency to ignore minority-group problems, little attention was given to the principles of innovation as intellectual subject matter. Thus, while the interns advocated change, they seldom were encouraged to read the literature on change or to consider the effects of alternative strategies for implementing it. As a result, even promising projects were often resisted because of the manner in which they were introduced. These inadequacies can be traced to a number of problems.

1. There was no consensus in the program and, indeed, in the teaching profession, as to whether specialized knowledge is required to teach in low-income schools. And, if so, what should the content of that knowledge be? To a certain extent, this reflects a level of primitiveness in the state of the art, which was further compounded by the goal conflicts and role confusion within the program. But the program failed to resolve the question of what kind of knowledge a special training program such as this one must develop and disseminate. In fact, it failed to take notice of the question, despite the rationale used to justify the program to Congress, that the problems of teaching in low-income schools were so unique that they required a special training program.

2. Most of the professors themselves had very little of the formal training or practical experience in low-income schools that might have equipped them for this program. The majority of the interns rated "almost none" of their professors as superior teachers on these counts, and over four out of five rated less than half of their instructors as superior. On the other hand, one of the most important factors accounting for the changes that did occur in the colleges pertained to characteristics of the faculty, including their competence and their political liberalism. Probably the major obstacle here was the failure of the program to overcome the social isolation between schools and universities, that is, the failure to develop new forms of collaboration.

3. The tendency of interns to disparage the importance of cognitive knowledge, in favor of developing affective rapport with children as a basis for teaching, accounted for some of their negativism toward the professors and also discouraged the interns from seeking out other sources of information.

4. Vested interest groups within the universities often refused to make room for new courses in the college curriculum. The fact that it was necessary to *add on* changes to existing requirements without a change in priorities or redistribution of resources imposed unreasonable demands on personnel in the program. When changes did occur, they amounted to little more than superficial alterations of what already existed.

But no matter what the reasons were, *the program produced very little codified knowledge related to teaching in low-income schools, as distinct from other types of schools,* that could be disseminated to new generations of teachers. This might signify that there are neither unique learning principles nor special skills required; that the same skills can be applied to any setting; and that the teachers who are effective with bright middle-class children will be as effective as possible with academically retarded lower-class children. If that were true, it would indicate that the problems in low-income schools cannot be rectified by training better teachers or through a special teacher-training program.

Nevertheless, I am reluctant to reach this conclusion. *Although the learning principles may not differ, certainly the settings to which the principles were being applied did.* In the schools I visited there were severe language problems, even between teachers and students of the same ethnic background, and there were differences in values and in subcultures. The teachers often appeared to be almost oblivious or apathetic to many of the differences that separated them from their children. I observed cases of insensitive white, middle-class teachers in Indian schools who had never visited an Indian home and could not speak the language. I observed cases of equally insensitive middle-class black and white teachers in the large cities who punished lower-class children for fighting on the playground or running in the halls while winking at middle-class children who sought to destroy one another in intense status competition and through slanderous gossip. Although the special training did not deal with these problems either, it seems that the kind of detailed information needed to understand a particular subculture can be conveyed only by a special training program.

In retrospect, it appears that the political dimensions of the program were quite large, precisely because the program did not produce a clear consensus on what skills a technically competent teacher would need for teaching in low-income schools. Since individuals in the program could not readily establish their authority on the basis of their *specialized technical competence,* they turned for authority to their *positions* in the official structure of the schools and colleges. But because this basis of authority presumed a degree of commitment to the present system that the interns could not accept, they tended to discount it. This left teachers and professors without legitimacy in the eyes of many of the interns, which forced the teachers and professors to fall back on their *personal influence* and *power.*

Similarly, the interns failed to develop a specialized set of skills that they could use to justify their authority as leaders of educational reform, but they did not occupy positions of authority that would have permitted them to carry out their aspirations for leadership. Therefore, they, too, turned to power tactics. But they did not have sufficient power in most cases to have a real effect. In short, if there had been a special body of knowledge that people in the program could have pointed to as a basis of their authority, there might have been fewer problems and more change. Lacking this sense of technical competence, participants in the program were forced to rely on their official positions and "experience" or to use power; and the forces for change were not as strong as the sources of resistance.

New Forms of Collaboration and New Activities

Although, logically, the university and the school district had a common interest in educational reform, each institution had its own vested interests, clientele, and independent resources, and it was subject to different incentives. The university was oriented to the academic-prestige system, and the schools were plagued with day-to-day problems. A negative relationship between innovation in the schools and the quality of the university signifies the marked remoteness of the most prestigious institutions from the local schools. The social distance was reinforced by the fact that most of the local program headquarters were located on university campuses away from school districts. A plan by the universities and the schools to have courses jointly taught at the schools seldom materialized because of different hiring and evaluation practices and different schedules used by the two institutions. The hoped-for "hybrid" professional, trained in the social sciences but concerned with the application of knowledge to educational practice, seldom appeared. This was largely because the social scientists were primarily oriented to the academic system and were not provided with sufficient inducements to turn their attention to other matters.

The presence of very liberal interns seemed to have an adverse effect on the relationship between schools and colleges and seemed to reduce their willingness to cooperate with one another. Conversely, cooperation was better where interns endorsed an ideology of close control over the pupils and rejected "permissiveness." The competence of the university faculty members, as rated by the interns, and the liberalism of the team leaders also had an important positive influence on the extent of co-operation.

The program tried to promote new relationships among schools, the community, and the home. But since community activities were not part of the daily routine, they were the first to be slighted under the pressure of time, even though they were less bound by established routines and offered more latitude for experimentation. Teachers preferred to have the interns help them in the classroom, and principals were concerned about the tendency of some interns to engage in "social action" in the community (as opposed to social service). The interns tended to define their community-activity responsibilities more broadly than did the teachers. The teachers considered community activities to be of value only when the activities had an immediate bearing on their own classrooms.

New Teaching Institutions

The program introduced an internship in the schools that, generally, was very useful, in principle, for both the interns and classroom teachers. It provided for direct experience with children in actual school settings, facilitated their understanding of disadvantaged children and the communities in which they live, and taught the interns about the "political realities" of schools. But the apprenticeship enabled the school to control a large portion of the training experience. The fact that the classrooms had not been selected for their known innovative qualities implied that the internship was designed to teach the interns to adapt to typical classrooms rather than to depart from tradition. Few interns had learned to become more "innovative" by virtue of their apprenticeship. The teachers, of course, complained of the opposite kind of problems: interns did not spend enough time in the classroom; interns did not provide teachers with enough assistance; interns were too "permissive"; they were unrealistic about the changes that could be accomplished within the school system; and they were so protected by the contrived team situations that they were not really prepared to assume responsibilities for large, unruly, self-contained classrooms.

Specialized Roles

The special roles in the program were not well integrated into the status structure and did not carry sufficient authority to support the interns, team leaders, and other people in the program against traditional role obligations. Consequently there were numerous role conflicts. Over one half of the principals and interns and one fourth of the cooperating teachers reported disagreements, usually with team leaders, about the amount of time interns should spend in the schools, the appropriate degree of permissiveness in the classroom and the amount of control that should be exercised over the children, who should supervise the interns, and the resistance of team leaders to trying out interns' proposals.

Each member of the program advocated the role definition that would reinforce his own status. Professors emphasized the intellectual foundations of teaching, that is, the importance of their subject matter and of cognitive skills, while classroom teachers regarded their practical experience as the critical ingredient for leadership in education. The interns, wanting to "humanize" teaching, regarded their own ability to establish rapport with the children as the critical factor. When the interns tried to encourage "permissive" classrooms in schools that were experiencing a high incidence of assault, extortion, drug use, and sexual attacks, the veteran teachers became more convinced that interns were naïve and poorly informed.

Although the team structure provided some protection for the interns' nebulous status, it contributed to the role conflict. The teams, after all, had been assigned contradictory objectives. There was not a clear-cut division of labor among the members nor a consensus within the school about the team's function; this undermined the authority of members of the program to act as change agents. Teams seldom operated as viable social groups in the classrooms largely because veteran teachers were in full control of the self-contained units. The only exceptions occurred where teams were given complete responsibility for a classroom or for implementing a program and, in some cases, where they could work together on a community project after school hours without being constrained by the school schedule. In these cases the teams seemed to work cooperatively and were able to institute new programs.

Full-Time Statuses and Units Responsible for Implementing Innovation

A major obstacle to the success of this program was that there had been no provision for a special organizational unit in the universities and schools that would be explicitly responsible for implementing it. If special departments had been created that were directly responsible to the chief administrator of the university and of the school system, they might have provided better protection from local pressures. There were, of course, some "full time" positions assigned responsibility for implementing the program, but a high rate of rotation among program directors, team-leaders, and coordinators reduced their effectiveness. Mobile teachers and administrators used these positions as stepping-stones into school or university administration.

Team leaders could have provided stable leadership because they supervised the day-to-day operations, but federal guidelines prohibited them from serving more than two years in their positions; and, as employees of the local schools who served subject to the principal's discretion, they had little reason to be committed to the success of the *program*. Because they were dependent on the cooperation of other teachers and were assigned largely administrative responsibilities, they seldom functioned as master classroom teachers who provided role models for the interns. Even so, the team leaders were more sympathetic to the interns' objectives than were most other classroom teachers; this put the team leaders in a position to mediate conflicting pressures on the team.

THE NATIONAL OFFICE AS A GUIDANCE SYSTEM: *WHAT IS THE GOVERNMENT'S ROLE IN EDUCATIONAL REFORM?*

Where does the federal government fit in this framework of events? Although the American fear of federal control over education perhaps makes this program an atypical case, the fact that it was an extreme test of local control enhances its utility as a social barometer for the evolving role of the federal government. In this case a federal agency served as the "control center" identified in the foregoing model. How well did the national Teacher Corps office function as a goal-directed feedback system, and what problems were encountered?

The National Teacher Corps Office as a Control Center

As a federal agency and a creature of the Congress, the national office was responsible for translating the broad legislative mandate into operating priorities and for establishing the means to attain them. Although it was able to exercise "control" only in the loosest sense, its involvement in reform nevertheless represented a very important development. Although agencies of the federal government have been part of a lateral network of groups influencing education, traditionally they have had a subdued influence in comparison to the welter of universities (that set administrative standards and train teachers), accrediting associations, professional

associations, and even textbook publishers.[3] Moreover, in contrast to the
many regulatory agencies responsible for enforcing compliance to legal
and administrative guidelines and to the many formula grant programs,
which have little discretionary power over funds distributed on the basis
of fixed criteria, the Teacher Corps sought to promote institutional *reforms*
by using a strategy that goes far beyond persuading *individuals* to change
their habits (as in the case of birth-control campaigns). This program
attacked professional prerogatives and aimed at structural reform.

FEDERAL INTERVENTION AS A THROTTLING MECHANISM. Why did an agency
of the federal government assume the responsibility for promoting reform?
There are, of course, many answers. First, the fact that the major educational issues today are national in scope means that they must be resolved
at that level. Since low-income people are mobile, everyone must pay the
costs of unemployment, of an uninformed citizenry, and of similar problems that result when a pocket of the country fails the poor. A single type
of organization or a single level of society does not have the answers or
the necessary resources to implement needed institutional reforms.

As a corollary, it takes a *coordinating agency*, with its own sources of
power and resources, functioning as an *outside* third party, and *national*
in scope, to mobilize coalitions of national organizations, to mediate conflicts among member organizations, and to effect institutionwide reforms.
In an organizational society, organizations specialize in small aspects of
major problems and monopolize skills and resources needed by other
organizations. Therefore, institutional change requires a concerted attack
by a coalition of organizations. But because local, autonomous organizations are often immobilized by local traditions and are trapped by local
power structures and vested interests, they must be prodded into cooperation with special incentives, and there must be a structure for transmitting
successful innovations. A federal agency has the best chance to fulfill these
functions.

But these factors do not fully explain why it is advantageous for the coordinating agencies to be part of the federal government. Of course, the
institutions involved were themselves quasigovernmental organizations and,
for that reason, perhaps, they were vulnerable to the influence of a
higher level of government. But the key is that the need for educational
reform had become a matter of bitter *public* controversy that had nearly
paralyzed the local institutions. Once the problem became political, the
issues were necessarily forced to the federal level. Hence, only federal
agencies could respond to national issues and mediate conflict among state
and local agencies, and only federal agencies had access to the discretionary

funds necessary to attack nationwide problems. Moreover, by fixing responsibility for reform in a specific federal agency, Congress could monitor and influence the direction of change more thoroughly than if responsibility for reform had been more widely diffused throughout the federal government or throughout the society. Furthermore, the authorities most concerned about federal intervention were even more fearful that, unless the government became directly involved, groups beyond congressional control would attempt to push through more radical reforms. *Federal intervention was a way of heading off these more radical efforts.* By creating a special office to administer the program, subject to congressional control, Congress assured that control over education would be retained in the hands of the middle-class professionals and bureaucrats instead of either the low-income clientele, whom the program was designed to serve, or radical reformers representing them.

The fact that a federal agency was involved had at least two other costs. First, the thrust of reform became compromised by the political process. The self-interests of the agency, Congress, and the schools and colleges had deflected attention from the problems that initially justified the program. Second, the likelihood was increased that education would be more politicized. The change agents who were most dedicated to educational reform subscribed to politically liberal and radical doctrines and sought to use their professional positions to proselytize their political dogma.[4]

The Administrative Apparatus

Before a deliberate change can be institutionalized, a structure must be established to maintain the momentum. Therefore, the administrative procedures used by the national office were of crucial significance for the outcomes.

DELEGATED CONTROL. The national office was dependent on subcontractors whom it could not control. That is, the management responsibilities for day-to-day operation had been delegated to the local universities, which shared authority with local school districts. Local program directors sometimes became paralyzed when they attempted to establish cooperation with wary school districts while being responsible for enforcing federal guidelines (for example, to assure that schools would not use interns illegally as substitute teachers). Program directors usually were faculty members without official authority over other professors or the teachers and team leaders. Supervisory responsibilities necessarily fell back on the national office that was not properly equipped to exercise effective supervision.

PARALYSIS FROM INSTITUTIONALIZATION. Although the agency attempted to develop its own constituency and to undertake lobbying on its own behalf with members of Congress, its ability to control the subcontractors was compromised by its opponents in Congress, by competition from other agencies, and by controls within the federal hierarchy itself. Despite efforts of Teacher Corps officials to obtain discretionary status for this program, its operations became increasingly institutionalized. In addition to the already mentioned legislative provisions that delegated control to local institutions, the national office was handicapped by its failure to gain control over several instrumental administrative tools including: (1) full authority to negotiate and rescind contracts with member organizations and to set funding and fiscal policies as conditions for performance (these functions were shared with separate departments and higher administrative echelons); (2) a substantial discretionary budget that would have provided for needed flexibility in the internal operations of the national office; (3) a public relations department; and (4) authority to lobby with Congress.

Feedback and Evaluation Mechanisms

The agency was further handicapped by the fact that the Congress and the bureaucracy refused to provide the discretionary funds and personnel to carry out evaluation, and to provide a sufficiently large professional staff, and to enable the agency to engage in the travel needed to maintain its information-gathering capacity. This chronic shortage of funds not only virtually excluded any meaningful or systematic monitoring of local programs but, ironically, limited the opportunities and channels available for *local* institutions to exert influence on the national office.

Corrective Action

The model presumes that once deviations from the goals have been detected, the control center will be able to take corrective action to restore the proper direction. However, again the national Teacher Corps office was seldom in a position to exert the necessary leverage except by rescinding contracts (which only produced a high turnover rate among member organizations that diluted its impact).

In short, there appear to be inherent limitations on the power of federal agencies because of the political nature of organizational networks. Now we shall consider these limitations.

The Role of Federal Agencies in the Change Process

There was little evidence in this program that federal funding had posed an imminent threat of control over public education by the federal bureaucracy. The authority of the national office was restricted on all sides by controversy, congressional restraints, internal bureaucratic controls, and resistance from member institutions. Indeed, some of the major obstacles confronted by the program had been erected by the same Congress and federal bureaucracy that created it. Operating without a clear public mandate for reform or the benefit of centralized power, the agency had to attempt to *bargain* for whatever influence it was to exert. Each bargain placed constraints on its power, which maximized local diversity and initiative, permitting local institutions to help shape the program. At best, the national Teacher Corps office bided its time and waited for ripe opportunities where it could exercise a modest influence on changes already developing, and it tried to tap vulnerable spots in the system of public education.

THE FEDERAL GOVERNMENT AS A COUNTERVAILING POWER. The loss of control at local levels, in other words, does not imply that control was therefore becoming centralized at the federal level. Control shifted outward and upward, and became diffused among many organizations existing between local communities and federal bureaucracy. The federal government could do no more than play a mediating role. It was only one element in a larger system of checks and balances, functioning primarily as a *countervailing power* to local institutions.

Moreover, whatever influence it was able to accrue developed because of the incapacity of locally and professionally controlled service institutions to respond on their own initiative to emerging national problems. Federal intervention helped to overcome the provincial insulation that has traditionally shielded schools from societal changes.

A TYPOLOGY OF FEDERAL INTERVENTION. The role that federal agencies can and do play in the change process is determined by at least two conditions: the level of consensus within the society on the need for reforms and the distribution of power necessary for implementing those reforms. From various combinations of these two conditions, four types of roles can be identified (see Table 11–1).[5]

When there is a complete mandate for change and power is centralized, a *corporate* arrangement (Type I) can be said to exist (Levine and White, 1961; Warren, 1967). The coordinating agency will encounter

Table 11-1 Conditions that influence the role of federal agencies
in the change process

Distribution of power with the government system	Degree of consensus on the need for reform within the society			
	High		Low	
Centralized	Type I		Type II	
	Corporate role		Empire role	
	Consequences	Basis	Consequences	Basis
	+change	+authority	+change	-authority
	-conflict	+power	+conflict	+power
	-coercion	-bargaining	+coercion	-bargaining
Diffuse	Type III		Type IV	
	Voluntary role		Feudal role	
	Consequences	Basis	Consequences	Basis
	+change	+authority	±change	-authority
	-conflict	-power	+conflict	-power
	-coercion	+bargaining	-coercion	+bargaining

+ = presence of the characteristic.
- = absence of the characteristic.

little resistance, and it will have sufficient power and authority to mobilize necessary resources and to coordinate a broad frontal attack on problems. The agency's responsibility is confined simply to *implementing* innovations that are needed, with a minimum of conflict or coercion.

However, in a dynamic complex society, it is unlikely that a full consensus will develop. Nevertheless it is possible that power will become centralized in the absence of consensus. This is an *empire* arrangement (Type II) guided by an elite that dictates policy. The central agency plays a coercive, regulatory role, concentrating on ways to maximize its own power as well as the task of implementing change. Under these conditions the most effective way to produce change is from the top down; conversely, permitting widespread participation in planning for change would have the effect of dissipating and compromising plans formulated at the top.

There is a third possibility: national consensus on objectives but a diffuse power structure. This might be described as a *voluntary* network (Type III), cemented by devotion to community values and mediated by informal collaboration and exchanges of information. The consensus permits the federal agency to play an effective coordinating role even though power is not centralized. It can concentrate its energies on identifying needed changes and experimenting with strategies to achieve them. The agency's role, however, is not confined simply to implementing change. It may also help to develop and maintain a consensus.

The fourth type, a *feudalistic* network, involves little consensus and decentralization of power. It comes closest to describing the Teacher Corps environment. Not only was the program deprived of coercive power but it could not rely on a public mandate or the weight of its authority to influence the local institutions. Without a minimum of consensus on even the elementary objectives, bargaining often broke down into open conflict and terminated relationships. In this controversial and politically hostile environment, much of the program's energies necessarily focused on (1) finding a common thread of consensus around which to orient the program, and (2) striking feasible compromises. Indeed, *a primary responsibility of a coordinating agency under these conditions is to mediate value conflicts, not merely to implement a given conception of the innovation or simply to explore alternative strategies.* It must function like a gyroscope, constantly sensing environmental pressures and constraints and seeking new levels of consensus.

CONCLUSIONS

The implications for several issues discussed go beyond the specifics of this particular case. Therefore, we shall now consider (1) what the paradigm developed in this chapter means for the nature of program evaluation; (2) what it means for the role of agencies or groups responsible for implementing innovation; (3) what can be extrapolated from the study about the conditions that would be most conducive to reform; and (4) what extensions and refinements now can be made in the model introduced earlier.

Implications for Evaluation

The political nature of organization has serious implications for the use of research for evaluation purposes. The concept of "evaluation" itself is at variance with the paradigm presented earlier. Before a program can be "evaluated," there must be a fixed, identifiable, achievable goal. The implication is that if the goal has not been achieved, something "has gone wrong." These assumptions are unreasonable in most cases, because in practice organizations constantly elaborate new goals and shift priorities as a condition of their existence; they are faced with constraints beyond their control; and *seldom is power sufficiently concentrated either to permit the kind of internal control necessary to implement a program as planned or to allow for a well-controlled study of it.* These factors must be viewed as conditions inherent to the innovation process, not merely as incidental inconveniences to be overcome. Simplistic approaches to evaluation, designed to determine whether a program is "effective" according to a single criterion variable, at best can produce an incomplete picture and at worst can lead to distorted and misleading conclusions.

Implications for the Role of Innovators

It would be naïve to hold the Teacher Corps responsible merely for implementing an innovation as though that function were its sole responsibility. The Washington office had neither the necessary authority to define the objectives nor the power to implement them. But it did have three other major functions: (1) to sustain the momentum for social reform by counteracting inertia; (2) to advance alternative conceptions of innovation with the hope that some form of the program would survive; (3) to facilitate debate and compromise. In a conflict-ridden democratic society, these *consensus-seeking* functions are as important as implementing a specific plan for innovation. To the extent the coordinating agency is able to play an effective *mediating* role, it cannot at the same time be effective at implementing a *given* innovation. *The dilemma is that change can be achieved most effectively if coercion is exercised through a centralized power structure; whereas consensus is effectively achieved through the bargaining process that compromises the innovation.* The challenge is to find the proper balance between consensus and power, between democratic consensus-seeking processes and a concerted social-reform effort. Irrespective of any concrete reforms the Teacher Corps did or did not produce, the fact that it attempted to cope with this larger problem has provided useful insight for future efforts of this kind.

Conditions Conducive to Reform

Examining more general issues, it is clear that the capacity of a coordinating agency to promote social reform can be enhanced only if one or more of at least four conditions prevail:

1. A higher level of consensus develops within the society on the need for a given form of change.

2. Some groups demonstrate their technical competence to lead ch
and thus establish sufficient authority to implement change peacefully
3. Power becomes more centralized within the network of relevant
organizations responsible for reform.
4. A coordinating agency increases its access to the resources needed
for bargaining with member institutions.

Notice that, throughout the program's existence, change was stifled by
an apparently fundamental dilemma. Attempting to unravel the roots of
this dilemma will highlight some of the critical aspects of the study. On
the one hand, organizations in which there had been a prior consensus
on educational philosophy, work roles, and the goals of the schools and
colleges appeared to be relatively static and resistant to change. Consensus in these cases usually had been formed around existing procedures
and traditions, or it depended on a precarious compromise among the
participants that could be upset by any proposed change. On the other
hand, direct confrontation and conflict seldom produced extensive change,
either. The conflict tended to create status threats to veteran teachers
and professors who often became defensive and resorted to the power and
authority that their positions might afford them to resist change. Under
what conditions, then, might more change have occurred? At least four
can be identified:

1. If the most liberal, reform-minded professors and interns had been
able to demonstrate that they possessed the technical competence to
identify promising innovation, they might have been granted more authority by the other participants to lead change, and change could have
been implemented peacefully.
2. If the interns had been provided with the necessary information and
training in the tactics of making changes in complex organizations, they
might have been able to more effectively exert informal influence without
provoking so much resistance.
3. Another alternative is to seek to reduce the ability of the teachers and
professors to *resist*; for example, by curbing their participation in making
policies for the program by centralizing decisions at the national level, or
by selecting low-status universities or schools with less competent staffs
to participate in the program.
4. Another recourse would be to *increase* the strength of the force for
change by recruiting a critical mass of interns or by placing them in positions of control within the program.

In other words, one could attempt to influence the change process
either by altering the amount of resistance to change or by increasing the

force for change. Specifically, one could attempt to increase the *authority* of the change agents by making available the necessary knowledge to legitimate their actions, or increase their *influence* by providing the necessary tactical skills to increase their overt power, or minimize the *power* and authority of those people in the system who are most likely to oppose change while maximizing the power of the change agents.

These general propositions suggest several derivative corollaries. Although many of these conditions were not present in the case examined, they can be extrapolated from the program's failures. An *ideal type* of social system, likely to be highly responsive to deliberate efforts to change it, would consist of the following conditions:

1. A public mandate for institutional reform (a) based on a broad consensus and (b) supported by a dominant social elite.

2. An outside coordinating agency with a single overriding commitment to change, and responsible for leading change.

3. Substantial resources strategically concentrated on high-status member organizations that have been deliberately selected for their capacity to exert institutional leadership.

4. A centralized decision-making structure within the organizational network in which authority is centralized at the national level and also centralized within each member organization in such a way as to permit little opportunity for employees at the lowest levels to influence policies.

5. Full backing for the plan from the central units within the member organizations.

6. A clear-cut division of labor and authority structure and effective coordinating mechanisms throughout the organizational network.

7. Boundary positions staffed by competent personnel in each of the member organizations.

8. A critical mass of professional apprentices recruited from outside traditional channels into several echelons of the member organizations, backed by an outside organization and trained in both the local mores and change strategies.

This ideal-type organization is not only complex but presumes the simultaneous presence of many conditions that seldom exist even in isolation. For example, a clear mandate for reform will rarely evolve because some groups will always benefit from the status quo. Moreover, although modern societies cannot be reformed without the aid of complex large-scale programs, the programs themselves will develop their own internal problems and will be forced to appease many different publics; this dissipates resources and shifts goal priorities.

Refinement of Model

Earlier, a model was introduced as a framework for this chapter and to help to understand the reform process. Other subsidiary processes were identified that will help to extend and refine this model and to make more explicit how the critical political status, structural, and economic dimensions of this program shaped its fate. These variables include:

- Value consensus as a primary source of incentive and constraint motivating reform programs.
- Goal-setting as a bargaining strategy.
- Rhetoric as a persuasive form of influence and a device for protecting goals.
- The use of slack resources as a way of enhancing and altering bargaining power.
- Discretionary funds as a source of flexibility and leverage for the coordinating agency.
- Dispersal of resources as a means of promoting support with its dissipating consequences.
- The use of marginal utility principles as a way of optimizing the impact of funding.
- Promoting change by maximizing the leverage of the more change-oriented, cosmopolitan member institutions.
- Recycling funds by reserving funds for capital investments at the critical initial stages of the innovation cycle.
- Checks and balances produced by a diffuse distribution of power.
- Selective recruitment of vulnerable member organizations subject to co-optation.
- Prestige of member organizations used as a bargaining resource and source of constraint on other organizations in the network.
- The need for internal control within member institutions and the adverse effects of decentralized decision-making structures on member organizations' commitment to a reform program.
- Organizational structure and status threats as fundamental sources of inflexibility.
- Promoting the development of latent subcultures within organizations as a way of promoting change, and the conflict that can result.
- The interjection of team structures as a way of promoting structural looseness.
- The dynamic tension and antagonistic forms of cooperation produced by the interdependence of member organizations in face of their autonomy and independent incentive systems and resources.

- The strategic importance of boundary personnel for linking organizations into a viable network.
- Federal intervention as a means of throttling the rate of change.
- The paralyzing effects of delegated control and institutionalization.
- The countervailing powers exercised by coordinating agencies operating within a feudal type of network.
- The significance of consensus-seeking and mediating functions of coordinating agencies attempting to implement reform.
- Reform as a political, compromising process.

NOTES

1. The term "political" applies to organizations only in a restricted sense. It refers to the power struggles and compromises at the basis of organizations. It is not intended to confuse organizational bases of power with the political institutions in the larger society.

2. In taking this approach, I am suggesting a crude hierarchy of variables in which there is a tendency for some variables to dominate the situation but also in which there can be two-way influence between variables and shifts in the usual priorities under certain circumstances. For example, just as power often determines the hierarchy of prestige, so prestige in some cases can become the basis of power. Thus power can be seen as a central dimension in the sense that it is a necessary condition for change in the many instances in which ambiguity of dissent prevails, but it is not a sufficient condition.

3. For example, the federal government stayed in the background during the efforts to develop new math and science courses under the National Defense Education Act, and the bulk of the money in the 1965 Elementary and Secondary Education Act was given directly, with few controls on a formula grant basis and administered by state departments of education.

4. Conversely, it must be recognized that *local* control also has a politicalizing effect: school boards are highly political bodies that often impose political criteria for hiring, promotion, and curricular policies (Gross, Mason, McEachern, 1958).

5. The typologies in the literature do not adequately recognize the diverse types of coordinating structures that fall between the federated (decentralized) and the corporation (centralized) types of coordination.

A Postscript: Long Range Implications of the Study

In one sense, this has been another study documenting the disappointing failures and modest successes of another government program. The federal program attempted to cooperate with relatively autonomous local organizations to bring about reform from within the established system by adding resources to the present system and making minor adjustments in it. But strong opposition, nationally and locally, prevented the program from receiving the full share of authorized funding; structural concessions were made to local organizations, giving them greater freedom to run the program, and in many instances to go against the policy and purposes of the legislation. On the local level, the program had to face the reality of strong opposition by organizations and professions whose established positions might be threatened by visible accomplishment of the program's goals; the resources available to the federal program were too little and too thinly dispersed to make a striking impact on the organizations they were designed to change. In order to survive, the federal organization had to keep subtly redefining its goals behind a smoke screen of ideologies used to disguise and compensate for the fact that extensive change was not occurring. The federal program sought acceptance, legitimacy, and institutionalization within the federal bureaucracy. Some of its power was given to other agencies; and, internally, a succession of leaders and personnel resulted in less emphasis on "reform" and more emphasis on technical specialists. In short, this program demonstrated the tendency of such organizations to remain prisoners of the coalition of conflicting forces that created them. In final analysis, the Washington office was bargaining the possibility of creating a dramatic and visible effect for a more modest impact and ultimately for its very survival.

I suspect that many of these same observations—the frustrating obstacles

393

the Teacher Corps encountered at each turn, and the subsequent goal displacements, co-optation, and disillusionment of its participants—could be made with equal validity about a host of other government programs, ranging from the New Deal's Tennessee Valley Authority (Selznick, 1949) to more recent Office of Economic Opportunity Community Action and Model Cities antipoverty programs (Moynihan, 1969), the Head Start program, the Ford Foundation's Gray Area programs (Marris and Rein, 1967), and the Peace Corps.

The valiant, yet frustrating history of these governmental efforts raises serious questions about the federal government's capacity to lead social reforms and, indeed, about whether it is possible to make marked improvement solely by working from within the established institutions. Was the price of survival too high, in terms of limiting the effectiveness that it might have had? Can the federal-local coalition inducement strategy be made to work? Or is it necessarily self-defeating? My answer is that unless there is a rather unusual combination of circumstances, identified in Chapter 11, government programs are doomed at best to only modest accomplishments. Without the right conditions, modest improvement is about all that one should expect. Perhaps this is better than no improvement, regardless of how inefficient the programs may seem.

But in another sense, I have also tried to show that failure is not entirely inevitable. The failures in this program were caused by the particular circumstances identified here, some of which *are* amenable to change. I have said that such programs always will be partially compromised by organizational principles, but the probability of complete failure is virtually assured as long as the nation's leadership continues to concoct program after program in complete disregard of known constraints that will vitiate the strategies, and without any attempt to provide at least some of the conditions necessary for programs to survive and thrive.

As I have already argued, realistically such programs often come about only as concessions made by citizens and government leaders who do not really want change; thus *the government itself is responsible for many of the barriers that compromise these programs.* Nevertheless, these programs would be more successful if the persons who conceive and administer them devoted as much attention to the problem of cultivating and propagating them, once instituted, as they devote to the program's original design. We know now that innovations cannot be installed simply by announcing that they are available; and through this and other studies, we are beginning to learn more about how to implement them. With this knowledge, the nation's leaders can do a better job in the future, if they should choose to use it. Otherwise, perhaps in the future it will be necessary to circumvent the established institutions in order to implement reform—without government leadership. The establishment of *competitive,* privately run organizations is one such strategy. Perhaps this sobering alternative will encourage government officials to plan more seriously for reform in the future.

APPENDICES

Appendix 1

Scales and Indices Developed for the Study

ITEM

1. Index of Commitment to Teaching in Low-Income Schools

   a. How likely is it that you will work in an impoverished school next year?

      1. Very likely   2. Probably
      3. Maybe   4. Very unlikely

   b. In five years?

      1. Very likely   2. Probably
      3. Maybe   4. Very unlikely

   c. Indefinitely?

      1. Very likely   2. Probably
      3. Maybe   4. Very unlikely

      Scale range: 3-12

2. Attitudes Toward Racial Integration

   a. If children of different races went to school together, this would lead to better academic achievement for all students concerned in the long run.

      1. Strongly agree   2. Agree   3. Undecided
      4. Disagree   5. Strongly disagree

   b. "Neighborhood" elementary schools should be maintained regardless of any racial imbalance produced.

      1. Strongly agree   2. Agree   3. Undecided
      4. Disagree   5. Strongly disagree

    c. Any difference in intelligence between nonwhites and whites is mainly due to lack of opportunity for the nonwhites and will eventually disappear under an integrated school system.

        1. Strongly agree   2. Agree   3. Undecided
        4. Disagree   5. Strongly disagree

    Scale range: 3-15

3. <u>Initiative and Compliance Scale</u> (corrected split-half reliability r_n = .85)
Below is a list of incidents which have occurred in different schools throughout the country. We are interested in getting your reactions to these situations. There is no right or wrong answer. Just imagine yourself as a teacher in each situation. Indicate (1) what you would do as the teacher in each of these situations and (2) what is likely to happen when such a situation arises at the school or school system in which your Teacher Corps team is working.

<u>Alternatives</u>

A. What would you do as the teacher in the situation?

    (1) Comply with the superior's request
    (2) Try to compromise
    (3) Seek support of colleagues
    (4) Ask for an investigation by a professional organization
    (5) Refuse to comply with the request
    (6) Quit the job

B. What do you anticipate will happen if you do not comply?

    (1) No disapproval or mild disapproval from the administration
    (2) Strong disapproval but no formal action from the administration
    (3) Loss of reputation
    (4) Loss of deserved promotion or deserved salary increase
    (5) Transferred to less desirable position
    (6) Dismissal from the school system

Choose one alternative for each question.

<u>Incident A</u>: The assistant principal told a teacher that he was too "outspoken" in criticizing certain policies of the school and that it was causing unrest among faculty members. The teacher continued to be critical of certain administrative policies.
    What would you have done as the teacher in the situation described above? (Enter one alternative from A listed above.)

What do you anticipate would happen to you if you did not comply
with the above request?   (Enter one alternative from B above.)

Incident B: A mathematics teacher was told by the principal that he
was not presenting his subject in the most effective way and that he
should revise his course content and the methods of teaching it.   He
refused to change his practices on the grounds that his professional
society had recommended his procedures.
   What would you have done as the teacher in the situation described above?   (Enter one alternative from A listed above.)
   What do you anticipate would happen to you if you did not comply
with the above request?   (Enter one alternative from B above.)

Incident C: The school board rules explicitly stated that teachers
should not participate in the local school-board elections.   One
teacher made a public statement that one of the present board members
was a professional politician and otherwise actively engaged in the
campaign.   He was told to desist.
   What would you have done as the teacher in the situation described above?   (Enter one alternative from A as listed above.)
   What do you anticipate would happen to you if you did not comply
with the above request?   (Enter one alternative from B as listed
above.)

Incident D: The administration issued a directive that teachers
should help to improve parent-teacher relations.   A parent-teacher
committee was established to select textbooks.   One math teacher
refused to participate, stating that the parents on such a committee
are not qualified to select textbooks.
   What would you have done as the teacher in the situation described above?   (Enter one alternative from A as listed above.)
   What do you anticipate would happen to you if you did not comply
with the above request?   (Enter one alternative from B as listed
above.)

Incident E: One school system did not permit students to read several American literature classics by Faulkner, Hemingway, Steinbeck,
and others.   One teacher actively sought to have the policy repealed
by soliciting the support of certain influential citizens in the community.   The principal asked her to desist her campaign against the
policy because she was stirring up trouble for the school.   She refused, saying that her action had the support of the National English
Teachers' Association.
   What would you have done as the teacher in the situation described above?   (Enter one alternative from A as listed above.)
   What do you anticipate would happen to you if you did not comply
with the above request?   (Enter one alternative from B as listed
above.)

Incident F: In one school, male teachers received preference in pro-
motions. A group of women teachers at the school complained to the
school board. They were told that the situation would be changed,
but it was not. One female teacher who was passed over for a promotion wrote a letter to the NEA and State Department of Education.
The principal ordered her to stop stirring up trouble.
   What would you have done as the teacher in the situation described above? (Enter one alternative from A as listed above.)
   What do you anticipate would happen to you if you did not comply
with the above request? (Enter one alternative from B as listed
above.)

Incident G: A principal occasionally changed the grade given by one
of his teachers if a student's complaint seemed to him to justify a
higher grade. One teacher protested and was told by the principal
that he had the final authority over whatever happened in his school,
and he asked her to understand.
   What would you have done as the teacher in the situation described above? (Enter one alternative from A as listed above.)
   What do you anticipate would happen to you if you did not comply
with the above request? (Enter one alternative from B as listed
above.)

Incident H: The administration requested teachers not to use a
standard textbook in American Government because it was "socialis-
tically inclined." A history teacher felt that the book was the best
available and proceeded to submit an order for it.
   What would you have done as the teacher in the situation described above? (Enter one alternative from A as listed above.)
   What do you anticipate would happen to you if you did not comply
with the above request? (Enter one alternative from B as listed
above.)

Incident I: The administration changed a course of study that included philosophy and music appreciation to one that was based
strictly on the sciences and mathematics. A committee of teachers
went to see the principal and voiced disapproval; they were told
that the administration was in a better position to make the decision,
due to the complexity of the issue. One teacher complained to the
school board.
   What would you have done as the teacher in the situation described above? (Enter one alternative from A as listed above.)
   What do you anticipate would happen to you if you did not comply
with the above request? (Enter one alternative from B as listed
above.)

4. Professional Role-Orientation Scale (corrected split-half mean
    reliability $r_n = .65$)

1. Strongly agree   2. Agree   3. Undecided
4. Disagree   5. Strongly disagree

A. Orientation to students-Interitem correlation r = .42

   (1) It should be permissible for the teacher to violate a
       rule if he/she is sure that the best interests of the
       students will be served in so doing.
   (2) Unless he is satisfied that it is best for the student,
       a teacher should not do what she is told to do.
   (3) A good teacher should not do anything that he believes
       may jeopardize the interests of his students regardless
       of who tells him to or what the rules state.

B. Orientation to the profession and professional colleagues

   (4) Teachers should try to live up to what they think are the
       standards of their profession even if the administration
       or the community does not seem to respect them.
   (5) One primary criterion of a good school should be the de-
       gree of respect that it commands from other teachers in
       the state.
   (6) A teacher should try to put his standards and ideals of
       good teaching into practice even if the rules or proce-
       dures of the school prohibit it.
   (7) Teachers should subscribe to and diligently read the
       standard professional journals.
   (8) Teachers should be active members of at least one profes-
       sional teaching association, and should attend most con-
       ferences and meetings of the association.
   (9) A teacher should consistently practice his/her ideas of
       the best educational practices even though the adminis-
       tration prefers other views.

C. Orientation to knowledge as basis of competence

   (10) A teacher's skill should be based primarily on his ac-
        quaintance with his subject matter.
   (11) Teachers should be evaluated primarily on the basis of
        their knowledge of the subject that is to be taught and
        their ability to communicate it.
   (12) Schools should hire no one to teach unless he holds at
        least a bachelor's degree.
   (13) In view of the teacher shortage, it should be permissible
        to hire teachers trained at nonaccredited colleges.

D. Orientation to decision-making authority

   (14) A teacher should be able to make his own decisions about

problems that come up in the classroom.
(15) Small matters should not have to be referred to someone higher up for final answer.
(16) The ultimate authority over the major educational decisions should be exercised by professional teachers.

5. Employee Role-Conception Scale

A. Loyalty to the administration (corrected split-half reliability r_n = .81)

(1) Teachers should adjust their teaching to the administration's views of good educational practice.
(2) The school administration should be better qualified than the teacher to judge what is best for education.
(3) In case of a dispute in the community over whether a controversial speaker should be permitted in the school, the teachers should look primarily to the judgment of the administration for guidance.
(4) Personnel who openly criticize the administration should be encouraged to go elsewhere.
(5) Teachers should not be influenced by the opinions of those teachers whose thinking does not reflect the thinking of the administration.
(6) The only way a teacher can keep out of "hot water" is to follow the wishes of the top administration.

B. Emphasis on rules and procedures (corrected split-half reliability r_n = .84)

(7) Teachers should be completely familiar with the written descriptions of the rules, procedures, manuals, and other standard operating procedures necessary for running the classroom.
(8) The school should have a manual of rules and regulations that are actually followed.
(9) Rules stating when the teachers should arrive and depart from the building should be strictly enforced.
(10) To prevent confusion and friction among the staff, there should be a rule covering almost every problem that might come up at the school.
(11) There should be definite rules specifying the topics that are not appropriate for discussion in a classroom.
(12) When a controversy arises about the interpretation of school rules, a teacher should not "stick his neck out" by taking a definite position.

6. Pupil-Control Ideology Index

(intern's mean r = .30;   interitem range r = .35 – r = .36)
(teacher's mean r = .23; interitem range = r = .25)

1. Strongly agree   2. Agree   3. Undecided
4. Disagree   5. Strongly disagree

> (1) Teachers should consider revision of their teaching meth-
> ods if these are criticized by their pupils.
> (2) Pupils should not be permitted to contradict the state-
> ments of a teacher in class.
> (3) The opinions of students should not influence teaching
> methods.
> (4) It is more important for pupils to learn to obey rules
> than to make their own decisions.
> (5) Student governments are a good safety valve but should
> not have much influence on school policy.

7. Alienation

A. Alienation from the Teacher Corps
    (interns mean r = .63)
    (teachers mean r = .34)

1. Strongly agree   2. Agree   3. Undecided
4. Disagree   5. Strongly disagree

> (1) What I personally think does not count very much in the
> way the Teacher Corps program is managed.
> (2) The people running the Teacher Corps program are con-
> cerned about how the program affects people like me.

B. Alienation from the school
    (interns mean r = .39)
    (teachers mean r = .37)

> (1) I am just a cog in the machinery of this school.
> (2) Every time I try to do something worthwhile in this
> system, somebody or something stops me.

8. Liberalism Scale (corrected split-half reliability r = .60)

1. Strongly agree   2. Agree   3. Undecided
4. Disagree   5. Strongly disagree

> (1) The government should have the right to prohibit certain
> groups of persons who disagree with our form of govern-
> ment from holding peaceable public meetings.
> (2) Police are unduly hampered in their efforts to apprehend
> criminals when they have to have a warrant to search the
> house.

(3) Capital punishment (the death penalty) should be abolished.
(4) Legislative committees should not investigate the political beliefs of college or university professors.
(5) The government should do more than it presently is doing to see that everyone gets adequate medical care.
(6) Labor unions these days are doing the country more harm than good.
(7) Conscientious objectors should be excused from military service in wartime.
(8) The welfare state tends to destroy individual initiative.
(9) Individual liberties and justice under laws are not possible in socialist countries.

9. Self-Identification with Political Beliefs

A. Do you consider your political point of view to be generally:

1. Quite conservative 2. Fairly conservative
3. Fairly liberal   4. Very liberal   4. Radical

10. Satisfaction with the Faculty Index (mean of interitem correlations, $r = .48$; range from $r = .56$ to $r = .36$)

(1) What proportion of the college faculty members who have taught you during the past year would you say are superior teachers?

1. Very few   2. Less than half
3. More than half   4. Almost all

(2) In relation to the kind of education you are seeking, how satisfied are you so far with the various competencies and specialties of those who are supervising your training?

1. Very dissatisfied 2. Somewhat dissatisfied
3. Fairly satisfied   4. Very satisfied

(3) In relation to the kind of education you are seeking, how adequate would you say is the choice of college courses and availability of suitable field experiences?

1. Very inadequate   2. Somewhat inadequate
3. Fairly adequate   4. Very adequate

(4) In general, are you enjoying your studies in the college this term as much as you had expected to?

      1. No, I am definitely enjoying them less than I had
         expected.
      2. No, but I am only mildly disappointed.
      3. My expectations for this term are reasonably well
         satisfied.
      4. I am enjoying my studies this term more than I had
         expected.

(5) So far this year, how successful would you say your instructors at the college have been in challenging you to
produce to the limit of your intellectual and creative
capacities?

      1. They have been wholly unsuccessful.
      2. Several have been somewhat successful.
      3. Several have been quite successful.
      4. Almost all have succeeded in continuously challenging
         my intellectual capacities.

(6) Have you had the feeling in the past year or so that some
of your instructors have judged (e.g., graded) you more
on the basis of extraneous or irrelevant factors than on
the basis of the quality of your work?

      1. Quite often   2. Once in a while
      3. Very rarely   4. Never

11. Four Teaching Competence Scales

1. Poor   2. Below average   3. Average
4. Good   5. Excellent   6. No opportunity to observe

A. Innovativeness in the classroom (mean interitem $r = .58$;
range from $r = .68$ to $r = .52$)

    (1) Brings latest developments in subject area into lessons
    (2) Makes efforts to try new ideas in the classroom
    (3) Goes beyond the curriculum if class will benefit from it
    (4) Takes into account pupils' interests in planning lessons

B. Respect for and understanding of pupils (mean interitem $r =$
.53; range $r = .38$ to $r = .7$)

    (5) Respects the viewpoints of the pupil
    (6) Teaches students to be sensitive to the problems and
        opinions of others
    (7) Shows respect for his pupils
    (8) Avoids making derogatory personal remarks about pupils
    (9) Has a good understanding of the home backgrounds and

different types of children and their problems

C. Rapport with pupils (mean interitem r = .54; range r = .77 to r = .38)

(10) Commands the respect of his pupils
(11) Has ability to win the cooperation of students
(12) Shows sincere concern when confronted with personal problems of pupils
(13) Has a willingness to go beyond the call of duty for his students
(14) Is consistent in administering discipline

D. Community relationship (mean interitem r = .54; range from r = .67 to r = .51)

(15) Has ability to win the cooperation of parents
(16) Makes effectual use of community resources in his teaching
(17) Visits parents frequently
(18) Participates in the activities and events of the local community in which the school is located.

12. Index of Preferred Teaching Style

Answer the following questions by entering the appropriate type of teacher, using the code here:

Teacher No. 1 is most concerned with maintaining discipline, seeing that students work hard, and teaching them to follow directions.

Teacher No. 2 feels it is most important that students know their subject matter well, and that he (she) cover the material thoroughly and test their progress regularly.

Teacher No. 3 stresses making the class interesting and encourages students to be creative and to figure things out for themselves.

Teacher No. 4 thinks it is most important that a teacher be friendly and well liked by students and able to understand and to handle their problems.

This question to be answered by interns and team leaders and regular teachers only. Although teachers have to concern themselves with the many different things in their jobs, some teachers emphasize certain things more than others. We would like to know which one of the above four types of teachers you think best describes you.

Which one of the four types of teacher do you think most
of the mothers of the students in your class prefer?
How about your principal? Which type do you think he (she)
prefers?

13. <u>Organizational Change Measures</u>
A. Global Change Index

1. <u>School-college cooperation</u>
... Has the Teacher Corps program been in any way responsible
for the following:

More effective cooperation between the local school and the
teacher-training program in the college or university?

(1) No   (2) Yes, largely responsible
(3) Yes, partially responsible (4) Not sure

2. <u>Introduction of new techniques into the schools</u>
... Has the Teacher Corps program been in any way responsible
for the following:

The introduction into at least one local school of new
techniques for teaching the impoverished?

(1) No   (2) Yes, largely responsible
(3) Yes, partially responsible (4) Not sure

3. <u>Involvement of the school in community projects</u>
... Has the Teacher Corps program been in any way responsible
for the following:

More involvement on the part of the school in local community
projects?

(1) No   (2) Yes, largely responsible
(3) Yes, partially responsible (4) Not sure

4. <u>Change at the college</u>
... Has the Teacher Corps program been in any way responsible
for the following:

(a) The introduction of new courses into the college curriculum?

(1) No   (2) Yes, largely responsible
(3) Yes, partially responsible (4) Not sure

(b) The introduction in the college curriculum of new

procedures or techniques for training future teachers?

(1) No   (2) Yes, largely responsible
(3) Yes, partially responsible   (4) Not sure

(c) Basic modifications of existing college courses resulting in more attention to educating the impoverished?

(1) No   (2) Yes, largely responsible
(3) Yes, partially responsible   (4) Not sure

B. Objective Weighted Index
This set of 5 indices was constructed from a content analysis of the interviews. Each specific change reported was (a) classified into one of four areas -- new techniques of teaching, school-college cooperation, change in college and community activity -- and (b) rated on several dimensions as outlined below:

1. Introduction of new techniques
   a. Primary (Planned) changes (each change was weighted from 1 to 5 on each of the following categories):
      (1) Methods--Traditional (weighted 1) to Innovative (weighted 5)
      (2) Materials--Standardized (weighted 1) to Developed by user (weighted 5)
      (3) Clientele--Prescribed and homogeneous (weighted 1) to Unprescribed and diverse (weighted 5)
      (4) Personnel--Carried out by people in established roles (weighted 1) to Requires new (non-existent) roles (weighted 5)
      (5) Activities--Extracurricular and/or optional (weighted 1) to Integral part of the formal schooling process and/or required (weighted 5)

   b. Secondary (by-product) changes (each change was weighted 1 to 4 on the following categories):
      (1) Attitudinal change of classroom teachers
         (a) Toward colleagues, self (e.g., more self-motivation of individual classroom teacher)
         (b) Toward students (e.g., more compassionate toward their problems)
      (2) Educational change (e.g., greater access to equipment; action-oriented teaching)
      (3) Relational change (e.g., pupil evaluation of classroom teachers)

   c. Assumptions for the weightings given above:
      (1) Changes involving reorganization, changed relationships, or new basic educational activities

were more significant than additive or peripheral changes.
(2) Behavioral changes and changes effecting numerous personnel and/or different subgroups were more significant than individual or attitudinal changes.

2. <u>School-college cooperation</u>
   a. Primary changes (each change was weighted from +5 to -5 on each of the following categories):
      (1) Frequency of contact
      (2) Quality of relations
      (3) Amount of cooperation
      (4) Attitudinal change toward the other party

   b. Assumptions for the weightings given above:
      (1) Changes limited to members of the Teacher Corps would tend to be more temporary than changes in relations involving members of the permanent organizations.
      (2) Cooperative relations and positive attitudes were more desirable than conflictful relations and negative attitudes.

3. <u>Change in college</u>
   a. Primary changes (each category was assigned a 0 or 1, multiplied by the weights given below):
      (1) Instructional changes
          (a) Methods
          (b) Methods of teacher training
          (c) New content
          (d) New courses
          (e) New programs
          (f) New materials
      (2) Administrative changes
      (3) Relational changes
          (a) Among university faculty
          (b) Between university and community
      (4) Attitudinal changes--among faculty
          (a) Toward educational matters
          (b) Toward the community
          (c) Toward other factors
      (5) Noninstructional activities

   b. The above scores were multiplied by a weight assigned to the unit in which the various changes occurred as follows:
      (1) Teacher Corps program and associated faculty only (weighted 1)

(2) Both Teacher Corps and university (weighted 2)
(3) University organization and faculty only (weighted 3)

c. Assumptions for the weightings given above:
(1) Changes occurring only within the university were more significant and more permanent than changes related to the existence of a temporary system.

4. Community projects
   a. Primary changes (each change was weighted from 1 to 4 on the following categories):
   (1) Activities
       (a) Noninstructional supplementary services (weighted 1)
       (b) Noninstructional school affairs (weighted 2)
       (c) Educational programs outside regular curriculum (weighted 3)
       (d) Integral educational programs (weighted 4)
   (2) Clientele
       (a) Students (weighted 1)
       (b) Students and parents (weighted 2)
       (c) Parents and/or community (weighted 3)
       (d) Parents and/or community and school personnel (weighted 4)
   (3) Teacher Corps--community relations
       (a) Teacher Corps/labor--community/employer (weighted 1)
       (b) Teacher Corps/service--community/recipient (weighted 2)
       (c) Teacher Corps/leader--community/participant (weighted 3)
       (d) Teacher Corps/support--community/leader (weighted 4)

   b. Secondary changes, i.e., changes in parent/community/ school relations (each change was weighted 1 to 4 as follows):
   (1) More sensitivity to parents' opinions (weighted 1)
   (2) Greater participation of parents (weighted 2)
   (3) More involvement of parents in decision making (weighted 3)
   (4) Parents assume leadership positions (weighted 4)

14. School System Centralization Index

To what extent can schools in this system follow different practices in each of the following issues:

Responses

(1) Schools are permitted to pursue different policies with-
    out informing the central office.
(2) Schools are permitted to pursue different policies if the
    central office is informed about it.
(3) Schools are often permitted to pursue different policies,
    but permission from the central office must be obtained.
(4) Schools are seldom permitted to pursue different policies,
    although permission to do so may sometimes be given by
    the central office.
(5) Schools are rarely or never permitted to pursue different
    policies.
(6) Does not apply in our system.
(7) Do not know.

Issues

(a) Selection of textbooks
(b) Selection of books for recommended reading
(c) Use of films, filmstrips, or other audiovisual materials
(d) Team teaching, independent study, or similar teaching
    practices
(e) Separated classes in the same subject for rapid and slow
    learners
(f) Use of schools or school equipment for nonacademic functions,
    such as hobby club meetings for students or garden club
    meetings for adults
(g) Grading system

15. Evaluation of Principals and Team Leaders (6 items)
    (intern's mean $r = .52$; interitem range $r = .70 - r = .41$)
    (teacher's mean $r = .56$; interitem range $r = .73 - r = .49$)

    Please indicate how accurately each of the following statements
    describes the behavior of (1) your principal and (2) the one
    team leader in the Teacher Corps program with whom you associate
    most closely.

    (1) Never   (2) Once in a while   (3) Fairly often
    (4) Always   (5) Do not know

	Principal	Team Leader
He (she) refuses to explain his (her) actions.	___	___
He (she) allows me to make contributions to the program.	___	___
He (she) puts suggestions made by the staff into operation.	___	___
He (she) has sound ideas about the types of curriculum materials that		

are more suitable for children in
this school.   _____   _____

He (she) demonstrates innovative
approaches to teaching low-income
children.   _____   _____

He (she) is one of the most competent
educators in the school system.   _____   _____

16. Flexibility Index (5 items)
(intern's mean r = .56; interitem range r = .74 - r = .38)
(teacher's mean r = .47; interitem range r = .54 - r = .34)

(1) Never   (2) Once in a while
(3) Fairly often   (4) Always
(5) Do not know

(a) Degree of restrictions placed on activities (personal,
    professional)
(b) Opportunity to engage in experimental and innovative
    activities--depart from routine and procedures
(c) Amount of flexibility permitted in the curriculum
(d) Extent to which the administration encourages teachers to
    exercise initiative and innovation in the curriculum and
    teaching program
(e) Extent to which the school administration will back the in-
    tern if he gets into trouble with other teachers in the
    course of what he considers a worthwhile Teacher Corps
    activity

17. Index of Quality of Local School (4 items)
(intern's mean r = .61; interitem range r = .74 - r = .56)
(teacher's mean r = .47; interitem range r = .57 - r = .44)

How satisfied do you feel with each of the following aspects of
of your school? Answer each of the following by indicating in
the space provided in the margin the number of the statement
that best expresses your answer.

(1) Very dissatisfied   (2) Moderately dissatisfied
(3) Slightly dissatisfied   (4) Slightly satisfied
(5) Moderately satisfied   (5) Very satisfied

(a) The level of competence of most of the teachers in this
    school
(b) The method employed in the school for making decisions on
    pupil matters
(c) The attitude of the faculty toward the students in this
    school
(d) The quality of the curriculum and its suitability for the
    students here

18. <u>Respect for School Administration Index</u> (3 items)
    (intern's mean r = .51; interitem range r = .59 - r = .45)
    (teacher's mean r = .57; interitem range r = .63 - r = .49)

    (1) Very dissatisfied   (2) Moderately dissatisfied
    (3) Slightly dissatisfied   (4) Slightly satisfied
    (5) Moderately satisfied   (6) Very satisfied

    (a) Evaluation process that my superiors use to judge my
        effectiveness
    (b) The amount of recognition that teachers are given by the
        administration for their efforts and contributions
    (c) The administration's respect for you as a professional per-
        son to which your level of expertise, training, and experi-
        ence would entitle you

19. <u>Long-Range Career Plans</u>

    Your plans may not be definite at this time, but please indicate
    your present expectations.

    (1) Expect to continue teaching until retirement
    (2) Expect to continue in the field of education, but hope to
        move from classroom teaching into some other area of educa-
        tion
    (3) Expect to leave teaching in order to devote my time to
        homemaking, would not want to return to teaching later
    (4) Expect to leave teaching for homemaking, would want to re-
        turn later
    (5) Expect to leave education for another vocation (please
        specify) _____

20. <u>Preference for Racially Mixed Schools</u>

    What kind of school do you prefer to work in, as far as racial
    composition of students is concerned?

    (1) In an all-white school
    (2) In a mostly white school but with nonwhite students
    (3) In a school that has about half white and half nonwhite
        students
    (4) A mostly nonwhite school but with some white students
    (5) In a school with all nonwhites
    (6) No preference

21. <u>Index of Principal Support</u>

    How would you rate the adequacy of . . . support of program by
    principal?

416

(1) Excellent   (2) Average   (3) Unsatisfactory
(4) Nonexistent   (5) No opinion

22. <u>Participation Index</u>

Did you participate in preparing the proposals for the Teacher Corps program?

(1) Yes   (2) No

Appendix 2

A MATRIX OF FIRST-ORDER INTERCORRELATIONS AMONG 37 INDICATORS OF
DIFFERENT INNOVATION STRATEGIES

Table A-1 A matrix of first order intercorrelations among 37

	1	2	3	4	5	6	7	8	9	10	11
1	1.00	.08	.01	-.59	-.07	.18	-.60	-.40	.06	-.31	.32
2		1.00	.13	-.07	.16	.10	-.11	-.05	-.22	-.04	-.08
3			1.00	.12	-.21	.47	.14	.12	-.07	-.29	.04
4				1.00	.06	.03	.18	.55	.003	.54	-.20
5					1.00	-.16	.13	.16	.08	.13	.14
6						1.00	-.10	-.11	-.13	-.22	-.08
7							1.00	.39	.08	.23	.07
8								1.00	.18	.53	.04
9									1.00	-.04	.55
10										1.00	.005
11											1.00
12											
13											
14											
15											
16											
17											
18											
19											
20											
21											
22											
23											
24											
25											
26											
27											
28											
29											
30											
31											
32											
33											
34											
35											
36											
37											

The numbers in the table are explained below. Variables 36, 37, and
32 are the dependent variables, technological change, number of
community projects, and school-college cooperation, respectively.

indicators of different innovation strategies

12	13	14	15	16	17	18	19	20	21	22
.01	-.11	-.60	.07	-.02	-.09	-.26	-.25	-.15	-.30	.11
.17	-.13	-.03	-.16	.001	-.13	-.11	.03	-.12	.23	-.54
-.13	.05	-.26	-.03	-.11	-.49	.07	.31	-.20	.06	.47
-.16	.34	.62	.06	.18	.25	.20	.05	.49	.43	.21
.04	.11	.26	-.10	-.11	.02	.11	-.13	.03	.18	.000
.02	.21	-.14	.07	-.07	-.43	.15	.12	-.10	.05	.35
-.09	.30	.12	-.09	-.08	.05	.31	.20	.21	.18	-.31
-.12	.62	.29	.14	.15	.29	.26	-.19	.47	.33	.07
-.16	.04	.17	.52	-.07	-.08	-.25	-.13	.16	-.09	-.22
-.10	.50	.17	-.11	.22	.66	.25	-.18	.66	.51	-.06
-.20	.12	-.22	.37	.03	-.02	-.06	-.05	.07	-.04	-.13
1.00	-.14	.10	.01	.05	.07	.12	.05	.03	.10	-.25
	1.00	.04	.14	.14	.33	.35	-.04	.42	.31	.08
		1.00	.11	.01	.20	.14	-.12	.18	.31	-.14
			1.00	.06	-.11	-.12	-.04	.12	-.15	-.06
				1.00	.21	-.002	-.25	.05	.04	.21
					1.00	.20	-.50	.55	.11	-.42
						1.00	.09	.002	.16	-.12
							1.00	-.24	.24	.01
								1.00	.33	-.10
									1.00	.10
										1.00

23	24	25	26	27	28	29	30	31	32	33
-.41	.51	.13	-.13	-.32	.35	.44	-.38	.29	.10	-.72
-.15	-.19	.17	.20	-.13	.40	-.10	.09	.46	-.06	-.12
-.40	-.45	.02	.30	.24	.15	.30	.17	.19	-.31	-.33
-.25	.08	.11	.28	.54	-.52	-.43	.24	-.42	-.37	.65
.13	.000	.11	.04	.15	-.07	-.36	.20	-.20	.14	.30
-.30	-.09	-.08	.10	-.10	.14	.10	.04	.22	-.13	-.24
-.43	-.35	-.19	.05	.32	-.31	-.04	.14	-.31	.31	.58
-.15	-.10	-.01	.33	.57	-.38	-.17	.31	-.43	-.30	.46
.07	.03	-.004	-.05	.18	-.09	-.15	.08	-.13	-.05	.13
-.28	.21	.09	.29	.49	-.42	-.17	.22	-.44	-.01	.44
-.18	.11	-.05	.14	.20	-.05	.14	.03	-.08	.23	-.14
.18	-.03	-.38	-.03	-.08	.05	-.05	-.23	.04	-.02	-.09
-.24	.10	-.13	.30	.42	-.30	-.03	-.19	-.35	.07	.29
.38	-.16	.04	-.02	.18	-.34	-.87	.34	-.19	-.29	.78
.05	.12	-.24	.004	.13	.04	.06	-.07	-.11	-.31	.05
-.13	.19	-.14	.03	-.05	-.03	.05	-.05	-.12	-.23	.06
-.16	.24	.11	.06	.20	-.44	-.14	.02	-.28	.17	.30
.07	-.11	.01	.28	.25	-.29	-.16	.23	-.20	-.002	.24
.12	-.15	-.39	.23	.17	.08	.04	.05	.18	.09	-.03
-.28	.28	.09	.16	.47	-.57	-.13	.10	-.43	.004	.43
-.13	-.14	-.23	.48	.43	-.23	-.50	.46	.05	-.14	.38
-.44	-.07	.32	.21	.12	.20	.11	.20	.07	-.40	-.23
1.00	-.23	-.22	-.38	-.29	.06	-.29	-.07	-.09	.14	.46
	1.00	.08	-.19	-.07	-.11	.22	.61	-.32	.08	-.03
		1.00	.07	.01	-.07	-.02	.04	-.02	-.08	-.03
			1.00	.64	-.12	-.09	.27	.02	-.15	-.01
				1.00	-.52	-.15	.30	-.35	-.16	.33
					1.00	.25	-.16	.42	-.15	-.51
						1.00	-.58	-.09	.13	-.65
							1.00	.26	-.08	.25
								1.00	.06	-.45
									1.00	-.01
										1.00

34	35	36	37
-.41	-.70	-.32	-.20
-.03	-.05	.20	-.19
-.48	-.44	-.16	-.02
.45	.25	-.19	-.16
.37	.26	.12	.05
-.27	-.26	-.32	-.10
.44	.38	.66	.51
.50	-.01	.43	-.02
.22	-.02	-.15	.01
.63	.06	-.12	-.04
.09	-.27	-.05	.09
-.12	.07	.02	.25
.40	-.07	.53	.01
.57	.70	-.17	-.03
.05	-.16	-.07	-.10
.10	-.12	-.01	.22
.61	.03	-.11	.20
.17	.16	.14	.17
-.41	.24	.33	.03
.62	-.05	.32	.05
.38	.25	-.09	-.16
-.29	-.30	-.26	-.50
.18	.69	.39	.32
.03	-.29	-.33	-.16
.08	-.15	.25	-.38
.06	-.12	-.05	-.22
.32	-.02	-.05	.02
-.55	-.22	.28	-.10
-.57	-.73	.14	.17
.34	.35	.10	-.19
-.34	-.05	.04	-.31
.18	.35	.35	.30
.81	.72	.13	.14
1.00	.45	-.02	.10
	1.00	.19	.14
		1.00	.42
			1.00

Indicators of Different Strategies of Innovation

I.   Indicators Associated with the Replacement Approach

1. Mean political liberalism of interns
2. Interns' emphasis on pupil control
3. Difference in political liberalism of teachers and interns
4. Proportion of interns with liberal arts major
5. Quality of interns' undergraduate college
6. Mean percentage difference in status of interns and teachers in education, race, and sex

II.   Indicators Associated with the Diffusion Variables

7. Proportion of university faculty who consider themselves very liberal politically
8. Political liberalism of the team leader
9. Competence of the school principal
10. Political liberalism of the classroom teachers
11. Principals' support of the program
12. Tenure of the principal

III.   Indicators of the Competence of the Primary Socialization Agents

13. Interns' satisfaction with university faculty
14. Quality of the university
15. Quality of the school
16. Competence of the team leader
17. Teachers' emphasis on pupil control
18. Proportion of teachers who prefer creative teachers

IV. Indicators of Organizational Size and Decision-
Making Structure

    19. Centralization of decision-making within the
         school
    20. Size of the university
    21. Size of the school
    22. Proportion of teachers who participated in
         the proposal

V. Indicators of Resources Available

    23. Ratio of federal funds allocated for the
         program per intern

VI. Indicators of Status Security

    24. Proportion of program funds controlled by the
         local school
    25. Proportion of teachers who are members of unions
    26. Professional orientation of classroom teachers
    27. Client orientation of teachers
    28. Administrative orientation of classroom teachers
    29. Quality of teachers' undergraduate college
    30. Proportion of teachers with M.A. degree
    31. Rules and procedures orientation of classroom
         teachers

VII. Indicators of Environmental Context

    32. Cooperation between the school and college
    33. Modernization of the state
    34. Number of other training programs at college
    35. Size of the city
    36. Technological change in schools
    37. Number of community activities

Appendix 3

MEANS OF NEW AND EXPERIENCED TEACHERS, INTERNS, AND TEAM LEADERS ON
10 OPINION SCALES

	Interns						Teachers		
	New (3rd cycle)			Experienced (2nd cycle)			New		
	Mean	SD	N	Mean	SD	N	Mean	SD	N
Client orientation[a] Ranks[d]	8.45 (1)	1.88	120	8.04 (2)	2.20	92	7.29 (3)	1.98	248
Professional orientation[a] Ranks[d]	6.20 (4)	1.90	85	6.50 (2)	1.91	91	6.51 (1)	1.99	248
Administrative orientation[a] Ranks[d]	4.06 (4)	1.57	108	4.33 (3)	1.65	52	5.78 (2)	1.57	210
Initiative-compliance[c] Ranks[d]	4.13 (1)	1.64	91	3.92 (2)	1.54	53	3.54 (3)	1.78	112
Racial integration[b] Ranks[d]	6.99 (2)	3.54	166	5.39 (1)	2.31	93	7.96 (4)	2.52	291
Commitment to teaching[b] Ranks[d]	3.55 (1)	2.15	112	4.54 (2)	3.02	92	5.44 (4)	2.71	135
Pupil control[a] Ranks[d]	2.38 (4)	1.22	65	2.75 (3)	1.25	55	3.47 (2)	1.33	123
Liberalism[a] Ranks[d]	7.83 (1)	1.70	108	7.04 (2)	1.92	52	5.82 (3)	1.71	121
Rules and procedures orientation[b] Ranks[d]	3.83 (4)	1.23	108	4.35 (3)	1.28	52	4.95 (2)	1.39	210
Alienation from the Teacher Corps[b] Ranks[d]	4.38 (4)	2.07	122	5.10 (1)	2.22	91	4.65 (2)	1.61	139

[a] High score indicates high orientation.
[b] Low score indicates high orientation or high liberalism.
[c] High score indicates high rebelliousness.
[d] The categories in the table are ranked from high orientation or commitment to low orientation or commitment; the figures in parentheses indicate the rank.

425

| Teachers | | | | | | Totals | | | | | |
| Experienced | | | Interns | | | Teachers | | | Team leaders | | |
Mean	SD	N	Mean	SD	N	Mean	SD	N	Mean	SD	N
6.81 (4)	2.07	570	8.28	2.02	220	6.89	2.04	701	7.14	1.93	42
6.38 (3)	1.99	570	6.37	1.91	184	6.38	2.00	701	5.55	1.85	42
6.02 (1)	1.54	409	4.17	1.59	163	5.88	1.56	494	4.81	1.55	32
2.96 (4)	1.61	317	4.07	1.61	148	3.11	1.68	428	3.18	1.49	28
7.32 (3)	2.53	701	6.44	3.24	267	7.13	2.51	863	7.78	3.72	58
5.16 (3)	2.79	464	4.01	2.61	209	5.23	2.77	598	3.11	2.31	45
4.05 (1)	1.49	365	2.57	1.29	125	3.91	1.47	486	3.39	1.38	36
5.20 (4)	1.66	367	7.55	1.82	166	5.36	1.69	486	5.50	2.04	36
5.19 (1)	1.31	409	3.99	1.27	163	5.11	1.32	494	4.81	1.28	32
4.54 (3)	1.52	524	4.71	2.17	220	4.57	1.54	662	4.08	1.89	47

Appendix 4

INTERRECORRELATIONS AMONG 10 ATTITUDE MEASURES FOR INTERNS, TEAM
LEADERS, NEW TEACHERS, AND ALL TEACHERS

Variable[a]	1.				2.			
	I	TL	NT	T	I	TL	NT	T
1. Client orientation	1.00	1.00	1.00	1.00				
2. Professional orientation	.54	.42	.54	.55	1.00	1.00	1.00	1.00
3. Administrative orientation	-.40	-.21	-.21	-.22	-.11	-.02	.09	.05
4. Rules and Procedures orientation	-.32	-.13	-.12	-.15	-.02	.26	.22	.17
5. Racial integration	.09 (.31)[c]	.02	.01	.09	.14	.14	-.05	.06
6. Initiative-compliance	.35	.28	.31	.26	-.02	-.15	.09	.21
7. Commitment to teaching	-.08 (.25)[d]	-.09	.01	-.003	.01	-.002	-.001	.01
8. Teacher Corps alienation[b]	.03	-.12	-.15	-.09	.05	-.05	-.09	-.09
9. Pupil control	-.43	-.20	-.19	-.22	-.21	-.09	.01	-.06
10. Liberalism	.34	.06	.33	.22	.07	-.25	-.04	.09

[a] N's vary by scale and by position.

N By position	$\overline{X}$ of N's for all scales	Range
Interns	136	54-216
Team leaders	28	9-47
New teachers	118	42-248
All teachers	405	115-701

[b] Not included in the ideal type.
[c] For second-cycle interns.
[d] For third-cycle interns.

	6.				7.				8.		
I	TL	NT	T	I	TL	NT	T	I	TL	NT	T
1.00	1.00	1.00	1.00								
.10 (−.16)[d]	.08	−.05	−.02	1.00	1.00	1.00	1.00				
.12 (.25)[c]	.20	−.01	−.06	.26	.06	.20	.12	1.00	1.00	1.00	
−.31	.01	−.24	−.21	−.01	−.01	.20	.14	−.02	−.18	.12	.12
.43	.39	.49	.33	−.27	−.09	−.12	−.08	.04	.46	−.10	−.03

429

	3.				4.				5.			
	I	TL	NT	T	I	TL	NT	T	I	TL	NT	T
	1.00	1.00	1.00	1.00								
	.60	.48	.65	.61	1.00	1.00	1.00	1.00				
	-.11	-.08	-.33	-.23	-.04 $(-.38)^{c}$	.10	-.13	-.10	1.00	1.00	1.00	1.00
	-.53	-.17	-.35	-.39	-.41	-.23	-.43	-.31	.30	.52	.11	.19
	-.03	-.18	.34	.08	.04	.11	.13	.06	-.23	-.19	.04	-.08
	-.30	.12	-.05	-.05	-.30	.29	.09	.05	.06	.04	.06	-.01
	.53	.46	.30	.23	.37	.50	.33	.26	-.33	-.22	-.18	-.29
	-.69	.20	-.62	-.44	-.58	.70	-.60	-.35	.39	.38	.28	.38

	9.				10.		
I	TL	NT	T	I	TL	NT	T

1.00 1.00 1.00 1.00
-.52 -.24 -.34 -.41 1.00 1.00 1.00 1.00

Appendix 5

CHARACTERISTICS OF THE INTERVIEWERS

Field research teams were recruited primarily from among graduate students in sociology at The Ohio State University, although at two sites sociology graduate students from other universities also were involved. Leaders of the research teams were, in all cases, specially recruited graduate students from The Ohio State University who were closely associated with the project from its inception. A total of 43 persons served as interviewers for the 15 visits. Less than half of this number (44 percent) did two-thirds of the interviewing; seven persons interviewed 38 percent of the sample, and 11 did half of the interviewing. The majority of interviewers were over 25 years of age, with a median age of between 25 and 29 years. Forty percent of them, and more than half of those who did most of the interviewing (including the leaders of the interview teams), had previous teaching experience and previous experience with the disadvantaged.

Each interviewer was given pertinent materials explaining the project and outlining standard interviewing procedures, and he participated in a training session before interviewing and review sessions during the field work. During the course of the study the interview team leaders accumulated 22 hours of training. The average interviewer accumulated 11 hours of training; those who did most of the interviewing had a total of 14 hours. Site-visit leaders accumulated a total of 15 days in the field during the course of the study, and the average interviewer spent seven days in the field.

Appendix 6

A LIST OF SELECTED TEACHER CORPS ACTIVITIES

Statistical treatments of the innovations obscure the qualitative difference between innovative activities. Therefore, the following descriptions of intern activities are provided to illustrate some of the variety of techniques introduced into the educational system by the interns and the range of activities in which they were involved.

Where facilities were available on a permanent basis, it was possible for the team to set up laboratories or centers to which other classes could come periodically, for example, a science lab or a multi-ethnic center. These cases were the only ones observed in which the interns could work as a team. Such an activity was observed in one program, conducted by a consulting teacher and two interns out of a group of five. In this case one intern presented a particular unit on geography; the other intern role-played with the teacher in recapitulating the previous lesson. In the latter half of the hour all three circulated among the students as they examined various science "stations," or displays around the room. Since this was only the third session, much confusion existed as well as a lack of directed student behavior. As the interns and teacher met to evaluate the session afterward, the different levels of tolerance for undirected and unstructured learning were evident between the teacher and interns.

When interns had responsibility for an entire class, many attempted to individualize instruction. In one small class the intern attempted such instruction and the class members proceeded at their own rate, using self-direction through preassigned lessons. Although it was a group of third graders, there was a minimum of wasted effort and undisciplined behavior. One intern who had been a strong supporter of the "process" approach, however, expressed discouragement because he spent so much time on simply trying to administer and organize classroom activities for individualized learning that he did not have much opportunity to teach.

In cases in which an intern worked with a teacher, individualized or small-group instruction seemed the pattern. Primarily, this included the intern working in the same classroom with the teacher, or in some other available spot, with certain students needing extra help. In most cases observed, this was directed toward reading skills.

433

Perhaps because of the emphasis on these reading groups, there was great interest in this as a specialized area by the interns as they discussed future plans. In one program in which there was a bilingual emphasis, one intern taught English to three Mexican boys. While one listened to tapes made by the intern, the other two worked with the intern. After using flash cards, the intern produced articles such as a clothespin, stapler, ruler, and magic marker. The boys then described the articles, the various materials used, and the colors, using comparative words such as long, longer, and longest.

Tape recorders were used by a few interns in small groups for a variety of purposes. With a group of poor readers, one intern emphasized student identification of his own mistake after reading a passage. Members of another poor reading group recorded their own compositions and identified errors. Another intern worked with a group on listening skills. Six third-graders in an urban, black area school discussed gang warfare and then made an attempt to evaluate their discussion skills. After this session the intern remarked, "These six drive me up the wall in half an hour. What'll I ever do with a whole class?"

In one program a number of husband-wife teams were used. One such team was observed in which they took poor readers and other problem children out of different classrooms. While the wife gave individual help to one poor reader after another in a partitioned-off section of the stage, the husband worked with five to seven other children of varying ages. This included playing pick-up-sticks with them; listening to a disturbed, hyperactive boy read; and reviewing a scrapbook another boy was making. Other children were acting out a play or drawing pictures.

In this and other instances, interns were observed capitalizing on children's interests and activities as the starting point of their teaching activities. One intern, however, developed a fictitious experience through role playing as the basis for her work on handwriting and composition. The children acted out a sequence portraying slave conditions in the old South, including clandestine meetings, a discussion of slave relations with the master, fear of being sold and being caught. This was followed by a slave auction in which various children assumed the roles of auctioneer, buyer, wives and children of the auctioned slaves. Although some attempt was made by the teacher to examine the various attitudes and values of the participants, the children unanimously identified with the auctioned slaves. According to the intern, the written results from these experiences were fruitful and the children were very motivated to write up reports of what had happened and their reactions to the various characters.

Classroom control constituted a major problem as the interns tried to use more unstructured creative approaches. The intern who conducted the role-playing session experimented with a few techniques. One was the use of lights to give direction. When she turned the classroom lights off, the pupils would return to their desks and put their heads down. Or, during the role playing, when the pupils became

15. Setting up experimental science lab centers using team teaching
16. Use of a word game with cards for small-group tutoring in reading
17. A multiethnic center in which forums and parent-teacher meetings are held, consisting of:
    Listening centers - phonographs and head sets
    Typewriters for student use
    Records of African music
    Library, including books on black history, Africa
    Projectors
    Team teaching
    Display of teacher's art work
18. A role-playing session reenacting a slave sale
19. Creative writing sessions in which children write their own materials from personal experiences, using black dialect, and so on
20. Cameras for students to use as means of expression
21. Anthropological approach to a unit in black history
22. Construction of individualized reading sheets for the first grade
23. An enrichment center to teach a variety of practical subjects, including sex education
24. Bilingual tutoring program

F. Secondary Changes
   25. Introduction of "openness" into school faculty meetings
   26. Supplying audiovisual equipment to teachers
   27. Introduction of recent black literature and professional literature to school teachers

G. Supplementary School Activities
   28. A bookmobile
   29. A Black Arts Festival
   30. A garden developed in conjunction with pupils
   31. Experimental program with 14 students to develop curriculum materials for multiethnic center
   32. After-school tutorial centers for school children of all ages
   33. Home tutoring
   34. Social noon-hour programs for students and parents
   35. School-sponsored teas for parents to give them a chance to observe their students in activities such as plays
   36. Home visitations made by Corpsmen with specific purpose of interpreting the school program to parents, effecting better turnout at parent-teacher meetings
   37. An evening program to introduce the school multiethnic center to parents. Slides by school assistant principal on Africa

overinvolved, by turning the lights on she reinstated the regular classroom atmosphere and norms.

Also, when control was needed, she would instruct the pupils either to "freeze" in their positions or to make themselves into "little balls." This provided activities that the pupils enjoyed but that concentrated their energies and attention on immobility and silence and effectively reversed the trend toward uncontrolled behavior.

The following is a listing of various activities connected with the school and community observed in the course of the site visits. Those innovative activities connected with the school (part I) are categorized on somewhat the same dimensions used in the construction of the Objective Weighted Change Index.

PART I: SCHOOL ACTIVITIES

Some of the activities listed below involve only one area of change, that is, a new method for presenting standard material (sections A-D). Other activities, however, incorporate multiple changes, that is, new material presented by a new method (section E).

A. New Methods
1. Team teaching (two per classroom)
2. Clustered desks
3. Unit on reading and history through folk music
4. Taped discussion of first and second grades - to teach listening and speaking skills, and courtesies
5. Math laboratories in which children learn to manipulate objects

B. New Materials or Content
6. A unit on astrology taught to black students in an inner-city area of a large city
7. Charm-school classes to teach manners, discuss guidelines for baby-sitting, and so on
8. Intern-produced language tapes
9. Music centers (records bought by interns)
10. Outside reading lists by individual interest

C. New Clientele
11. Mixed-age grouping
12. Flexible subgrouping by subject, ability, and problem areas

D. Implementing Personnel
13. A "cross-age" teaching program in which junior high students with learning and emotional problems taught younger children and thus learned to handle their own problems

E. Multiple Changes
14. Use of tape recorder with small groups in reading class

PART II: COMMUNITY ACTIVITIES

A. School-Related Community Projects
   38. Cooperation with a local Head Start program to prepare
        children for better adjustment to kindergarten
   39. A neighborhood center for preschoolers (and their
        parents) who had not gotten into Head Start
   40. Tutoring girls in a Job Corps center for their high
        school diplomas
   41. Teaching in a school for young mothers
   42. A parent center to teach new math to parents
   43. Tutoring children and adult education in a neighborhood
        community center (an OEO affiliate)
   44. Adult education programs for underprivileged seasonal
        agricultural workers
   45. A program for teaching English to Puerto Rican adults
   46. A Great Books discussion group for adults and parents
        in the school neighborhood

B. Community-Based Projects
   47. A community center in which materials on black history
        and culture were displayed, including movies, records,
        pictures, and books
   48. Community surveys of attitudes toward the schools and
        other agencies
   49. A project to organize a buying co-op between parents
   50. Setting up sales outlets for a quilting club of parents
        in a Southern community
   51. Intern activity on welfare rights organization
   52. Intern activity on Area Council
   53. Intern activity on Fair Housing boards
   54. Surreptitious participation in civil rights activities
        in a Southern town
   55. Individual work with children attending a center for
        the mentally retarded and handicapped
   56. Initiation of a new Girl Scout troop
   57. Participation in a community recreation club
   58. Work with city recreation departments and other service
        agencies during the summer
   59. Coaching Little League baseball and participation in
        Cub Scout activities
   60. A Saturday afternoon arts, crafts, and nature club

REFERENCES

Aiken, Michael, and Jerald Hage. "Organizational Interdependence and Intra-Organizational Structure." American Sociological Review, 33:912-929; December 1968.

_____. Social Change in Complex Organizations. New York: Random House, 1970.

American Association of Colleges for Teacher Education. Teacher Productivity. Washington, D.C., 1967.

Anderson, K. E. "A Frontal Attack on the Basic Problem Evaluation: The Achievement of Objectives in Specific Areas." Journal of Experimental Education, 18:163-174; March 1950.

Applebaum, Richard P. Theories of Social Change. Chicago: Markham, 1970.

Baldwin, J. M. The Individual and Society. Boston: Richard G. Badger, 1911.

Barnett, Homer G. Innovation: The Basis of Cultural Change. New York: McGraw-Hill, 1953.

Barrington, Thomas M. The Introduction of Selected Educational Practices into Teachers Colleges and Their Laboratory Schools. New York: Teachers College, Columbia University, 1953.

Barton, Allen H. Studying the Effects of College Education. New Haven, Conn.: Edward W. Hazen Foundation, 1959.

_____. "Studying the Effects of College Education." The College Student and His Culture: An Analysis. (Edited by Kaoru Yamamoto.) Boston: Houghton-Mifflin, 1968.

Becker, Howard S. "Role and Career Problems of the Chicago Public School Teacher." Unpublished doctor's thesis. Chicago: University of Chicago Press, 1951.

_____, and Blanch Geer. "The Fate of Idealism in Medical School." Harvard Educational Review, 28:70-80; Winter 1958.

440

_____, and Frank Stafford. "Some Determinants of Organizational Suc-
cess." Journal of Business, 40:511-518; October 1967.

Becker, Selwyn, and Thomas L. Whisler. "The Innovative Organization:
A Selective View of Current Theory and Research." Journal of
Business, 40:462-469; October 1967.

Ben-David, Joseph, and Randall Collins. "Social Factors in the Origins of a New Science: The Case of Psychology." American Sociological Review, 31:451-465; August 1966.

Benson, Charles. "The Socio-Economic Political and Fiscal Environment
of Educational Policy-Making in Large Cities." (California Study,
reported by Allen K. Campbell.) American Political Science Association, 1966.

Bereiter, Carl, and Mervin Freedman. "Fields of Study and the People
in Them." The American College: A Psychological and Social Interpretation of the Higher Learning. (Edited by Nevitt Sanford.)
New York: Wiley, 1962.

Berelson, Bernard, and Gary Steiner. Human Behavior: An Inventory of
Scientific Findings. New York: Harcourt, Brace, & World, 1964.

Berkowitz, Joanne E., and Norman H. Berkowitz. "Nursing Education and
Role Conception." Nursing Research, 9:218-219; Fall 1960.

Bessent, Warland, and Hollis A. Moore. "The Effects of Outside Funds
on School Districts." Perspectives on Educational Change.
(Edited by Richard I. Miller.) New York: Appleton-Century-
Crofts, 1967. Pp. 101-117.

Blalock, H. M., Jr. "Correlated Independent Variables: The Problem
of Multi-Collinearity." Social Forces, 42:233-237; December 1963.

Blau, Peter. The Dynamics of Bureaucracy. Chicago: University of
Chicago Press, 1955.

_____. "Orientation Toward Clients in a Public Welfare Agency."
Administrative Science Quarterly, 5:341-361; December 1960.

_____, and W. Richard Scott. Formal Organizations. San Francisco:
Chandler, 1962.

Bonjean, Charles M., Richard J. Hill, and S. Dale McLimore. Sociological Measurement. San Francisco: Chandler, 1967.

Boocock, Sarone S. "Toward a Sociology of Learning: A Selective Review of Existing Literature." Sociology of Education, 39:1-45;
Winter 1966.

Borgatta, Edgar F. "Research Problems in the Evaluation of Health
    Service Demonstrations." Milbank Memorial Fund Quarterly, 44:
    182-201; October 1966. (Milbank Memorial Fund, 40 Wall St.,
    New York.) (Quote, p. xii.)

Brademas, John. House Resolution 9627. Washington, D.C.: General
    Subcommittee on Education Hearings; July 7, 13-15, 1967.

Buckley, Walter. Sociology and Modern Systems Theory. Englewood
    Cliffs, N.J.: Prentice-Hall, 1967.

Burns, Tom, and G. M. Stalker. The Management of Innovation. Lon-
    don: Tavistock, 1961.

Bushnell, Margaret. "Now We're Lagging Only 20 Years." The School
    Executive, 77:61-63; October 1957.

Caplow, Theodore. Principles of Organization. New York: Harcourt,
    Brace, & World, 1963, p. 207.

Carlson, Richard O. Executive Succession and Organizational Change:
    Place-Bound and Career-Bound Superintendents of Schools. Chicago:
    Midwest Administrative Center, University of Chicago, 1962.

_____. "School Superintendents and Adoption of Modern Math: A
    Social Structure Profile." Innovation in Education. (Edited by
    Matthew B. Miles.) New York: Teachers College, Columbia Univer-
    sity, 1964.

Carroll, Jean. "A Note on Departmental Autonomy and Innovation in
    Medical Schools." Journal of Business, 40:531-534; October 1967.

Cass, James, and Max Birnbaum. Comparative Guide to American Col-
    leges, 1970-71. New York: Harper & Row, 1969.

Central Advisory Council for Education. Children and Their Primary
    Schools: A Report of the Central Advisory Council for Education,
    Vols. I and II. London: Her Majesty's Stationery Office, 1967.

Chin, Robert. "Models and Ideas About Changing." Paper presented at
    the Symposium on Identifying Techniques and Principles for Gain-
    ing Acceptance of Research Results of Use of Newer Media in Edu-
    cation. Lincoln, Nebraska: November 1963.

Cillié, Francois. Centralization or Decentralization? A Study in
    Educational Adaptation. New York: Teachers College, Columbia
    University Press, 1940.

Clark, Burton R. "Organizational Adaptation and Precarious Values: A
    Case Study." American Sociological Review, 21:327-336; June 1956.

442

_____. The Open Door College: A Case Study. New York: McGraw-Hill, 1960.

_____. "Interorganizational Patterns in Education." Administrative Science Quarterly, 10:224-237; September 1965.

_____. The Distinctive College. Chicago: Aldine, 1970.

Clark, Kenneth B. Dark Ghetto. New York: Harper & Row, 1965.

Clark, Terry N. "Institutionalization of Innovations in Higher Education: Four Conceptual Models." Administrative Science Quarterly, 13:1-25; June 1968.

Clausen, John A. "A Historical and Comparative View of Socialization Theory and Research." Socialization and Society. (Edited by John A. Clausen.) Boston: Little, Brown, 1968. Pp. 18-72.

Cloward, Richard A., and James A. Jones. "Social Class: Educational Attitudes and Participation." Education in Depressed Areas. (Edited by Harry Passow.) New York: Teachers College, Columbia University, 1963.

Cohen, David K. "Politics and Research: Evaluation of Social Action Programs in Education." Review of Educational Research, 40:213-238; April 1970. (Quotes, pp. 216 and 231.)

Coleman, James S., Ruth Janowicz, S. Fleck, and Nea Norton. "A Comparative Study of a Psychiatric Clinic and Family Agency." Social Case Work, 38:3-8; 74-80; January and February 1957.

_____, and others. Equality of Educational Opportunity. Washington, D.C.: Government Printing Office, 1966.

Coles, Robert. Children of Crisis: A Study of Courage and Fear. Boston: Little, Brown, 1967.

Cooley, C. H. Human Nature and the Social Order. Revised edition. New York: Scribner's, 1922.

Cort, H. Russell, Jr., and Ann O'Keefe. Teacher Corps: Two Years of Progress and Plans for the Future. Washington, D.C.: Washington School of Psychiatry, October 1968.

Corwin, Ronald. A Sociology of Education. New York: Appleton-Century-Crofts, 1965.

_____. "Education and the Sociology of Complex Organizations." On Education: Sociological Perspectives. (Edited by Donald A.

Hansen and Joel E. Gerstl.) New York: Wiley, 1967.

_____. _Militant Professionalism: A Study of Organizational Conflict in High Schools_. New York: Appleton-Century-Crofts, 1970.

_____, Marvin J. Taves, and Eugene Haas. "Professional Disillusionment." _Nursing Research_, 10:141-144; Summer 1961.

_____, and Marilyn Schmit. "Teachers in Inner-City Schools: A Survey of a Large-City School System." _Education and Urban Society_, 2:131-155; February 1970.

Cronbach, Lee J. "Evaluation for Course Improvement." _Bureau of Educational Research_. Urbana: University of Illinois Press, November 1962. (Mimeo.)

Crotty, William J. "Democratic Consensual Norms and the College Student." _Sociology of Education_, 40:200-218; Summer 1967.

Davis, James A. _Great Aspirations: The Graduate School Plans of America's College Seniors_. Chicago: Aldine, 1964. Table 1-4C.

Deutscher, Irwin. "Looking Backward: Case Studies on the Progress of Methodology in Sociological Research." _American Sociologist_, 4:35-41; February 1969.

Dewey, John. _Human Nature and Conduct_. New York: Holt, 1922.

Douty, Harriet. "Learning To Teach the Disadvantaged." _The New Republic_, 158:14-15; June 29, 1968.

Dubin, Robert. "Deviant Behavior and Social Structure: Continuities in Social Theory." _American Sociological Review_, 24:147-164; April 1959.

Duncan, Roger. "An Experimental Study of the Effect of Parents' Knowledge on Student Performance in SMSG Mathematics." _The Journal of Educational Research_, 58:135-157; November 1964.

Durkheim, E. _On the Division of Labor in Society_. (Translated by G. Simpson.) Macmillan, 1933.

Educational Testing Service. Certain items adapted from _College Student Questionnaires_. Copyright c. 1965 by Educational Testing Service. All rights reserved. Adapted and reproduced by permission. Princeton, N. J.

Ehrlich, Howard J. "Attitudes, Behavior, and the Intervening Variables." _American Sociologist_, 4:29-33; February 1969.

Eisenstadt, S. N. "Social Change, Differentiation, and Evolution."
American Sociological Review, 29:375-386; June 1964.

Etzioni, Amitai. Modern Organizations. Englewood Cliffs, N.J.:
Prentice-Hall, 1964.

Evan, William. "Superior-Subordinate Conflict in Research Organizations." Administrative Science Quarterly, 10:52-64; June 1965.

_____, and Guy Black. "Innovation in Business Organizations: Some
Factors Associated with Success or Failure of Staff Proposals."
Journal of Business, 40:519-530; October 1967.

Farward, John. "Towards an Empirical Framework for Ecological Studies
in Comparative Public Administration." Comparative Perspectives
on Formal Organizations. (Edited by Henry A. Landsberger.)
Boston: Little, Brown, 1970.

Fitzpatrick, Robert, and Michael J. Blum. Evaluation of the Pittsburgh Preservice Training Program for the National Teacher Corps.
Research pursuant to a subcontract with the University of Pittsburgh, under Master Contract No. OEC-1-6-48-1110-1118. Washington,
D.C.: U.S. Office of Education. (Mimeo.)

Flanagan, J. C., and others. The American High School Student. Pittsburgh: University of Pittsburgh (Project Talent Office), 1964.

Foskett, John M. "The Influence of Social Participation on Community
Programs and Activities." Community Structure and Analysis.
(Edited by Marvin B. Sussman.) New York: Thomas Y. Crowell,
1959.

Freeman, Howard E., and Clarence C. Sherwood. "Research in Large-
Scale Intervention Programs." Journal of Social Issues, 21:
11-28; January 1965.

Friedenberg, Edgar Z. "Requiem for the Urban School." Saturday
Review, 50:77-79; November 18, 1967.

Fusco, Gene C. School-Home Partnership in Depressed Neighborhoods.
U.S. Department of Health, Education and Welfare, Office of Education. Washington, D.C.: Government Printing Office, 1964.

Gamson, William A. Power and Discontent. Homewood, Ill.: Dorsey,
1968.

Gerard, R. W. "Problems in the Institutionalization of Higher Education: An Analysis Based on Historical Materials." Behavioral
Science, 2:134-146; April 1957.

Giddings, F. H. The Theory of Socialization. New York: Macmillan,
1897.

Ginzberg, Eli, and Ewing P. Reilly. (Assisted by Douglas W. Bray
and John L. Herma.) Effecting Change in Large Organizations.
New York: Columbia University Press, 1957.

Goffman, Erving. Stigma: Notes on the Management of Spoiled Identity. Englewood Cliffs, N.J.: Prentice-Hall, 1963.

Gogswell, Betty E. "Some Structural Properties Influencing Socialization." Administrative Science Quarterly, 13:417-440; December
1968.

Goldman, Harvey. A Study of Multiple Failures at Rufus High School:
A Report of a Social Welfare Field Project. Milwaukee, Wis.:
Rufus King High School, 1966.

Goode, William J. "A Theory of Role Strain." American Sociological
Review, 25:483-496; August 1960.

Gordon, Robert. "Issues in Multiple Regression." The American Journal of Sociology, 73:592-616; March 1968.

Gottlieb, David, and Benjamin Hodgkins. "College Student Subcultures:
Their Structure and Characteristics in Relation to Student Attitude Change." School Review, 71:266-289; Autumn 1963.

Gouldner, Alvin. Patterns of Industrial Bureaucracy. New York:
Free Press, 1954.

_____. "Organizational Analysis." Sociology Today. (Edited by
R. K. Merton and others.) New York: Basic Books, 1959.

_____. The Coming Crisis of Western Society. New York: Basic
Books, 1970.

Graham, Richard. Statement before the Committee on Education and
Labor. Washington, D.C.: U.S. House of Representatives, March
2, 1967.

_____. "Teacher Corps: More Help in the Classroom." Occupational
Outlook Quarterly, 11:1-4; September 1967.

_____. "The Teacher Corps and the Education Professions Develop-
ment Act." Contemporary Education, 39:185-186; March 1968. Re-
printed with the permission of the editor and Indiana State University.

_____. "The Teacher Corps: One Place to Begin." NAASP Bulletin, 52:49-61; October 1968.

_____. "Educational Change and the Teacher Corps." Phi Delta Kappan, 51:305-309; February 1970.

Greiner, L. E. "Organization Change and Development." Unpublished doctor's thesis. Cambridge, Mass.: Harvard University, 1965.

Griffiths, Daniel E. "Administrative Theory and Change in Organizations." Innovation in Education. (Edited by Matthew Miles.) New York: Teachers College, Columbia University, 1964.

Gross, Edward. Work and Society. New York: Crowell, 1958.

Gross, Neal, Ward S. Mason, and Alexander W. McEachern. Explorations in Role Analysis: Studies of the School Superintendency Role. New York: Wiley, 1958.

Gross, Neal, Joseph B. Giacquinta, and Marilyn Bernstein. Complex Organizations: The Implementation of Major Organizational Innovations. Presented at the Annual Meeting of the ASA. Boston: August 1968.

Guest, Robert. "Managerial Succession in Complex Organizations." American Journal of Sociology, 68:47-54; July 1962.

Guetzkow, Harold. "The Creative Person in Organizations." The Creative Organization. (Edited by Gary A. Steiner.) Chicago: University of Chicago Press, 1965.

Gusfield, Joseph R. "Social Structure and Moral Reform: A Study of the Women's Christian Temperance Union." American Journal of Sociology, 61:221-232; September 1955.

Guthrie, J. W., G. B. Kleindorfer, H. M. Levin, and R. T. Stout. Schools and Inequality. Washington, D.C.: The Urban Coalition, 1969. Chapter 5.

Hage, Jerald, and Michael Aiken. "Program Change and Organizational Properties: A Comparative Analysis." American Journal of Sociology, 72:503-519; March 1967.

Hage, Jerald, and Robert Dewar. "The Prediction of Organizational Performance: The Case of Program Innovation." Denver, Col.: paper read at the American Sociological Association Meetings, August 1971.

Hagen, Everett E. On the Theory of Social Change. Homewood, Ill.: Dorsey, 1962.

Hanna, Elizabeth. "The Small Group-An Instrument of Organizational Change." Unpublished paper presented at the Spring Symposium on Conflict and Change in Contemporary America, The Ohio State University, May 1971.

Hanson, Robert. "The System Linkage Hypothesis and Role Consensus Patterns." American Sociological Review, 27:304-313; June 1962.

Havemann, E., and Patricia West. They Went to College. New York: Harcourt, 1952.

Herriott, Robert E., and Benjamin Hodgkins. "Sociocultural Context and the American School: An Open-Systems Analysis of Educational Opportunity." Tampa, Fla.: Florida State University, January 1969.

Herriott, Robert E., and Nancy St. John. Social Class and the Urban School. New York: Wiley, 1966.

Hertzog, Elizabeth. Some Guidelines for Evaluative Research: Assessing Psychological Change in Individuals. Technical Study Branch, Division of Research, U.S. Department of Health, Education and Welfare, Office of Education. Washington, D.C.: Administrative Children's Bureau, 1959.

Himmelweit, Hilde T., and A. P. Sealy. "The School as an Agent of Socialization." London, 1966. (Unpublished mimeo.)

Holland, John. "Undergraduate Origins of American Scientists." Science, 126:433-437; May 6, 1957.

Hollingshead, August deB., and Frederic C. Redlich. Social Class and Mental Illness: A Community Study. New York: Wiley, 1958.

Hovland, Carl I., Arthur A. Lumsdaine, and Fred D. Sheffield. Experiments on Mass Communication. Princeton, N.J.: Princeton University Press, 1949. Pp. 33-45.

Hunt, David E. Evaluation of National Teacher Corps Trainees by a Situational Testing Approach. U.S. Department of Health, Education and Welfare, Office of Education (part of Contract #OEC-1-6-421-600-1112). Syracuse, N.Y.: Syracuse University, 1967.

Husén, Torsten. International Study of Achievement in Mathematics. New York: Wiley, 1967.

Ingmire, Alice E. "Attitudes of Student Nurses at the University of California." Nursing Research, 1:36-39; October 1952.

Jacob, Philip E. Changing Values in College. New York: Harper, 1957.

448

Johnson, Lyndon B., in "The National Teacher Corps . . . to reach and teach the children of poverty." Washington, D.C.: U.S. Government Printing Office, 1966.

Kandel, Denise B., and Gerald S. Lesser. "Parental and Peer Influence on the Educational Plans of Adolescents." American Sociological Review, 34:213-222; April 1969.

Katz, Fred E. Autonomy and Organization. New York: Random House, 1968.

Kohl, Herbert. Thirty-Six Children. New York: New American Library, 1967.

Koos, Earl. The Health of Regionville. New York: Columbia University Press, 1954.

Kozol, Jonathan. Death At An Early Age. Boston: Houghton Mifflin, 1967.

Kroeber, Alfred L. Configurations of Culture Growth. Berkeley: University of California Press, 1944.

Labovitz, S. "Some Observations on Measurement and Statistics." Social Forces, 46:151-160; December 1967.

Leavitt, Harold J. "Applied Organizational Change in Industry: Structural, Technological, and Humanistic Approaches." Handbook of Organizations. (Edited by James March.) Chicago: Rand McNally, 1965.

Lefton, Mark, Simon Dinitz, and Benjamin Pasamanick. "Decision-Making in a Mental Hospital: Real, Perceived, and Ideal." American Sociological Review, 24:882-889; December 1959.

Levine, Sol, and Paul White. "Exchange As A Conceptual Framework for the Study of Interorganizational Relationships." Administrative Science Quarterly, 5:583-601; March 1961.

Lipset, Seymour Martin, and others. Union Democracy. Glencoe, Ill.: Free Press, 1956.

Litwak, Eugene, and Lydia Hylton. "Inter-organization Analysis: A Hypothesis on Coordinating Agencies." Administrative Science Quarterly, 6:395-420; March 1962.

Litwak, Eugene, and Josephina Figueira. "Technological Innovation and Theoretical Functions of Primary Group and Bureaucratic Structures." American Journal of Sociology, 73:468-481; January 1968.

Loomis, Charles P. "Tentative Types of Directed Social Change In-
     volving Systematic Linkage." Rural Sociology, 24:383-390;
     December 1959.

Lortie, Dan. "Laymen to Lawmen: Law School, Careers, and Profes-
     sional Socialization." Harvard Educational Review, 29:352-369;
     Fall 1959.

Luszki, M. B., and R. Schmuck. "Pupil Perceptions of Parental Atti-
     tudes Toward School." Mental Hygiene, 47:289-299; April 1963.

McDill, Edward, Leo Rigsby, and Edmund D. Meyers. "Institutional
     Effects on the Academic Behavior of High School Students." Soci-
     ology of Education, 40:181-199; Summer 1967.

March, James G., and Herbert A. Simon. Organizations. New York:
     Wiley, 1958.

Marris, P., and M. Rein. Dilemmas of Social Reform. New York:
     Atherton, 1967.

Martyn, Kenneth A. "Report on Education to the Governors' Commission
     on the Los Angeles Riots." November 1965. (Unpublished mimeo.)

Mead, G. H. Mind, Self, and Society. Chicago: University of Chica-
     go Press, 1934.

Mechanic, David. "Sources of Power of Lower Participants in Complex
     Organizations." Administrative Science Quarterly, 7:349-364;
     December 1962.

Menzel, Herbert. "Innovation, Integration and Marginality: A Sur-
     vey of Physicians." American Sociological Review, 25:704-713;
     October 1960.

Merton, Robert. Social Theory and Social Structure. Glencoe, Ill.:
     Free Press, 1957.

Messinger, Sheldon L. "Organizational Transformation: A Case Study
     of a Declining Social Movement." American Sociological Review,
     20:3-10; February 1955.

Meyer, Genevieve Rogg. Tenderness and Techniques: Nursing Values in
     Transition. Los Angeles: Industrial Relations Monographs of the
     Institute of Industrial Relations, No. 6, 1960.

Meyer, Henry J., Eugene Litwak, and Donald Warren. "Occupational and
     Class Differences in Social Values: A Comparison of Teachers and
     Social Workers." Sociology of Education, 41:263-281; Summer 1968.

450

Meyer, Marshall W. "Harvard Students in the Midst of Crisis." Sociology of Education, 44:245-269; Summer 1971.

Moore, Wilbert E. Social Change. Englewood Cliffs, N.J.: Prentice-
Hall, 1963.

Mort, Paul R. "Studies in Educational Innovation from the Institute
of Administrative Research: An Overview." Innovation in Education. (Edited by Matthew B. Miles.) New York: Teachers College,
Columbia University, 1964.

Moynihan, Daniel P. The Negro Family: The Case for National Action.
U.S. Department of Labor, Office of Policy Planning and Research.
Washington, D.C.: Government Printing Office, 1965.

_____. Maximum Feasible Misunderstanding: Community Action in the
War on Poverty. New York: Free Press, 1969.

Mulder, Mauk. "Power Equalization Through Participation?" Administrative Science Quarterly, 16:31-38; March 1971.

Myers, J. K., and L. Schaffer. "Social Stratification and Psychiatric
Practice: A Study of an Out-Patient Clinic." American Sociological Review, 19:307-310; June 1954.

Nasatir, David. "A Note on Contextual Effects and the Political Orientation of University Students." American Sociological Review,
33:210-219; April 1968.

Nash, George. "A Description of the 1444 Accredited Four-Year Institutions of Higher Education." Bureau of Applied Social Research.
New York: Columbia University, January 1969. (Mimeo.)

National Education Association, Research Division. The American Public-School Teacher, 1960-61. Washington, D.C.: The Association,
1965-1966. Table 9, p. 15.

Nations Schools. "School Men Mix Their Views on Teacher Corps Program." (Opinion Poll.) Nations Schools, 79:91; May 1967.

Newcomb, Theodore, K. E. Koenig, R. Flacks, and D. P. Worwich.
Persistence and Change: Bennington College and Its Students
After 25 Years. New York: Wiley, 1967.

Ojemann, R. H., and F. R. Wilkinson. "The Effect on Pupil Growth of
an Increase in Teachers' Understanding of Pupil Behavior."
Journal of Experimental Education, 8:143-147; December 1939.

Olsen, Marvin. The Process of Social Organization. New York: Holt, 1968.

Pace, C. R. They Went to College. Minneapolis: University of Minnesota, 1941.

Pareto, Vilfredo. The Rise and Fall of the Elites. (Introduction by Hans L. Zetterberg.) Totowa, N.J.: Bedminster, 1968.

Parsons, Talcott. "Evolutionary Universals in Society." American Sociological Review, 29:339-357; June 1964.

Putney, Snell, and Gladys I. Putney. "Radical Innovation and Prestige." American Sociological Review, 27:548-551; August 1962.

Riessman, Frank. The Culturally Deprived Child. New York: Harper, 1962.

Riley, John W., Jr., and Matilda White Riley. "Mass Communication and the Social System." Sociology Today: Problems and Prospects. (Edited by Robert K. Merton, Leonard Broom, and Leonard S. Cottrell, Jr.) New York: Basic Books, 1959.

_____. "Sociological Perspectives on the Use of New Educational Media." New Teaching Aids for the American Classroom. (Edited by Wilbur Schramm.) U.S. Department of Health, Education and Welfare, Office of Education. Washington, D.C.: Government Printing Office, 1962.

Roberts, Bryan R. "An Experiment in Teacher Education." Innovation in Mass Education. (Edited by David Street.) New York: Interscience, 1969.

Rock, Donald A., John A. Centra, and Robert L. Linn. "Relationships Between College Characteristics and Student Achievement." AERA Journal, 7:109-130; January 1970.

Rogers, E. M. Diffusion of Innovations. New York: Free Press, 1962.

Rokeach, Milton. The Open and Closed Mind. New York: Basic Books, 1960.

Rose, Peter I. "The Myth of Unanimity: Student Opinions on Critical Issues." Sociology of Education, 37:129-149; Winter 1963.

Rosenthal, R., and L. Jacobsen. Pygmalion in the Classroom. New York: Holt, 1968.

Ross, Donald (editor). Administration for Adaptability. New York: Metropolitan School Study Council, 1958.

452

Sapolsky, Harvey M. "Organizational Structure and Innovation."
    Journal of Business, 40:497-510; October 1967.

Sarason, Seymour B. The Culture of the School and the Problem of
    Change. Boston: Allyn and Bacon, 1971.

Schiff, Herbert Jerome. "The Effect of Personal Contractural Rela-
    tionships on Parents' Attitudes Toward and Participation in Local
    School Affairs." Unpublished doctor's thesis. Evanston, Ill.:
    Northwestern University, 1963.

Scott, W. Richard. "Some Implications of Organizational Theory for
    Research on Health Services." Milbank Memorial Fund Quarterly,
    44:35-64; October 1966. (Milbank Memorial Fund, 40 Wall St.,
    New York.)

Selvin, Hanan C., and Warren O. Hagstrom. "Determinants of Support
    for Civil Liberties." British Journal of Sociology, 11:51-73;
    March 1960.

Selznick, Philip. TVA and the Grass Roots. Berkeley: University of
    California Press, 1949.

Sharpe, Donald M. "National Teacher Corps--Where To?" (Editorial)
    Journal of Teacher Education, 18:131f; Summer 1967.

_____. "Lessons from the Teacher Corps." NEA Journal, 57:21-22;
    May 1968.

_____. "Lessons from the Teacher Corps," and "National Teacher
    Corps--Where To?" Teacher Corps: A New Dimension in Education.
    (Edited by V. J. Kennedy and Robert E. Rousch.) Bureau of Educa-
    tion Research and Services. Houston: University of Houston,
    1969. Pp. 69-72; 204-208.

Shepard, Herbert A. "Innovation-Resisting and Innovation-Producing
    Organizations." Journal of Business, 40:470-477; October 1967.

Sieber, Sam D., and David E. Wilder. "Teaching Styles: Parental
    Preferences and Professional Role Definitions." Sociology of
    Education, 40:302-315; Fall 1967.

Silberman, Charles E. Crisis in the Classroom. New York: Random
    House, 1970.

Sills, David L. The Volunteers. New York: The Free Press, 1957.

Simmons, Ozzie G. "Implications of Social Class for Public Health."
    Human Organization, 16:7-10; Fall 1957.

References

Sjoberg, Gideon, Richard A. Brymer, and Buford Farris. "Bureaucracy and the Lower Class." Sociology and Social Research, 50:325-337; April 1966.

Smelser, Neil J. Sociology: An Introduction. New York: Wiley, 1967.

Sontag, Marvin. "Attitudes Toward Education and Perception of Teacher Behaviors." AERA Journal, 5:385-401; May 1968.

Stevens, Sylvia. "An Ecological Study of Child Guidance Intake." Smith College Studies in Social Work, 25:73-84; October 1954.

Stone, James C. Breakthrough in Teacher Education. San Francisco: Jossey-Bass, 1969.

Strauss, Anselm. "The Hospital and Its Negotiated Order." The Hospital in Modern Society. (Edited by Eliot Friedson.) New York: Free Press, 1963.

Suchman, Edward. "The Values of American College Students." Long-Range Planning for Education. Washington, D.C.: American Council on Education, 1957.

Sudnow, David. Passing On. Englewood Cliffs, N.J.: Prentice-Hall, 1967.

Tarde, Gabriel de. Laws of Imitation. Revised edition. Gloucester, Mass.: Peter Smith, 1962.

Terreberry, Shirley. "The Evolution of Organizational Environments." Administrative Science Quarterly, 12:590-613; March 1968.

Thomas, W. I., and F. Znaniecki. The Polish Peasant in Europe and America. Four volumes. Boston: Richard G. Badger, 1918-1920.

Thompson, James D., Robert W. Hawkes, and Robert W. Avery. "Truth Strategies and University Organization." New York: paper read at American Sociological Association meetings, 1960.

Thompson, James O. Organizations in Action. New York: McGraw-Hill, 1967.

Thompson, Victor A. "Administrative Objectives for Development Administration." Administrative Science Quarterly, 9:91-108; June 1964.

_____. Bureaucracy and Innovation. University, Ala.: University of Alabama, 1969. P. 6.

Turk, Herman. "Interorganizational Networks in Urban Society: Ini-

454

tial Perspectives and Comparative Research." _American Sociological Review_, 35:1-18; February 1970.

Turner, Richard L. "The Acquisition of Teaching Skills in Elementary School Settings." _Bulletin of the School of Education_ (Indiana University), 41:1-96; January 1965

Vreeland, Rebecca, and Charles Bidwell. "Organizational Effects on Student Attitudes: A Study of the Harvard Houses." _Sociology of Education_, 38:233-250; Spring 1965.

Wallace, Walter L. _Student Culture: Social Structure and Continuity in a Liberal Arts College_. Chicago: Aldine, 1966.

Warren, Roland. "The Interorganizational Field as a Focus for Investigation." _Administrative Science Quarterly_, 12:396-419; December 1967.

Watson, Bernard C. "The Taming of a Reform." _Phi Delta Kappan_, 50: 99-104; October 1968.

Wayland, Sloan. "Structural Features of American Education as Basic Factors in Innovation." _Innovation in Education_. (Edited by Matthew B. Miles.) New York: Teachers College, Columbia University, 1963.

Wayson, William W. "Securing Teachers for Slum Schools." Adopted from address to the Annual Meeting of American Association of School Administrators, Syracuse University, New York, February 19, 1964.

Webster, Harold, Mervin Freedman, and Paul Heist. "Personality Changes in College Students." _American College: A Psychological and Social Interpretation of the Higher Learning_. (Edited by Nevitt Sanford.) New York: Wiley, 1967.

Weiss, Robert S., and Martin Rein. "The Evaluation of Broad-Aim Programs: Experimental Design, Its Difficulties and an Alternative." _Administrative Science Quarterly_, 15:97-109; March 1970.

Willie, Charles V. "The Social Class of Patients that Public Health Nurses Prefer to Serve." _American Journal of Public Health_, 50:1126-1136; August 1960.

Willower, Donald, Terry L. Eidell, and Wayne K. Hay. _The School and Pupil Control Ideology_. Philadelphia, Pa.: Penn State University, 1967.

Wilson, James Q. "Innovation in Organization: Notes Toward a Theory." _Approaches to Organizational Design_. (Edited by James D.

Thompson.)   Pittsburgh, Pa.:   University of Pittsburgh Press,
1966.

Wilson, O. Meredith. Highlights of the April 20 Report of the National Adivsory Council on the Education of Disadvantaged Children:
Evaluation of the Teacher Corps. Washington, D.C.; April 1967.

Wolff, Kurth H. (translator and editor). The Sociology of Georg
Simmel. Glencoe, Ill.: Free Press, 1950. Pp. 402-408.

Yamamoto, Kaoru. The College Student and His Culture: An Analysis.
Boston: Houghton Mifflin, 1968.

Yankelovich, Daniel. Generations Apart. New York: Columbia Broad-
Casting System, 1969.

Yuchtman, Ephraim, and Stanley E. Seashore. "A System Resource Approach to Organizational Effectiveness." American Sociological
Review, 32_891-903; December 1967.

Zald, Mayer N. Organizational Change: The Political Economy of the
Y.M.C.A. Chicago: University of Chicago Press, 1970.

Author Index

Subject Index

motivation and performance of children,
201, 204–205, 221–222, 235–
236
opinions and roles, 201–202, 204, 205
school-community relations, 201, 203,
205
teacher-student relationships, 205
techniques for teaching the impoverished,
201–202, 205, 235
see also Organizational innovation
Change, strategies of, by addition, 122–123,
151, 377
broad-front approach, 316
diffusion approach, 248, 260, 280
economic surplus approach, 252, 260, 265,
266, 382, 391
and environmental conditions, 252, 260
interorganizational approach, 252, 260
and organizational differentiation, 250,
260
power equalization approach, 265
replacement approach, 219, 249, 250,
259, 280
socialization approach, 249, 260
and status maintenance, 252, 260
from the top down, 151
as a two-step process, 248
use of change agents, 321
use of force, 157, 389
see also Organizational innovation
Change, measurement of, 310
theories of, 225, 254, 355–356, 362
and value climate, 284
see also Organizational innovation
Client orientation, of interns, 93
changes in, 168–169, 173
measured, 45
"Cognitive dissonance," 341
Colleges, commitment to teacher training,
307
dominating role of, 262
marginal leverage of, 343
and "organizational slack," 252, 337,
340, 343, 365, 382, 391
overlapping authority of, 154
prestige of, 6, 368, 391
quality of, 282, 284, 285, 289, 291, 298,
300, 304, 307, 310, 328–329, 340,
342
relationship with schools, 121, 122, 135,

224, 262, 287–291, 304, 307, 339,
344, 370, 376, 378
selective recruitment of, 289, 330, 367,
380, 391
and level of funding, 334, 350
and organizational change, 334, 350
and recruitment of students, 334, 340,
350
size of, 310
teacher training, 330
see also Change in college
Commissioner of Education, 315, 338
Commitment to teaching, of interns, 82, 92,
159, 184, 187, 189, 213, 231, 239
changes in, 168, 169, 173, 184, 187,
226, 231, 239
measured, 44
Community field work, and characteristics
of colleges, 291, 293, 294, 305
anc characteristics, of interns, 293–294,
305, 339
of schools, 291, 293–294, 305
versus classroom teaching, 148, 152
evaluations of, 146
role conflicts over, 121–122, 147–150,
159, 214, 218, 233, 235, 236, 241
social action versus social service aspects,
148
susceptibility to politicalization, 149
types of, 145
and urbanization and modernization, 266
see also Community relationship to
schools
Community relationship to schools, community control and, 24, 73
disaffection between teachers and low-
income clientele, 3, 19, 21, 23, 34,
36, 356
effects on learning, 23
parental participation in schools, 24
see also Community field work
Conflict among participants, and their
liberalism, 300, 306, 339
and organizational flexibility, 303, 306,
309
and other characteristics, 285, 289–302,
309
and other problems, 339
and quality of their undergraduate college,
300